WHY VIETNAM?

TIME: United States

The '50s, '60s, and '70s, with rock 'n' roll, peace signs, Afros, joints, 'tune in, turn on, drop out'.

PLACE: Vietnam

Vietnam, with its jungles, tunnels, mud, 100 per cent humidity, snakes, monsoons, tigers, blistering sun, red dirt, brown water, peopled with smaller men and women, speaking a sing-song language our soldiers didn't know.

WAR: 1950–1975

A crazy war. 'Grunts' rotating in to replace another grunt whose tour was over or who was seriously injured or dead; weapons field-tested in the war, no front line, no territory to hold, some territory off-limits (such as the Ho Chi Minh Trail, the resupply route to the VC), take no prisoners, 'just kill gooks'.[1]

Marines riding on an M-48 tank. (Courtesy D. Phillips)

Two soldiers wading through a muddy hole.
(Courtesy D. Phillips)

WHY VIETNAM?

REFLECTIONS ON THE EFFECT OF WAR

MARGARET COLBERT BROWN

Pen & Sword
MILITARY

AN IMPRINT OF PEN & SWORD BOOKS LTD.
YORKSHIRE - PHILADELPHIA

First published in Great Britain in 2025 by
Pen & Sword Military
An imprint of
Pen & Sword Books Ltd
Yorkshire - Philadelphia

Copyright © Margaret Colbert Brown, 2025

ISBN 978 1 03611 155 7

Typeset by SJmagic DESIGN SERVICES, India.

Printed and bound in the UK by CPI Group (UK) Ltd.

The Publisher's authorised representative in the EU for product safety is
Authorised Rep Compliance Ltd., Ground Floor, 71 Lower Baggot Street,
Dublin D02 P593, Ireland.
www.arccompliance.com

For a complete list of Pen & Sword titles please contact

PEN & SWORD BOOKS LIMITED
George House, Units 12 & 13, Beevor Street, Off Pontefract Road,
Barnsley, S71 1HN, UK
E-mail: enquiries@pen-and-sword.co.uk
Website: www.pen-and-sword.co.uk

or

PEN AND SWORD BOOKS
1950 Lawrence Rd, Havertown, PA 19083, USA
E-mail: uspen-and-sword@casematepublishers.com
Website: www.penandswordbooks.com

Contents

Preface

'Each of us carried in his heart a separate war which in many ways was totally
different, despite our common cause. We had different memories
of people we'd known and the war itself, and we had different
destinies in the postwar years.' (Bao Ninh, North Vietnam
soldier and writer, *The Sorrow of War*, 232)

How do we talk about a war? Do we talk about the how or the why?[2] The question of how
we got involved in Vietnam is a description of what happened. There is an easy answer:[3]
We supported the French until they lost the Battle of Dien Bien Phu; we then supported
the South Vietnamese government, fearing the loss of Southeast Asia to the communists.

But why we got involved in Vietnam leads to blame. Do we blame those who ignored Ho
Chi Minh's plea for independence at the end of World War I and II? Do we blame Truman for
not heeding President Roosevelt's policy of not supporting the French in Indochina (Loewen,
249)? Do we blame President Eisenhower's belief in the Domino Theory, which proved
prophetic. Do we blame President Kennedy for strengthening our commitment to the South
Vietnamese, and allowing the American ambassador and the Vietnamese generals to kill
President Diem and promise no repercussions, or do we blame President Johnson for his total
commitment to the undeclared war and for tying the military's hands, making the conflict
defensive, protecting South Vietnam; rather than offensive, sending troops across the DMZ
(Demilitarized Zone) and into Laos and Cambodia? Was the war ever winnable? Should we
have ever gotten involved? Those questions, the 'whys', have been debated for the past fifty
years because 'we tend to avoid single-cause explanations and prefer to situate the big events
of the past within complex swirls of social history and political culture' (Blight, 3).

Do we blame the fact that many historians believe that the Vietnam War was a proxy
continuation of the First World War, Second World War, Cold War and Korean War?
'That same generation [who fought in the two world wars] then immediately entered
the Cold War, again a continuation in many ways of World War II, but fought out
through the proxy wars in Korea, Vietnam and elsewhere' (Shanken, 2). Having fought
in these previous wars, it is thus no wonder that we fought in Vietnam.

In the United States, wars are won, never lost. The government issues reports on
the money spent, the jobs created, the number of troops sent, and the number brought
home. It also issues reports on technical improvements to weapons, equipment, armored
vehicles, and airplanes. The government seems busy collecting information and
churning out information. No matter what we face, no matter what the cost, we will win.

What happens, however, if who won and who lost is in dispute? One Vietnam vet
told me that of course we won the war: 'You don't see a Vietnam flag flying at the White

House, do you?' His buddy, another Vietnam vet, frowned and said the government didn't let us win because it was all politics. The military watched Washington run the war. So we couldn't shut down the Ho Chi Minh Trail, North Vietnam's supply route, because it entered Laos and Cambodia, providing safe access to South Vietnam. No, we had our hands tied. We didn't take territory and hold it; we took some prisoners and killed others. We didn't know who the enemy was, so we couldn't shoot unless we were fired upon. In Saigon, people we thought were innocent civilians pushed booby-trapped baby carriages, tossed grenades, and stole what they could (Vietnam Vet Program 4/9/93).

But those were not the only issues which made this war maddening. Soldiers were trained to fight as they had fought in the First and Second World Wars, but received no training in jungle warfare. The soldiers were taken to Louisiana to learn to fight in conditions like Vietnam, but if you have seen the movie *Southern Comfort*, you know how those living in the area responded, like the guerillas the soldiers faced in Vietnam.

The clothing the soldiers initially wore was not intended for the jungle but for the desert. The heat and humidity wreaked havoc on their clothes and boots, but there were no instant replacements. The rifle the military sent with soldiers to Vietnam, the M-16, had not been field-tested. Soldiers preferred the M-14, good out to 1000 yards or M-15, good out to 400 yards. But the military insisted on the M-16 because in a jungle the soldiers didn't need to shoot that far. After several modifications, the M-16 worked well. Soldiers preferred a more reliable weapon. They asked for and received more ammunition than they could use. Their packs became too heavy, so they discarded extra ammunition, just as the French soldiers had done in the early Fifties. And like with the French, the Vietcong made use of this ammunition, as well as anything else the soldiers discarded, although some were booby-trapped. Our discards armed the Vietcong.

The US military placed untested, untrained lieutenants at the head of platoons. Some soldiers, fearing that the lieutenants would get them killed, tried to kill them. It happened so often that it even had a name – fragging. Even the little things were maddening to the soldiers: an Afro comb did not fit in their pockets; they were paid in scrip, military certificates, only useful in base camps; and mail from home often took several weeks to arrive, creating a feeling of loneliness and despair.

Everybody has got an opinion as to the madness that was the Vietnam War, so whom can we trust? Should we turn to the government and the military, who told their feel-good stories – often called 'dog-and-pony shows' – which journalists could report back home, or to the soldiers who were there? The soldiers watched, listened, talked, fought, hid, and killed. Many died doing what the government asked of them, so they can't tell their stories; but others can.

Let's listen to them. Yes, it has been over fifty years. They come to us as strangers, but they won't always be. After all, one of them might be your uncle who flies an American flag in the yard every day. Or he might be your mechanic, who wears a POW button on his uniform. One might be your bank's president, who has a vanity license plate for his car that reads *Semper fi* ('always faithful', the motto of the US Marine Corps); once a Marine, always a Marine. One could also be your ex-husband, who took his secrets from the war with him when he left. One could even be your mother, who teaches nursing. Others might be men who were wary of attending my college English course on Thursday evenings. He said he'd 'think about it'; another, the man who paced around the room during his first visit to my program; and a third might be Randall who never went anywhere without his weapons. One of my vets told me that before Randall came to my class, he was able to remove every weapon but his knife. Listen to them: they have a lot to teach us about the war.

One might be Bobby Ward, a Vietnam vet from Vietnam Veterans of America (VVA) Virginia Chapter 138, who attended my college English course on Thursday evenings. I thought the topic would relate to my students' family experiences in the '60s and early '70s. That First Thursday program with Bobby could have lasted all night. My students and I had endless questions that Bobby graciously answered. Even the one I was not prepared for: 'How many people did you kill?' Bobby said he didn't know. When his unit was fired upon, he shot back – into a triple-canopy jungle. 'I wasn't going looking for no dead bodies.' Four hours later, I asked everyone to save their remaining questions until next week. One of my students whose arm I twisted to take my course, Chris, wrote in his journal: 'Last night was Magic.' Indeed, it was.

I found out later that Bobby Ward came just to check us out; he worked on our campus anyway, so he was the chapter's natural choice to find out what I had planned for those Thursdays. Several chapter members' experiences with college students once they came home had not been positive. They wondered why I invited them. After that first Thursday, Vietnam vet Chapter 138 advertised the Thursday evening program, which brought more veterans, different vets, two, three, or four of them at a time. I never knew who was coming. Our class had a core of four men, with others dropping in for a Thursday or two. Eventually, the wives and adult children of some of these vets wanted their own session, which added to our understanding. We learned so much from all of them because we just talked – no lectures, no handouts, no ties-and-jackets. 'Our vets', as we came to call them, were gracious with their time, their energy, and their patience. Going to the Wall (the Vietnam Memorial) with them is something all of us will treasure. One of our vets who couldn't make himself go for years walked through holding the hand of one of my students. 'I did it, I did it,' he said to my student – and both were in tears. Me too!

This book is written in our soldiers' shared language, a code of sorts. Our American soldiers learned the code from other soldiers around them. So, here's the code that I hope unlocks the door that separates the soldiers who went to war from those who love them and those who want to know about history. The code is infantry-speak, grunt-style. Their words, their photos, and their poetry are all history to respect, to remember, and to pass on to others.

The grunt was an infantry soldier (Army or Marine), drafted or more likely a volunteer. One tour was twelve months for the Army infantry, twelve months plus an extra twenty days for a Marine. One Vietnam vet told me he could count down to the minute how much longer until his tour was over. Soldiers planning for 'one and done' kept count on what they called their 'short-timer's stick', or cartoon, or girlie poster: breaking off part of the stick after the day was over, whenever that happens to be, or tearing off a piece of poster, saving the funniest or sexiest for last. When there was no more stick, or a final rip on the poster, they knew they could head back to the real world on their 'Freedom Bird', the plane that took them away from Vietnam. Some soldiers thought Vietnam didn't exist, that it wasn't part of any world. They will explain that and more, maybe more than we thought we wanted to know.

The soldiers' reflections and the reflections of others reveal the effect the war had not only on those who fought in it, sacrificing their lives and sometimes their families and livelihood, but also on those demonstrating for or against it. It also had an effect on those no longer able to trust their government, on those living through it and fighting in it in North and South Vietnam, on the countryside torn apart by defoliation and war, and on those escaping the communists' victory to forge a new life for themselves in another country. Finally, it affected those staying behind to rebuild a devastated country now known as Vietnam. Their world and our world would never be the same after the War in Vietnam.

A Note on Language

> 'Swearing can be so satisfying that it can help us withstand pain. It can shock, offend and entertain. It can release tension or increase it. It can foster intimacy.' (Roache, 1)

'Like most wars, the Vietnam War provoked a vocabulary of its own. Many of the hundreds of words and phrases coined during the war appear in this book and require explanation' (Anderson, *Grunts*, xvii). Like Anderson, my book contains many, if not hundreds, of words used by the grunts, each with their own special meaning. 'In all the language dealing with Vietnam – whether fiction, poetry or film – you will notice the obscenities. Most writers and filmmakers argue that this is done on purpose, to reflect the real-life happenings. If this is so, then we are asked not to condemn the language merely because we are outsiders. If the language is true to the experience, then the language is defined by the community that shared the Vietnam experience – and we cannot judge it by standards our community shares' (Farb, 102, 18).[4]

'Oh, how the grunts could swear! The four-letter words came out of the young faces as smoothly as they flowed from a forty-year-old whore's mouth in a Singapore alley. It lost its profanity, even started to sound a little beautiful against the absurdities of the day' (Anderson, *Grunts*, 60). Our language conveys violence in a violent world – 'Get that motha-fucker'. Sexual words used in non-sexual situations show violence and aggression – 'Fuck you'. Language can show indifference when the real feeling is exactly the opposite – 'It don't mean nothing', said over one of our dead soldiers, is a survival technique; we toss it off and go on about our business. Language comforts when the absurdity of Vietnam comes at us – 'there it is',) when a body bag tumbles out of a helicopter. What else can we expect in this crazy war that other grunts say isn't real, doesn't exist, is a dream? Language also puts icing on a shit cake: 'neutralize', not 'kill'; 'navigational misdirection' for bombing errors. Military operations hide behind their names: 'search and destroy' means go find some gooks and kill them; Operation Ranch Hand means dropping defoliants and herbicides to destroy trees, grasses, and bushes over at least 1.7 million acres of land, possibly forever.

'[Reporter Michael] Herr [who wrote *Dispatches*] … used the troops' own vocabulary and made it into a new literary language. Some of the language was army slang – words and phrases by which soldiers separated themselves and their world from the outside world of civilians, a way of expressing their conviction that if you weren't there you can't understand. Some of it was the common obscenities of the American street … [Herr] saw that language [as described above] was appropriate for the story of the Vietnam War' (Hynes, 204–205). 'The language of war helps us to deny what war is really about, and in doing so it makes war more palatable' (Grossman, 93, see also 92).

We are now grunts, with some drop-ins such as reporters, photographers, a television crew, movie stars, and a general now and then, coming to support the troops. We personalize our equipment and use nicknames, all to create a familiarity with everything around us in this strange country. Puff the Magic Dragon (a C119 aircraft, later a C47 and still later a C130, a gunship), Freedom Bird (our ride home, not an army plane), White Mice (Saigon police and their white gloves), shake-and-bake (an instant lieutenant, with a new bar on his uniform, barely through basic), Monopoly money (we're not paid in money but in certificates), the Jolly Green Giant (a helicopter used for rescue missions), Mad Minute (fire like crazy), WHAM (Winning Hearts and Minds), Ho Chi Minh sandals (made from cast-off rubber tires), and the Korean phrase SNAFU (Situation Normal, All Fucked Up – it refers to a stupid action, a boss who forgets to send ammo). We can laugh at these because laughter and humor are natural impulses; why should they disappear in a war? Why can't we laugh at a grunt that sleeps with his M16 that somehow goes off?[5] There it is. That's the 'Nam.

A NOTE ON STYLE: I have chosen to spell Vietcong as one word to be consistent. I have, for the most part, used American spellings of Vietnamese words. I also have chosen to put in bold important ideas and words, like **Domino Theory** and **Ho Chi Minh Trail**, which I have defined or will define in this book.

Vietnam headstone. (Courtesy E Brown Jr)

Introduction

'Silent Battlefields'

'War is an ugly thing, but not the ugliest of things. The decayed and degraded
state of moral and patriotic feeling which thinks that nothing is worth
war is much worse. The person who has nothing for which he is
willing to fight, nothing which is more important than his
own personal safety, is a miserable creature and has no chance
of being free unless made and kept so by the exertions of better
men than himself.' (John Stuart Mill, *Principles of
Political Economy*, 1848)

The war is over now; only silent battlefields remain. But when the US put boots on
the ground in Vietnam, it had no idea what would happen to the grunts after landing
at Da-Nang Air Force base. From there, they traveled to the Replacement Center in
Chu Lai, known as Repo-Depo, to pick up orders, then the grunts went their separate
ways. Training together didn't mean fighting together. This separation was one of only
a hundred silent battles that took place in this ten-year guerrilla war.

The rock 'n' roll generation meets the crewcut lifers. Marijuana, Afros, long hair,
boonie hats with peace symbols, necklaces as well as dog tags, individual decisions –
take off that twelve-pound ceramic bullet-proof vest, it's no good against automatic
weapon fire; kick a little dirt over your trash, smoke even though it can be smelled a
mile away, join a unit to replace a combat-ineffective (Army-speak for 'dead') grunt.
You're a country boy from Alabama and your lieutenant is blacker than black. You
don't know any of them. They don't know you, but they are asking themselves: 'Can
he read a map to call in the coordinates for air support? Does he have the magic eyes to
walk point? Can he snap up a body bag, turn and say, "It don't mean nuthin'?"'

Silent battlefields twenty-four hours a day for your twelve-or-thirteen-month tour.
Silent because the battles in your head were often worse than the real ones: do I step
there or *there*?; is the man in black pajamas working in a rice field a Vietcong?; I see
night shadows that move; we killed some gooks but there are no bodies – I *know* we
killed some.[6]

Charlie. Singular and plural; refers to a Vietnamese man or the enemy. 'It was ghost
country, and Charlie Cong was its main ghost. The way he came out at night. How you
never really saw him, just thought you did. Almost magical – appearing, disappearing.
He could blend with the land, changing form, becoming trees and grass. He could
levitate. He could fly. He could pass through barbed wire and melt away like ice and
creep up on you without sound or footsteps' (O'Brien, *The Things They Carried*, 229).

Dig. Digging a foxhole for shelter; most soldiers considered this to be a make-work project, since they were likely to be ordered to advance, thereby leaving their foxholes for someone else to use. Marines apparently never dug in.

DIG
By Raymond Bolton (Marine, from the ninety-day siege at Khe Sanh)

What do you see?
I see nothing! A mute night
        as thick as death.
        It must be death.
                Dig deeper!
I cannot penetrate the darkness
        and the aloneness.
                Dig deeper!
        What do you see?
Ideas and dreams, hope and
        fantasies and innocence.
                Dig deeper!
        What do you see?
Young men and birds,
        water and the blue sky.
                Dig Deeper!
I hear voices and weeping.
        I hear the flutter of wings
        on the other shore.
Don't weep! Don't weep!
They are not on the other
        shore. The voices, the
        Weeping and the wings are
                your own heart. (Eichler 17)

Garbage. What passed for garbage to Americans was a treasure trove for the VC. They repaired broken equipment, carved brass shells into bowls, empty meal cans became booby traps. 'In Vietnam, our soldiers were a major part of the enemy's supply system. The US soldier, by nature, was rather wasteful, a trait that carried over from his civilian life. He tended to discard anything he considered extra and the idea of policing the battlefield was distasteful to him' (*A Distant Challenge*, 83).

Tin Trap
By Randy Cribbs

That peanut butter tin
Became a must keepsake,
Not left for the
Surprise Charlie could make.

Never eat it,
Caused too much thirst,
There in the boonies
Nothing worse.
But with it
Those C's* you could heat,
By mixing slowly with
A squirt of OD* Deet*.
Hot chow for
The whole team;
Important then,
Silly as that
May seem;
And
Better to keep
It now than to
Feel it later in our lap,
Among the innards
Of Charlie's booby trap. (41)

* Cs = C4, a pinch or two would light a fire to cook your food
* OD = olive drab
* Deet = insect repellant, not effective in Vietnam

Grunt. A soldier in the infantry. 'Doughboy' in the First World War; 'Yanks' or just 'soldiers' in the Second World War. A grunt got his proud name from the sound he made picking up his rucksack, which might weigh 50 pounds. His daily battles were exhaustion, lack of sleep, humping 50 pounds and taking turns carrying extra ordnance such as a 28-pound mine detector, heat over 100 degrees, humidity 100 per cent, and expecting to be fired upon any minute by an unseen enemy.

'To the dirt-eating grunt, Vietnam was an endless succession of bummers. Besides the never-ending fear of death, we had to endure a host of miseries: merciless humps through a sun-scorched landscape packing eighty pregnant pounds, brain-boiling heat, hot house humidity, dehydration, heat exhaustion, sunburn, red dust, torrential rains. Boot-sucking mud, blood-sucking leeches, steaming jungles, malaria, dysentery, razor-sharp elephant grass, bush sores, jungle rot, moaning and groaning, meals in green cans, armies of insects, fire ants, poisonous centipedes, mosquitoes, flies, bush snakes, vipers, scorpions, rats, boredom, incoming fire, body bags, and a thousand more discomforts. Despite all this the grunt did his job well' (Alfano).

Reptiles of Southeast Asia
By Larry Rottman

There are two kinds of snakes in Vietnam
Mr. One Step
And Mr. Two Step
Named for how far you go after being bitten. (Rottmann, 27)

Mantras. For the grunts, there were three mantras: 'It don't mean nuthin', 'There it is', and 'That's the 'Nam'. Although the mantras may sound callous, unfeeling, or indifferent, they provided another form of self-preservation. Along with drugs, alcohol, DEROS[7] – the time a grunt's tour was over, which he knew down to the minute – and R&Rs (a one-time Rest & Relaxation break to places such as Thailand, Japan, the Philippines, even Australia), grunts did their job.

Dr John Parish, in *An Autopsy of War*, comments on the grunts' mantra 'It don't mean nuthin': 'The grunts who did the fighting and those who supported them in the rear were not concerned with abstract morality, politics, opinion polls or military strategy. Once they were in the field their goal was simple survival, to do what they were told to do, to make war, to protect their buddies, to wear down "the enemy" and to kick ass. They did not see themselves as liberators, bullies, or imperialists; however, after being in Vietnam a very short time, many came to feel the country could not be saved, only destroyed. In that mission there was clarity' (46).

They said 'It don't mean nuthin' when it really did – the death of another grunt nearby, the war itself, looking at the aftermath of a skirmish or battle, or a 'Dear John' letter from a girlfriend saying she was breaking off the relationship. 'There it is' was said when a grunt saw the unexpected but was not surprised given the circumstances: watching a grunt drop ammo into a stream because he'd asked for too much. 'That's the 'Nam' was a recognition that it could only happen there, a *hope* that it happened only there, in the 'Nam – a grunt caught in a wait-a-minute vine discharging his weapon as he tried to extricate himself from its thorny streams of vines; or white monkeys throwing sticks at a unit as it passed by; or mud so thick it pulled boots off the grunts.

Nicknames. Combat units had revolving doors. Grunts came in as needed: to replace a grunt whose tour was over or to replace a seriously injured or dead grunt. The new grunt might be a newbie facing the start of his twelve-month tour; the lieutenant might have just two months left in his tour. Usually, every grunt in a unit had a different length of service left because each came to the unit one at a time. Usually, every grunt had a nickname: from his appearance (Bug Eyes), his home state (Okie, from Oklahoma), his favorite team (Yankee), or maybe his hobby (Surfer-Boy). Nicknames were another way of self-protection. If Surfer-Boy bought the farm[8] (died), PFC Rick Anderson (Surfer-Boy) from California died too. Somehow, Surfer-Boy's death, real as it was, became less important than the death of PFC Rick Anderson from California – hence the nicknames. Grunts chose nicknames that could provide some humor, but at the same time, they distanced themselves from the real person. It was a safety device. Grunts didn't want friends; they wanted to know somebody was watching their back.

The Vietnam Memorial, 'the Wall', became a silent battlefield when a grunt walked the 500 feet looking at 140 polished black granite panels filled with names. Where was Surfer-Boy? Where was Okie? Where was Bug Eyes? In his mind, they existed; he could see them. But where were they on the Wall? It was a cruel irony. That's why you see many vets run their hands down the Wall. That's why you hear many vets say 'they're all my brothers'. That's true. But Surfer-Boy is not only dead, he's also lost.

My college students met with local chapter 138 of Vietnam Veterans of America once a week for a semester. Anne, a student, said later that none of our vets knew any names or unit numbers. A Vietnam vet can find an approximate date on the Wall, usually by knowing when a battle occurred; he might then scan the names, names, and more names, but Surfer-Boy isn't there.

Night. The night belonged to Charlie. He was on his land, his trails, and in his tunnels. He could move without a sound, disappear into a tunnel – one of over 4,800. Honeycombed to make a small village, they contained caches of rice, water, weapons, and ammo. There were meeting rooms, a hospital, kitchens, places to live and sleep, and workshops that produced weapons.

Night Enemy
By Randy Cribbs

Through the night nothing stirred;
Pleasing to the ear, nothing heard.

They come in the dark
Leaving barely a mark,
Slipping through shadows hidden,
Guests unbidden.

But not this night,
Now giving way to light.
So rest easy you may;
            Soon comes the day. (27)

Race. Thoughts battling in grunts' heads: 'Why am I fighting in Whitey's war? Did they send young black men to kill little yellow men? What's with that grunt with a rebel flag on his helmet? I'm the only black guy and they got me walking second, so if the point man screws up, I'll be next to get it. That new lieutenant is black. What the hell do you think he knows? Is he any good? And I have to obey him?'

Volunteers accounted for 46 per cent of those men in the war; a disproportionate number were from the South. War was a duty and an honor to Southerners. 'Young blacks from large northern cities were brought into close contact with a kind of white man they had only heard about secondhand from parents and grandparents who had migrated from the rural South' (Anderson, *Other War*, 154).

One of our vets explained that racial tensions didn't exist out in the field. First, everybody had a weapon. Then everybody knew you had to depend on everybody else to make it to the next day. It was a learning experience. 'One vet [who attended my Thursday Evening Programs] when asked about trust said, "When I arrived in Vietnam, I only knew the guy I had met beside me on the plane. I wouldn't have called myself prejudiced, but a lot of those boys were when they got there. One thing is for sure they weren't for long; it didn't matter who you were we were in it together and you trusted them with your life"' (Ramsey, 59).[9] Harold Bryant, a Black grunt (they called themselves Bloods), said: 'I did get to find out that white people weren't as tough, weren't the number one race and all them other perceptions that they tried to ingrain in my head. I found out they got scared like I did' (Terry, 23).

AMERICA'S WHITE TABLE

- This table, set for one, is small, symbolizing the frailty of one prisoner, alone.

- It is set for one, symbolizing the fact that some are missing from our ranks.

- The tablecloth is white, symbolic of the purity of their intentions to respond to their country's call to arms.

- The black napkin represents the sorrow of captivity.

- The single red rose in the vase signifies the blood that many have shed to ensure the freedom of the United States of America. This rose also reminds us of the family and friends of our missing comrades who keep the faith, awaiting their return.

- The yellow ribbon on the vase represents the yellow ribbons worn on the lapels of the thousands who demand a proper accounting of our comrades who are not among us tonight.

- A slice of lemon on the plate reminds us of their bitter fate.

- The salt sprinkled on the plate reminds us of the countless fallen tears of families as they wait.

- The glass is inverted because they cannot toast with us.

- The chair is empty because they are not here.

- The candle is reminiscent of the light of hope that lives in our hearts to illuminate their way home, away from their captors, to the open arms of a grateful nation.

On an empty table in Chili's Restaurant. (Courtesy E. Brown, Jr)

The World. When your tour was nearly over, you were *short* – a *short timer*. Forty years later, a vet told me he knew down to the minute how much more time he had left to serve: 'I started with months, then at three months left, I went to weeks, then three weeks, to days, then at three days, I went to minutes. Three's my lucky number.' Grunts played a game with short timers. 'How short are you?' 'I'm so short you can see my head sticking out of my boot.' 'I'm so short I could parachute off a dime.' Then it was boarding your Freedom Bird to take you back to 'The World'.

The World meant more than home, more than baseball and apple pie. For most grunts, Vietnam had been a geographical unreality – sun so hot it burned your fingernails; rain so hard it put dents in your helmet; mud so thick it sucked your boots off; jungles so dense you couldn't see the elephant looking at you; rivers full of leeches and tiny barbed fish that could swim up a penis (some wore condoms when taking a river bath or just cooling off); humidity that rotted uniforms; black boots that the sun and water turned white.

One grunt said: 'I ain't never gettin' hit in Vietnam. ... 'Cause [Vietnam] it don't exist' (Herr, 125). This statement reveals the dichotomy the grunts felt: the grunts in Vietnam made a distinction 'between where [they are] and the rest of the world. [Even after returning home, they still say] "back in the World" with a capital "W" just like the grunts used to say it. Like [they're] in war now. A free-fire zone. A place where the normal rules are suspended' (Iles, 143).

'To [grunts], logic looks absurd, absurdity looks logical. They can't make realistic decisions about the future because they are no longer sure what reality is. The war was madness in motion; it was a surrealistic landscape brought to life and yet it was an historical event, real enough to wrench once solid values out of all recognizable and useful shape. Now for the confused veterans the mad play of life on the planet Earth goes on, bouncing back and forth between reality and illusion, and they feel strapped to a seat before that stage. Action is okay, passivity is okay, brutality is okay, love is okay – they're all okay, they're all worthless, "who gives a shit?"' (Anderson, *The Grunts*, 231).

A 'No-Bullshit' War Story
By Jim Gray

We went to Vietnam
And some of us came back
That's all there is –
Except for the details. (21)

SECTION ONE

The United States in the '50s, '60s, and '70s

'I was proud of the youths who opposed the war in Vietnam because they were my babies.' Dr Benjamin Spock (1988)

♦ ♦ ♦

'Above all, Vietnam was a war that asked everything of a few and nothing of most Americans.' Myra McPherson (1984), author of *Long Time Passing* about Vietnam and journalist for *The Washington Post*

♦ ♦ ♦

'This war has already stretched the generation gap, so wide that it threatens to pull the country apart.' Senator Frank Church (May 1970)

♦ ♦ ♦

'When history is denied and forgotten by society, it is bound to happen again.' Lieutenant Bernadette Harrod (2015)

Introduction

At the end of the Second World War, the GIs returned home from the fighting eager to take advantage of the free college tuition through the GI Bill and to resume their lives. Eisenhower promised peace and prosperity. General Electric promised progress – 'progress is our most important product'. Everywhere you looked, you could see signs of progress. With the construction of Levittown in Long Island, owning your own

Peace symbols. (Courtesy E. Brown, Jr)

home became a reality. The three automakers couldn't build cars fast enough. Life seemed perfect: barbecues in the backyard, freedom to travel on the newly constructed interstates, and with more families owning cars, shopping malls were constructed where everything you could want was available. The affordability of cars also meant many could and would move to the suburbs. Kids no longer had to play in the big city streets, but could play football and baseball in their backyards after school. Cars also provided teenagers with opportunities to drive down suburban Main Streets at night listening to Wolfman Jack playing rock 'n' roll on their car radios. But at the end of the George Lucas movie *American Graffiti*, some of these young men went off to war in Vietnam.

Yet all was not rosy. The USSR lowered the Iron Curtain and built a wall between East and West Berlin. The Cold War started in earnest, heating up in Korea and then Vietnam. By the early Sixties, communism was on our doorstep in Cuba. Presidents Eisenhower, Kennedy, and Johnson, believing in the Domino Theory, feared that communism would control all Southeast Asia. Eisenhower supported the French in Indochina, and when the French were defeated, he took over the responsibility to save Southeast Asia from communism. Kennedy and Johnson followed Eisenhower's lead, increasing their commitment to Southeast Asia, in particular Vietnam, first with advisors and then with troops.

The promise of the Fifties had disappeared in the increasing tensions brought about by the Cold War. Many young people protested against our increasing involvement in Vietnam, even disrupting the 1968 Democratic Convention in Chicago. Other young people heeded the words of Dr Timothy Leary, inventor of LSD, to 'turn on, tune in, and drop out'. Greenwich Village and Haight-Ashbury in San Francisco became the center of the drug culture and the Hippy movement. As Scott McKenzie sang, 'If you're going to San Francisco, be sure to wear a flower in your hair.' The musical *Hair* and other shows and movies depicted drug culture and flower power. *Godspell* took advantage of the movement to sing about love for Jesus.

Chapter 1

Foreign Affairs

'There's a definite split between what people believe history to be and what actually occurred.' (Moriah Richard, Managing Editor of *Writer's Digest*)

'Are there truths about the past that have been deliberately covered up?' (Moriah Richard)

The 1950s and 1960s were a turbulent time. The Soviet bloc increased tensions: the Cuban Missile Crisis, raising the Berlin Wall, and then the attempt to spread communism to Southeast Asia. The United States had been involved in Vietnam since the early Fifties, supporting the French colony financially. The US feared that if South Vietnam lost to the communist North, all Southeast Asia would become communist, one country at a time. This became known as the Domino Theory.

Domino Theory. President Eisenhower explained the Domino Theory, the underpinning of the Vietnam War, as follows: 'You have a row of dominoes set up, and you knock over the first one and what will happen to the last one is the certainty that it will go over very quickly. So you have the beginning of a disintegration that will have the most profound influences' (*Vietnam War Almanac*, 35). Staff Sergeant Browne knew all about the Domino Theory: 'you know, the Communists taking South Vietnam and then the Philippines and marching across the Pacific to Hawaii and then on to the shores of California' (Terry, 156).

'Americans were always talking about freedom from Communism, whereas the freedom that the mass of Vietnamese wanted was freedom from the exploiters, both the French and the indigenous. The assumption that humanity at large shared the democratic Western idea of freedom was an American delusion' (Tuchman, 256). 'Vietnam was never a patriotic war for America. There were no calls for people to save the country "from the invading yellow hordes!" only weird talk of a domino theory, the red spread of communism' (Page, 11). Daniel Phillips, who served in Vietnam, stated: 'We were there to bring democracy to South Vietnam, and the Communists were there to bring their way of life to the people. All the [Vietnamese] people [we worked with] just wanted to be left alone so they could raise their family, grow their crops, and be left in peace. Democracy or Communism was not going to affect them at all' (26).

Because each of the countries of Southeast Asia had its own traditions, culture, and history, the Domino Theory, although prevalent in US government circles, did not consider these differences. The US government never considered whether these differences made them ripe for communist takeover. By defending Vietnam, the US also made a commitment – although never spoken or acknowledged – to defend the other Southeast Asian countries if they lost in Vietnam; but, of course, they would not lose in Vietnam, so the other countries became a non-issue. Robert McNamara said that the Domino Theory's purpose was 'to save some fantasized Southeast Asian dominoes from tumbling' (Hendrickson, 123). The United States and its allies attempted to thwart the communist advance into Southeast Asia through the creation of a regional defense system, known as SEATO.

SEATO. Southeast Asia Treaty Organization. All signers of the 1954 treaty – the US, France, Great Britain, New Zealand, Australia and several nations in Southeast Asia – would come to the aid of any member under attack. Even though the Geneva Peace Accords of 1954 forbade Vietnam, Laos, and Cambodia from signing any international treaty, the treaty signers agreed to come to their aid in the event of a communist attack. Developed by the Truman administration, the treaty's purpose was to thwart the prevailing Domino Theory that if one Southeast Asian nation fell to the communists, they all would.

Reporter Michael Herr offers one reason United States troops were in Vietnam: 'Not that you didn't hear some overripe bullshit about it: Hearts and Minds, Peoples of the Republic, tumbling dominoes, maintaining the equilibrium of the Dingdong by containing the ever-encroaching Doodah; you could also hear the other, some young soldier speaking in all bloody innocence, saying, "All that's just a *load*, man. We're here to kill gooks. Period"' (20).

In his inaugural address, President Kennedy stated that 'The United States would pay any price, bear any burden, meet any hardship, support any friend, oppose any foe, to assure the survival and success of liberty [which] reinforced Americans' vision of their country as a muscular force for good around the globe' (*The Atlantic Magazine*, October 2017, 3). He realized that to preserve democracy in South Vietnam, the government would have to gain popular support of the people – 'Victory would be impossible without it' (*Vietnam: Special Newsweek Edition*, 9). To help the South Vietnamese government gain that support, the US would provide materiel support and advisors. When the Catholic President Diem proved unpopular and unable to win the support of the South Vietnamese people because of his oppression of Buddhists, President Kennedy supported the overthrow of that government, although he was shocked that Diem and his brother had been killed. But who would now govern South Vietnam? Kennedy thought he might have been too hasty in supporting the overthrow, for without a stable government, fighting the Vietcong would be difficult (*The Atlantic Magazine*, October 2017, 3). In May 1964, '[President] Johnson confessed to National-Security Advisor McGeorge Bundy that he did not know what to do. ... "It's just the biggest damn mess I ever saw. ... I just thought about ordering those kids in there, and what the hell am I ordering (them) out there for. ... What the hell is Vietnam worth to me? ... What is it worth to the country?"' (*The Atlantic Magazine*, October 2017, 3). Yet later in 1964, Johnson stated: 'This is not a jungle war, but a struggle for freedom on every front of human activity' (*Public Papers*, 931). He also acknowledged, 'we are not about to send American boys nine or ten thousand miles away from home to do what

Asian boys ought to be doing for themselves' (Speech at Akron University, 21 October 1964). But he did, not wanting to be the first US Commander-in-Chief to lose a war. 'In 1965 Defense Secretary McNamara told the President that even if he committed more men, the chances of victory were no better than one in three' (*The Atlantic Magazine*, October 2017, 4). That advice did not stop the escalation of troops. Believing his own credibility and America's credibility were at stake in Vietnam (Herring, 2), Johnson authorized the immediate dispatch of 50,000 troops in July 1965, increasing the draft to 35,000 each month. He explained why he sent those troops to Vietnam: 'The first reality is that [communist] North Vietnam has attacked the independent nation of South Vietnam' (Appy, 1). Some anti-war factions disputed 'the claim that South Vietnam was an "independent nation" established by the Geneva accord' (Appy, 1). Others claimed that the war was not fought to protect Southeast Asia from Soviet or Chinese influence. Nixon, by toasting the leaders of the Soviet Union and China in a trip to both nations in 1972, made it clear that the concern was not the spread of Soviet and Chinese influence in Southeast Asia. So if it was not fought to keep the Soviet Union and China out of Southeast Asia, was it, in fact, a civil war (Appy, 2)? Jessica Chapman, a historian at Williams College, thinks so: 'The Vietnam War was, at its core, a civil war greatly exacerbated by foreign intervention. Others have described it as a civil war that became internationalized.' Still others said it was part of the anti-colonial struggle for independence that occurred throughout the world at the end of the Second World War (Appy, 2).

Was it fought to gain access to the oil reserves off the coast of Vietnam? One of the phrases used by the grunts at one of my Thursday Evening Programs to refer to the Vietnam War was **Lady Bird's War**. It was so named because many felt that President Johnson continued the war so that the US could gain control of the oil to be found off the Vietnamese coast. In a conversation with my father-in-law in 1970, he told me that we needed to support South Vietnam to protect our investment in the offshore oil reserves (conversation with Dr Earl Brown). In fact, the first traces of oil were not discovered off the coast of South Vietnam until 28 August 1974, when the war had all but ended (Spiker, 1).

In 1965, President Johnson explained to the nation: 'We are there because we have a promise to keep. … We are also there to strengthen world order. … We are also there because there are great stakes in the balance. We need to continue to provide aid to [the] South Vietnamese to show our confidence in their ability to stop communist aggression. If we deserted South Vietnam, that would only be the beginning of our endless wars in Southeast Asia, each country demanding our support due to the SEATO Treaty of 1954' (*Public Papers*, 156–157).

Yet at the same time, President Johnson was trying to find some way out, some way to bring our boys home. He offered incentives to North Vietnam, with 'a vast economic uplift plan for Southeast Asia … if they agree to sit down at the bargaining table'. He also suspended air strikes as a further demonstration of his serious intent (*Vietnam: Special Newsweek Edition*, 31).

Yet this peace overture, like all others, was met with contempt. Although Johnson offered the North Vietnamese a way to end the war, they never offered the United States a way to save face, or what Sun Tzu, author of *The Art of War*, referred to as a 'golden bridge', so that the United States could find a way to retreat. For the North, there would be no compromise, and no offer of compromise.

Project 100,000. In August 1966, the demand for more troops created a logistical problem for President Johnson and Secretary of Defense McNamara. Johnson did not want to remove the deferment for students in post-secondary education. Johnson and Secretary McNamara created a plan, known as Project 100,000, to draft those men who had previously been rejected by the military. It took two years for them to convince Congress and the Pentagon to lower requirements for draftees, but by 1966, Congress and the Pentagon relented. The program was not a success, as the new draftees were not mentally and physically equipped to handle basic training, much less combat – some were even illiterate. They thus endangered their fellow soldiers. By late 1971, the program was phased out (Fitzgerald, 2–5).

'By late 1967, the war had become the most visible symbol of malaise that seemed to grip the nation as a whole. Noisy street demonstrations, rioting in Detroit and Newark and a spiraling national crime rate' created greater anxiety. One responder to a national survey about the war said 'he wanted to get out but not give up. … But the public mood – tired, angry, frustrated – posed perhaps a more serious threat to the [Johnson] administration than the anti-war movement itself' (Herring, 5).

In a nationwide address delivered on 31 March 1968, President Johnson explained why he had ordered the end to the bombing of the North: 'Our objective in South Vietnam has never been the annihilation[10] of the enemy. It has been to bring about a recognition in Hanoi that its objective – taking over the South by force – could not be achieved' (*The American Presidency Project*, 8).

At the end of 1968, future US National Security Advisor and Secretary of State Henry Kissinger wrote in an essay for *Foreign Affairs*: 'A denial strategy cannot in itself produce victory. We fought a military war; our opponents fought a political one. … We sought physical attrition; our opponents aimed for our psychological exhaustion. In the process we lost sight of one of the cardinal maxims of guerilla war: the guerilla wins if he does not lose. The conventional army loses if it does not win' (Elliott, 3).

During the 1968 campaign for president, Nixon had constantly stated that he would get America out of Vietnam. He said he had a plan to end the war in Vietnam and bring the boys home. All he would say is that it involved 'peace with honor'. Secretly, however, he believed that if South Vietnam was to fall, better after the election than before (*The Atlantic Magazine*, October 2017, 4).

The same thinking occurred as he ran for reelection in 1972: better that Saigon fell after he won reelection. But he promised during his campaign that the United States would not leave Vietnam until all Americans came home. Christian Appy wrote: 'The idea that Vietnam posed a threat to Cold War America was so discredited, it sometimes sounded as if the only remaining war aim was to get back its P.O.W.s' (2).

When the last helicopter lifted off the American Embassy roof in Saigon on 30 April 1975, it ended the illusion of American invincibility; it made Americans reexamine their sense of morality and 'undermined the country's faith in its most respected institutions, particularly the military and the presidency' (*The Atlantic Magazine*, October 2017, 1). General H.R. McMaster, US National Security Advisor from 2017–2018, wrote that even thirty years later, 'after the end of the Cold War, the shadow of the American experience in Vietnam still hangs heavy over American foreign and military policy, and over American society' (xiii).

Leaving Vietnam. (Wikipedia)

At approximately the same time, former Secretary of Defense McNamara said in two books, *In Retrospect 1995* and *Argument Without End*, that he regretted his involvement in the Vietnam War, and 'the United States had been "terribly wrong" to intervene in Vietnam. He attributed the failure to a lack of knowledge and judgment. If only he had understood the fervor of Vietnamese nationalism … if only he had realized that the Domino Theory was wrong, he might have persuaded his presidential bosses to withdraw from Vietnam. Millions of lives would have been saved. If only' (Appy, 1).

Chapter 2

The Draft

'[Draft Boards,] by exercising their vast discretion in choosing who
would be drafted and enforcing existing social hierarchy, …
were organizations "that effectively ensured social, economic and racial
inequality throughout the 20th century from World War II to
the Vietnam war".' (Jason Higgins, quoted in C. Wilson,
'What "It's A Wonderful Life" Teaches us about American History')

The peacetime draft, established in 1940 and ended in 1973, provided a means to fill military vacancies. In 1968, defense officials announced that 302,000 men faced the draft – this was still lower than 1966, but these men were needed to replace men with completed tours. In a few cases, a judge volunteered a young man, offering him prison time or a stint in the Army. It was mandatory to register with Selective Service at the age of 18 and always carry your draft card. Government drafting for the armed forces was employed for the first time since 1942.

In 1965, President Johnson needed additional troops 'because the aggression of others has increased in Vietnam. There is not, and there will not be, a mindless escalation' (*Public Papers*, 211). There were, however, never enough troops. On 1 December 1969, when General Westmoreland desperately needed more troops overseas, the draft boards instituted a lottery system, based on the date of one's birth, with every birth date minus the year drawn out one-by-one, and numbered accordingly. The first date chosen would be #1 – it was 14 September – and any young man at least 18 born on 14 September knew he would be drafted first. Those young men whose birth dates were lower numbers knew they were at risk of being drafted, while individuals with higher numbers had less chance of being drafted. The best number was 24 September, number 366, including 29 February. The second determiner was alphabetical order. Those with the same birth date were selected according to their last name. The draft/lottery ended in 1973. 'Men with numbers of 96 and above … will remain in a holding category, 1-H. [This] "readily inductible pool" will contain about 500,000 men. Because of a high physical disqualification rate and various deferments, [the Selective Service acting director] estimates that 100,000 … would be qualified for service' (*NY Times*, 9 March 1973, 30).

'The draft in the Vietnam era was full of inequities. Applicable standards for deferments and exemptions varied from place to place, depending in part on whether

Draft card.

a local board was having trouble meeting its quota. Reserve and National Guard units became safe havens – for those with the right connections or who happened to be at the right place at the right time' (*Roanoke Times*, 21 September 1992, A10).

The draft policy had even wider implications. Because the draft placed a higher priority on certain occupations and on certain college majors, those students and professionals had a better chance of avoiding the draft. Those who did not fit into these categories, especially those on lower incomes and minorities, were more likely to be drafted, a blatant form of discrimination (Anderson, *Other War*, 149).

With a draft in place, young men found themselves in a waiting game. Some remained ambivalent, willing to conform to draft board rules but hoping not to be called up. One man decided 'it was better to spend two years in the service than five years in prison. And I figured that for nineteen years I had enjoyed a whole lot of fruits of this society. I knew that you didn't get anything for free' (Terry, 55).

Some men received a 4-F classification, which meant that they were not qualified for the armed services for medical and/or psychiatric reasons. 4-F was final – if the draft declared you 4F, the board would not recall you for a physical. But 4-Fs were difficult to get, and the Army needed men. You were more likely to receive a 1-Y, whereby you could be recalled later to see if you were now fit to serve.

Johnny, who came to my Thursday evening programs, was 19 when drafted ''cause I couldn't afford no college. So, when I went to Vietnam, I was dumber than dirt' (Vietnam Vet Program, 28/1/93). Al, another former soldier who attended my program on Thursday evenings, thought there should never be a draft unless we were in an all-out war (Vietnam Vet Program, 4/2/93).

In a letter that appeared in *The Roanoke Times and World News* on 3 December 1990, Owen Schultz said: 'In 1969, the Smithtown, N.Y. draft board granted me classification 1-H following a hearing about my conscientious-objector status. This meant I awaited induction and assignment to alternative, humanitarian service in lieu of military duty. It also meant that I would not go to Vietnam, or to federal penitentiary for five years, or pay a $10,000 fine. I don't remember who got the money, but dissent had a clear price tag against which you could weigh your choices.'

In the 1960s, the draft board needed men to fight the war in Vietnam. But for the first time in US history, according to an article written in *Newsweek* on 11 April 1966, avoiding the draft became 'socially acceptable. "The old image of true red-blooded volunteers is for the birds"[11] says Georgia Selective Service Procurement Director. ... It is not merely an unpopular war; to vast numbers of the public, it is an unacknowledged war. Only one in every 850 U.S. citizens is in the combat zone, and the full tragedy of war hardly touches most Americans, save for the families of the 2762 who have lost their lives' (*Vietnam: Special Newsweek Edition*, 65).

Since avoiding the draft had become socially acceptable, many young Americans looked for ways to avoid being drafted and sent to Vietnam: moving to Canada, getting married, staying in school, or joining the National Guard. College students granted deferments could avoid induction into the military so long as they remained in good standing. Once they graduated or left school, they lost their deferment. In July 1965, a Selective Service document, 'Channeling', which wasn't published until 1967 in *New Left Notes*, stated: 'For the first time, students could see how the "club of induction" [joining the military] was used to control their lives: certain occupations [such as engineers], deemed important by the government, were to be allowed deferments' (Zaroulis and Sullivan, 105).

Other means to avoid or evade the draft were more creative and/or dangerous: building up one part of your body or tanning only one side of your body so you looked deformed or getting letters from doctors attesting to some medical problem which would keep you from serving.

Willard Gaylin, MD, in an article that appeared in the *LA Times* on 29 October 1992, said: 'I worried about what might happen to these young men [draft dodgers] ... in Federal prison. We needn't have worried. In 1967, when I began what turned out to be three years of research, there were all of 70 imprisoned political war resisters in the entire country.' Gaylin's research revealed that those in the middle or upper classes 'could use the loopholes and dodges' written into the Selective Service Act. Those who could avoid the draft did so and, in fact, were expected to do so. There would be no shame attached to their deferments (B7).

But some, unable to avoid the draft, were urged not to comply with their draft boards. In the film *Boys N the Hood* (1981), Furious Styles, played by Laurence Fishburne, 'mentions his time in Vietnam ... "Don't ever go in the Army, [son]," he says. "Black man ain't got no place in the Army."' (*Boyz N the Hood*, reviewed thirty years later by Lawrence Ware, *NYTimes*, 13 July 2021, section C, 3). Earlier, in July 1965, Clinton Hopson and Joe Martin made the same argument, '[urging] the African American Mothers of McComb, Mississippi to keep their sons from going to Vietnam, their words reflected private grief and anger rather than' the views of any civil rights group (L. Rosenwald, 383).

Unwilling to look for a way to avoid the draft, although a student at Cornell University, Matthew Goodman just refused to take part in the process altogether. He 'refused to register for the draft on general pacifist grounds. ... His method of refusal was not to recognize the draft system at all and to continue as usual, including ... his overt antiwar activity – now without a draft card" (Goodman, 440).[12]

On 6 January 1966, the Student Non-Violent Coordinating Committee (SNCC) issued a 'Statement on American Policy in Vietnam'. This said: 'We are in sympathy with, and support, the men in this country who are unwilling to respond to a military draft which would compel them to contribute their lives to United States aggression in Viet Nam in the name of the "freedom" we find so false in this country. ... We recoil with horror at the inconsistency of a supposedly "free" society where responsibility to freedom is equated with the responsibility to lend oneself to military aggression' (Rosenwald, 383).

Many in the United States, however, felt it was their patriotic duty, just as it had been their father's patriotic duty to fight against the Germans in the Second World War. Others felt that the US Army offered them opportunities that were not available otherwise, such as learning skills which they could use once their term of service had ended. Tim O'Brien has his narrator in 'On the Rainy River' say, 'I was a coward. I went to war' *(The Things They Carried*, 63). John Rempel said that he 'gladly went over because they needed me' (letter to Margaret Brown).

Our students did not ask the soldiers who came to our class why they joined. We did learn later that some who had no interest in higher education felt that by volunteering they would get better assignments. Bobby Ward told the class that he joined because he could get a 'cot and a hot'; another vet told the class he was given the choice of jail or the Army – 'it was no choice. I chose the Army.' Dee Phillips, a daughter of one of the soldiers, was so proud of her father who served in Vietnam that she later volunteered to join the Army. This was typical nationwide. Some volunteered, while others, who had no intention of pursuing higher education or had their deferments run out, were drafted; those convicted of a minor crime were given a choice of the Army or jail time. Still others, such as conscientious objectors (COs), argued their beliefs in letters to the draft board or in front of a judge. Many of those who objected conscientiously still served. Basil Paquet, a poet who objected to firing a weapon, served as a medic in Vietnam without a weapon. He said that he didn't want his friends and family to think him a coward.

Bestselling author Michael Connelly's fictional character, Dominick Santanello, also would not fire a weapon: 'Nicky, I remember being at chow on *Sanctuary* [a hospital ship] when I heard about you getting shot down. ... I remember begging you not to go out there to First Med. I begged you. I said, "don't get off the boat, man." But you didn't listen. You had to get that CMB [combat medical badge] and see the war' (98–99).[13] Yet, despite the draft and prison-or-the-Army sentences, the majority of those who served were volunteers. In the Second World War, 66 per cent of American military personnel were draftees; in Vietnam, only 25 per cent (or 648,500) were draftees. These draftees accounted for 30.4 per cent (or 17,725) of combat deaths in Vietnam.[14]

Vietnam
By James Griffin

12,000 miles, away from home.
Our Hearts are emptied, all but blood
Our bodies are covered with sweat and mud.
This is the life we choose to live
A year of lifetime is what we give ...
You never know what it's like to be here,
You, with your party girls and beer.
Over there, you aren't even trying,
While over here our men are dying.
March at dawn, and plant your signs on the
   White
House lawn.
Shout out, ban the bomb, and there is no war
 · in Viet Nam ... .
Pop some pills, and roll in the sun,
Simply refuse to carry a gun.
There's nothing else for you to do?
And I am supposed to die for you?
Stand fast prepare for a blow,
I'll tell you something you do not know.
It's not for you and me this war goes on,
It's for the people of South Vietnam,
All they want to do is live and be free,
And to live in human dignity.
There is another thing I want you to know,
And that's where I think you should go.
We are already here and we are here to stay.
We'll be here tomorrow,
If we make it through today. (Eichler, 53–54)

Danny Phillips.
(Courtesy D. Phillips)

Volunteers[15]

'This is why we (well, most of us) serve – not because we are hellbent on killing but because we believe our country and its principles are worth dying for.' (Johnson, *The Bulwark*)

According to Jack Reacher, the fictional hero of Lee Child's novels, 'there are four types of people who join the military. For some it's family trade, [Lew Puller]. Others are patriots, eager to serve, [Jim Bowman]. Next you have those who need a job [Bobby Ward].[16] Then there's the kind who want the legal means of killing other people' (Christopher McQuarrie, director of the 2012 film *Jack Reacher*). A Japanese reporter who interviewed several men in a US field hospital, many of them volunteers, later wrote: 'What was common to all of them was that they had a very strong sense of duty and were of the opinion that it was right and proper for citizens to [do what their country asked of them. Despite that belief, they would not reenlist but] wanted to go home as soon as their obligatory term of one year would be over' (Honda, 32).[17]

Jim Bowman, one of the vets who attended my Thursday evening program, volunteered in 1965 at the age of 19. He said: 'Somebody has to do it, might as well be trained people. I didn't go on blind faith. I had an oath to serve/obey orders. I considered it my personal responsibility' (4/2/93). Bobby Ward, who volunteered at the age of 18, commented: 'For me, it was an escape, not just from poverty or college, but to make some money.' Unlike Bobby Ward, who had no friends, Jim Bowman said he had four good friends there; two of them died. 'Maybe the worst was the jungle rot, worse than in WWII. I got malaria, which was like being crushed in a car. When I got home, I had some mental problems but nobody to help me. Maybe the ABC (Alcohol Beverage Commission) store' (Vietnam Vet Program, 4/2/93).

Steve Flaherty, a college student with pro-baseball prospects, told his sister-in-law that he joined the Army willingly because he felt it was his obligation. She said: 'I was in tears (reading the letters) thinking of how he must have felt, how afraid he must have been yet determined to do his duty' (First, 9). He died in battle on 25 March 1969.

Many went gladly. 'Being the only son in my family, I did not have to accept the orders to Vietnam. I accepted the orders because I wanted to see what the war was all about. And I thought that if we were there it must be right. We have to stop communism before it gets to America. I was just like all the other dummies' (Terry, 63). Some, however, were forced to volunteer, like Robert E. Holcomb, who evaded the draft for over a year; when finally caught by the FBI, he was told to say the oath. He'd be a problem for the Army next time. When he refused, he was told either he served in the Army or he would spend the rest of his life in prison. 'I raised my hands and said the oath. I was sworn into the Army in manacles' (Terry, 200).

Many also felt that it was their duty to support 'my country, right or wrong'. But that was not the original intent of the phrase. The essence is that we, the United States, want to be right in our dealings with other countries. Within our own country, we can accept that we can be right, and we can be wrong. Johnny said in one program about the protestors that he 'didn't resent them. It was their right to protest' (Vietnam Vet Program, 1/93).

All the women who participated in the war were volunteers. Ninety per cent were nurses; others served in the United Service Organization (USO). Although approximately 260,000 women served in the armed forces during the Vietnam War – about 3 per cent of those being in uniform – the military did not provide numbers of women who served in Vietnam. As early as 1956, nurses were in Vietnam training Vietnamese. By 1963, the numbers of skilled nurses had increased. Because of the nature of guerilla warfare, nurses were always at risk; many were injured during their year in Vietnam. As well as attending to the wounded, nurses also aided in evacuating wounded soldiers and served on hospital ships off the coast of Vietnam.

The women returning from Vietnam faced the same hostile reaction as the men. And just like the men, many refused to talk about their experiences in Vietnam. 'Limited information about American women in Vietnam complicates knowledge regarding health issues. Many suffered complications from Agent Orange and post-traumatic stress disorder' (*Women Veterans*). Bernadette Harrod claimed 'that the most tragic part of the story of women in Vietnam is that the story has gone untold'. Untold is the 'pain, longing, and sadness' of women who risked their lives to save others (36).

Lifers. Then there were the Lifers, career Army personnel. Dr Lifton, a Vietnam vet who works with many vets, said: 'What he found was a chasm between the grunts and the lifers. [The grunts] brought to Vietnam some of the culture of the 60s: rock music, allowing their hair to grow long, Afros with a special comb that didn't fit in their front pocket to keep the style, pot-smoking, peace signs, and even antiwar literature. In contrast, the lifers were the regular military complete with a "conventional and authoritarian military ethos"' (230).

Lynda Van Devanter, who was a nurse, explains: 'One of our main targets for frustration was the attitude of the lifers who … probably questioned the war in private but would not voice their opinions because their precious career might be damaged' (210). Vietnam then became the site of the same generational war that was happening in many places in the US. Lifton speculates that this had a lot to do 'with the actual violence of "fragging" incidents' (231), the complete misunderstanding and non-acceptance of each group for the other.

This total misunderstanding led to fragging, the killing of a higher-ranked man considered to be dangerous to a squad or other unit, an assassination, usually by a grenade. Many of the incidents occurred because the grunts feared for their lives and felt that the platoon leader had asked them to do something which exposed them to greater danger. 'From 1969–1972, there were 96–126 incidents with 37–39 deaths; 290 incidents with 34 deaths; 333–335 incidents with 12 deaths; 37–59 incidents with 1–4 deaths' (Dunnigan and Nofi, 221).

'Every soldier, Marine, sailor or airman who fragged a unit leader believed at the time of the incident that he acted with more than ample justification. Such a view may sound incredible now, but anyone who has seen combat and perceived what it does to one's thinking processes can appreciate the extreme difficulty, perhaps even the folly of making value judgments on the thoughts and actions of men in a combat environment from a haven now made safe by both time and distance' (Anderson, *Grunts*, 217–218).

Explanations offered for the fragging of unit leaders indicated a belief that one's survival was threatened. Two specific and one general type of incident provoked all such assumptions. First, two dates were always in the minds of Americans in Vietnam: R & R and Tour Rotation, one's last day in the 'Nam, known as DEROS.[18] The last thing a trooper wanted to hear was that either of those dates had been changed. In his anxiety to leave the war, he could see no real justification for either being 'messed with by some paper-shuffling lifer in the rear'. Yet these important dates were changed, often with no explanation to the grunt.

One such fear occurred when the grunt had only few days left in 'country'. Although there was no official policy, many platoon leaders acknowledged the short-timer by allowing him to remain safe behind the lines, providing food or delivering the mail. 'Occasionally, however, the combat situation dictated that such a policy be set aside', in which case the reaction of the troops affected bordered on paranoia and 'unnecessary harassment' (Anderson, *Grunts*, 218–219).

James Fellows, writing for *The Atlantic Magazine* in 2017, concluded that there were two ways to classify Vietnam-era men's thinking about the war. **#1. 'Did they think anybody in the United States should be going to fight in Vietnam, Yes or**

No?' Some who answered 'no' protested the draft and the war, and, unfortunately, the soldiers who returned from Vietnam. Even though they answered 'no' to #1, many of them just looked after themselves, finding ways to avoid the draft. Because many of them only took care of themselves – keeping themselves out of harm's way – very few did anything to alter US policy; by doing little, they actually aided the government's increasing involvement in Vietnam (Fallows, 'The New Series', 4). If their answer was 'yes', they volunteered. **#2. 'Did they think that *they personally* should go to fight in the war, Yes or No?'** If their answer was 'no' to #1, they answered 'no' to #2, and like those who had answered 'no' to #1 they joined the protest movement, used every available means at their disposal to avoid being drafted or did both. If their answer was 'yes', once again they volunteered. However, many believed that the answer to #1 was 'yes', that people should go; but their answer to #2 was 'no', not me. James Fellows refers to them as 'chickenhawks' ('Chickenhawk in Chief, 2).

Deserters. 'The formal definition of "deserter" is someone absent without leave [AWOL] for thirty days or more, without extenuating circumstances' (Dunnigan and Nofi, 338). It is also defined as 'being absent with the intention to remain away permanently' (Kutler, 157). The first definition is easier to apply; an authority can determine if the 'extenuating circumstances' were reasonable. The second definition, however, is impossible to apply. How is one to determine another's 'intention' to do anything?

'During the Vietnam War, desertion rates reached an all-time high of 73.5 out of 1,000 soldiers in 1971, a 400 percent increase over the 1966[19] rate of desertion' (Kutler, 158). Johnny explained in one of my courses on the Vietnam War why Americans deserted: 'If caught, what could they do? Court Martial you and send you home?' (1/25/03). Desertion, in combination with AWOL incidents, cost the Army approximately 550,000, of whom approximately '92,000 were declared deserters' (Dunnigan and Nofi, 339).

Chapter 3

Basic and Advanced Training

Whether Uncle Sam wanted you or you wanted Uncle Sam hardly made a difference, except that if you volunteered, you had more options. Once you were in the Army or armed services, off you went to boot camp for basic training.

Boot Camp. Eight weeks of basic training. You would learn discipline, develop stamina and learn what it's like to be in the military, from buzz cuts – which you had to pay for – to taking aptitude tests, getting vaccinated and being outfitted. You also learned to hate your drill sergeants and the enemy. Journalist and Vietnam vet Holzwarth recalled that before he began basic training, he had to swear 'to support and defend the Constitution against all foreign and domestic enemies, obey the orders of the President and our officers, and abide by the Uniform Code of Military Justice[20] and the Military Code of Conduct' (#24).[21]

All that processing made you realize that it was not just basic training: it was whole life training, from the clothes you wore to the haircut you received. You were issued with a military combat uniform (fatigues), including blouse or jacket with hook-and-loop attachments to strap on things, and flak jacket to protect against shrapnel, not bullets; most didn't wear them because they were hot and heavy, and they were already carrying at least 40 pounds of equipment. There were also trousers with Velcro pouches for knee-pad inserts, two forward-tilted thigh storage pockets and two calf storage pocket, plus a helmet, T-shirts with moisture wicking to keep them as cool as possible, and footwear (Ruck For Miles, 1–2), sometimes referred to as jungle boots. These boots were partly stainless steel, with holes to keep the water from staying in the boot. They were supposed to dry out quickly, but the boots tended to stay wet, causing jungle rot to feet, also called immersion foot. By the end of a tour, a grunt's boots would be ringed and stained white, very different from the spit-shining so important in basic training. According to Olsen's *Dictionary of the Vietnam War*, the jungle boot had 'DMS', a Direct Molded Sole (508). The Goodyear Tire & Rubber Company was already advertising its part in the jungle boot – when the Marines were arriving in Vietnam without jungle boots, because none were available. Despite their boots not being available, Goodyear placed ads in magazines: 'Boots with '"Chemivic synthetic rubber vinyl" soling compound outlasted old boots by 300 percent in Vietnam' (Ebert, 196). Of course, there were also socks to keep your feet dry; but they didn't.

During the war, the military changed fatigues to camouflage – greens and yellows.[22] Because of the wet weather or 100 per cent humidity on dry days, plus elephant grass, dirt and dust, fatigues didn't last long. They ripped and shredded. Some Marines lost

17

Danny Phillips holding an M16.
(Courtesy D. Phillips) (Below dog tags)

the seat of their fatigues. Tops were loose. In the heat and humidity of Vietnam, the clothes might have given out before a soldier's tour was over. Firebases didn't always have replacements. More than one soldier came to his bunker with his pants falling off; and too much crawling in dirt and water made the fatigues wet or damp all the time.

They wore a cap, like a ball cap, called a 'cover'. Some wore soft camouflage hats known as 'boonie' hats. Many soldiers put peace buttons and their slang names on them ('Rocky', 'King Kong' or 'Okie'); they were generally scrunched, out of shape. Early in the war, the Army issued uniforms that were available. Some of the clothing soldiers wore was not suitable for the ground and weather in Vietnam. With 100 per cent humidity, nothing stayed dry. Soldiers were always requesting socks from home due to theirs rotting. 'Fatigue uniforms were … deplorable; the constant dampness rotted the seams and weakened the threads and the jungle constantly clenched and tore at the clothing, making short work of the hardiest material' (Ebert, 198). Because of the fungus that caused immersion foot (and affected other parts of the body), many soldiers chose to skip underwear as it stayed damp all the time – as did their feet. So, with fatigues rotting and falling apart, some soldiers were left 'with their asses hanging out' (Ebert, 198).

And, of course, there were Dog Tags. The Army gave each GI two tags on metal chains with identifying information. Some men laced one of the tags around shoelaces in case a serious wound made the other tag illegible. Many grunts had as many as four or five, thinking of them as lucky charms. Grunts in the bush often put one on an ankle and one around the neck in case killed in action, in the hope they could be identified. 'Dog tags were oval or rectangular (with rounded ends) tags worn by servicemen on a chain. Stamped data varied between services and period,

but typically included name, serial number, blood type, and religion. Examples of other entries were tetanus inoculation dates and home address. If a soldier were killed, one tag was left with the body and the other turned in. One tag had a notch in one end, and it was rumored that this was to be inserted between the teeth of the dead man. This is a myth; it was a positioning notch for a stamping machine' (Rottmann, *FUBAR*, 41).[23]

Although trained to follow all forms of military courtesy – everything spit and polished, senior officers saluted, decorum always maintained – when they arrived in Vietnam, they quickly learned not to salute their officers to keep them from being targeted by the enemy. In country, many abandoned the spit and polish of boot camp, wearing unconventional, unauthorized clothing and accessories, but only in the field. 'Military decorum [however] remained in place at base and facilities' (Holzwarth, #14).

Not only were they given clothing to wear and trained in tactics and strategy, but they were also given a backpack or rucksack to carry. 'All of the weight carried in a soldier's back is set by the army commanders and their subordinate leaders based on what they deem most appropriate based on their circumstances' ('Ruck For Miles', 3). Each soldier carried a pack weighing approximately 40 pounds, strapped to his back. Caputo gave us a summary of what he carried in his: 'Signal flares, smoke grenades, dry socks, a poncho, and three days' rations … an entrenching tool and machete. … In my pockets, I carried a map, compass, hand grenades, more flares, halazone tablets [to purify water], malaria pills, and a spare magazine, a pistol, two clips of ammunition, knife, first aid kit. … Two full canteens hung from my belt. The gear weighed over forty pounds altogether' (Caputo, 247). Tim O'Brien had a different list, based on necessities: 'Among the necessities or near necessities were P-38 can openers, pocket-knives, heat tabs, wristwatches, dog tags, mosquito repellent, chewing gum, candy, cigarettes, salt tablets, lighters, matches, sewing kits, Military Payment Certificates,[24] C rations, and two or three canteens of water' (O'Brien, 4). Nurse Mary Powell, in her book *A World of Hurt*, remarks on when and how nurses were resupplied: 'Firebase Mace resupplied them every three days, not only with water – they carried six liters [approximately six quarts] in their backpack – and ammo, but with critical morale-raising letters and packages from home. Chocolate-chip cookies became the most tangible connection to a past life' (63).

'Soldiers carry different items depending on whether they're training or in the battlefield. The two most noteworthy weight loads soldiers carry in their backpack … Fighting load (68.9 pounds) or Approach march load (96.8 lbs). The Approach march load [occurs] when soldier is in direct contact with the enemy' ('Ruck For Miles, 3).

Many soldiers lightened their load as best they could. Carrying all the equipment you were expected to carry weighed from 30–70 pounds. 'It was an exercise that had more to do with mental health than weight' (Anderson, *Grunts*, 65). The act of lightening usually resulted in leaving only a pound behind – a grenade sacrificed for old letters, a picture of a girlfriend, and one of Mom's cookies (Anderson, *Grunts*, 65–66, 78). Sometimes, however, they threw away something that might protect them from shrapnel. Some ditched the fiberglass plates in their flak jackets, which reduced their 8.6 pound flak jacket by about 4 pounds. 'Just getting rid of something – anything – made them feel better, made tomorrow look a little more tolerable' (Anderson, *Grunts*, 78). Some soldiers lightened their load by not carrying three meals of C-rations per day, as they added 4½ pounds to their already heavy load. 'Instead, most [settled] for a single complete meal per day and extra cans of crackers, cakes and fruit to supplement until the next resupply – all stuffed into a sock and tied to the back of a rucksack' (CherriesWriter, 2).

Man carrying rucksack. (Courtesy D. Phillips)

Advanced Training. Now that they all looked alike – same uniform, same hair style and backpack – it was time to train them to fight the enemy. 'Basic Training was eight weeks, for some, nine. From the day I enlisted (September 26, 1966) to the day I set foot in Vietnam (March 26, 1967), it was exactly six months. ... Anybody sent into combat with only two weeks of training would last about three minutes (if that) into his first fire fight. But far worse, he'd get half the guys around him killed' (Zabecki).

> '[During those eight to nine weeks of training:] you practiced carrying all your gear ... your morning usually started before dawn ... you had to run 5–6 miles before breakfast ... you hit the horizontal ladder before every meal ... you were taught education lessons along with combat training ... you hit the firing range ... you took hand-to-hand combat training which included bayonets ... you endured confidence and obstacle courses ... you would have to learn what it felt like to be tear-gassed ... after breakfast and lunch you ran even more ... you were required to wash dishes, pots and pans ... you were terrorized by your drill sergeant at first ... you were often required to stay up at night on "fire watch"' (excerpted from Seemayer, 1–7).

While instructors taught inductees the Uniform Code of Military Justice, basic hygiene and first aid, to fight and to hate the enemy, they were not 'prepared to deal with the Asian population: [its] language, customs, traditions, and psychology. So, a soldier might have received excellent hands-on training at assorted military skills' (Seemayer, 3), but little to no training in dealing with Vietnam or the Vietnamese.

According to Richard Ford III, whom Terry interviewed for *Bloods*, that excellent hands-on training meant nothing once they got to Vietnam. He expressed disdain for the tactics taught in stateside training: 'The tactical thing was we fought it different from any way we was ever trained to fight in the states. They tell you about flanks, platoons, advance this. It wasn't none of that. It was just jungle warfare. You jumped up and ran where you could run' (52).

Although they were not prepared for dealing with the conditions in Vietnam, instructors taught them to hate Asians: 'For most people not killing another human being is instinctive. It has to be taught. ... Brutalization and desensitizing the individual were necessary to overcome the instinct not to kill and they were applied from the moment a recruit arrived at boot camp through the rest of his training' (Holzwarth, #20).

'As soon as you hit boot camp ... they tried to change your total personality. Transform you out of that civilian mentality to a military mind. Right away they told us not to call them Vietnamese. Call everybody gooks, dinks. ... They were like animals, or something other than human. They ain't have no regard for life. They'd blow up little babies just to kill one GI. ... That killer instinct. Just go away and do destruction' (Terry, 90). Doc Holley expressed much the same sentiment in a letter to his wife: 'It's amazing how much hate man can build up against his enemy. I'll sure be glad to get back home where I can experience love instead of hate. I'm so tired of hate and killing and death' (141).

David Cline, another Vietnam veteran, comments on the indoctrination after killing an enemy: 'I looked at this guy; he was about my age, and I started thinking, "why is he dead and I'm alive?" ... I wonder if he had a girlfriend? How will his mother find out her son is dead? What I didn't realize at the time, but did later, was that I was refusing to give up his humanity. And that's what a lot of war is about: denying your enemy's humanity' (*Vietnam: Special Newsweek Edition*, 5).

Once you had graduated, you often went for advanced training, depending on your **Military Occupational Specialty**. Your MOS might be 11B Infantry Rifleman, 13B Artilleryman, 91B Medical Specialist (Reinberg, 145), or 92G Culinary Specialist, often a bartender. Dunnigan and Nofi note that 18,465 men designated 11B died in Vietnam, 'accounting for 31.76 percent of American deaths in Vietnam' (3). The Navy called their classification system NEC, **Naval Enlistment Classification**. One Navy man said he served as a radio operator out of Cam Ranh Bay. But what your MOS was meant little to the Army. Bobby Ward, who attended my Thursday evening programs, was trained as a cook but his MOS was a truck driver.

Advanced Infantry Training (AIT). Those going to AIT camp, at Fort Benning, also known The Benning School for Boys, were the grunts, those assigned to the infantry. They were sent to a place which simulated a Vietnam village, 'which included tiger traps, sharpened bamboo stakes, and various forms of traps designed to cripple or kill' (Holzwarth, #10). Some simulations included walking through swamps, as fictionalized in the allegorical movie "Southern Comfort," which supposedly took place in Louisiana among alien peoples, the Cajuns, who spoke a foreign language, Pidgin French. But it was more than that. Being trained to leave base camps and pursue the enemy wasn't enough, so advanced training meant being proficient in light weapons and military tactics. They were also 'trained to search villages for supplies and weapon caches ... to defend secured villages ... and to prepare them for the conditions they would encounter and the duties they were expected to perform in Vietnam' (Holzwarth, #10). In training, soldiers were rewarded for shooting at man-shaped targets that popped up sporadically.

The target fell backwards (as if shot), and the shooter was praised. Soldiers not firing quickly enough to engage (that is, kill) the target were punished lightly. This training was called 'quick shoot' (Grossman, 253). Through training and rehearsal of this process, the soldier, 'when he does kill in combat, he is able to, at one level, deny to himself that he is actually killing another human being … he has only "engaged" another target' (Grossman 255–256). As one of our vets said, he was brainwashed by the Army (Vietnam Vet Program, Bobby Ward, 1/14/93).

ARS (Army Ranger School). This school trained two separate forces, Rangers and LRRPS (Long Range Reconnaissance Patrols). The Rangers were aggressive fighting men who were supposed to lead the troops. LRRPS were men who went behind enemy lines to observe and report. Although not new to the military, the LRRPs played a significant role in Vietnam because of the difficult terrain and elusiveness of the enemy. The more elusive the enemy, the more the military needed these patrols to ferret them out. With the help of helicopters and LRRPs, the military were able to avoid ambushes and better able to fight the enemy. One LRRP, Lewis Bruchey, who led a five-man Patrol of Army Rangers, wrote a poem about his experience. I include the first and last two stanzas:

> They pin
>   A star
> Upon my chest,
>   A subtle nod
> No more, no less.
>   Alone
>   I stand
> I AM THE BEST

> Save your judgment,
> Your sorrow,
> Your pity,
> Your prayer.

> For I am
> A cold, stone man
> Of Vietnam.
> Beware! Beware! (Reston, 15, 17)

John Wayne High School. Nickname for the home of Studies and Observation Group (SOG) in Fort Bragg, NC, which often worked closely with the CIA. The SOG included Green Berets and locals (such as the Montagnard), but no officers. Their missions were so secret that not even those in command knew all of them (Dunnigan and Nofi, 199). Their missions usually focused on one target in Cambodia or Laos, or even sometimes in North Vietnam, to free a prisoner valuable to the war effort. This group, also known as the joint unconventional warfare task force, was responsible for the 'provocative maneuvers of the U.S. Navy destroyers[25] … [resulting] in the Gulf of Tonkin episode in 1964' (Reston, 93).

The Cheerleaders
By Harrison Kohler

John Wayne
Leads
A charge of leathernecks against the japs or jerries,
He's tough and not afraid to die.

George Jessel
Is
Lean and mean in his tailored American legion uniform,
Grizzled veteran of hellish vaudeville campaigns.

Martha Raye
Has
Her green beret and combat infantry's badge,
She goes where the action is.

Bob Hope
Travels
All over the world
To entertain 'our boys'.

War
Is
A paunchy worn out old movie
A tired old man
A menopaused hag
A grotesque comedian
Parading
Patriotic
Obscenities. (Rottmann, 43)

Jungle Survival School (JSS). Until the situation arose, soldiers often did not understand the need for rescue gear. The Jungle Survival School taught them the importance of rescue gear – radios, flares, and parachutes – and how to call for the rescue helicopter, the Jolly Green Giant, that rescued hundreds of downed airmen. Knowing these skills made survival more likely.

'The jungle itself wasn't the only danger downed airmen faced. ... You also had to know how to hide and evade the enemy. For that reason the JSS employed local Negrito tribesmen [diverse ethnic groups who inhabited isolated parts of Southeast Asia] to teach evasion and survival skills. [Although] they spoke little English ... they knew the jungle' (Pendergrass, 8).

The Marines, later in the war, learned that they needed to teach survival skills, known as **Individual Combat Training (ICT)**. US Marine recruits were sent to Camp LeJeune to learn to bivouac in the field, techniques of infantry combat, concealment, and other skills which were required for survival in the field (Holzwarth, #13).

Basic and advanced training soldiers involved more than just teaching them to become soldiers; they also needed to learn common sense, what they needed to know to survive in Vietnam.

You have gotta have eyes in the back of your head. Watch out. Everything is dangerous. Not just booby traps: poisonous snakes, leeches, mosquitoes, tigers, monkeys. Spec 5 Emmanuel J. Holloman took this lesson he learned when he was in boot camp with him after returning home from the war. 'I keep reverting back to Vietnam, when I had to watch all the time. I stayed over there so long if a rocket would fire 10 miles away, I'd be up and out of there and out of reach when the rocket hit because I could hear 10 miles away. I've conditioned myself. I see stuff that other people don't see, so I'm always looking for something. I'm always on guard' (Terry, 88).

What you don't know can kill you. Every unit was constantly getting a replacement. You had to listen to those in your unit who had experience that basic training couldn't teach you. Watch your back; be aware of everything around you. Johnny Phillips said they were lied to, that they weren't there to save South Vietnam; he said basic training 'psyched us up so bad; we were scared into thinking the VC can move without making a sound – they shouldn't scare you so bad' (Vietnam Vet Program, 1/21/93).

Stay off the trail. 'I made it a policy not to follow trails and paths. That way you avoid ambushes and punji sticks [booby trap stakes placed in the ground and covered with jungle debris]' (Terry, 23). An identical statement was made by an Army sergeant: 'Make yer *own* way through the jungle out there. It's a lot safer and you'll avoid the mines and booby traps' (Anthony, 61).

Stay off the trail. (Courtesy D. Phillips)

Do it right or don't do it. If you didn't do something the right way, you could get killed and get others killed. You might not be able to learn from experience because you might never get a second chance. As a new lieutenant, Lewis Puller, Jr. got an invaluable lesson. Most of the company had eaten when it was still light and heated their food with little pieces of C-4 (a plastic explosive). Puller had neglected to bring any rations, so he thankfully took a can of beans and franks from a member of another platoon. 'They're better hot,' he was told. But then he got his 'first lesson in field comfort. Food can be eaten hot only during the daylight hours since the light from the heat tabs and plastique can be spotted by the enemy. I would remember next time, but hungry as I was and as newly acquainted to C rations, even cold, the grub tasted delicious' (*Fortunate Son*, 88–89).

Doing it wrong was called **John Wayne Tactics** – crazy, risky military tactics designed to glorify the troop leader without concern for the troops. Dr Lifton, in working with Vietnam veterans, learned that many went into service with the image of John Wayne as a soldier. It was a powerful image to take into battle. 'All men in battle require elements of that imagery, having to do with courage and male group loyalty, or bonding, in order to cope with their fear of death, the concern with manhood, and the quest for higher purpose' (220). 'A lieutenant or platoon sergeant who would want to carry out all kinds of crazy John Wayne tactics, who would use their lives in an effort to win the war single-handedly, win the big medal and get his picture in the hometown paper' (Anderson, *Grunts*, 219). The John Wayne mentality was gung-ho – don't let anyone stop you, go it alone and don't worry about it, use whatever weapons are handy, kill the enemy one at a time, guerilla-style. Go after the government if you have to. 'Now we don't want to see no John Wayne performances out here. Just do your job and listen to your fire team and squad leaders – they're the ones who'll teach you everything and help you get through the next few months' (Anderson, *Grunts*, 106).

'There were people over there that were just putting their time in, and I [Rifleman Randy Hoelzen] was one of them. We did what we had to do but we weren't out to be

John Wayne
visiting the
troops in 1966.
(Wikipedia)

John Wayne. There were "John Waynes" who loved what they were doing and would **re-up** (re-enlist for another term in the field). And then there were some that were there because they had to be there and weren't doing what they had to do' (J. Ebert, 137).

'There is much evidence of the currency of Wayne's name in the combat zone as a term identifying all those daring individual acts that succeed in the movies but are only dumb stunts that will get you killed in a real war' (Hynes, 215). A young enlistee just out of basic training summed up her basic training: 'War becomes more impersonal. Will war now become like playing a video game?' (Dee Phillips, daughter of Johnny Phillips, Vietnam Vets Program, 1/28/93).

Once trained, many of them flew to Vietnam to the Replacement Depot (**Repo Depo**), located at the Long Binh US Army base. 'When our country sent soldiers into Vietnam, they did not send them in groups from an American base. … [One vet] told us that he was sent to Vietnam on a plane full of complete strangers that would have to trust each other with their lives' (Ramsey, 59).[26] There, the incoming replacements picked up their assignments. They dragged their bags with them and deplaned at Repo Depo. Because they were replacing soldiers with the same Military Occupational Specialty (**MOS**), who were **combat ineffective** (dead) or had served their year, most of them would never see each other again, assigned to different platoons and to their individual MOS. Since replacements came one at a time, it often disturbed whatever cohesiveness the platoon had developed. It was also the place where a grunt picked up his paperwork to go home. Since most soldiers in a given unit had a different Date of Expected Return from Overseas (**DEROS**), soldiers went home one at a time: no debriefing, no welcome homes, no parades. They could watch their fellow soldiers continue the war on television sets.

Long Binh Army Base in October 1967. (Wikipedia)

Chapter 4

Domestic Dissent

'Hey, Hey, LBJ, how many kids did you kill today?' Protest chant that first became
popular in late 1967

'Time has shown that these young people who protested the war had a
better understanding of it than those government officials who
perpetuated the war. Youth does not imply ignorance of foreign
affairs nor are age and high office any guarantors of wisdom.'
(Secretary of Defense Clark Clifford, May 1978, Reston, 273)

'Vietnam is a painter's illusion, a nightmare; a
dream without an ending, forcing upon young
men and women death and destruction.

Vietnam is a black man screaming in a
strange world, fighting for freedom he is yet
to have.

Vietnam is a loss of dignity, identity, and pride.
It becomes a struggle from within – from the
hunting of human lives.

Vietnam is America, for in America black men
Continue to lose their lives. Bang!'
(Ulysses Marshall, Sinaiko, 115)

At home, political tensions also increased. Lyndon B. Johnson, US President following
the assassination of John F. Kennedy on 22 November 1963, continued the Kennedy
policy to aid South Vietnam. In 1965, two years into Johnson's presidency, the infantry
arrived in South Vietnam. There has been much speculation about what JFK's actions
would have been. Al Davis, a Vietnam vet who attended my Thursday evening program,
thought that JFK would have gotten troops out faster. That's one reason why he was
killed, because war was a money-making proposition. And everybody knows that LBJ
and his wife, Lady Bird, were interested in oil and there was a lot of drilling off the
coast that could have been done (Vietnam Vet Program, 2/4/93). For that reason, many
soldiers referred to the war as **Lady Bird's War**.

The murders in 1968 of Robert Kennedy – President Kennedy's brother – and Martin Luther King, Jr, one of the leaders of the Civil Rights Movement, further increased tensions, as did the protests in Chicago during the 1968 Democratic Convention. Both men opposed the war in Vietnam. King opted for Gandhi-like pacificism: sit-ins, marches, admission to segregated schools, and voting rights. He became increasingly opposed to the war for several reasons: that the US was doing nothing but provoking violence, and his perception that young black men couldn't get the college deferments that young white men could.

In April 1967, the Reverend Dr Martin Luther King, Jr, gave a speech, 'Beyond Vietnam', in Manhattan's Riverside Church. He called for an end to the bombing and the declaration of a unilateral truce, with a move towards peace talks. His advisors recommended that he not give this speech because it may harm the Civil Rights Movement (Rosenwald, 407). But King realized the connection between the Civil Rights Movement and Vietnam. When asked by other Blacks 'why be a pacifist when we see what America is doing in Vietnam?', he responded: 'What about Vietnam? They asked if our own nation wasn't using massive doses of violence to solve its problems, to bring about changes it wanted. Their question hit home, and I knew I could never again raise my voice against the violence of the oppressed in the ghettos without first having spoken clearly to the greatest purveyor of violence in the world today: my own government. For the sake of those boys, for the sake of this government, for the sake of the hundreds of thousands trembling under our violence, I cannot be silent' (Rosenwald, 411).

During that speech, King summarized United States violence against the Vietnamese and implied the connection to the violence done to the Negro in the United States: 'We have destroyed their two most cherished institutions: the family and the village. We have destroyed their land and their crops. … We have corrupted their women and children and killed their men' (Loewen, 247).

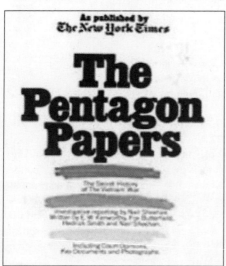

Book cover of *Pentagon Papers*.

Ebert, in his book *Life in a Year*, summed up King's speech: 'During the conflict, apart from the usual brutalizing process to which soldiers are exposed in any war, "we are adding cynicism to the process of death, for our troops must know after a short period that none of the things we claim to be fighting for are really involved"' (292).

The growing involvement of the United States in the war, which people saw every day on their television set, increased anti-war sentiment, as did an article appearing in *The New York Times* on 13 June 1971. This article reported on Daniel Ellsberg's theft of papers belonging to the Pentagon detailing the history of the war in Vietnam from

1945–1967. These documents proved that President Johnson and his administration had lied about American involvement and lied about their objectives – not so much to support South Vietnam as to contain China. These documents verified what 'the North Vietnamese government had been claiming for years that American military involvement was illegitimate' (Nguyen, Lien-Hang, 1). Elizabeth Becker, a former war correspondent in Cambodia for *The Washington Post* reflecting on the fiftieth anniversary of *The Pentagon Papers*, stated that they revealed the numerous lies told 'to the public, to Congress, in closed-door hearings, in speeches and to the press' (Section F, 2) by the Eisenhower, Kennedy, Johnson, and Nixon administration. Becker quotes McNamara saying in a speech in spring 1965: 'In the past four and one-half years, the Vietcong, the Communists, have lost 89,000 men. … That was a lie. From confidential reports, McNamara knew the situation was "bad and deteriorating" in the South' (Section F, 2). The release of *The Pentagon Papers* had a 'seismic impact in [North] Vietnam – fortifying the country's military and public with evidence that their cause had been just' (Nguyen, Lien-Hang, 1).

Most of the anti-war demonstrators were not countercultural or sexually promiscuous; they were just ordinary people. They were not cowards, afraid to fight. Many were harassed, put under surveillance, put on trial, or sent to jail (Zaroulis and Sullivan, xii). To protest against the war, men burned their draft cards in public. Since a man was supposed to always have his draft card with him, it was illegal to burn it. Another form of protest was not paying the 10 per cent surcharge[27] on your phone bill, asked for by President Johnson and established by Congress in 1966.

Not everyone who marched against the war was a pacifist or a liberal. Many conservatives also opposed the war. But even at the height of the anti-war movement, many Americans were not moved to join it; either they were indifferent, it didn't affect them, or they were in favor of the war (Dunnigan and Nofi, 260). '[One man] enrolled at Wayne State University [Detroit, MI] with the secret mission of getting a degree in sociology so that [he] could work with high-school age Mexican-Americans and African-Americans, convincing both to stay the hell away from the meat grinder that was the military' (Jones, *Dead of Winter*, 289). According to a student in my course, 'there were three types of protestors: (a) minority who believed in cause; (b) leaders who would protest so long as they remained leaders; and (c) professional protestors who would protest anything' (1/3/93).

Although some youths were active politically, demonstrating for equal rights and against the war, others chose to 'tune in' to Harvard Professor, Dr Timothy Leary, creator of LSD, 'turn on' to LSD and other drugs, and 'drop out' of society. Many dropped out because of the tensions created by the war, the Civil Rights and feminist movements: they advocated to make love, not war, and listened to psychedelic music. They created a counterculture of love, flower power, and drugs.

Americal Division
By Sgt Dudley Farquhar

Was it really that long ago?
They called us the Flower Generation,
Children of the '60s, the Beatles,
Hula Hoops and Woo-Woo Ginsburg,

But along came Vietnam.
They sent us to Basic Training,
To learn about 'Mr. Charles'.
We were young, and it seemed exciting,
But why don't the faces go away?
We left our American Bandstand world,
But America wasn't behind us.
We fought the gallant fight,
But weren't allowed to win.
Some of us were lucky: we came back.
The POW/MIAs can't say the same.
The media did a job on us,
A portrayal that wasn't fair.
The drug addicts and baby killers came home,
And we lived with Calley's mistake.
For years we hid in our closet world,
And hoped America would come around.
We watch the 'Hot Spots' with vivid reality,
Knowing it could happen, once again.
The war is over, but the battle lingers on,
So Washington erected 'THE WALL'.
Names on top of names,
But one meant so much to me
DAWSON
To most everyone, just a name among the thousands,
But to his platoon, he was the best.
He gave his life for his men.
Six letters on a wall, no thank you.
Words don't tell the story.
VIETNAM
The Hurt Lives On.

Dedicated to the memory of SSG ROBERT C. DAWSON, KILLED IN ACTION 18 JUNE, 1970, CHU LAI, VIETNAM. Some people come into our lives and quickly go. Some stay for a while and leave memories on our hearts, and we are never, ever the same. Bob Dawson was more than a soldier in a strange land – he was my friend. (Written in 1982 after attending the dedication of the Vietnam Veterans Memorial in Washington, DC.)[28]

These youths, the children of the 60s – the Flower Generation, were often referred to as Hippies,[29] youths who wanted to drop out of a 'corrupt' society. They congregated in New York City's Greenwich Village and San Francisco's Haight-Ashbury district. The counterculture movement began in San Francisco. It was the time of do your own thing, be your own person, say what you think, believe that you know best. The usual rules didn't apply. The stereotypical Hippies wore their hair long, wore flared jeans, love beads, bracelets, sandals (or went without shoes), leather fringed belts, vests, or jackets. Grass (marijuana) was shared freely; they sometimes traveled in vans and cars painted with peace symbols and were considered anti-establishment.

DOMESTIC DISSENT

Thomas Aloysius Meade
By Patrick J. Fitch

'Hippiecrits' he called them.
Students in the World
Did they know? Did they care?
His name was Thomas
Apostle of Doubt
Penultimate Aloysius
Surname Meade

The rocket; round
Directly taken
'Chest high, No Cry'

He had a name, and it wasn't Corporal.
Left a twin brother
And a father who asked:
'How did he die?'

But the letter was a lie
No body bag need apply
A backpack sufficed
for the arms and the watch.

We tagged remains.
Just another stat
Body count ours
On a damp little mesa.

Just a faded memory of the 26th Marines
In a place called Khe Sanh.

His death was obscene. (Eichler, 40–41)

President Nixon showed his contempt and cynicism at the same time: 'You know, you see these bums, you know, blowin' up the campuses. Listen, the boys that are on the college campuses today are the luckiest people in the world, going to the greatest universities, and here they are, burnin' up the books, I mean, stormin' around about this issue, I mean, you name it – get rid of the war, there'll be another one' (Isserman, 167).

The same was true of the career military, also known as lifers, who made known their antipathy to those who protested:

'America is the greatest country in the history of the world; the duty of every American citizen is to do all in his or her power to keep America the greatest; the best way to help keep America the greatest and to show one's love of country is to serve in the military; the line between dissent and treason is so vague that it can safely be ignored; communists and hippies are the most despicable life on earth and should be locked up forever if they can't be killed on sight; and, this Vietnam War is a great patriotic crusade that got off to a good start but recently turned into a chickenshit no-win thing because the pinko socialistic professors and politicians back in Washington won't get their hands off it.' (Anderson, *Other War*, 17–18)

Some, however, were not as antagonistic: 'When I returned from Vietnam I was asked, "Do you resent young people who have never been in Vietnam, or in any war, protesting it?" On the contrary, I am relieved. I think they should be commended. … What they are against is our boys *being* in Vietnam. They are not unpatriotic. Again, the opposite is true. They are opposed to people, our own and others, dying for a lie, thereby corrupting the very word democracy' (Duncan, 'Ramparts,' 96).

The protestors were not organized groups; they were not 'anti-American' (Zaroulis and Sullivan, xiii) – they wanted to know what the government was doing and why. One of the Vietnam veterans from SW Virginia said when he came home, he thought he'd been fighting for the government; he didn't know he *wasn't* fighting for the American people as well. This distinction between the government's policy and the citizens' eventual understanding of that policy was made by Johnny, who was 17 when he enlisted. Later, he sat with his daughter, who joined the Army in 1993. Dee Phillips,[30] Johnny's daughter, said: 'I have a lot of resentment towards the peace movement during the war, and towards those who dodged the draft.' Her father had a different view: 'A lot *did* want to stop war. A lot didn't want to go. That was their right. I wasn't no hero for going when I got drafted. I was there to survive' (Vietnam Vet Program, 1/3/93).

Lynda Van Devanter, a nurse in Vietnam,[31] wrote: 'It hurts so much sometimes to see the paper full of demonstrators, especially people burning the flag. Fight fire with fire, we ask here. Display the flag, Mom and Dad, please, every day. And tell your friends to do the same. It means so much to us to know we're supported, to know not everyone feels we're making a mistake being here' (Edelman, 233).

PFC Stephen W. Pickett commented: 'We were well informed about the demonstrations by both sides. Even though I'm here, I still have an open mind – realizing, of course, that an immediate pullout or anything of the sort is out of the question. It would degrade the heroic deaths of those who never returned because it would mean going back on everything that we have done. There are many here who feel as I do, but we will continue to fight for the country in which we believe' (Edelman, 222).

Although grunts served in different areas of South Vietnam, they knew about the protestors. After all, television at base camps and USOs showed what was happening, and they heard from home about them. Their obvious adversaries were the Hippies, whose anti-war demonstrations 'poisoned' the minds of many Americans and whose anti-war chants encouraged the enemy. No wonder the antipathy lingered even after the soldiers came home (Anderson, *Grunts*, 226–227).

Marine Lewis Puller, Jr. – with devastating wounds, amputations, many surgeries, and struggles with prostheses – was angry both with the protestors and at himself: 'It made me angry to see these college kids, with no frame of reference outside a classroom, second-guessing the decisions that had almost cost me my life, and it made me angrier still to think that they might be right' (269).[32] Both groups shared, however, the same problem: their government's apparent lack of will and its abuse of authority and deception (Anderson, *Grunts*, 233).

Some researchers after the war saw a different picture. 'Critics of the war claimed that their opposition was a principled one, rooted in pacifism, respect for human dignity, and anti-imperialism. Many were, but not all. (Dunnigan and Nofi, 261). Some anti-war protestors were pro-communism and criticized those who attacked the lack of human rights in North Vietnam (261).

Protestors were seen as 'communist dupes'. But although investigated by government agencies, no links were ever found between the protestors and foreign communist governments (Zaroulis and Sullivan, xii). Some were quiet protestors who felt guilty because they didn't know what to do. A high school student wrote the following poem, identifying with the grunts while at the same regretting what she saw.

I Am A Veteran of Vietnam
By Sue Halpern

I
am a veteran
of Vietnam
I've been from
Hamburger Hill to the DMZ
and back again
with a mere flick
of my wrist.
Through my own eyes
I've seen people
Tortured
Bombed
Burned
Destroyed
Beyond hope of recovery
While I
sit contently
Watching …
and let it
go on. (Rottmann, 113)

Sue Halpern believes that anyone living through the war were Vietnam veterans. A son of a vet tried to buy USAA insurance because his father fought in Vietnam. He was told by the insurance agent that, although he may not be a vet, '[he] served under [his] father' (Boylan, 4). Many also experienced the fear that the vets felt every minute of every day. Jennifer Boylan, a contributing writer for *The New York Times*, recalls: 'What I remember most of all was the constant sense of dread, that the world in which I was growing up was one of violence and peril, that our government could not be trusted, that the older brothers of my friends were dying in a war whose purpose even some of its most passionate supporters could not articulate' (2).

Those protesting against the war often witnessed horrible deaths. On 4 May 1970, members of the Ohio National Guard fired on a crowd gathered at Kent State University to protest the war in Vietnam, killing four students. 'The tragedy was a watershed moment for a nation divided by the conflict in Southeast Asia. In its immediate aftermath, a student-led strike forced the temporary closure of colleges and universities across the country. Some political observers believe the events of that day in northeast Ohio tilted public opinion against the war and may have contributed to the downfall of President Richard Nixon' (*History Com., The Kent State Shooting*, 1).

Eventually, the protests at the Chicago Democratic Convention, in Washington DC, and at many other sites throughout the nation had an effect: they led to the Democratic Party becoming anti-war. 'The crazy thing is, y'all did affect national policy! The Vietnam War ended. That's how democracy should work – an anti-war movement shook up a major political party and pulled us out of a fight ... because our involvement was not in line with what they believed our country should stand for' (Fallows, 'New Series', 3).

In November 1969, James Quay[33] and others carried the names of those who died in Vietnam around their necks on a placard in the 'March Against Death'. 'In that March, 45,000 people each with the name of an American killed in action in Vietnam and a lighted candle, walked to 1600 Pennsylvania Avenue. There [in front of the White House] each marcher ... said the name he or she carried. ... It took nearly 40 hours to say all the names. ... In November 1982, the names were spoken again in the candlelight vigil of names that preceded the dedication of the Vietnam Veterans Memorial' (Ezell, 19).

'The war in Vietnam was not lost in the field, nor was it lost on the front pages of the *New York Times* or on college campuses. It was lost in Washington, D.C., [the result] of a uniquely human failure: arrogance, weakness, lying in the pursuit of self-interest, and, above all, the abdication of responsibility to the American people' (McMaster, 333–334). Bobby Ward, a Vet who attended my class, agreed: "We were not allowed to win the war because of the decisions made by the government in Washington, D.C.' (Vietnam Vet Program, 1/28/93).

Karl Marlantes, a Marine lieutenant in Vietnam, believes that 'America didn't just lose the war, and the lives of 58,000 young men and women; Vietnam changed us

Protest at Kent State University. (Wikipedia)

as a country. In many ways for the worse. It made us cynical and distrustful of our institutions, especially of government' (1).

War On Poverty. To further the aims of the Civil Rights Movement and to deflect attention from the war in Vietnam, President Lyndon Johnson declared a War on Poverty. He would end poverty and racial injustice through such programs as Medicare, Medicaid, Head Start, and Jobs Corps. 'These programs ... would give poor people "a hand up, not a handout"' (The 1960s History, 2). But Civil Rights was not the only movement which wanted to increase their rights. Feminists fought for equal pay and equal rights for women, including the right to control their own bodies.

For some, the programs to establish a 'Great Society' and the pacifism of King's Southern Christian Leadership Conference (SCLC) were not moving quickly enough. Several other more violent leaders and more active groups emerged: Malcolm X, Stokely Carmichael, and the Black Panthers, and even some white groups including Students for a Democratic Society (SDS) and the Weather Underground. These groups led riots, bombings, and more violent protests, like the anti-war protestors who took over Columbia University, the protests at the 1968 Democratic National Convention in Chicago, and the destroying of draft board records in Catonsville, Maryland and Milwaukee, Wisconsin in 1968.

Television War

> 'Thanks to television, for the first time the young are seeing history made before it is censored by their elders.' Margaret Mead

> 'The War America waged in Vietnam, the first to be witnessed day after day by television cameras, introduced the home front to a new intimacy with death and destruction.' Susan Sontag

Walter Cronkite in Vietnam in 1968. (Wikipedia)

'The postwar [Second World War] generation was the first to grow up with television, a medium of communication whose profound effects are still not fully understood. ... Television glorified violence and at the same time kept it at a safe distance. The viewer was encouraged to accept the idea that swift and violent action usually yielded positive results. ... Television helped many Americans, young and old, to adopt an escapist mentality' (Anderson, *Grunts*, 193–194).

Television provided its viewers with instant solutions to common everyday problems – acid indigestion, rings around their shirt collars, body odor, and aches and pains. For the grunt, there were no instant solutions; no escape from a remorseless enemy. They drank their Kool Aid to hide the taste of halogen tablets used to purify the water; they swallowed salt tablets to keep hydrated against another remorseless enemy – nature. They were ever on the alert for ambushes and traps. 'They were frantic to find some relief, from an agony that defied relief. Slowly the hard reality came through: there was no alternative, no time-out, no falling out from this "field problem". The grunts were being beaten to a psychological pulp. The dream of returning to the great dreamland America was looking more hopeless every minute' (Anderson, *Grunts*, 62).

Many of the vets on leave told their families about their feeling of hopelessness. 'Mogie [Crocker]'s sister Carol notices something else. They were watching television together ... when Mogie suddenly held his face in his hands. "I don't want to go back," he said. "I was dumbstruck," Carol remembered, "and said to him, 'But this is what you want to do.' It had never occurred to me that he was torn about this, that he was afraid. It confounded me that he had made so many sacrifices and yet was afraid and yet determined to go"' (Ward, 123).

They Watched Television Together
By Kellan Kyllo

Late at night
the house was still and quiet
His best friend,
killed
in Vietnam,
sat on the basement sofa with him
and shared
only a glance and a few words. (Eichler, 70)

Private First-Class Reginald 'Malik' Edwards, home now from Vietnam, watched from his seat on an Amtrak train as Morley Safer reported on the destruction at Cam Ne.[34] Looking back on what he saw, he commented: 'Safer didn't tell them to burn the huts down with their lighters. He just photographed it. ... When you say level a village, you don't use torches. ... You use a Zippo. That's why people bought Zippos. Everybody had a Zippo. It was for burnin' shit down' (Terry, 3).

Reporters. General Westmoreland caught hell from the military that wanted him to control reporters. Herr says the '**higher Highers**' kept saying they were winning the war; it was 'you people' who are making them look like losers (228–229). 'In Vietnam, television, most of journalism, merely confirmed to Americans that the entire affair had a certain stench to it. Westmoreland and many others fully believed the stench came from the lies, inexperience, and manipulations of journalists' (Safer, 134). Covering a war was a dilemma for Herr, and no doubt for others, too. '[If] you photographed a dead Marine with a poncho over his face and got something (money, prestige, something) for it, you were some kind of parasite. But what were you if you pulled the poncho back first to make a better shot, and did that in front of his friends? Some other kind of parasite, I suppose. Then what were you if you stood there watching it, making a note to remember it later in case you might want to use it?' (228).

Herr writes about his observations of the reporters near the end of his time there: 'So there we all were, no real villains and only a few heroes, a lot of adventurers and a lot of drudges, a lot of beautiful lunatics and a lot of normal, come to report what was ultimately the normals' war. ... There was a lot that went unsaid at the time, but just because it was seldom spoken didn't mean that we weren't very much aware of it or that, in that terrible, shelterless place, we weren't grateful for each other' (223–224).

Reporters and photographers, such as Tim Page, learned how to survive during the war – you kept moving. Herr reports a conversation with Page and Errol Flynn, Jr: 'The more you moved the more you saw, the more you saw the more besides death and mutilation you risked, and the more you risked of that the more you would have to let go of one day as a "survivor". Some of us moved around the war like crazy people until we couldn't see which way the run was even taking us anymore, only the war all over its surface with occasional, unexpected penetration' (8).

Another dilemma faced by Morley Safer (CBS) and Susan Brownmiller (ABC) was 'photo opportunities'. Morley Safer, watching Marines arrive on a beach, said that was his introduction to the phrase 'photo ops'. The Marines were greeted by 'cameramen and photographers fetched up from Saigon to record the event. ... For Marine Corps recruiters it would be an especially stirring device to remind eighteen-year-olds that they, too, could stand in the same salty Pacific that John Wayne had liberated so many times before' (161–162).

Print reporter Michael Herr saw the effect of television on the grunts: 'I keep thinking about all the kids who got wiped out by seventeen years of war movies before coming to Vietnam to get wiped out for good. You don't know what a media freak is until you've seen the way a few of those grunts would run around during a fight when they knew that there was a television crew nearby. ... They were insane, but the war hadn't done that to them' (209).

The TV News: What increased the support for the anti-war movement was the *6 0'Clock News*. Over a TV dinner, the public could watch the day's results from the war: the body count, the helicopters whumping away, the tired faces. Vietnam quickly became 'no longer a war in which a few people were being killed. Large, large numbers of people were being killed. And everybody knew about it. It was in the papers, on television' (Terry, 194). It was a new fight, an 'all-out war against the countryside. Its aim is to make the rural areas in which the Vietcong operate unlivable' (Scheer, 75).

Adrian Cronauer,[35] who served as a DJ for Armed Forces Radio in Vietnam, called the war the First Electronic War – one that revealed in living rooms all the horrors of war. The military was unprepared for the American people's reaction, so it tightened up the news. As an example, Cronauer said a pilot returning from a raid might be 'exhilarated', but bureaucratic censorship changed the word to 'gratified'.[36]

Bob, a Vietnam vet from Virginia, watched as the lieutenant snapped closed his buddy in a green body bag: 'Then a shit bird wrote a note and stuck it in. The LT and I reached it about the same time: "Thank you for the loan of your boy's body. So sorry we couldn't return it in the same condition we received it in." There it is. That's the 'Nam. You don't know who you are anymore. The LT and I brought him in. He was nineteen with a wife and a new child. He had been writing letters home to his baby just in case' (Vietnam Vet Program, 1/28/1973).

Television reporters did not find many heroes to celebrate or courage to describe. The courage that was often reported in the news was not the heroic ideal of an Audie Murphy, a Sergeant York, or a John Wayne, who defined courage as 'being scared to death but saddling up anyway' (*Newsweek*, 63). The war stories of men killing Vietcong were often horrific and not for mass viewing. What was reported were 'the protective acts – recovering one's own wounded, or the dead, or covering withdrawal – that carry moral and emotional weight. Courage and heroism were possible in Vietnam narratives; the *ideal* of courage, the Heroic Man of the war tradition, wasn't' (Hynes, 214).

This was especially true for many grunts whose concern was only to get out of this place, to survive for one more day and then another day and another until they could fly home on their Freedom Bird. 'The concepts of bravery, honor, heroism, justice, war and even peace were overwhelmed by a personal plan to survive for one year. Stay away from FNGs (fucking new guys), whose mistakes could get you killed, and "short-timers" because they were jinxed and often got blown away with only few days left to go. ... Enter – stay alive – exit' (Parish, 47).

Despite the need to stay alive, many soldiers still believed in the heroic ideal as represented by John Wayne. 'In the Western movies, John Wayne usually played a man of honor, loyalty, and courage. That image, however, doesn't work so well in war. Instead, the John Wayne image became "Violence-prone super-maleness"' (Lifton, 255). But this war wasn't that kind of war. 'For the Vietnam generation, "John Wayne" was the Hollywood war-in-their-heads, exposed and mocked by the real, bitter thing. It's a sign of how completely the old values had faded that Wayne had become a soldier's joke, an anti-hero, everybody's example of how *not* to fight a war' (Hynes, 215). The Hollywood image, however, didn't fade away. One veteran said in group therapy: 'I'm sorry. I don't know why I felt sorry. John Wayne never felt sorry' (Lifton, 121).

Atrocities. What television news reported, but did not show, were the atrocities committed by both sides. Lieutenant Calley's Charlie Company, under the leadership of Captain Ernest Medina, massacred an entire village. My Lai 'remains a horrifying example of the ways in which war can shatter basic precepts of conscience and honor'. Although initially hushed up by the US Army, 'when reports of the My Lai massacre, as it has come to be known, reached the American public late in 1969, they unleashed a tsunami of national shame and self-examination' (Knauer, 110).

But this was only one of many atrocities committed during the war. Indeed, General Westmoreland noted that killing civilians 'deprived the enemy of the population, doesn't it' (Loewen, 244). Many demonstrators referred to the soldiers as baby-killers,[37] one of the worst names returning soldiers were called. Vietnam vet Johnny Phillips told a group of university students: 'Soldiers were just like you – kids – forced into it. Not child-killers' (Vietnam Vet Program, 1/28/1973). Many denied it bothered them: '"No, it never really bothered me … You get used to [the name-calling]." This defensive repression and denial of emotions appear to have been one of the major causes of post-traumatic stress disorder' (Grossman, 279).

Viet Thanh Nguyen remembers, at the 'age of 12 or 13', reading about a fictional atrocity in Heinemann's *Close Quarters*, a book written in 1974 by a Vietnam veteran. Nguyen recalls being horrified at what Heinemann wrote, but later came to realize that Heinemann did not sympathize with the atrocity; instead, 'he wasn't endorsing what he depicted. He wanted to show that war brutalized soldiers as well as civilians caught in their path. The novel was a damning indictment of American warfare and the racist attitudes held by some nice average Americans that led to slaughter and rape' (4).

The North Vietnamese and the Vietcong had a different view of US atrocities: 'Frankly, we exaggerated stories of the brutal activities of the Americans. … We needed that talk in order to encourage our comrades on the battlefields' (Nguyen, 6). Another Vietcong concurred: "I harbored hatred for the US Army because they killed my brother … but I recognized that American soldiers valued humanitarianism. When they saw our villagers, even our comrades, wounded they cared for all on the spot or sent them to the hospital immediately' (Nguyen, 6).

Jim Gray, a Vietnam vet from Athens, GA, served in the First Air Cav in 1967 and 1968. He found his voice after the war in poetry.

Married and Settled
By Jim Gray

I would like to be married and settled
Bouncing plump, healthy babies on my knee
Teenagers asking for use of the family car.

But a hot, humid wind
Tinted with kerosene and sweat
Carries my soul
To an eternal unknown.

My job is not finished yet
There's a final mission to be flown. (19)

Atrocities made the news because there weren't long, protracted battles for the print or television news to follow. US soldiers would give the prisoner a 'flying lesson'. When they were unable to interrogate him because of the language barrier, they would dispose of the prisoner by tossing him out of an airplane (Terry, 94–95). In addition to beatings and rapes, there were Zippo raids that destroyed whole villages. And then there was white phosphorus, also known as 'Willy Peter'. Although banned by the Geneva Convention, a white phosphorus grenade proved one of the more horrific ways to die. 'White phosphorus is a very potent, caustic, and deadly agent, which will burn straight through any human tissue it comes into contact with. It will also burn through most human-caused materials as well' (Holley, 133). Washing it off with water serves no purpose. It is still deadly. Despite it being banned, both sides in the war used it. Herr was told this while riding in a helicopter that encountered misty, white smoke.

Other atrocities included taking body parts of dead soldiers as souvenirs. Tom Magedanz couldn't understand why people back home 'were always appalled by stories of taking ears, but not about killing' (Ebert, 361). The Vietcong collected ears off US soldiers they killed to create necklaces. Many Americans did the same. 'What's with the funky necklace? Those, son, are human ears. …One from each human kill I had. … I looked more closely at the photo; they were indeed human ears threaded together with twine' (Jones, *Dead of Winter*, 291–292).

The Montagnard, an indigenous mountain people of northwest South Vietnam, also collected ears. Herr tells of one such man who held a plastic bag in front of him. 'It was full of what looked like large pieces of dried fruit. Someone had told me once, there were a lot more ears than heads in Vietnam; just information. When I handed it back, he was still grinning, but he looked sadder than a monkey' (Herr, 34).

Some in Vietnam didn't know about the human ears. After the war, CBS reporter Morley Safer was speaking with a Vietnamese professor, who had been a soldier, about hearing war news at the time. The professor said he'd heard on the radio about Americans' cruelty, about Americans cutting ears off dead enemy soldiers. When Safer confirmed this, the professor said: 'Then it's true? They did cut the ears off our soldiers?' Safer told him: 'This was not a policy. Something happens to ordinary men during and after battle. For the most part American soldiers were decent men who did what was asked of them' (102–103).

'Most of the mutilation, however, probably resulted from frustration, a desire for revenge, or outright callousness. … After the death of [a popular] machine-gunner, a member of his squad carved their unit designation across the chest of a nearby corpse and tacked an Ace of Spades [a bad omen for the Vietnamese] to his forehead'[38] (Ebert, 359).

Vietnam vet Charles R. Anderson shares his thoughts on atrocities: 'There were several physical and cultural characteristics[39] about the Vietnamese which set the foundation for an environment in which atrocities could occur. The first thing any Westerner notices about the Vietnamese is their small physical size. Half the adult population is under five feet tall and weighs less than 120 pounds. Also … the Vietnamese were unarmed. Those two observations together invited the impression that the Vietnamese were unable to effectively answer injustices done them' (Anderson, *Grunts*, 204).

Language barriers also led to atrocities. Unable to understand them, the Americans assumed that the Vietnamese were constantly plotting against them rather than discussing the current weather or when to harvest their crops. Pearl Harbor confirmed the American belief that Orientals have always been a sly and cunning race. 'When Americans expressed their frustration or anger against the Vietnamese … No matter how loudly the Vietnamese might protest, the grunts couldn't understand. Thus, whatever feelings of guilt that might follow an atrocity were either considerably lessened or completely precluded' (Anderson, *Grunts*, 205).

David Gelman in *Newsweek* (28 August 1989, 62–64) blamed ethnocentrism. A student in one of the Vietnam Vet Programs, Paul, agreed: 'Whether "Gooks" in Vietnam or "Yellow monkeys" in Japan, the less we know, the more we hate.' His priest told him: 'There is no way to kill unless you hate … and that it's not as simple as it may seem: "How much hate does it take to fly in an airplane, and press a button that drops thousands of bombs?"' In one of the Vet Programs, Al said that units controlled behavior if they could, but some guys were like animals (2/25/93).

Combat Engineer Bryant would agree. After a firefight, he and others went looking for a body count, shot two wounded VC until they were dead, and then 'this guy – one of the white guys – cut off the VC's dick and stuck it in his mouth as a reminder that the 1st Cavs had been through there. And he left the ace of spades on the body' (Terry, 24).

Chapter 5

The Music

Music connected the 'World' to Vietnam. It also connected the soldiers to the protestors. It reminded the soldiers of home and friends, listening to the music in their cars, riding down Main Street on a Friday night. No one could live through this period without listening to music. It was everywhere: on the radio, on television, in your shopping mall, in your elevator, and in Vietnam.[40]

Musicians and some of their music reflected the drug culture: songs by Jefferson Airplane, the Beatles, The Doors, Fleetwood Mac, and the Rolling Stones. Many musicians died of overdoses: Janis Joplin, Jim Morrison, Keith Moon, and Jimi Hendrix, to name just a few. Drugs became an integral part of the rock scene and Vietnam, although many singers did write and sing anti-drug songs, such as Eric Clapton and Neil Young. The culmination of this musical period occurred at the Woodstock music festival on 15 August 1969: 400,000 young people attended, 'representing the best of the peace-and-love [and-drug] generation' (*1960s History*). 'Billed as "An Aquarian Experience: 3 Days of Peace and Music" … [it] became synonymous with the counterculture movement of the 60's' (History.com, Woodstock, 1).

Music also became a means to protest against the war. Some of these anti-war songs became number one on the hits charts: *The Eve of Destruction* (Barry McGuire), one week in 1965; *Ballad of the Green Berets* (Sgt Barry Sadler), five weeks in 1966; *People Got to be Free* (The Rascals), five weeks in 1968; *Aquarius/Let the Sun Shine in* (The Fifth Dimension), six weeks in 1969; *War (What is it good for? Absolutely nothing)* (Edwin Starr), three weeks in 1970; and *Give me Love/Give me Peace on Earth* (George

Woodstock
Music Festival,
1969.

Harrison), one week in 1973. Other popular anti-war songs were Stephen Stills' *For What it's Worth*, Buffy St Marie's *Universal Soldier*, and Bob Dylan's *Where Have All the Flowers Gone?* Although the song *I Ain't Marchin' Any More* by Phil Ochs never reached number one, it did have a tremendous anti-war following. One song that stayed around forever was Country Joe and the Fish's *I-Feel-Like-I'm-Fixin'-To-Die-Rag*, which was played at Woodstock and also on Armed Forces Radio Vietnam (**AFRVN**), a surprise because of its powerful anti-war lyrics. What follows is the opening stanza:

I-Feel-Like-I'm-Fixin'-To-Die-Rag

Oh this is, this is just a try out. It's not ...
Fixin'-To-Die-Rag, Fixin'-To-Die-Rag, Take 1.
One, two, three, four.

Well, come on all of you, big strong men,
Uncle Sam needs your help again.Yeah, he's got himself in a terrible jam
Way down yonder in Vietnam.
So put down your books and pick up a gun,
Gonna have a whole lotta fun.

And it's one, two three,
What are we fighting for?
Don't ask me, I don't give a damn,
Next stop is Vietnam

And it's five, six, seven.
Open up the pearly gates,
Well, there ain't no time to wonder why,
Whoopee! We're all gonna die.

The wicked satire in the lyrics points to a war nobody understands – unless it's Uncle Sam; and he's keeping it a secret. Then there's the prediction that death is unavoidable, followed by a contradictory 'Whoopee!'. Not only were anti-war songs written by protestors, men in Vietnam also wrote and sang songs full of what Marine Lieutenant Caputo calls 'gallows humor' (216). An officer in A Company wrote a song popular with the soldiers:

Belly-Full of War
By an officer in A Company

Oh they taught me how to kill,
Then they stuck me on this hill,
I don't like it anymore.
For all the monsoon rains
Have scrambled up my brains.
I've had a belly-full of war.

Oh the sun is much too hot,
And I've caught jungle rot,
I don't like it anymore.
I'm tired and terrified,
I just want to stay alive,
I've had a belly-full of war.

So you can march upon Hanoi,
Just forget this little boy,
I don't like it anymore.
For as I lie here with a pout,
My intestines hanging out,
I've had a belly-full of war. (Caputo 216)

One of the paratroopers' favorites, used both in the Second World War and Vietnam, had this chorus: 'Gory, Gory, what a hell of a way to die'. In its eight verses, it recounts the failure of a paratrooper to check his equipment before he jumped – 'Gory, Gory, what a hell of a way to die'.[41]

As the war slogged on, musicians – especially Bob Dylan, Phil Ochs, and Tim Buckley – turned their attention from songs about drugs to more political songs. Even songs which seemed to have no political basis became political in the context of the Vietnam War. 'More than the Vietnam War, music defined the 1960s, and the music followed the troops to Vietnam' as they listened to AFRVN (Dunnigan and Nofi, 157).[42] 'Those songs provided the war with its own distinctive music; but they provided more than that. They offered the men who were there a rhetoric and a set of attitudes – brash, anti-establishment, often explicitly anti-war. Armies are traditionally and necessarily authoritarian and disciplined; but the music this army moved to was neither of those, was indeed the opposite' (Hynes, 185).

AFRVN (Armed Forces Radio Vietnam). Adrian Cronauer, an airman from Roanoke, Virginia, who was in Vietnam beginning in 1962, found himself a radio announcer on AFRVN in May 1965. In a speech at Radford University, Radford, Virginia, in 1992, Cronauer said: 'I tried to make AF radio sound like a stateside radio station.' He then said 'he wanted music to be a morale factor. Many of our young men, just in their teens, had never even been out of their own state. The music I hoped would be an antidote to culture shock.' Cronauer is the DJ who began what became a ritual: '*G-O-O-D M-O-R-N-I-N-G V-I-E-T-N-A-M!*'

Cronauer brought American top-40 songs, ads, and gimmicks to Vietnam. He made his own public service announcements: 'Malaria pill, special, Tuesday only', 'Mail Christmas packages by November 1 to beat the rush', or 'New fatigues on the way. Reserve yours now.' He also sponsored gag contests – for example: 'Send $37.50 plus eight copies of orders for a free getaway to Point Barrow, Alaska.'

Was it appropriate for the AFRVN to have humor? Cronauer said yes: 'How can you ignore this aspect of our lives – all aspects, even humor in a war, exist over a year's time.' Cronauer's favorite compliment came from an Air Force pilot who, on hearing the station, thought he was back home. 'Thanks for getting me through 'Nam,' the pilot told Cronauer.

THE MUSIC

Since the AFRVN paid no royalties, there were copyright problems. To solve them, record companies sent a master tape to LA; a master record was cut on an AFR label, and then sent overseas. Any DJ could play any record; there was no censorship in the music. The military did, however, have material censored. The military command had to approve certain reports before Cronauer could broadcast them. Cronauer said there were some legitimate reasons why certain information wasn't on the radio: a one-person guerilla incident in Saigon; the bombing of a popular restaurant in Saigon; General Westmoreland had called for an additional 200,000 troops. Don't give them news they (the communists) can use, he was told. Not even the weather.

The AFR bureaucracy wouldn't allow him to share over the network anything that might prove embarrassing to the United States. They didn't permit him to warn the soldiers about prostitutes. He couldn't even broadcast the Pope's message for peace because it might be interpreted as anti-war. The military also changed words for him to report. What the bureaucracy didn't realize was that its own network was passing on information to the troops; its DJs, between the rock music, used double-entendres that went right over the heads of the censors: for example, 'be on the lookout for roaches in the walls' – which meant get your marijuana cigarettes (roaches) someplace safe.

Cronauer said that what served the United States well was that the military didn't trust the media and the media didn't trust the military. In ideas, he said, freedom works best; in wartime, the military rules by fiat. He said the best solution, however, was freer speech, freer media that can be accurate. Then he explained that not every soldier was in the field. Support troops did the work that allowed enlisted combat soldiers to serve out in the field and be resupplied when needed. **Cronauer said it took between twelve and fifteen people – cooking, cleaning, resupplying, checking helicopters, servicing vehicles, putting in gas, unloading planes – to keep one combat soldier in the field.** [mmphasis mine] He predicted there would be billions of different stories of the war in the future: like a mosaic, billions of tiles, to represent the billions of stories (speech at Radford University, 16 September 1992).

Dr Byron Holley, drafted in late 1967 as a surgeon, wrote on 10 April 1969 to his girlfriend, later to become his wife: 'Well, Baby, I am lying around the old aid station tonight, listening to AFRVN radio, and they are playing *Please Release Me* by Engelbert Humperdinck. It really reminds me of you and just how much I love you and miss you. Music is such an important morale factor over here. Between mail call and the music from AFRVN, I somehow manage to avoid going out of my tree. There is one real crazy DJ over here who starts off each morning show with a long-drawn-out "Good morning, Viet-Nam!" and then he starts cracking on the place and what a bummer it is for us to have to be over here, halfway around the world away from our loved ones. I don't know how he gets away with it, but the troops really love him' (154).

Herr reports hearing him say, 'moving right along here with our fabulous Sounds of the Sixties, AFRVN, Armed Forces Radio Network, Vietnam, and for all you guys in the First of the Forty-fourth, and especially for the Soul Brother in the Orderly Room, here's Otis Redding – the *immortal* Otis Redding, singing *Dock of the Bay*' (137). Another DJ was Pat Sajak [retired June 2024], now host of popular game show *Wheel of Fortune*. He joined the Army, was assigned to be a finance clerk, a job in the rear, but managed to get transferred to AFRVN in Saigon as a morning disc jockey. He said: 'The Good Morning thing was already in place' (email to Margaret Brown, 8 November 2010).

45

The popular music chosen by the disc jockeys or played by bands at proms in the US was simply groovy or hip. At the senior proms back home, girls wore pink carnation corsages, boys yanked at ties that didn't fit, as chaperones, with arms crossed, shook their heads while watching the kids do the monkey and the boogaloo to the rock 'n' roll music. A boy would slip cheap vodka into the punch of orange sherbet and ginger ale, couples slipped out of the gym to make out in cars in the parking lot, and a few fast girls smoked joints outside with an English teacher, celebrating with McDonald's hamburgers, the new fast food chain. Few at the prom were thinking about college, student deferments, or the war.

Thousands and thousands of miles away, it was a rock-and-roll war (Hynes, 185). Those same songs had grunts in a Jeep in Vietnam singing along, poking each other, one grunt standing, bopping to the music. 'These were last year's football players, pool-playing dropouts from down the block, drag-racing steelworkers' sons who got their girls in trouble at the drive-in movie on warm summer nights, crew-cut ranchers' sons from Kansas' (Anderson, *Grunts*, 74). But the music was part of them and part of the war. 'The music said much about the war, and the troops knew it' (Dunnigan and Nofi, 159). You listen to the lyrics differently when you're in a war. What the soldiers heard in the Beatles' song *Yesterday* or The Rascals' *People Got to Be Free* was quite different from what those at the prom heard. Even the song titles suggested something about war. *The Letter* (The Box Tops) indicated how important mail from home was. *Leaving on a Jet Plane* (Peter, Paul, and Mary) was all about the most important event in a soldier's experience, the end of his tour and his trip home on a Freedom Bird. *We've Gotta Get Out of This Place* (Eric Burden and the Animals) expressed a widely held sentiment about life in the bush. Everybody said it. Everybody felt it. 'This was the national anthem for guys in 'Nam. The song was simply the *geographical cure* for what ailed the soldiers. It made sense to want to get the hell outta 'Nam. Even so, we had to put in our 365 days. If we made it through every one of those days – one day at a time – it meant we were going home alive' (Anthony, 35).

Another song which was popular with the troops was *Paint It Black* (the Rolling Stones), while *The Dock of the Bay* (Otis Redding) was liked because of the way it referred to San Francisco, the last part of America many soldiers saw before being flown to Vietnam. Creedence Clearwater Revival produced numerous songs that were very popular with the troops, among the most heard being *Proud Mary* (made famous by Ike and Tina Turner) and *Bad Moon Rising*. Soldiers favored tunes with a driving beat. Most popular was *Wooly Bully* (Sam the Sham & the Pharaohs), and the already mentioned, *War (What is it good for? Absolutely nothing)* (Edwin Starr) was often chanted by the troops.

'And then there was Vietnam Veteran and Special Forces NCO S. SGT Barry Sadler who had three hit songs, all of them hitting a responsive chord with the troops in the bush: *The Ballad of the Green Berets, I'm a Lucky One* and *Trooper's Lament*' (Dunnigan and Nofi, 159).

Of course, opinions about the rock 'n' roll radio show differed. Back in Vietnam after a quick trip home for a funeral, Ed Emanuel, a member of an all-black LRRP team called the Soul Patrol, woke up his first morning to hear 'Goooooood Morning Vietnam!'. He was thinking, not that again. 'The Armed Forces Radio disc jockeys felt a need to entertain the troops in Vietnam with a cheerful beginning to the day. The

THE MUSIC

"Gooooood Morning" commentary was for those "REMF" (rear echelon motherfuckers) who didn't have to go to the boonies and fight the war. Each morning that we had to listen to that noise, other [LRRPs] and I routinely responded to the expression with a loud and vocal chorus of "Kiss my ass!" Yeah, it was easy for those REMF to have a good morning; they didn't have to face Charlie' (77–78). Jim Ward, Vietnam vet, thought that the music was not entertaining, but instead was a great divider: 'There were the **Heads** – who smoked pot and listened to rock. Then there were the **Juicers** – who drank and listened to country music' (Vietnam Vet Program, 2/4/93).

Many of the songs of the day not only reflected the war but also either the passing of time or hearkened back to an earlier golden age. Otis Redding sang about sitting on the dock of the bay, just wasting time, nowhere he needed to go; nothing he needed to do. Bob Dylan, meanwhile, wrote about the passing of time with 'Where have all the flowers gone', then in a following verse 'Where have all the soldiers gone'. Don McLean sang about the past, a time when 'good ole boys were drinking whiskey and rye' down by the levee but now 'the levee was dry' in *American Pie*. Jim Croce wanted to put 'time in a bottle', and the Rolling Stones sang of time being on their side. But Elvis sang about how time had slipped away since his love had found someone new. The Beatles sang about yesterday, when 'all my troubles seemed so far away', but 'now it looks as though they're here to stay'. Dion reminisced about the loss of Abraham, Martin, and John, and the effect it had on the nation. Whether these songs were love songs, protest songs, or songs about the past, they all reflected the growing concern with time and how it was not now on their side.

Herr noticed his friend singing two songs, reflecting an earlier golden age – 'When you go to San Francisco' – and the war – 'There's something happening here/What it is ain't exactly clear/There's a man with a gun over there/Tellin' me I've got to beware' (Herr, 123, 138).

No Americans in the Sixties and early Seventies could avoid thinking about time; either counting the days until they could come home from Vietnam or reminiscing about that golden age, in the Fifties, under President Eisenhower, when all things seemed (or so they thought) peaceful and prosperous – when the soldiers came home victorious, when 90 per cent of the nation, many of them veterans, owned their own home, many in the suburbs (Molotsky, L1, 1), and the Second World War had become a distant memory. The Sixties and early Seventies, however, were a different time; to misquote the Rolling Stones, 'Time was not on their side'. Some youths retreated from or dropped out of the increasingly hostile society. Scott McKenzie reminded them, 'If you go to San Francisco, be sure to put some flowers in your hair'. For those who didn't drop out or retreat, the Sixties and early Seventies were a time of chaos, assassination, drugs, hostility, protests, and a place called Vietnam.

SECTION TWO

Vietnam, Understanding the Enemy

'Now we have a problem making our power credible, and Vietnam is the place.'
(President Kennedy, 1961)

***

'I can't say what made me fall in love with Vietnam – that a woman's voice can drug
you; that everything is so intense. The colors, the taste, even the rain.'
(Graham Greene, *The Quiet American*, 1956)

***

'They say whatever you're looking for, you will find here. They say you come to
Vietnam and you understand a lot in a few minutes, but the rest
has got to be lived. The smell: that's the first thing that hits you,
promising everything in exchange for your soul. And the heat.
Your shirt is straightaway a rag. You can hardly remember
your name, or what you came to escape from.'
(Graham Greene, *The Quiet American*, 1956)

Introduction

What is a place: Does the word refer to a continent, a country, a city, a town, a community, or a home? Home is the place where they have to take you in when you have nowhere else to go. Home is the life blood of a community, composed of multiple homes; home is the place to raise your children, the place to make memories, the place to feel safe. But what if you are not at home? What if you are in a place called Vietnam as an American soldier? What then? US soldiers did not think about place, only about time – 'how much time do we have left before our tour of duty is over?' All they wanted was to go home. But was it really home they were missing? Joseph Kanon wrote that it was not home they were missing but their youth: 'But it was the homesickness of an exile – what [they] missed was [their] own youth, not a place' (Kanon, 111).[1]

They created calendars to mark the time left: '**two-digit midgets**' (under 100 days) and '**short-timers**' ('I'm so short I can parachute off a dime'). They called the airplane that took them home the **Freedom Bird**. They never felt comfortable in that place called Vietnam; they never wanted or needed to understand its traditions, culture, geography, and people.

Vietnam has had several names over its long history. The French adopted the Chinese name, Annam, meaning 'pacified south'. The French colonies in Southeast Asia were known as Indochina, because they served as a buffer between India and China. Not until the mid-twentieth century did Annam become Vietnam. Colonel (Ret) Keith Nightingale describes Vietnam, its attractions and insidious nature: 'Indochina, our Vietnam, was a beautiful lady who easily obsessed the visitor with her quite deadly charms. Lush beauty, vast landscapes, and the combination of heat, danger, and exotica joined to create a mystique that quickly captured all but the most jaded of visitors. ... Such was Vietnam for much of her history – a beautiful woman with a terminal effect on those who attempted to possess her' (1).

That terminal effect was felt by the Chinese, the French, and later the Americans. Ruled by the Chinese and then the French, the Vietnamese spent centuries fighting off oppression. They had a brief period of independence under successive Nguyen dynasties from the late fifteenth century until the conquest by the French in the late nineteenth century. Despite the turmoil, most Vietnamese still lived in rural hamlets consisting of five or six families. They lived as their ancestors had lived in one- or two-room huts, known as **hooches**, planting rice, raising chickens and oxen, living from hand-to-mouth. They would bring their produce to open-air markets, bartering with others for what they could not produce themselves. Those who lived in major urban centers had adopted French and Chinese languages, religion, customs, and culture. Pictures of Saigon in the Fifties show French architecture, modern cars, and people dressed in modern European clothing. The contrast was startling.

Above: Saigon, 1968. (Wikipedia)

Right: Older woman. (Courtesy
D. Phillips)

In 1954, all of this changed. After the French defeat at **Dien Bien Phu**, although most Vietnamese still followed traditional ways, the Geneva Accords would affect and alter their lives. Many did not know or care about the Accords, only wishing to live their lives in peace, while those in cities wanted freedom for their country. But that was not to be. The Accords created three countries from what the French colonizers referred to as Indochina: Cambodia, Laos, and Vietnam. Vietnam was further divided into North and South, with elections scheduled in 1956 to reunite the country.

After the French defeat and the signing of the Geneva Accords, the United States – which had been providing materiel support to the French ever since the end of the Second World War – assumed responsibility for the development of South Vietnam into a viable democratic nation. The United States provided advisors, materiel support, and eventually soldiers to the new government of South Vietnam. Since neither the United States nor South Vietnam had signed the Geneva Accords, they would not honor the section of the Accords authorizing 1956 elections that would reunite the country, fearing that Ho Chi Minh, head of the communist North, would win. The US also believed that if South Vietnam was to fall to the communist North, it would not be long before all Southeast Asia became communist. That fear, known as **'the Domino Theory'**,[2] led to war between South Vietnam and its allies (chiefly the Americans) and the communist North and its allies.

51

Chapter 1

A Place Called Vietnam

Many Americans had never heard of Vietnam; even fewer knew where it was, despite the fact that in 1967, during the height of the war, the South Vietnam government 'touted the country as an enticing destination, with its sophisticated mountain resorts, fine white beaches, extensive hunting reserves and numerous other attractions' (Laderman, 1).

Although our soldiers were fighting a war there, Americans had 'very little knowledge about the country itself, and in particular its people and their way of life' (Rempel, 1). To the American soldiers, Vietnam was 'the other': they were either in that place or in 'the world', the latter referring to home, the United States. What does that say about where they were now? A place not in the world? A place that didn't exist? 'In a crazy war with no clear objectives, grunts could see, 'Nam was hell. For many grunts, Vietnam is not part of the world. In fact, according to one grunt, it doesn't exist: "I ain't gonna die here 'cause Vietnam, it don't exist"' (Herr, 125).

Even to the Vietnamese, Vietnam was hell. One North Vietnamese spoke with his driver: 'I've had nightmares since joining this team, but last night's was the worst.' A North Vietnamese soldier 'watched the white rain, the mountains, the endless forests, battlefield after battlefield, stretched out all the way to the horizon. This vast space swarming with soldiers, armies of black ants, red ants, winged ants, fire ants, bee ants, termites, all paddling about in the mud, running through scorched, desolate fields' (Huong, 246).

To Americans, Vietnam was not a place but a war. 'Were you in Vietnam?' means 'Were you in the war?' Twelve years earlier, the Korean War did not become Korea; Korea was Korea. But Vietnam simply didn't exist. To so many veterans, Vietnam was unreal, didn't mean anything – spooky, ghostly, it existed in dreams, nightmares, flashbacks of the war.

'The grunts were no longer in a geographical place named Vietnam. They were in a box full of adversity and suffering, all the things one could think of to complete the old phrase, "anything but that". But this box had no limits – they would walk but they would never reach the other side, the end' (Anderson, *Grunts*, 49–50).

Viet-Nam
By Robert C Hahn

> Land of volcanic hills, time warped mountains,
> Lichened rivers and rain scented heat,
> Land of rice, palms and poverty,
> Patience, struggle and violence.
> Land of war – Land of silence.

52

Proud people whose ravished children
Speak the beggar's tongue,
Whose girls whore the invader,
Whose men salute the rapist,
At night, hunt the rabid beast.

Enslaved in the name of Freedom;
You watch invader kill invader,
You watch your children die,
Watch the others speak of peace,
Suffer sorrow without cease. (Rottmann, 26)

For reporters, there was 'a standard question you could use to open a conversation with troops, and [former Saigon CBS bureau chief] Fouhy tried it. "How long you been in-country?" he asked. The kid half lifted his head; that question could *not* be serious. The weight was really on him, and the words came slowly. "All fuckin' day"' (Herr, 179). There it is.

In 1966, Captain John Rempel, a doctor operating in Vietnam, wrote in his diary: 'Viet Nam is a land of contrasts and variety: a melting pot of old and new, of many faiths and customs, of towering mountains and flat beaches, of subtropical heat in the lowlands and bitter cold nights in the mile high mountain highlands.' In the 1960s, Saigon – now Ho Chi Minh City – was known as the 'Paris of the Orient', with wide boulevards, modern dress, cars, and more substantial buildings. In the country, conditions were much worse: roads were often unpaved; people were poor; carts drawn

Farmer on his land in the 1960s (Courtesy D. Phillips)

by oxen were the usual means of transportation; people lived in wooden huts, often with straw roofs (Rempel, 2).

One soldier related his joy in gazing on the Vietnamese countryside. He wrote: 'As we passed field after lush field of ripening rice, we would watch the fat kernels of grain turn slowly, then rapidly, from straw color to sunset saffron to burnished copper in the afterglow. We had enjoyed the cool, moving air, the visual and aural panorama and the pungent rural odors. ... Occasionally we would stop for a minute or two in some red-tiled or thatch-roofed hamlet, where people were settling in for the evening as they and their ancestors had done for hundreds of years [while we rediscovered] what ordinary sane life and ordinary sane beauty and truth in ordinary sane people were all about' (Hastings, 413).

A view of the land. (Courtesy D. Phillips)

Chapter 2

Geography, People, and Culture

The Map of Vietnam [its first few lines]
By Dang Minh Tri [2.5]

Yesterday I practiced drawing a map
My teacher drew neat squares on the board

The border was made easy-to-find yellow chalk
From Southern Gate to Ca Mau

He knew each place by place
This was Dong Thap, this was Hien Luong Bridge

The East Sea was with a deep shade of blue
The mountains were drawn with brown spots

His hand moved and curved
Drawing the arcs of rivers and the swaths of jungles

Then he spoke with a deep voice
"The race of Dragons and of Fairy/God shine all the jungle and mountain

They have seen growth, fall, lost, prosperity
Have brought their blood to water each and every tree

To make up the air we now breathe
To make the road we walk and the house we live

Much bitter our ancestors have tasted
To leave the land to us" (H. Friedman 31-32)

Geography. Vietnam has over 1,000 miles of border: to the north and northeast with China, to the west with Laos and Cambodia, to the south and east with water. It is about the size of New Mexico, approximately 127,000 square miles, with a population of more than 98 million in 2020.[3] The country is divided into three geographic areas: (1) in the north, Hanoi and the Red River valley; (2) the long central part, with scenic beaches, the imperial city of Hue, and Da Nang, a large port city; (3) in the south, the Central

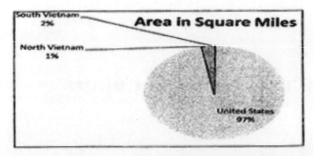

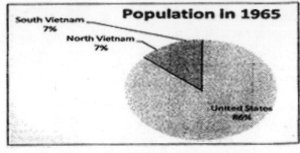

Relative size and
population in 1965.

Highlands – comprising almost 50 per cent of South Vietnam, the Mekong Delta – lying south and west of Ho Chi Minh City – and Ho Chi Minh City itself, formerly Saigon.

Ecologically and ethnically diverse, there are mountains in the northwest, the Red and Mekong River deltas, highland plateaus, and coastal plains. Its people represent fifty-four ethnic groups, with the Kinh or ethnic Vietnamese making up 86 per cent of the population. The two most important features of its location are water, the life blood of Vietnam, and its neighbor to the north, China, which had dominated Viet Nam for centuries.

Landscape with river. (Courtesy D. Phillips)

Water. Water has had a dominant influence over the lives of the Vietnamese people.

'Water motifs retained their cultural power as distinguishing features of the Vietnamese landscape. An early thirteenth-century [Vietnamese] folktale … (the chronicle of the catfish and the frog) satirizes a Confucian [Chinese] bureaucrat's unfamiliarity with the Vietnamese environment. In a lawsuit over the paternity of a brood of tadpoles, the mandarin and his corrupt inspectors award custody to a catfish, only to be confounded by a famous legal scholar who advises the frogs to wait until their tadpoles mature. The catfish had to confess to its theft, pay the frogs' costs, and submit to exile. … The Chinese-style mandarin [attempted to] thwart the concrete realities of his environment.' (Kiernan, 173)

Water, including the two great river systems – the Red River in the north and the Mekong River in the south – provides water for rice, the major crop, and fish, the major industry. It also provides a means of communication, as much of the country's early transportation from village to village occurred by water. A Vietnamese geographer in 1820 described the importance of water: 'The mountains are like the bones of the earth. Water is its blood' (Kiernan, 1).

Climate. Vietnam's tropical climate not only influences agricultural production, but also the economy, the culture, the flora and fauna, and the clothing people wear. Their deep familiarity and folk wisdom born from many generations in Vietnam allowed them to understand the cycles of the seasons. They knew when to expect heat and monsoons. 'Nam was dry and hot. 120–130 [degrees] Fahrenheit half of the year. ... The second half of the year, December to March, was wet due to the monsoons. It would rain for days, weeks, and months' (Harrod, 7). '"I sat in water," [Marine John] Musgrave recalled. "I slept in water. I ate in water because our [fox] holes were full. A flooded fox hole can drown a wounded man"' (Ward, 229).

Rain
By Jim Gray

I hate rain, low gray clouds and mist,
Tensed at the controls over my fate,
My senses strained beyond my visibility
Looking for the obstacle
Whose gut-wrenching, split second avoidance
Is the gossamer thread between life and death

On which I hang.
I much prefer clear, blue spring skies
Where all the treacheries of the earth
Are plain, small, and harmless
Maybe even beautiful.

I tell myself what I see
Through this Huey windshield, tired eyes and rain,
Is just an aberration
Of fear's flawed lens. (11)

'Temperatures were irrelevant – the climate in Indochina does not lend itself to conventional standards of measurement. … [The] numbers [98, 110, 105] can no more express the intensity of that heat than a barometer can express the destructive power of a typhoon' (Caputo, 57).

The Weather in Vietnam
By Larry Rottmann

There are two kinds of weather in Vietnam
Hot and dry and
Hot and wet

During the hot and dry
The dust is as fine as talcum powder
And hangs like a gritty mist in the air

During the hot and wet
The monsoon winds blow so hard
That it rains sideways. (8)

Monsoons. The most debilitating season is the annual monsoon. In the north of South Vietnam, the rainy season is from September to January. In the south, especially, in the Mekong Delta and the land bordering Cambodia and Laos, the rains come between May and September. Monsoons took away physical comfort and changed attitudes as well, writes Surgeon Holley to his wife: 'Well, today is truly a "blue" Sunday as it's been gray and overcast and rainy all day long. The monsoons have arrived, and I've never seen such huge raindrops. I know that sounds crazy, but sometimes it looks like it's raining grapes, and it's not hail, just huge raindrops, and lots of time it comes down in buckets' (181).

'One of [Nurse Van Devanter's] clearest, most oppressive memories … was the fall monsoon season. The unrelenting rains and violent winds began in early October and lasted until January with hardly a break. Together these four months felt longer than any other full year I've noticed before or since. The people who warned me about the season were right. These were the "real monsoons". The red mud was everywhere – on the buildings, in our rooms, on our clothes and on every casualty the helicopters brought in' (179).

Spec 4 Strong and his guys got caught on a mission during the monsoon season. It wasn't anything like he'd ever seen before: 'It rained 15 days and 15 nights continuously. We stayed wet 15 days. We started catching cramps and charley horses. And guys' feet got messed up. Well, they were trying to get supplies into us. But it was raining so hard, the helicopter couldn't get in. After five days, we ran out of supplies' (Terry, 55).

Claude Anshin Thomas, who went to Vietnam aged 17 (he's now a Buddhist monk), found that rain 'for want of a better word [is a flashback]. For me, every time it rains I walk through war. For two rainy seasons I experienced very heavy fighting. During the monsoons in Vietnam, the tremendous volume of water leaves everything wet and muddy. Now when it rains, I am still walking through fields of young men screaming and dying. I still see tree lines disintegrating from napalm. I still hear seventeen-year-old boys crying for their mothers, fathers, and girlfriends. Only after reexperiencing all of that can I come to the awareness that right now, it's just raining' (3).

Monsoon Season
By Yusef Komunyakaa

A river shines in the jungle's
wet leaves. The rains finally
let up but whenever wind shakes
the foliage it starts to fall.
The monsoon uncovers troubled
seasons we tried to forget.
Dead men slip through bad weather,
Stamping their muddy boots to wake us,
their curses coming easier.
There's a bend in everything,
In elephant grass & flame trees,
raindrops pelting the sand-bagged
bunker like a muted gong.
White phosphorus washed from the air,
winds sway with violet myrtle,
beating it naked. Soaked to the bone,
jungle rot brings us down to earth.
We sit in our hooches
with too much time,
where grounded helicopters
can't fly out the wounded.
Somewhere nearby a frog
begs a snake.
I try counting droplets,
Stars that aren't in the sky.
My poncho feels like a body bag.
I lose count. Red leaves
whirl by, the monsoon
unburying the dead. (130)

The weather, especially the monsoons, affected everything. 'Everything rotted and corroded quickly over there: bodies, boot leather, canvas, metal, morals. Scorched by the sun, wracked by the wind and rain of the monsoon, fighting in alien swamps and jungles, our humanity rubbed off of us' (Caputo, 217). It rained so hard for four months that it became difficult not only to fight a war, but to grow crops and live a normal life. Everything shut down.

The monsoons also provided the moisture for tropical triple-canopy jungles, the bush and tropical plants (such as what the soldiers called the wait-a-minute vine and elephant grass), and animals (poisonous snakes, leeches, mosquitoes, tigers, monkeys, blood-sucking leeches, armies of insects, fire ants, poisonous centipedes, mosquitoes, flies, bush snakes, vipers, scorpions, and rats).

Triple-canopy jungle. In a triple-canopy jungle, plants grow at three levels: the canopy layer, also known as the overstory, with the tallest trees 100–140 feet in height; the

Triple canopy jungle. (Courtesy D. Phillips)

second layer, called the understory, with smaller trees and shrubs, where most of the wildlife lives; and the forest floor, which is mostly clear of vegetation except for decaying plant and animal matter. The three intertwine, making the growth so dense that no sun gets through, making it a perfect place to rest or hide. Because this jungle was impenetrable and the enemy knew how to fight in this arena, Americans used defoliants, such as Napalm and Agent Orange, to clear it, resulting in fewer places for the enemy to hide and ambush our troops.

Bush. Infantry term for field or boonies. In the triple-canopy jungle, there was much that attacked the human body: sunburn, dehydration, 106° temperatures in the morning, exhaustion, diarrhea, cramps, elephant grass that cut the skin, jungle rot, sprained ankles, there always being yet another hill to climb, and hunger. Furthermore, there was never enough water. Al, a vet who attended my program, said that the CDC (Center for Disease Control) couldn't even identify some diseases people came home with (Vietnam Vet Program, 2/4/93). The bush was home to poisonous snakes, monkeys, an elephant or two, giant insects, quicksand, and tigers.

Plants of Vietnam. So many species of plants in Vietnam could make you sick or even kill you that some men created a deck of playing cards, called Survival Cards for Southeast Asia, with the names of deadly plants (Pendergrass, 7). The soldiers found that trees with sturdy, low-lying branches made for good cover, allowing them to climb as high as 15 feet (Pendergrass, 9) and forget for a few moments that they were fighting a war. Climbing these trees reminded some grunts of life back home – 'climbing trees and racing go-carts back home' (Anderson, *Grunts*, 143).

Wait-a-minute. This was a vicious vine. Ed Emanuel, a member of the Soul Patrol, the first all-black LRRPs, said: 'The vines hung down from the canopy of the jungle, sprouting sharp barbs at one-foot intervals. I … had to cover up all exposed skin

In the Bush. (Courtesy D. Phillips)

Above left: Wait-a-Minute vine. (Wikipedia)

Above right: Elephant grass. (Courtesy D. Phillips)

because the "wait-a-minute" vines would always triumph when it came to the slice-and-dice battle. It was unbelievable how badly the vines or even tall blades of grass [probably Elephant grass] could cut up your arms and hands, anything that was exposed' (45).

Elephant grass. A tall (approximately 6 feet) razor-sharp tropical plant. Because it is so sharp, it is nearly impenetrable. 'Forget the Cong, the *trees* would kill you, the elephant grass grew up homicidal, the ground you were walking over possessed malignant intelligence, your whole environment was a bath' (Herr, 66).

Snakes and other reptiles. The triple-canopy jungle and the tall elephant grass served as excellent hiding places for constrictors, cobras, extremely venomous kraits, vipers, and 20-foot pythons. Lying out in the sun, snakes were often startled by the point man, who moved as cautiously and silently as possible. Most of the snakes they encountered were not fatal, but some, especially cobras and kraits, were quite dangerous. '[Soldiers] believed that cobras traveled in pairs, mated for life, and sought revenge if you killed its mate. For that reason, killing a snake in a bunker or hut did not bring relief but anxiety over where the vengeful mate was' (Dunnigan and Nofi, 101).

Reptiles of Southeast Asia
By Larry Rottmann

There are two kinds of snakes in Vietnam
Mr. One Step
And Mr. Two Step
Named for how far you go after being bitten. (Rottmann, 27)

Not only snakes but other reptiles, like lizards, inhabited the jungles. One such lizard, a gecko, known as 'the fuck-you' lizard because of its distinctive call, would sometimes crawl up to a guard tower and scare the American guard.

Leeches. These were in the water wherever the grunts went. The soldiers took as many precautions as they could – tightening laces on their shoes, pulling the web belt tighter. Some grunts even wore condoms to protect themselves. After crossing water, they checked each other to pull off all the leeches. The VC were not magically immune from leeches. A retired colonel from the People's Army of Vietnam (PAVN) explained to Morley Safer that a 'man could lose two hundred grams of blood every day from the leeches. The leeches have an anticoagulant … many of my men bled to death' (32).

People. The Kinh, ethnic Viet or Mongolian in origin, made up 86 per cent of the population. The other 14 per cent were mountainous people, including the Hmong, Cham, Nung, Negritos, Degar, and ethnic Khmer. The French called them Montagnard, or mountain people.

Montagnard. The name the French gave to the indigenous mountain people of Vietnam. Although they had different tribal names, the French referred to them all as mountain dwellers. They are the original inhabitants of Vietnam. They were forced into the mountains, away from their fishing places, 'prior to the ninth century by the invading Vietnamese and Cambodians' (Baxter, 206). 'Strictly speaking, the Montagnard are not really Vietnamese at all, certainly not *South* Vietnamese, but a kind of upgraded, demi-enlightened Annamese[4] aborigine' (Herr, 93).

Hmong. One of the other ethnic groups originally inhabited China, Vietnam, and Laos. They are an indigenous, anti-communist ethnic group now living in the northern mountains of Vietnam. An anonymous source told me that the Hmongs were good fighters, whom the CIA often used as guards. After 1973, a number emigrated to the

Vietnamese children with their mothers. (Courtesy D. Phillips)

United States; many others were slaughtered by the North Vietnamese (Dunnigan and Nofi, 184–185). During the Vietnam War, the United States recruited thousands of Hmong people in Laos to fight against North Vietnam.

Amerasians. One soldier, Chuck, new to his unit, learned about a different, dark side of the war from Thanh, his Vietnamese female interpreter. She introduced him 'to the most shameful facet of the American involvement in Vietnam. … The unmentioned result of sending over two and a half million Americans to Vietnam without wives were several hundred thousand illegitimate children. … Most fathers simply [deserted their families] by following their transfer orders back to the States. Mothers left with mixed-blood illegitimate children [called *bui doi*, "dust of life"] were usually ill-equipped to support young children – the only job "skills" most had were those required by bar hostesses and prostitutes. More devastating was the humiliation and discrimination to which unmarried mothers and their illegitimate offspring were subjected' (Anderson, *Other War*, 97–98).

Later, Thanh took Chuck to visit a Catholic church in a part of town off-limits to Americans. More than 300 children lived there. Chuck tries to put this into perspective. 'So here it is, another kind of Body Count. More than three hundred. Most Americans in Vietnam were interested in the body count of dead enemy troops. But here was another kind of body count, produced by Americans, a body count of the living, not the dead. The living and the rejected – rejected by all the world except a handful of French Catholic priests and nuns' (Anderson, *Other War*, 99).

Spec 5 Emanuel J. Holliman married a Vietnamese woman, Tran Thi Saly, in 1968. The couple had not completed the papers required to allow her to come to America by the end of Holloman's tour. He says: 'When the paperwork did get approved, it was too late. I was shipped home.' He didn't get back to Vietnam until 1971, but couldn't find her right away. About all he could do was buy gifts for her and her mother. But after 1974, he didn't hear from the mother again. 'I'm told that they mistreat or maybe killed a lot of kids that, you know, were black. I just hope the baby was able to pass for Cambodian. Then she won't have a problem' (Terry, 84–85).

Refugee or DP (displaced person). The total number of Southeast Asian people who fled their homeland for fear of reprisal is astounding. Many nations refused to accept any more boat people – the primary, cheap way to escape. By 1975, 20,000 boat people had fled; by 1979, the number was up to 100,000. In 2000, it was estimated that two million people had fled Vietnam. Hmong tribal people, who had been anti-communist, settled in California and Minnesota – by the early 1990s, half a million were in this country (*Encyclopedia of the New American Nation*).

In 1984, the United States announced that over the next three years 'it will admit 8,000 Vietnamese children fathered by American servicemen. The law regards these children as US citizens' (*Vietnam War Almanac*, 355).

Daily Life. The problem of poverty dominated the life of the Vietnamese peasant. Often, the family had only one pair of pants, which the husband and wife would share. Most of the men wore what the Americans referred to as black pajamas. They were designed for a tropical climate

Above left: Vietnamese women wearing Ao dai. (Wikipedia)

Above right: Man wearing black pajamas. (Courtesy D. Phillips)

Memorial For Man In Black Pajamas
By Jan Berry

Trinh Vo Man was a poet
In his own land a scholar
To his own people a venerable
and wise old man
in his village
throughout his native land
a warm and kind man
to his wife and children
and grandchildren
a humorous and tolerant man
to his neighbors
an hospitable man to all

til the blue-eyed visitors
came uninvited
and shot him

Because a Man wearing
black pajamas to them
was just a slope, a dink, a gook
was Vietcong (Rottmann, 94)

Little Man in Black
By Randy Cribbs

Minutes ago, my enemy;
Probably neither of us knew why.
Just two soldiers trying to survive
And it was he to die.

Strange that I feel sad
For this little man in black,
Just another number
In the body count,
Added to the stack.

But I do mourn him
As I hope others will,
And pray he is at heaven's door;
This little man in black
Is my enemy no more. (13)

The daily labor involved caring for the rice paddies, often having to paddle water uphill to irrigate the crop. Many communities worked together to lessen the workload for an individual family. 'Many in the rural South "idealized the simplicity of peasant life" before the war with Americans' (Hastings, 36–37).

The peasants cooked their food over an open fire in the middle of the one-room home. They ate rice and, when available, a little meat, which they flavored with spices and sauces not available in the United States. Rice and tea were the major staples of their diet. They did not use tables, but sat cross-legged and ate from bowls with chopsticks. In many cases their food was placed on a banana leaf and eaten with their fingers. Like most countries, Vietnamese farmers took their produce to markets, carrying them in wicker baskets suspended on a bamboo pole across their shoulders. Oxen pulled the heavier loads.

City dwellers did not idealize simplicity. French architecture, food, and clothing were modern. Men in the city wore ties and jackets. Most of their clothing was made of cotton or hemp, but the women usually wore silk-like long skirts which emphasized their slimness.

Women wore long gowns over trousers, often quite colorful, called **Ao dai**. 'The *ao dai* is fitted tight around the waist and over the hips and makes these slim, fragilely constructed women even more willowy. A street filled with them, their hair falling down their backs to their waists … is a remarkable sight. The swaying hair, glistening black in the sun, the gentle flapping of the *ao dai* make the street shimmer, as if seen through a heat haze' (Safer, 204).

Culture. Vietnamese society valued family and community, with an emphasis on harmony and humanity. The structure was hierarchal and patriarchal, based on

65

Confucian teachings of self-development, reliance on moral teachings, and experiential judgment. The family was patriarchal, with the mother and father assuming traditional roles. No one would eat until their father began to eat. Families looked to the father to make the decisions which would be best for the family. They lived together in a one- or two-room hooch. Despite these traditional roles, sometimes the whole family had to work in the rice paddies or the gardens.

Work ceased during **TET**,[5] the Vietnamese lunar new year festival and the most important Vietnamese holiday. It occurs between the last ten days of January and mid February. 'The Vietnamese Tet holiday is an occasion for an entire people to share a common ideal of peace, concord and mutual love. The Tet holiday is officially three days long but is often celebrated for seven days. It comes at a time when there is a pause for the farmer after twelve months of labor. During this holiday the people take extra care to be kind and not show anger or act in a rude way toward anyone' (excerpted from Anon, 22).

Cultural and other changes occurred during colonial occupation. Many foreign ideas entered through travel and conquest. Among these were religion, manufacturing, Western languages, culture, racial hierarchies, and colonial laws and government. Because of the invasion and colonization by the Chinese and later the French, the Vietnamese people assimilated many of their occupiers' customs and traditions. From the third through to the ninth centuries, 'A variety of cultures … took root across the Vietnamese lowlands, coast and highlands. Locally diverse indigenous beliefs (such as those represented in the spirit cults), the standard Northern culture of the elite, the strong transnational Buddhist presence, and other ethnic patterns in the mountains and along the coast. … [Many of the changes to daily life occurred during this time:] the use of Chinese characters in writing, chopsticks for eating, money in the form of Chinese copper cash, and the Tang's dynasty poetry and laws' (Dutton, 11), as well as elements of Chinese religion in its political system and philosophy. When the French colonized the region, they had less effect on the country, which had already adapted many Chinese customs. The greatest impact the French had on the Vietnamese was in the areas of architecture, religion, language, and preparation of food.

Despite exposure to Western ideas and ideology during the French occupation, the greatest culture shock for soldiers landing in Vietnam was that the country was 130 years behind: they noticed people defecating in public and other things that we in the US would consider vulgar. 'The Vietnamese have no sense of time the way we understand it, their mental and body clocks are tuned more to history than to the ticking urgencies of ordinary life. That is why small, seemingly weak men and women were able to lug tons of supplies hundreds of miles through impassable and dangerous foot trails for years on end. [That is why] many of them will cycle thirty to forty miles [in the middle of the day] simply to say hello to a cousin or to deliver some firewood to a sick granny' (Safer, 4).

Captain Rempel, in his 1966 article, wrote about the differences between Eastern and Western culture: humility not confrontation, more subtle and less direct methods, and respect for elders rather than glorification of youth (13–14). In an earlier section of his article, Rempel explains these differences more fully:

'The Westerners have a dynamic concept of life full of needs and desires to be satisfied. The Easterners view the world, its social order, and man's place as predetermined. He aims at complete harmony with the outer world and is inclined to adapt to the environment and thereby create a balance with nature. ... He is not pressed for time ... but rather uses patience to replace speed. ... In the West, family means the immediate family, and family needs often give way to individual rights. In the East, family means all relatives as well, and it enjoys the dominant position in every level of society, thereby superseding the individual. Family ties are much stronger and the Easterner acts in accord with his parents' or relatives' feelings, even to the point of pronounced ancestor worship.' (3–4)

No wonder many US soldiers felt as if they didn't belong: what with the humidity, the jungle, the exotic wild flora and fauna, the monsoon season, the foreign, strange-sounding language, and pre-modern living conditions. No wonder many thought they were in a world with which they were not familiar.

Vietnam Clouds
By Stephen Hatch

> The clouds seem to say
> we do not belong here
> They are long and thin
> like cotton candy going
> on a paper cone
> Sometimes vanilla, orange
> or cherry
> Our own sunsets wait
> for us at home. (Rottmann, 74)

The United States military, aware of these cultural differences, created a list of rules of conduct and other advice to remind US soldiers that they were guests here: try to learn words in their language, be humble and respectful, and be observant of their customs, culture, and traditions.[6]

Vietcong soldier. (Courtesy D. Phillips)

Despite the rules of conduct and other advice offered by the military command, the United States and its soldiers were 'ignorant of Vietnam's history, tradition and national character. … But the longevity of Vietnamese resistance to foreign rule could have been learned from any history book on Indochina [or from the French or the advisors the United States sent into Vietnam in the late Fifties]. Not only did the United States underestimate the determination of the Vietnamese people but it overestimated the strength of the South Vietnamese government' (Tuchman, 376).

During the war, many soldiers, especially the Vietcong, had difficulty finding food. Many would come into a village or hamlet and demand rice and other produce, threatening not only their lives but their livelihood. In an interview with Morley Safer, Bui Tan, a retired Vietcong colonel, recalls the food shortage he and his men faced: 'Food was a constant worry for Vietcong and NVA, especially for the big units. I remember we shot an elephant once, and for five days we had meat. Men drowned; they fell off cliffs; they died of malaria and snake bites. I used to look up in the sky and envy you in those helicopters' (Safer, 32).

Above left: Nine rules.

Above right: Listing of nine rules.

Chapter 3

Colonial Rule

Early Vietnam was ruled by various dynasties until the mid-nineteenth century, when France took control of much of Southeast Asia. The Chinese, the French, and Indian traders brought with them their culture, religion, and customs. China dominated – if not ruled – Vietnam both culturally and economically from the first millennium CE until the Chinese were defeated in 938 and driven out in 1426. During that period, the Chinese attempted to 'civilize' Vietnam. One Chinese writer argued that 'with the right "polishing" southerners could yet become civilized. ... People of cities and countries are all comfortable in and used to their own customs.' But if these people were not so comfortable in their customs, they could become gentlemen (Kiernan, 76). The Chinese also changed Vietnam into a patriarchal society, based on the teachings of Confucius. They taught the Vietnamese advances in farming and introduced schools, although they were mainly for the Chinese (Kiernan, 77). Over time, 'this conquest ... [led to] the local adoption of what became a shared classical high culture that outlived nine centuries ... and weathered the storms of subsequent imperial invasions and occupations. Chinese political models and vocabulary and China's writing system and literary canon all helped shape Vietnamese culture' (Kiernan, 13).

Although China supported North Vietnam during the wars for independence against the French and then the Americans, supplying military and supplies, the Vietnamese and Chinese have had ongoing conflicts and disagreements over the centuries.

Because Vietnam is bounded on two sides by the Gulf of China, it was easy for foreigners to invade its port cities. Just as the Vietnamese objected to and fought Chinese control, they objected to and fought other attempts to colonize them. The first Europeans arrived in Vietnam in the early sixteenth century, when Portugal established the first European factories; 100 years later, the Dutch became the leading traders. Nguyen Anh signed a treaty with Louis XVI in 1787, granting land to the French in exchange for helping him defeat the Nguyen lords, which he succeeded in doing in 1802, thereafter taking the title Gia Long. Gia Long, a name which is a contraction of two provinces, north and south, thus uniting the country.

'[Gia Long, whom the Chinese referred to as King of the Southern Viet country] built his new Nguyen dynasty on the Chinese bureaucratic model and the traditional neo-Confucian base' (Kiernan, 270). He established his capital at Hue and asked the Chinese to refer to his country as 'Nan Yue', which the Chinese reversed to 'Yue Nan', Chinese for Viet Nam. But the Chinese still preferred calling Viet Nam 'An-Nam', the pacified South. Although Gia Long had good relations with the Chinese, he was ever mindful of the help the French provided in overthrowing the previous Nguyen dynasty: he asked the French for advice on military matters, also asked them to keep other invaders away, and he favored French Catholic missionaries.

Taking advantage of its treaty with Gia Long, France seized control of the southern third of Vietnam in the 1860s. By 1886, it had conquered all of Vietnam, which it divided into three states – Annam, Tonkin, and Cochin-China – finally amalgamating them into Indochina in 1887. Although France did not gain outright control of Vietnam until that year, the French had exerted influence on Vietnamese culture since the 1780s. The French colonized Cambodia and Laos in 1893. The French administration imposed significant political and cultural changes on Vietnamese society. A Western-style system of modern education introduced new humanist values, language, and culture into Vietnam. 'A schoolboy recalls being taught in his class that his forebears were Gauls.' However, his father proudly told him that his 'ancestors were Vietnamese' (Hastings, 4).

These values did not alter the cruelty towards the Vietnamese imposed by French plutocrats, namely the planters, rubber magnates, and coal-mine owners. These colonizers promoted goods that were easy to export – rice, coal, rubber, and silk – and manipulated the economy by importing goods made in France. Roosevelt called French rule 'the most exploitative in Asia' (Tuchman, 237).

Religion. In attempting to civilize the country, the Chinese and the French colonizers, as well as other traders, introduced the Vietnamese to their religions. The three most prominent strands in Vietnam's religious tradition are Buddhism, Taoism, and Confucianism, known collectively as Tam Giao, the three religions. Indian traders brought Buddhism into Vietnam, but the Vietnamese developed its own version of the religion. Tim Page, a photo-journalist in Vietnam, remarks on this fact in his book *Mindful Moment*: 'Vietnam has a penchant for throwing a new cult or sect into its spiritual blender. Heroic religious leaders have often adapted strands of beliefs imported by invaders' (66).

In 1967, in his book, *Vietnam: Lotus in the Sea of Fire*, Thich Nhat Hanh, introduced engaged Buddhism. This form of Buddhism is a social program, basing its adherents' actions on enlightenment, compassion, and wisdom while traditional Buddhism focuses on the individual. Its adherents strive for perfection on the way to awakening (Wikipedia).

The other two religions, Confucianism and Taoism – brought to Vietnam by the Chinese, that form the triad, Tam Gaio, were modified to meet the spiritual needs of the Vietnamese. Confucianism's code of ethics teaches hierarchy and patriarchy and a sense of duty to the state. Taoism teaches the 'Way' to live in harmony with the universe.

Although not part of the Vietnamese religious triad tradition, the French brought Catholicism to Vietnam. Approximately 8.5 per cent of the population today is Christian, most of whom are Catholic. It is the Catholics whose religion dominated South Vietnam during the war years. The nation's leader, Ngo Dinh Diem, was Catholic. Many Catholics in North Vietnam, fled to South Vietnam, not because Diem was Catholic but because the North was a communist nation.

In the 1920s, Ngo Van Chieu created the Cao Dai sect of Tam Giao, a combination of the three traditional faiths of Vietnam plus a dose of Catholicism and French spiritualism. 'Its beliefs and practices drew on Sino-Vietnamese Daoism [Taoism], a Buddhist concept of salvation, Chinese immigrant secret society ritual, the institutional structure of Catholicism, and French secular urban spiritualism and seances. The Cao Dai movement's eclecticism contributed to its appeal [especially to the peasantry] but also made it more likely to fracture.' By 1938, because of its eclecticism, it had fractured into twelve subsects. Despite the fractures and its geographical limitations, mainly in southern Vietnam, 'the Cao Dai movement [met] the cultural and material needs of its faithful' (all of the above is excerpted from Kiernan, 352–355). [I have paraphrased most of the section on religion. There are other authors in this section whom I have named and quoted.] It expands on Tam Giao, the three most prominent strands of Vietnamese religious traditions, in the following ways: its adherents believe that all religions are unified 'because the nature of all religions is unity; [they] promote the idea of the Three Religions in harmony' and promote their universality, all worshipping Dao or God, 'thus expanding Tam Giao into Tam Dao Dao' (Du, 7–8).

In 1966, Captain John Rempel commented on religious freedom in Vietnam: 'There is a free choice of worship with plural religions present, i.e. it is possible to find Christ, Confucius, and Mohammed all honored in the same temple. [I also saw] large statues to the Buddha' (10).

Language. The two major colonizers, the Chinese and the French, brought with them their language. Many of the words now in use in Vietnam are derived from the French, especially words for commerce and communication with the local people. American soldiers picked up these words to converse with the Vietnamese: '"number one" for best, "number 10" for worst, "dau" for pain, "bac si" for doctor, "di di" [also "dee dee maahhh"] for go away [or go quickly], … [and] that memorable army phrase "sin loi" (sorry 'bout that!)' (Rempel, 9). The grunts also used other words to communicate to and with the Vietnamese. The following words are a pidgin mixture of Chinese, French, and Vietnamese:

Bao chi! Bao Chi! Journalist; *Bao chi fap!* for Vietnamese French journalist; but according to Herr, it also meant 'Don't shoot! Don't shoot' (135).

Beaucoup. French for many or a lot; in grunt speak it became 'boo-coo', as in 'boo-coo money'.

Chop-chop. Of Asian origin, The term came into everyday American usage even before it was used in Vietnam. Chop-chop means do it now, don't wait. The phrase was also often used by Vietnamese children to ask for food from GIs (Clark).

Cumshaw. Chinese for tip or bribe; US for theft or corruption. Then there's the Standard Operating Procedure (SOP). Cumshaw was a necessary augmentation of an official (i.e., military) system that was not in fact as efficient as its designers and managers claimed. Cumshaw was not to be confused with the black market. Soldiers involved in cumshaw did not get rich. What they provided supported the troops, for example, a new engine part or other necessary items. The black market handled any item, and its purveyors, civilians, got rich. 'No one ever starved, ran out of ammunition, or bled to death because of [cumshaw]' (Anderson, *The Other War*, 121). Ketwig, author of *A Hard Rain Fell*, remarking on the cold at night in the highlands, 'cumshawed air force parkas and sleeping bags' (99). Cumshaw methods[7] worked by getting food and equipment – bartering with somebody who knew somebody who knew somebody.

Commanding officers had to rely on the army way (SOP): the right form (which may have been the wrong form yesterday) filled out in triplicate, black ink only, and turned over to the appropriate person. In two months you would be notified that the part you requested was no longer available; you were to use part # f2948750923875 instead!

Six weeks later, the soldier might be told that the part had been lost – try again. In two months he would be notified that the part he requested was no longer available. Anderson remarks in *Vietnam: The Other War* that it could take up to six months for a part to finally arrive. To the military, that was efficient (120–121). One resourceful man, Senior Chief Petty Officer B.G. Feddersen, was known as the king of cumshaw. According to a story in *Time*, Feddersen unclogged within twenty-three days a harbor loaded with 2,600 pounds of spare parts for trucks, bulldozers, and other items. He provided aluminum for a jetway 'and made Mobile Construction Battalion 10 the only outfit on the base with a perpetual supply of beer, steaks, lettuce, tomatoes and lumber' (*Vietnam War Diary*, 61).

Dinki dow. Crazy. When nothing made sense, when you knew it was all wrong, it was *dinki dow*, a Vietnamese phrase grunts used to describe the war – another example of the madness that was Vietnam. Sometimes you just had to expect it, such as when one of your men did something you couldn't explain away, like carrying 200 pounds of ammo up a hill (they could get as much as they wanted), only to drop it into a stream before he reached the top: 'when I got to the hill to set up for the night, I said, "Taylor, where's my ammo?" he said, "Man, you know that song about loose my shackles and set me free? I had to get free about a mile down the road. I got rid of that stuff in that stream. Them chains of slavery"' (Terry, 47).

Hooch, or Hootch. Vietnamese word for a rural house. Rural people lived in thatched homes, made of bamboo, wood, or straw, reinforced with mud or baked clay tiles. Floors were usually the ground itself and wooden planks. Thatched palms covered roofs. Hooches were much longer than wide and built on stilts for protection during the rainy season. The Vietnamese did not realize that many Americans considered their hooches hovels; for them it was home, home to many in the same family who shared the one- or two-room hooch. Soldiers adopted the term, referring to their own barracks and primitive dwellings as hooches. 'They [the Vietnamese] lived the most basic life [many soldiers] had ever seen. They lived the same way their forefathers lived' (Phillips, 26).

Vietnamese hooch. (Courtesy D. Phillips)

Mama-San. (Courtesy D. Phillips)

Mama-san and Papa-san. Names the soldiers used for the mother and father within a family. *San* is of Japanese origin and is a polite honorific attached to a noun.[8] Soldiers usually referred to older women as Mama-san, who were raising a family and planting rice while their husbands fought in the war.

Mama-San
By Jim Gray

Yours was a village of a dozen thatched roofs
Surrounded by palm trees and rice paddies.
I guess you were born in that village
Somewhere near Song Mao
Its name escapes me now.

I'd say you were a dark-eyed beauty once
Before the paddy sun faded you.
Raising children and crops
Long before the war
Finally reached your door.

WHY VIETNAM? REFLECTIONS ON THE EFFECT OF WAR

We came to your village not expected or invited,
Impolite teenagers in noisy helicopters.
Not respecting your age
We came with the sun
Before your sleep was done.

We landed by your house, in the garden
You guarded from the village boys.
In a huge flying insect we landed
Tearing up the rows
You so neatly hoed.

We saw you in your anger charge
Shuffling down the path to the garden.
Your gray hair back in a bun
Chasing off the boys
Playing with their noisy toys.

We had little to report of that morning mission
Just minor damage to a single helicopter.
A dented right side pilot's door.
You made quite a shot
With your cast-iron cooking pot.

Titi. A little, from the French.

Ville. From the French for village. A collection of hamlets and hooches.

Chapter 4

Resistance

'The Vietnamese still know only their family and do not know their country.'
Phan Chau Trinh, in a speech delivered in 1925, 'Monarchy and Democracy',
(quoted in Kiernan, 343)

'There is a privilege in being raised in a time of peace. A luxury that your life
is not under immediate threat. War becomes something labelled heroic, often
patriotic, nationalistic. There is a cause, it is just and right, and it somehow
excuses all the pain and loss.' (Page, 10)

Throughout the twentieth century, the Vietnamese resisted French rule. Part of this
resistance occurred in literature and speech. One such speech, 'Monarchy and
Democracy', given by Phan Chau Trinh, a political activist, called on the Vietnamese to
'sail with the wind, to follow the world trends towards democratic, liberal, revolutionary
and socialist ideas'. But as Trinh's speech made clear, 'the winds were still blowing in
all directions' (Kiernan, 342). Dutton, a professor of Asian Languages and Culture at
UCLA, sums up this speech: 'Only when the people exercise their popular rights …
will they truly learn to love their country and achieve self-determination' (376). Trinh
and others furthered the transformation of the Vietnamese people by writing in Western
script, although at that time, 1925, few Vietnamese could read it. 'The Romanized script
enabled a revolution in print media and literature … which [transformed the culture and]
fostered a new sense of national identity. … From 1920 to 1945 the French authorities
not only "lost control of language strategy" but also lost control of Vietnamese politics'
(Kiernan, 343). The French may have lost control of the Vietnamese people, but they
still maintained control of the country and all Southeast Asia.

When the Japanese invaded Southeast Asia in 1940 to cut off supply routes to
China, the French had controlled the region for six decades. The Japanese left the pro-
Nazi French Vichy government in place, but they controlled Southeast Asia. Many
Vietnamese, under the leadership of Ho Chi Minh with the support of the OSS,[9] fought
the Japanese and pro-Nazi French occupation. They fought a guerilla war against the
occupiers, just as later they fought another guerilla war against the South Vietnamese
and the Americans.

Nguyen Sinh Cung, later known as Ho Chi Minh, then in exile in France, attended
the Versailles peace conference at the end of the First World War, 'advocating' for
Vietnamese independence. When he returned to Vietnam in 1941, he adopted the name
Ho Chi Minh, meaning bringer of enlightenment. He created the Viet Minh, the League

for the Independence of Vietnam, a national independence coalition, on 19 May 1941. It established itself as the only organized anti-French and anti-Japanese resistance group, and was initially formed to seek independence for Vietnam from the French Empire. When the Japanese occupation began, the Viet Minh opposed Japan, with support from the United States and the Republic of China. Ho Chi Minh 'recognized that welcoming the Japanese as liberators was tantamount to "driv[ing] the tiger out the front door while letting the wolf in through the back"' (McMaster, 33). During the Second World War, Ho Chi Minh received secret help from the OSS in defeating the Japanese.

After the defeat of the Japanese, Ho Chi Minh established an independent Vietnam called the Democratic Republic of Vietnam on 2 September 1945. Its capital was Hanoi, where Ho Chi Minh declared: 'The French have fled, the Japanese have capitulated, Emperor Bao Dai has abdicated, our people have broken the fetters which for over a century have tied us down' (Hastings, 11–12). The French hadn't fled, but reoccupied Vietnam. Although Ho Chi Minh repeatedly called for US help in defeating the French, his pleas went unanswered as America was aiding the French in forming a new nation in the south. After the French were defeated at Dien Bien Phu in 1954, the United States provided support to South Vietnam, resulting in the Vietnam conflict.

At the end of the Second World War, De Gaulle refused to negotiate with Ho Chi Minh and the Viet Minh; instead, he reestablished French colonial rule in Indochina. The independence announced by Ho Chi Minh in September 1945, was short-lived. In December 1946, the French captured Hanoi, but not before the leadership fled to the mountains. When the exiled Emperor Bao Dai returned from France to Vietnam in 1948, he recognized French authority in Vietnam. Repression and guerilla warfare returned to the region as the Vietnamese demanded their independence. The Viet Minh military leadership, under the command of General Vo Nguyen Giap, finally defeated the French at Dien Bien Phu in May 1954.

Dien Bien Phu. A town in northwestern Vietnam. In June 1953, General Henri Navarre assumed command of the French forces in Indochina. He realized that 'the most serious danger still lay in the north, but that territory was firmly in the hands of experienced troops … They [the French] would prevent the enemy's offensive operations by smashing them before they were launched' (Roy, 39), and would cut off their supply routes.[10]

Dien Bien Phu pin. (Acquired by Margaret Brown in Vietnam)

By March 1954, however, the Viet Minh had blockaded the fort at Dien Bien Phu. Major General Rene Cogny, commanding French forces in northern Vietnam, realized the seriousness of the situation, and in April 1954 requested General Navarre to launch Operation Condor to send soldiers from Laos to relieve the blockade, although Cogny was not certain that the troops would arrive in time. Navarre believed that the loss of Dien Bien Phu would only result in the loss of thirteen battalions and four artillery batteries, 'not even a tenth of his troops', but if he launched Operation Condor the results could be catastrophic. Navarre did not fully realize what was at stake, believing that he had a better view of the French position in Indochina (Roy, 297).

In a battle lasting fifty-five days, from 13 March to 7 May 1954, the Viet Minh under the command of General Giap defeated the French. Although the French were beaten, skirmishes continued throughout Vietnam until a peace agreement was finally reached on 21 July 1954.

At the Geneva Peace Accords held from April–July 1954, the French agreed to give up all its colonies in Indochina. The French, British, United States and USSR divided French Indochina into three separate nations: Vietnam, Laos, and Cambodia. The Accords also stipulated that Vietnam be separated by a Demilitarized Zone (DMZ) at the 17th parallel until elections could be held in 1956, which would then remove the DMZ. 'The Geneva Accords ... merely settled terms of truce between the departing French colonialists and the communists' (Hastings, 90). Other nations who participated in the peace negotiations were not bound by any terms of the treaty.

Chapter 5

The Two Vietnams

The Demilitarized Zone, a 5-mile-wide strip established at the Geneva Peace Accords, separated North from South Vietnam. The Geneva Convention determined that there would be no firing across the DMZ. There were to be elections in 1956 to determine who would lead the united country. The US, however, was worried that the communist Ho Chi Minh of North Vietnam might win; consequently, there were no elections.

'To the diplomats who drew [the DMZ], the line represented a face-saving truce to a problem … a truce which saved but little western face and few Vietnamese lives. To the Vietnamese living south of it, the line meant a flimsy guarantee that rice could be planted and harvested in peace. … To the Vietnamese living north of it, the line was a constant and humiliating reminder that the reunification of a homeland and a way of life, ravaged by westerners for more than a century, was still unfinished … To the young grunts … the DMZ meant other things still … The DMZ was the reason the grunts were in Vietnam; if it had never been violated, the grunts would not be in Vietnam' (Anderson, *Grunts*, 124).

North of the Demilitarized Zone, Ho Chi Minh and his Viet Minh (Communist Party) created the Democratic Republic of Vietnam. On 2 September 1954, following the signing of the Geneva Accords, Ho Chi Minh proclaimed the establishment of a political communist government to half-a-million people in Hanoi's Ba Dinh Square. Ho Chi Minh had the support of the Soviets and the Chinese in his efforts to unify the country under a communist regime. In 1966, during the carpet-bombing of North Vietnam by the United States, Ho Chi Minh told the nation: '[President] Johnson and his clique should realize this: they may bring in 500,000 troops, a million, or even more troops to step up their war of aggression in South Vietnam. But never will they be able to break the iron will of the heroic Vietnamese people in their determination to fight for national salvation against US Aggression' (Dutton, 455).

Hanoi was home to the French prison of Hoa Lo, later known in the West as the Hanoi Hilton. My husband and I [Margaret Brown] visited the Hanoi Hilton in 2007. We saw bunk beds, neat prisoner cells, even the flight suit that future politician John McCain supposedly wore when he was shot down over North Vietnam, which he denies (*Vietnam, Special Newsweek Edition*, 87). The North Vietnamese state that they 'shot him down, but saved him, gave him clemency, released him and reunited him with his family' (*Vietnam: Special Newsweek Edition*, 86). Everything seemed according to the Geneva Convention. But from everything we read, that was not the case. We visited Ho Chi Minh's stilt house – a simple, minimalist home reflecting the Vietnamese leader, who rejected the grand palace built for him. We also saw US military equipment captured by the North Vietnamese and attended an exhibit, entitled 'Requiem', of photographs of those who died during the fighting. This exhibit was a gift from the people of the Commonwealth of Kentucky, sponsored by United Airlines, United Parcel Service, Brown-Forman Corporation, and several others. This only confirmed our impression of the extent of trade between the United States and Vietnam. Just as in Saigon (Ho Chi Minh City), motorcycles and cars were everywhere. People were prosperous and hard-working, a further indication of the capitalist economy even though the country was controlled by an authoritarian government.

North Vietnamese Army and Vietcong Guerrillas. North Vietnam never revealed the exact number of troops in the North Vietnam Army, the NVA, but this figure has been estimated at approximately 400,000, including both the NVA and the National Liberation Front (NLF). General Giap denied that the guerilla forces in the South, the **Vietcong**, took their orders from Hanoi, but said they would support them in their struggle for liberation. He claimed that they were a 'National Liberation Front' (NLF), also known as the Vietcong, made up of southerners opposed to the Diem regime. The Vietcong defended its villages, regions, and territory against the southern forces.

The Vietcong were trained in jungle guerrilla tactics. 'They relied on stealth, on ambush, on their personal skills and wile, as opposed to firepower. They knew it did not pay for them to stand and fight … They'd come back and fight another day' (Terry, 226). They had prepared defensive positions throughout their operational area, to which they could retreat if surprised by enemy forces. If these positions were attacked, the Vietcong would defend them until night, when they would escape (*Handbook*, 29).

The **North Vietnamese Army** was the regular army of North Vietnam. Like all armed forces, it was trained in conventional strategies and tactics, but although it would engage the enemy, it usually would not dig in. 'Every Viet Minh [NVA] combatant takes an "oath of honor", several points of which concern relations with the population. … He must not enter a house without the owner's consent; he must sweep and clean the place where he has been living. He may not share the inhabitants' food if doing so would make them go short' (Clos).

Colonel Huang Dai Hai, who commanded an artillery and aircraft unit, told Morley Safer: 'When you join the army you take seven oaths, the seventh is to swear to live together, die together, and share sorrows as if they were joys. I still maintain that oath, even now … but I have feelings of guilt that we didn't win the war more quickly. … Even though we now want reconciliation with the United States … I still hate those people who thrust war upon our country and those people who committed crimes in our country' (88–89).

Winning the war quickly is not a usual Vietnamese concept. For the Vietnamese, time is a wheel that always flows and never ends. A quick victory is a Western concept. There is little sense of progress in Vietnam. History possesses little value and few goals. Hence, the Vietnamese are not impressed by a need to rush. Their lifespan is already short; so make do with what you have. With patience, perhaps in the next existence, your Karma will permit improvement (The Religions of South Vietnam in Faith and Facts, US Navy, Bureau of Naval Personnel, Chaplains Division, 1967, at sacred-texts.com).

Even though they were fighting in their own country, the Vietnamese could not take for granted daily rations. This was due in part to the rice robbery which was a major United States psychological operation. Leaflets told the farmers they did not have to let the VC

North Vietnam troops on parade (Vets with a Mission)

take their rice. Because the VC had guns and the farmers did not, it was not that successful (Anon).[11] 'North Vietnam officers observed to each other that "rice is the field-marshal of our army"' (Hastings, 424). Just like their American counterparts, they too had problems with poisonous snakes, the rainy season, and feelings of remoteness from the outside world. One man 'suffering from acute malaria [was] told he should "go *chieu hoi*" – defect – if he wished to survive: continued jungle life would kill him' (Hastings, 425).

Both armies fought against the South Vietnamese Army (ARVN) and the Americans in their own way, the NLF as guerillas and the NVA as a conventional armed force. General Giap wrote in an article published in July 1965: 'The American imperialists cannot shake the determination of our people in both zones to fight them for national salvation, cannot cause any decrease in the wholehearted assistance of the northern people to the patriotic struggle of the southern people [NLF], let alone stabilize the very critical position of the puppet army and administration' (*Vietnam Special Newsweek Edition*).

The Draft. 'In North Vietnam, it was more difficult [than in the US] to "dodge the draft". ... North Vietnam had a very practical attitude towards reluctant soldiers. If a soldier in the north deserted, or refused to show up for military duty, some soldiers were sent to the man's village, city or neighborhood and spoke with his family. Avoiding military service was shameful' (Dunnigan and Nofi, 272–273). Just like Americans, the Vietnamese thought volunteering was a personal responsibility. 'I ran my fingers through the hair of a corpse, that of my youngest soldier, Hoang. ... He had taken first place in the math competition that selected students for study abroad. But he had volunteered for the army instead. [He had said:] "No, the college classrooms aren't as important as the battlefield. There have been and there always will be classrooms for those who want them. Only the war gives me a chance to participate in our country's historic mission. I've heard the sacred call"' (Huong, 219–220).

Desertions. According to Master-Sergeant Duncan, the number of recorded VC desertions cannot be trusted. 'In an effort to show waning popularity for the Vietcong,

80

great emphasis was placed on figures of Vietcong defections. Even if the unlikely possibility of the correctness of these figures is accepted, they are worthless when compared to ARVN desertions. The admitted desertion rate and incidents of draft dodging, although deflated, was staggering' (Duncan, 'Ramparts', 92–93).

Desertion was a universal problem. 'Desertion was rife throughout the [North Vietnamese Army] regiment at that time. … The authorities seemed unable to prevent desertions' (Ninh, 23). It was even worse in the South. 'Between 1965 and 1972, The Republic of Vietnam Armed Forces lost about 120,000 servicemen annually to desertion. Scholars attribute the difference in desertion rates … to the greater commitment and offensive, guerilla fighting style of the North' (Kutler, 158).

South of the Demilitarized Zone. In the non-communist South, Emperor Bao Dai, while in exile in France, appointed anti-communist Catholic Ngo Dinh Diem as his prime minister. 'In the end, Bao Dai recalled, he chose Diem … because he was well known to the Americans, who appreciated his intransigence. … Washington would not be sparing in its support for him' (Ward, 32). Once appointed, Ngo Dinh Diem formed the anti-communist Republic of Vietnam. The political structure 'concentrated power at the national level; most important decisions originate and are directed from Saigon'. Most of these decisions then are enacted by the forty-three province chiefs who administer their district, consisting of eight to twelve villages and the four to six hamlets which make up a village (*Handbook*, 1–2).

Diem's philosophy of Personalism became the country's official ideology. It combined Catholic modernism, Neo-Confucianism, and liberal democracy. He relied on the support of Vietnamese Catholics, who fled northern Vietnam, and the United States. In a speech to his countrymen, Diem stated: 'The text of the constitution does not create democracy. Democracy develops only when the spirit and will of the people enjoy favorable conditions'. In October 1955, Diem staged a one-sided 'referendum' on his regime. He campaigned strongly against Bao Dai and his supporters (who were forbidden to campaign) and suppressed all other resistance. Not surprisingly, the vote was heavily in his favor (Dutton, 477).

The republic's capital was Saigon (now Ho Chi Minh City), known to Herr and others during the war years as Sin City, the center of everything. 'Like a spider, it felt the trembles of action here, there, and everywhere. … Sitting in Saigon was like sitting inside the folded petals of a poisonous flower, the poison history, fucked in its root no matter how far back you wanted to run your trace. Saigon was the only place left with a continuity … it breathed history' (Herr, 42–43).

Saigon was protected by a 40-square mile jungle dominating land and river routes, known as the Iron Triangle. It was controlled by the **ARVN** (Army of the Republic of Vietnam) by day, but the Vietcong by night. The Iron Triangle contained Cu Chi, the largest Vietcong base, only 24 miles from Saigon. Like all Vietcong bases, most of it was underground. 'When they moved us from Cu Chi to Dau Tieng, that's when the shit got bad. The Iron Triangle. Oh, man. That place is not fit for God, let alone man. That was a tough assignment. After we got pinned down, that's when I began to rebel' (Terry, 177).

To distinguish the South Vietnamese from the Vietcong, all South Vietnam citizens had to have **Identity cards**. Of course, on the black market anything and everything was available, even identity cards, which deserters and those trying to avoid the draft would buy.

Street scene in South Vietnam during the war. (Courtesy D. Phillips)

Safe Conduct pass.

ARVN. 'Training the [South] Vietnamese army was a problem for the Americans throughout the war. ... The first Americans sent to Vietnam were military advisors, dispatched to train ... ARVN to defend themselves. ... It was largely a failure ... known by senior officers as early as the autumn of 1964' (Holzwarth, #4). Because of that failure, President Johnson ordered an escalation of troops in early 1965 'for ARVN was on the verge of defeat' (Holzwarth, #5). Even providing more troops did not really aid the war effort. It was the US failure to train the ARVN and its own troops in counterinsurgency techniques to combat the unconventional war waged by the Vietcong which would eventually lead to defeat. Instead, the US and its allies relied on conventional warfare techniques and body count as a measure of their success (Holzwarth, #5).

ARVN soldiers deserted at a high rate, some 73,000 in 1964 and 113,000 in 1965. The South Vietnamese government lessened the penalty for desertion by telling the deserted that if they rejoined their unit and promised not to desert again, there would be no punishment. This reduced the rate in 1967 to 10.5 per thousand. The rate, however, continued to climb, to a high of 16.5 per thousand. Many of those who deserted did so because of low pay – why subject yourself to fight and die for South Vietnam when you were not being paid enough for you and your family to survive? In April 1968, an

ARVN private earned US$467 per year; generals US$2,500 per year. This did not match the standards of living. The ARVN's enemy was not North Vietnam but the Vietcong; it would have preferred to handle its civil war itself (Kutler, 52, 54). In comparison, a US infantryman earned much more:

Wage and tax statement 1966 for American infantryman

Wages paid subject to withholding in 1966	$1,432.92
Social Security and Federal income tax withheld	146.70
After withholding wages paid monthly in 1966	**$1,286.22**[12]

The official numbers of ARVN soldiers killed doesn't tell the whole story. According to Fitzgerald, over 165,268 ARVN soldiers and about 380,000 civilians were killed. She writes that those awful numbers in proportion to the United States would mean we would have lost 20 million Americans in the war (537).

War Tribunal. In 1966, Bertrand Russell, an English philosopher, and Jean Paul Sartre, a French philosopher and writer, created a war crimes tribunal to judge American conduct in Vietnam. Included among those invited to attend was James Baldwin, a black activist and well-known author, who was currently living in Paris. Baldwin made the following comments about the tribunal and the war: 'There may be something suspect in the spectacle of Europeans condemning America for a war which America inherited from Europe, inherited, in fact, directly from France. ... The American war in Vietnam raises several questions. One is whether or not small nations, in this age of super-states and superpowers, will be allowed to work out their own destinies and live as they feel they should. For only the people of a country have the right, or the spiritual power, to determine that country's way of life.' (**Baldwin 428**). Baldwin also questioned why these underdeveloped countries were underdeveloped, why many of the inhabitants had too little to eat while others had too much. He called the American Negro the first Vietcong victim and wondered: 'What happens to the moral fabric, the moral sense, of the people [US government and its citizens] engaged in so criminal an endeavor [the war in Vietnam]?' (430).

Reunification. After the defeat of South Vietnam and US forces, Vietnam became a united nation. The Vietnamese people were free for the first time in over 100 years. Elections, which were supposed to have been held in 1956, had never occurred. Ho Chi Minh and the Viet Minh had to win on the battlefield – they succeeded.

Reparation. Why didn't the United States and its allies rebuild Vietnam and repay the Vietnamese for the destruction they caused during the war, especially the defoliation of their jungles and the bombing of their cities? The United States had a policy of paying money if it accidentally killed someone or destroyed their property. Forty dollars (or in Vietnamese currency, 4,000 piastres) seems such a small amount for the family of someone who was accidentally killed.[13] For a house, a family would receive $10 (Terry, 80). For destruction of their hooch, we would give 1,000 piastres, which was the equivalent of about $9 (Terry, 81). One vet killed a water buffalo, a working animal in Vietnam, and got fined $500; however, he couldn't remember how he paid the fine (Al, Vietnam Vet Program, 2/4/93). The Vietnamese were always out for money. 'People in villages were so poor they'd throw themselves in front of a Jeep just so the family could collect some money' (Banjo, Vietnam Vet Program, 2/4/93). The VC hid in rubber plantations to thwart US forces firing at them. Not only were they well-hidden, but they also knew that American soldiers weren't supposed to fire into a plantation, because if a tree got damaged, the US had to pay reparations. Damage to a rubber tree cost about $500, based on how much income it would have produced (Bobby, Vietnam Vet Program, 4/2/93).

In A Plantation
By Basil T. Paquet

> The bullet passed
> Through his right temple,
> His left side
> Could not hold
> Against the metal,
> His last 'I am' exploded
> Red and grey on a rubber tree. (12)

Although the US paid reparations for individual incidents, it never paid Vietnam for the destruction of its country. 'America has made no reparation to the Vietnamese, nothing. We are the richest people in the world and they are among the poorest. We savaged them, though they had never hurt us, and we cannot find it in our hearts, our honor, to give them help – because the government of Vietnam is communist. And perhaps because they won' (Jean Baudrillard, 1986).[14]

Rubber tree plantation. (Vis M, Wikicommons)

Chapter 6

Vietnam Today

'The scars of the war are being healed, the forgiveness being enshrined in the
Buddhist eight-fold path to enlightenment enabling
all parties to coexist' (Page, 149)

Post War Reflections. According to the *PBS Documentary on Vietnam*, Burns and
Novick interviewed 'many Vietnamese on both the winning and losing sides, and were
surprised to learn that the war remains as painful and unresolved for them [in 2017] as
it is for us' (Ward, 3).

Bui Tin, a North Vietnam colonel, wrote: 'We [did not] learn from the military
failures of the Tet offensive, 1968. … [We continued] to mount further major attacks
in May and September '68 and suffered even heavier losses. Our side also suffered
seriously from the social pacification plans dreamed up by the Americans, such as
Operation Phoenix, and the Chieu Hoi campaign … designed to induce our supporters
to defect. Yet, … [despite heavy bombing] we stood surprisingly firm in contending
with the bombers of the Rolling Thunder Operations' (Press Releases, 3).

Cao Ba Minh reflects on his turning from writing to painting: 'My works are washed
in the blood and tears of suffering, of annihilation, of brother killing brother – all the
baggage of humanity's shame. In my youth I was drawn and woven into the fabric of
Vietnam, into a history written in shame, not pride' (Sinaiko, 420).

CBS reporter Morley Safer, back in Vietnam listened to a retired, drunken VC
colonel praise his victory: 'I want my American friends to meet the brave fighters
whose courage defeated the expeditionary forces of the imperialists. I welcome you to
listen to the songs of our revolution, and you will understand how we were victorious
over the Americans and their puppet regime' (72). The colonel continued: 'The vile acts
and atrocities of the criminal American presidents, Eisenhower, Kennedy, Johnson and
Nixon, could not defeat the progressive sentiments of our courageous men and women.
Let us raise our glasses to their selfless sacrifice and their victory over the fascist war-
making machine' (73).

But in the United States, soldiers told a different story. If the government had
allowed them to fight, to really fight, they said, the war would have ended differently.
One US Army colonel 'famously told a North Vietnamese Colonel in 1975, "You know,
you never beat us on the battlefield." His counterpart responded, "That may be so, but
it is also irrelevant"' (Boot).

Modern Vietnam. 'Vietnam underwent a series of astonishing transformations while
finding its way into the modern age. By the early twenty-first century, Vietnam was

catching up economically with its more prosperous neighbors. Independent statehood ... had been resolved. But other issues – such as the most appropriate economic system, democratic rights versus state control, the rights of the individual versus those of the community and Western culture versus eastern values – continued to stir heated debates' (Dutton 449–450).

Despite these issues, Vietnam is thriving. No matter what they call themselves, the Socialist Republic of Vietnam is quickly becoming a capitalist economy with a political dictatorship. But the countryside has not developed economically as quickly. Farmers grow rice and wheat in the same way that their ancestors have done for generations. Traditional customs still predominate. They still ride bicycles everywhere.

According to the *Economist Magazine*, the Vietnamese government refers to its economic-political structure as 'capitalist communist' (12 April 2008). This is due, in part, to the privatization of land that occurred at the 1986 Sixth Party Congress, which 'privatized agriculture [and returned] confiscated land to its former owners. ... This package of reforms favored individual farmers and led to an "instant" rise in productivity' (Kiernan, 480). Today, so many imported products, especially clothing, say 'made in Vietnam'. Like all growing economies, labor is cheap, manufacturing plentiful. When my husband and I were there in 2007, we found free enterprise in both Hanoi and Ho Chi Minh City. For example, we bought a shirt and a hat from two people selling them on the streets. Cities are flourishing, with cars and motorcycles everywhere – the traffic is so dense it was hard to believe anyone could get anywhere.

Vietnam is thriving both politically and economically. It became a member of the UN in 1997. It has signed several trade agreements, including with the United States in 1999, and joined the World Trade Organization in 2007. Because labor is cheap and raw material plentiful, Vietnam has become the second-best performing economy in Asia, a most attractive country for foreign investment (Ghose, 15).

In a meeting in 2012, US Defense Secretary Panetta and Vietnam's Defense Minister Thanh 'agreed to expand sites for searching for the remains of American soldiers who are still listed as MIA'. They also exchanged three letters and a diary. Panetta gave Thanh a diary that belonged to a North Vietnamese soldier who died in the fighting. Thanh gave Panetta three letters taken off the dead body of Sergeant Steve Flaherty, who died in 1965. In one of these letters, he shared 'emotional accounts of his fears

Above left: North Vietnam. (Courtesy E. Brown, Jr)

Above right: North Vietnam. (Courtesy E. Brown, Jr)

Street scene, Ho Chi Minh City. (Courtesy E. Brown, Jr)

in the face of fighting and combat'. In another he wrote about the bloody nature of the fighting, in which his platoon lost nineteen of their thirty-five men as well as the squad leader (First Trip, 8–9). To continue building the US relationship with Vietnam, President Obama made a state visit to Hanoi in 2016, where he announced the lifting of bans on the sale of military equipment, a ban which had lasted for fifty years.

Rempel makes the following closing remarks: 'I have hardly scraped the surface of [Vietnam] as I try to pass on some understanding of a people and their land. This understanding can only come from being here and experiencing their way of life first-hand' (21). I can only agree, which is why I devoted Thursday evening programs to talking with those who had been in Vietnam – the vets, and their families.

SECTION THREE

WAR: Fighting the Enemy: The War in Vietnam, 1954–1975

'There's nothing so embarrassing as when things go wrong in a war.'
Michael Herr, *Dispatches*

♦ ♦ ♦

'Vietnam is what we had instead of happy childhoods.' Michael Herr, *Dispatches*

♦ ♦ ♦

'This is not a jungle war, but a struggle for freedom on every front of
human activity.' Lyndon B. Johnson (1964)

♦ ♦ ♦

'This War in Vietnam is, I believe, a war for civilization. Certainly, it is not a war of
our seeking. It is a war thrust upon us, and we cannot yield to tyranny'
Francis, Cardinal Spellman (*Vietnam: Special Newsweek Edition*, 9)

♦ ♦ ♦

'Some of the critics viewed Vietnam as a morality play in which the wicked must be
punished before the final curtain and where any attempt to salvage self-respect
from the outcome compounded the wrong. I viewed it as a genuine tragedy.
No one had a monopoly on anguish.' Henry Kissinger (1979)

♦ ♦ ♦

'It is not enough to fight. It is the spirit which we bring to the fight that decides the
issue. It is morale that wins the victory.' George C. Marshall (1948)

♦ ♦ ♦

'War is a procedure from which there can be no turning back without
acknowledging defeat' Tuchman (*March of Folly*, 325)

- An estimated 3.4 million US servicemembers deployed to Southeast Asia
- About 2.7 million deployed to Vietnam
- 265,000 women served during the Vietnam War
- 11,000 women were stationed in Vietnam
- Army Corps Nurses arrived in Vietnam as early as 1956
- 90 per cent of women who served were volunteer nurses
- Eight American military women were killed in the Vietnam War
- Fifty-nine civilian women were killed in the Vietnam War

Introduction

US and North Vietnam Reaction to War

'There are two types of war: **wars of necessity**, to protect vital national interests and involving the use of military force as a last resort, such as World War II and the Persian Gulf war of 1991; and **wars of choice** – armed interventions taken either in the absence of vital national interests or despite the availability of options not involving military force. Into this category fall the wars in Vietnam, Iraq and, after a limited initial phase in Afghanistan' (Haass).[1] Within this framework of choice or necessity, a war might be a **civil war**,[2] one of **counterinsurgency** (the Vietcong in South Vietnam), or one of **aggression** (Germany in the Second World War).

Why did the United States support South Vietnam in the first place? What were our obligations to the South Vietnamese? Our support of the French colonialists instead of Ho Chi Minh, despite his request for help, certainly indicated our interests in opposing any advance of communism. The Eisenhower administration believed in the **Domino Theory**; if Vietnam fell, Laos and Cambodia would be next. Our not signing the 1954 Geneva Accords that would have called for free elections in all of Vietnam in 1956 was certainly another indication that we intended to intervene in the war between North and South Vietnam. Since we did not sign the Accords, we were afraid that free elections would have resulted in Ho Chi Minh's victory. Our only option seemed to be to support South Vietnam against the aggressor, North Vietnam. If that meant war, so be it. But was that our only option? In the late Sixties, President Johnson offered 'a vast economic uplift plan' if the North agreed to negotiate. Would that have been an option in 1954?

What will the public remember about the war in Vietnam? Will they remember the struggle against communism for control of Southeast Asia? Will they remember, instead, a civil war between North and South Vietnam, in which the United States wrongly intervened? Or will they remember a resistance movement between a national liberation front (the Vietcong) and a puppet, oppressive government in South Vietnam? What they remember is not as important as its effect on US foreign policy.

'War is as big and horrible an event as man has yet devised to touch a massive number of lives at the same approximate time in an unforgettable way (Anderson, Grunts 155).' Yet there have always been many not touched by the war at all. On 25 May 1969, after the battle on Hill 174, there were some 125 people not in Vietnam (families and friends of those killed during the battle) affected by those who fought and died or were wounded during that encounter. But approximately 200 million others in the US were untouched by these events (Anderson, *Grunts*, 155). Not only the soldiers who fought on Hill 174 but others in Vietnam were affected. 'We lost our innocence. Once in country we were never the same again. The word war gained a new and terrible meaning' (Harrod, 24).

A North Vietnamese soldier remarked: 'The sorrow of war inside a soldier's heart was in a strange way similar to the sorrow of love. It was a kind of nostalgia, like the immense sadness of the world at dusk. It was a sadness, a missing, a pain which could send one soaring back into the past. The sorrow of the battlefield could not normally be pinpointed to one particular event or even one person. If you focused on any one event it would soon become a tearing pain' (Bao Ninh, 94).

War vs Conflict. Some historians and politicians called the conflict in Korea World War 2½. Whether Vietnam was referred to as a 'Conflict' or a 'War' made no difference to those fighting. The United States chose not to declare war on North Vietnam. It wanted its involvement seen as short-term, winning hearts and minds, keeping the North from invading the South, and keeping China and the USSR from entering "The War". Its goal was not to capture territory, not to drive an enemy away into its own territory, and not to invade another country, even though the North Vietnamese used Laos and Cambodia as supply routes (**Ho Chi Minh Trail**). When it became clear the war wasn't short-term, when the VC guerillas created havoc and fear, preventing the United States from changing hearts and minds. When we invaded Cambodia (called "an incursion") to keep supplies from reaching the VC, why didn't the United States *declare* war? John Ketwig, in his book *And a Hard Rain Fell*, couldn't 'refer to … Vietnam [as a] "conflict". LBJ saw it as a "Conflict". To a PFC, nineteen years old [Ketwig], that many dead guys earned it the title of war' (4). At one of my Thursday evening programs, the Vietnam veterans also objected to the term 'conflict'. For them it was a war, no matter what the administration called it.

For many reasons, the Vietnam War (though never technically declared a 'War') was unconventional when compared to the First and Second World Wars. There was no front line to advance, no territory to take and hold, and prisoners were taken and shut away, yet the United States had fought a similar 'unconventional war' just twelve years earlier in Korea. But politics played a major role in discussions about the Vietnam War; if it was 'unconventional', then the idea could be planted that we would win, as we had in Korea. Also, if it was 'unconventional', then the military would surely get as many troops, weapons, and money as it requested. Colonel Everett Smith, an early advisor in Vietnam, said the plans for the war included using guerillas – our Special Forces, LRRPs, SEALs – to counter other guerillas.[3]

Since Congress passed the Gulf of Tonkin Resolution, giving President Johnson free reign to wage war, it was not necessary to have a formal declaration of war. A declaration of war might have forced the Chinese and Russians to send troops, or even to use nuclear weapons. A war would also need the support of the American people, willing to shoulder the burdens that war entailed. Was it a **civil war**, with one part (the South) wanting a capitalist democracy while the North wanted a communist dictatorship? Was the American public ready to take a stand against communism, 17,000 miles away? Close by the United States, Castro was taking over Cuba. Was this a *war of counter-insurgency*, a supposed 'new war' against South Vietnamese insurgents – the Vietcong – demanding new tactics, new strategies, even new weapons? Or was this a *war of aggression*, with the NVA (North Vietnamese Army) having invaded the South? The United States actually decided to fight a *war of containment*. According to a colonel in the Army of the Republic of South Vietnam: 'The Americans had designed a purely defensive strategy for Vietnam. It was a strategy that was based on the attrition of the enemy through a prolonged defense and made no allowance for decisive offensive action' (Summers, 71).

Westmoreland wrote a defense of this strategy: 'The war in Vietnam was not against Asian hordes, but against an enemy with relatively limited manpower. ... in any case what alternative was there to a war of attrition?'[4] In a speech in 1966 at the Waldorf Astoria, he answered that question: 'The only alternative to a **war of attrition** is a **war of annihilation**'[5] (Reston Sherman, 131).

Just War. In the theory of a so-called 'just war' (a war of necessity), there are five sanctions for war: 1) are there goods or resources at stake?; 2) have they been seriously threatened?; 3) is violence the only way to protect them?; 4) is there a reasonable chance of success?; 5) and do the evils committed in war outweigh the value of the goods? (Seabury & Codevilla, 215). Those soldiers who participated in fighting against Nazi Germany and its allies considered they were fighting a just war, a war of necessity. People and countries were at stake, with minority groups singled out for death, peace talks and treaties being broken, and the United States – once it joined Germany's enemies – tipping the balance against the Nazis. What is important is that many American soldiers fighting in Vietnam – and more of them were volunteers than draftees[6] – knew their fathers had fought in a 'good war'. Father Charles Plater, in *A Primer of Peace and War*, wrote: '[T]here are many causes that can be considered just, but they can all be classified under two headings: self-defense and the defense of one's neighbor' (Shell, 85).[7] These two causes can be seen as wars of necessity.

An unjust war occurs when the evils committed do not outweigh the value of the goods being protected. In an article published in the *Cornell University Chronicle*, Lowery quotes the article 'Aerial Bombing and Counterinsurgency in the Vietnam War'[8] by Pepinsky, Kocher, and Kalyvas: 'Killing civilians is unjust, but our research shows it is also bad strategy.' That was because indiscriminate bombing did not distinguish allies from enemies and often turned allies into enemies (2).

'The essence of both the practical and the ethical problem of warfare is "**Whom shall we kill and why?**" ... The craft of the military leader is to cause death and destruction in the manner most likely to prevent the enemy from effectively continuing the fight' (Seabury & Codevilla, 226–227). A man in the post-Vietnam US Army said: 'In the army ... I had real objectives. Clear goals. Actual targets' (Jones, *August Snow*, 172). But in the Vietnam War, the '**whom?**' was the first problem. The enemy was not obvious. Any Vietnamese person could have been the enemy; so when soldiers counted dead bodies, they said 'if it's dead, it must have been VC'. Counting dead bodies became the only way to prove to the people back home, watching the news, that the United States was winning, since the military was not trying to take and hold territory. The second problem, '**why?**', was more troubling. 'Do we destroy a village because it may be harboring Vietcong or supplying the Vietcong with food and supplies? Do we kill the girl in the street because she may be carrying an explosive device?'

'Discussions of law and tactics – as important as they are – provide only partial answers. ... You can't simply merge law and tactics and declare everything that is legally and tactically sound is also moral, much less wise' (French, 'Escape', 1).

Rules of Engagement.[9] All wars and all nations at war are supposed to be governed by the **1864 Geneva Convention**, which established rules of engagement, rules governing the conduct of war, and the humane treatment of prisoners, the sick, wounded, and dead. All military personnel received a copy of the rules of engagement and was required to sign, agreeing to abide by these rules. 'It seemed odd to [Puller, Jr] that warring countries would expect their troops to kill each other in a gentlemanly and humane manner, and odder still that the Marine Corps would require its junior officers to undertake such an exercise in hypocrisy' (Puller, Jr, 78).[10] One soldier reflected on the Rules of Engagement: 'A lot of what I done over there seems like crimes to me. … The rules of engagement didn't cover half the situations you ran into. It was survival. Hindsight's a luxury we didn't have' (Iles, 175).

As atrocities on both sides attest to (not only in this war but in most other wars), neither side followed the Geneva Convention. In military school, a young artillery man had been told that the Geneva Convention prohibited firing white phosphorus at troops – 'So you call it in on their equipment. [The young artilleryman's logic was] if we're gonna find ways around the Geneva convention, what do you think the enemy is gonna do?' (Grossman, 203). According to H.L. Mencken, what helped 'desensitize' soldiers to atrocities was the use of swear words. 'Obscenity serves to desensitize him from atrocity but also to express the breakdown of conventional expression' (Lerer, 250).

Jan Berry, a veteran and poet, commented on the many US violations of the Geneva Convention:

> 'Every last Vietnam (Veteran) is guilty along with Calley[11] of committing war crimes. Because a "free-fire zone" – where anything that moves can be shot – is by definition a violation of the Geneva Convention of 1949 with respect to the treatment of civilians: because a "search-and-destroy mission" – where everything living is destroyed or removed – is also a violation of the Geneva Conventions; because massive defoliation, reconnaissance by fire, saturation bombing, mad moments, and forcibly relocating villagers are all violations of international law, and, therefore, war crimes.' (Reston, Sherman, 168).

POWs were especially ill-treated. The Third Geneva Convention, first adopted in 1929, last revised in 1949, detailed the treatment of prisoners of war. It defined prisoners of war and specified their treatment. All American soldiers were given the following card of instructions regarding treatment of prisoners of war: 'YOU CANNOT AND MUST NOT: mistreat your prisoner, humiliate, or degrade him, take any of his personal effects, which do not have significant military value, refuse him medical treatment if required and available. Always treat your prisoners humanely' (Reston, Sherman, xii). These instructions, like the rest of the Geneva Convention, were generally ignored by both North and South.[12]

The North Vietnamese tortured and held 'Sen. John McCain, a downed Navy pilot, for five years. He recalled, "asking to live just one more minute rather than one more hour or one more day, and I know I was able to hang on longer because of the spiritual help I received through prayer"' (Evan Thomas, *Newsweek*, 7 May 2007, 34). Charlie Plumb, six years as a POW, also found comfort in religion: 'I consider my confinement in prison to be spiritually beneficial. … I found that my previous value system was unrealistic. Stripped of all my material wealth, the only beacon I could home in on was my faith in an unchanging God' (232).

Colonel Fred Cherry 'was the forty-third American captured in the North. The first black. ... The first place they tried to interrogate me appeared to be a secondary school. And they put me in this hut. I did what I was s'posed to do. Name, rank, serial number, date of birth. And I started talking about the Geneva Convention. And they said forget it. "You are a criminal." ... The next place I end up was Hoa Lo Prison, which we called the Hanoi Hilton. The first place Americans were brought for serious interrogation and torture' (Terry, 272–274).

Another POW, US Air Force Colonel Robert Certain, related his experience at the Hanoi Hilton: 'The Interrogations began soon after [I] arrived at the prison. [I] was questioned on and off for 12 hours. [My] captors asked me about America's nuclear weapons. They demanded to know where [I] was headquartered and the number of planes there, details about the B-52 and their targets' (Redmon, 50). Some prisoners invented phony stories and details, using names from Heller's *Catch 22*, to avoid giving away any information (Redmon, 50).

James B. Stockdale, a commander in the US Navy, was also captured. A POW at the Hanoi Hilton for over six years, he was later a recipient of the Medal of Honor. Captain Charles Boyd, a prisoner of war for over seven years, caught while volunteering for a dangerous flying mission, was the only POW to become a four-star general. 'While captive, he was a model of impenetrable resistance to the enemy' (Seelye, 3) and helped the other POWs maintain morale despite the torture and depravity.

According to Charlie Plumb, a POW for over six years, he and other prisoners were ordered on Christmas 'to listen to a tape of a Vietnamese Catholic priest giving a sermon in his native tongue. An interpreter translated it into English, a phrase at a time: "We gather here of the occasion so to celebrate birth of Christ ... which we do so many years ... This time we have special reason ... multitudes of people are killed and injured ... by bombs you American pilots drop ... You are instrument of devil ... Hope is for you and hope for world ... Jesus came to save world ... Now your opportunity, you American Aggressors. ... You commit sin, but if repent them now, will be clean white like snow ... You be able to forward in life ... Admit wrongdoing and thank Jesus ... who born in lowly manger fight oppression from evil aggressors".' (231)[13]

Although the most famous Prisoner of War camp was the Hanoi Hilton in North Vietnam, the South Vietnamese and Americans also took and abused prisoners, despite the 3x5 card handed to all US military forces.

Picture on wall at Hanoi Hilton. (Courtesy E. Brown, Jr)

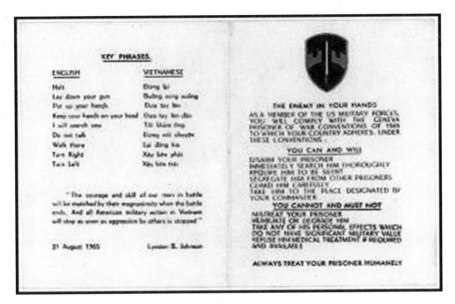

Orders regarding treatment of prisoners.

(See Appendix H for a legible copy of these orders as well as other orders regarding prisoners of war.)

US Military Code of Conduct. This was established as an Executive Order by President Eisenhower, after prisoners of war were tortured by North Koreans into making statements. The US military issued the following **Code of Conduct** for US military service members who were in combat or held in captivity as prisoners of war:

'**Article I**: I am an American fighting in the forces which guard my country and our way of life. I am prepared to give my life in their defense.

'**Article II**: I will never surrender of my own free will. If in command, I will never surrender the members of my command while they still have means to resist.

'**Article III**: If I am captured, I will continue to resist by all means available. I will make every effort to escape and aid others to escape. I will accept neither favors nor parole from the enemy.

Code of conduct.

'**Article IV**: If becoming a prisoner of war, I will keep faith with my fellow prisoners. I will give no information or take part in any action which might be harmful to my comrades. If I am senior, I will take command. If not, I will obey the lawful orders of those appointed over me and will back them in every way.

'**Article V**: When questioned, should I become a prisoner of war, I am required to give name, rank and social security number, and date of birth. I will evade answering further questions to the utmost of my ability. I will make no oral or written statements disloyal to my country and its allies or harmful to their cause.

'**Article VI**: I will never forget that I am an American, responsible for my actions, and dedicated to the principles which made my country free. I will trust in my God and in the United States of America.' (USAMM.com).

To win the war, both South and North covered up some of their illegal bombings, prisoner of war tactics, and their overall conduct of the war. In a letter published in the *New Yorker Magazine* on 16 April 2007, Master Sergeant Bob Schrynemakers, United States Air Force retired, from Torrance, California, wrote about one such cover-up: 'During 1971–72, I was assigned to the Air Force's 56th Special Operations Wing at *Nakhon Phanom*, Thailand, as an intelligence specialist. With us was Sergeant Lonnie Franks, who was on temporary duty from the air wing at Udorn Royal Thai Air Force Base, from which the strike missions in question were flown. Sergeant Franks, in de-briefing pilots after their missions over Vietnam, realized that they were being instructed to give fabricated information, and was told that he had to support this action by lying in official intelligence reports. Instead, Sergeant Franks wrote to his senator explaining that he had been ordered to lie in official reports documenting how the war was being fought. His action exemplifies the military's core ideal: when something is wrong, you must do something' ('In the Line of Duty,' 12).

Opposite Map Keys:
Vietnam Theatre of War, 1965–1970. (Encyclopedia Britannica)

Light Grey Arrows = North Vietnam supply routes (Ho Chi Minh rail along Laotian border)
Light Grey Triangle = NV air bases
Black Triangles = US air bases
Black Squares = US Corps HQ
Black ships = US aircraft carriers
Black arrows = US B-52 routes

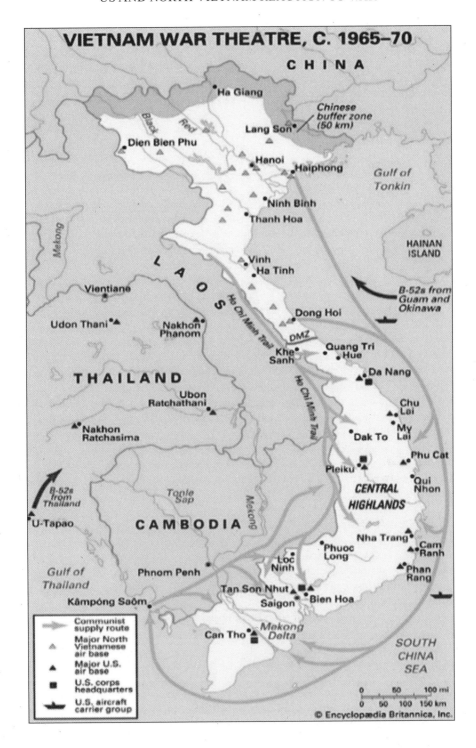

VIETNAM WAR THEATRE, C. 1965–70

CHINA

Ha Giang

Chinese
buffer zone
(50 km)

Lang Son

Dien Bien Phu

Black

Red

Hanoi

Haiphong

Gulf of
Tonkin

Ninh Binh

Thanh Hoa

HAINAN
ISLAND

Mekong

Vinh
Ha Tinh

L A O S

Vientiane

B-52s from
Guam and
Okinawa

Udon Thani

Nakhon
Phanom

Ho Chi Minh Trail

Dong Hoi

DMZ

Khe
Sanh

Quang Tri
Hue

THAILAND

Ho Chi Minh Trail

Da Nang

Ubon
Ratchathani

Chu
Lai

My
Lai

Nakhon
Ratchasima

Dak To

Phu Cat

Pleiku

Qui
Nhon

CENTRAL
HIGHLANDS

B-52s
from
Thailand

Tonle
Sap

U-Tapao

Mekong

CAMBODIA

Nha Trang

Cam
Ranh

Gulf of
Thailand

Phnom Penh

Loc
Ninh

Phuoc
Long

Phan
Rang

Tan Son Nhut

Saigon

Bien Hoa

Kâmpóng Saôm

Can Tho

Mekong
Delta

SOUTH
CHINA
SEA

Communist
supply route

Major North
Vietnamese
air base

Major U.S.
air base

U.S. corps
headquarters

U.S. aircraft
carrier group

0   50   100 mi
0   50   100 150 km

© Encyclopædia Britannica, Inc.

Chapter 1

War Stories

Five O'Clock Follies. The United States Information Agency (USIA) provided press briefings, known colloquially as the '**Five O'Clock Follies**', a public relations exercise. For example: the United States announced an 'incursion into Cambodia',[14] which was a joke because the unfamiliar word 'incursion' was deliberately used to hide an invasion where soldiers had been fighting long before the announcement. Herr refers to these briefings as 'an Orwellian grope through the day's events as seen by the Mission' (99). One vet in my Vietnam Vet Program talked about dragging a buddy back into Vietnam from Laos. 'We weren't supposed to be there either,' Bobby said. 'He was dead, but we couldn't put down where he got dead.' (Vietnam Vet Program 4/2/93). The USIA reported that the US continued to head to victory; body count charts of enemy dead showed success. Given the limited war we were fighting, and that we could take no territory or prisoners, the body count became Washington's way of indicating our wins to the public back home. An anonymous source told me that the purpose of body counts was not really for public consumption but to reassure Congress that we were winning the war so that they would authorize additional funding (Margaret Brown interview with Anon.). What made the body counts easier was that '[all] dead Vietnamese were by definition Vietcong' (Iles, 138).

For Orwellian lies to work, people needed to trust the reports coming out of Washington or from the media: 'Wooden-headedness, the "Don't-confuse-me-with-the-facts" habit, is a universal folly never more conspicuous than at upper levels of Washington with respect to Vietnam. Its grossest fault was under-estimation of North Vietnam's commitment to its goal' (Tuchman, 375–376).

George Orwell, writing about the Spanish Civil War, almost twenty-five years before the Vietnamese War, said: '**Political language** ... [is designed to make lies sound truthful and murder respectable]' (139). 'Defenseless villages are bombarded from the air. The inhabitants [were] driven out into the countryside. The cattle machine-gunned, the huts set on fire with incendiary bullets: this is called **pacification**. Millions of peasants are robbed of their farms and sent trudging along the roads with no more than they can carry: this is called **transfer of population**' (139, 136).

Linguist Peter Farb wrote:

> '[T]he Vietnam War inspired lying at a national level rarely seen before in history. ... An *air raid* [was] a momentary defensive strategy, [or] *a routine limited duration protective reaction*; defoliation of an entire forest [was called] *a resources control program*; the $34 given to South Vietnamese families who lost a family member by our mistake

[was called] *condolence awards*; and bombing errors against friendly villages [were called] *navigational misdirections*. Starving and homeless Vietnamese fleeing the horrors of war, did not seek survival in a *refugee camp* but instead discovered freshening experiences in what the Pentagon dubbed a *new life hamlet* or an *Open Arms Camp*. (155)

Farb called this language '*ornate euphemism*', meant to hide or soften the death and destruction of war. He said it led to 'a *credibility gap* [for President Johnson] ... and prove[d] to be an inefficient and hazardous strategy' (155–156).

He also noticed what he called '"before" and "after" terms which bestowed tremendous dignity before minor military objectives but only after they had been destroyed. What before had been simply a *straw-thatched hut*[15] became, after its bombardment, a structure. ... **a splintered set of logs thrown across a stream [after its destruction] became a *bridge*'[16] (155–156, I placed the words in bold)**.

Herr noticed another problem with language, which he called 'repetition'. Watching television news night after night, year after year, a news anchor or reporter would 'say that American casualties for the week had reached a six-week low, only eighty GIs had died in combat, and you'd feel like you'd just gotten a bargain' (215).

Thomas Merton, in *War and the Crisis of Language*, quotes a captain who solved 'the semantic problem of distinguishing the hostile citizen from the refugee, "In a V.C. area like this there are three categories. First there are the straight V.C. ... Then there are the V.C. sympathizers. ... I can't think of the third just now ... there's no middle road in this war."' Merton continues, '"**Pacification**" or "**winning the hearts**" of the undecided is thus very much simplified. "Soon" says a news report, "the government will have no need to win the hearts and minds of Bensuc, a small village.[17] There will be no Bensuc"' (491).

And then there were the **Dog and Pony Shows**. When visitors and/or VIPs (congressmen or senators) came to Vietnam to find out for themselves what was occurring on the front, the conversation, according to Herr, went something like this: 'Where are you from, son?' 'Macon, Georgia, Sir.' 'Real fine. Are you getting your mail okay, plenty of hot meals?' 'Yes, Sir.' 'That's fine, where you from, son?' 'Oh, I don't know, God, I don't know, *I don't know!*' 'That's fine, real fine, where you from, son?' This is the reason why Herr resisted joining these dog and pony shows in the field (216).

The Five O'Clock Follies and the Dog and Pony Shows were propaganda: to influence the attitudes of the people back home, to make them more comfortable with the war effort, and to make them more willing to accept the war and our ability to win. But it also served as propaganda aimed at the enemy: to show them that the United States supported the war effort.

American Soldiers' Stories. Rather than listening to the Five O'Clock Follies, Michael Herr spent time with the men in the field listening to their stories.[18] Herr found a story wherever he went. 'In war more than in other life you don't really know what you're doing most of the time, you're just behaving, and afterward you can make up any kind of bullshit you want to about it, say you felt good or bad, loved it or hated it, did this or that, the right thing or the wrong thing; still, what happened happened' (20–21). But some felt it could never happen in Vietnam; one soldier told Herr: 'I ain't never getting hit in Vietnam ... cause it don't exist.' It was an old joke, but this time he wasn't laughing (125).

The grunts Herr talked with sometimes told him stories that he'd heard before; sometimes the stories would tumble out, barely articulate as if they couldn't get it out fast enough. He found the 'mix [of grunts] so amazing; incipient saints and realized homicidals, unconscious lyric poets and mean dumb motherfuckers with their brains all down in their necks; and even though by the time [I] left [I] knew where all the stories came from and where they were going, [I] was never bored, never even unsurprised. Obviously, what they really wanted to tell [me] was how tired they were and how sick of it, how moved they'd been and how afraid' (30).

Herr continued: 'But once in a while you'd hear something fresh, and a couple of times you'd hear something high, like the corpsman at Khe Sanh [during the ninety-day siege] who said, "If it ain't the fucking incoming it's the fucking outgoing. Only difference is who gets the fucking grease, and that ain't no fucking difference at all"' (30).

Herr said the grunts told their stories differently: '[They] were afraid they might not get to finish, or saying it almost out of a dream, innocent, offhand and mighty direct, "Oh, you know, it was just a firefight, we killed some of them and they killed some of us"' (30). He heard so many stories that after a year he thought even the dead were trying to tell him theirs. It didn't matter 'whether he'd known them or not, no matter what I'd felt about them or the way they'd died, their story was always there and it was always the same: it went, "Put yourself in my place"' (31). '[My] war story – I worked at US Army, had a job, nothing more nothing less' (Bobby Ward, Vietnam Vet Program, 1994).

A LRRP (Long Range Reconnaissance Patrol) soldier on his third tour thought Herr was 'a freak because [he] wouldn't carry a weapon.

"'Didn't you ever meet a reporter before?" I asked him.

"'Tits on a bull," he said. "Nothing personal."

'But what a story he told me, as one-pointed and resonant as any war story I ever heard, it took me a year to understand it: "Patrol went up the mountain. One man came back. He died before he could tell us what happened." I waited for the rest, but it seemed not to be that kind of story; when I asked him what had happened he just looked like he felt sorry for me, fucked if he'd waste time telling stories to anyone dumb as I was' (Herr, 6).

That was part of Herr's problem about the war story that he didn't think had ended. An independent reporter, he hopped on helicopters and went wherever they were going. He talked to grunts. He humped his own gear. He spent overnights in the bush (67). 'I went to cover the war and the war covered me; an old story, unless of course you've never heard it. … It took the war to teach … that you were as responsible for everything you saw as you were for everything you did. The problem was that you didn't always know what you were seeing until later, maybe years later, that a lot of it never made it in at all, it just stayed stored there in your eyes. Time and information, rock and roll, life itself, the information isn't frozen, you are' (20).

Frozen in the Now
By Jim Gray

Murderer! Baby Killer!
I haven't heard that in awhile.
But then, I don't listen anymore
Frozen in the Now.

Returned and readjusted
To exist with proper style.
Discarded dreams of coming home
Frozen in the Now.

Gratitude and honor
Wreaths for the warrior's brow.
Belated gifts to the ambivalent
Frozen in the Now.

Take heed of me my son
While still your dreams can smile
A believer of empty promises
Frozen in the Now. (23)

North Vietnam Soldiers' Stories. The North Vietnamese soldiers also had war stories to tell. A half-buried coffin showed up in high water. 'Inside the coffin was a thick plastic bag, similar to those the Americans used for their dead, but this one was clear plastic. The soldier seemed to be still breathing, as though in a deep sleep. He looked so alive … Then before [the men's] eyes the plastic bag discolored, whitening as though suddenly filled with smoke. The bag glowed and something seemed to escape from it, causing the bag to deflate. When the smoke cleared, only a yellowish ash remained. They [the North Vietnam soldiers] fell to their knees around it, raising their hands to heaven praying for a safe flight for the departed soul' (Bao Ninh, 91).

Just as Herr discovered that the truth about the Vietnam War could be told only through the stories the grunts told, so too, Burns and Novick in their documentary on the Vietnam War, *The Vietnam War: A Film* (2017), realized that the best way to convey what happened was through oral histories. 'The documentary's power comes from those oral histories. An American veteran describes dragging insurgents' corpses into a village square "to see who would cry over them" so there would be more people to question. … A North Vietnamese officer recalls when she was assigned to a house abandoned by a South Vietnamese counterpart, an unfinished dress that the daughter had been sewing lying in place' (Poniewozik, 1). These are just two of the stories that made the documentary come alive.

The veterans of the Vietnam War who attended my course told their own stories, their own oral histories. Students that first night asked many questions of the Vietnam vets from the New River Valley Chapter that we discouraged others who attended later from asking: 'How many Vietcong did you kill?' 'What is it like to kill someone?' They did not know how many they killed because they just fired into the bush; 'it was either me or them'. One veteran said: 'It was not the killing that got to me but its effect, I lost my religion.'

Students also learned that the veterans thought they were fighting for America, only to realize that they were fighting for their government. When asked if we lost the war, Bobby Ward, one of the veterans, responded: 'Do you see a North Vietnamese flag flying over the White House?'

Chapter 2

Prelude to the Vietnam War

At the talks preceding the Versailles Treaty in 1919 at the end of the First World War, Ho Chi Minh advocated for an end to French colonization of Vietnam. During the Second World War, the OSS, a forerunner of the CIA, secretly aided Ho Chi Minh and the Viet Minh in their fight against the Japanese. '[In 1947, Truman] proclaimed before Congress what became known as the Truman Doctrine. "At the present moment in world history nearly every nation must choose between alternative ways of life. The choice is too often not a free one … I believe that it must be the policy of the US to support free peoples who are resisting attempted subjugation by armed minorities or by outside pressures"' (Hastings, 33).

Because of this doctrine, the US continued to ignore Ho Chi Minh's repeated requests for help against the French colonizers. Instead, the US continued to aid the French. After the French lost the Battle of Dien Bien Phu in 1954, the French agreed to a negotiated settlement known as The Geneva Accords of 1954. The Accords freed all Southeast Asia from French control, creating three nations: Cambodia, Laos, and Vietnam. The Accords divided Vietnam at the 17th parallel, a 5-mile strip known as the Demilitarized Zone until free elections in 1956 which would unite the country. The United States, fearing the communist takeover of Southeast Asia, took up the struggle against Ho Chi Minh and the communists, propping up an anti-communist

Southeast Asia during the Vietnam War.

government south of the DMZ, headed by Diem. Since the US and the Vietnamese delegations did not sign the Geneva Accords, the US argued that they and South Vietnam never agreed to elections in 1956, fearing – indeed knowing – that Ho Chi Minh would win a now unified nation that would be communist. Instead, they sent advisors to train South Vietnam soldiers and to shore up the government.

Dien Bien Phu. Located in the northwestern hills of Vietnam, west of Tonkin, Dien Bien Phu became the ultimate battle for control of Vietnam and all Southeast Asia. Wanting to stop the Viet Minh's supply routes, the French airlifted and then supported troops in these hills in 1954. General Giap, commander of the Viet Minh forces, surrounded the French, battering their positions with heavy artillery. The battle lasted fifty-five days, from 13 March to 7 May. What the French 'viewed … as a tactical issue … became a strategic opportunity for the Vietnamese' to defeat the French in Southeast Asia (Nightingale, 5).

Chapter 3

War Strategy

'There were few things more uncomfortable in the life of an officer than to be walking in front of a party of men all of whom knew that he was leading them in the wrong direction.' (Siegfried Sassoon, *Memoirs of an Infantry Officer*)

Introduction

'Tactics are the use of armed forces in a particular battle, while strategy is the doctrine of the use of individual battles for the purposes of war.' (Clausewitz, quoted in Pietersen, 3)

Military Strategy vs Tactics. Military Strategy is determined at the highest military levels. Clausewitz, in *On War*, writes: 'Strategy is concerned with defining an overall purpose and priorities. It is holistic. It clarifies how the individual battles fit together and why they are being fought ... Strategy is about picking the right battles. Tactics are about successfully executing those battles' (Pietersen, 3). **Tactics** are the means to realize a chosen strategy. Tactics are ever evolving, depending on the enemy's response, but the overall strategy remains constant. In most cases, politics do not come into play. But the United States government, fearing a wider war involving Russia and China, determined the military strategy: to contain communism, to insure that South Vietnam remained a viable democratic country and to provide a buffer to protect other countries in SE Asia. To execute this strategy, Westmoreland's tactics were to fight a limited war with limited means: not to invade or conquer the North Vietnam, not to cross the DMZ, not to bring the war to Laos and Cambodia and to train soldiers to fight a guerrilla war.

President George H.W. Bush seemed to acknowledge the limitations imposed on troops fighting in Vietnam when he declared in 1991 that the Gulf War would not be another Vietnam: 'Our troops ... will not be asked to fight with one hand tied behind their back' (Belew, 194). Clausewitz believed that wars were won or lost on the morale of the troops and the support at home (Pietersen, 4).

The same held true for the communist North. Military strategy and political strategy went hand-in-hand: both had as their goals reuniting North and South Vietnam under the leadership of Ho Chi Minh and the Viet Minh. To accomplish that end, they infiltrated the South through the **Ho Chi Minh Trail**, supplying guerillas in the South, the National Liberation Front (the Vietcong), with materiel and troop support. The North Vietnam Army (NVA) did not cross into the South until the Vietcong had softened the enemy.

The US and its allies wanted to engage the enemy in open combat, which is why they deforested South Vietnam. The Vietcong had a very different strategy, avoiding traditional methods of fighting. Instead, they would ambush, then retreat. '70 percent of all contacts were initiated by the Vietcong and North Vietnamese. The Communists were fighting the war on their own terms and chose when, where and how long to fight, which ultimately resulted in victory' (Milam, 5). Although Westmoreland had a vastly superior force and 'could move his troops anywhere he wished … he could not get the enemy to engage him in open combat. Instead, guerillas harassed his lines at every point and then receded. … To use Westmoreland's language, it was like fighting cockroaches' (Reston, Sherman, 30).

Both strategies relied on good weather. Monsoons affected both sides. In the North, they struck from September to January; in the South, Cambodia, and Laos, from May to September. During the monsoons, the North Vietnamese couldn't move troops who were walking in mud, which hampered getting supplies and troops through Laos and Cambodia to mount assaults across the border into South Vietnam. The US, meanwhile, could not use its main offensive weapon, the helicopter. In heavy rains, helicopters had to fly more slowly, there was no convenient place to hover and to disperse troops, so there was less conflict. If the weather was especially bad, the rain could come down the size of hail, meaning helicopters weren't flying at all. Both sides thus had to wait for the dry weather.

Another strategic problem the US encountered in Vietnam was a cultural difference in time. In the West, our calendar has a beginning (1 January) and an end (31 December). For the Vietnamese, however, time is a wheel that always flows, that never ends. A quick victory is a Western concept. In Vietnam, there is little sense of progress. History possesses little value and few goals. Hence, the Vietnamese are not impressed by a need to rush. Their life span is already short; make do with what you have. With patience, perhaps in the next existence, your Karma will permit improvement (The Religions of South Vietnam in Faith and Facts, US Navy, Bureau of Naval Personnel, Chaplains Division, 1967, sacred-texts.com). The US, with little support back home, needed and wanted a quick victory, not only to end the war and bring the troops home, but to keep China and the Soviet Union from sending military reinforcements. The Vietnamese had been fighting wars against invaders for centuries. Patience was a virtue. They could and would outlast any invader.

The Vietcong employed guerilla warfare tactics, the **Ho Chi Minh Trail**, a tunnel system, booby traps, and scavenger methods to hide and defeat the South and its allies. Because of these tactics, they controlled the ground war and made it dangerous for the United States to venture out at night. 'A night in the 'Nam always comes alive to some degree – things are either seen or heard. If something is both seen and heard, it usually turns out to be a tiger, rock ape or North Vietnamese' (Anderson, *Grunts*, 128–129).

Night Enemy
By Randy Cribbs

Through the night nothing stirred:
Pleasing to the ear, nothing heard.
They come in the dark
Leaving barely a mark,
Guests unbidden.
But not this night,
Now giving way to light.
So rest easy, you may;
Soon comes the day. (27)

Full Moon
By W.D. Ehrhart

We were on patrol last night;
As we moved along,
We came upon the enemy
Strange, in the bright moon
He did not seem an enemy at all.
He had arms and legs, a head ...
... a rifle.
I shot him. (Rottmann, 14)

Excelling at guerilla warfare, fieldcraft, and camouflage, the Vietcong tolerated hardships and sacrifice, to spread their message to the South Vietnamese. Their commander, General Giap, who defeated the French at Dien Bien Phu, was 'A Master of guerilla warfare and one of the great military minds of the twentieth century. ... Military strategist Giap was adept at compelling the opposing army to divide its forces into smaller units spread across a huge area, which could then be isolated and attacked with force' (Van Zyl, 174–175).

Guerilla Warfare. This involved a minor series of skirmishes. The Vietcong would use camouflage to hide from the enemy and then launch a sudden attack, followed by a quick retreat. During the monsoon season, the Vietcong had a tactical advantage since the South was unable to call in air support to protect their men from these assaults; the Vietcong thus became more active, following 'Mao Tse Tung's advice to guerillas to hit the enemy where [perhaps when as well] he is weakest' (*Vietnam: Special Newsweek Edition,* 27).

Because of the nature of guerilla warfare, no place above ground was safe. The US and South Vietnamese forces had nowhere they could hide. The Vietcong could hide underground in their tunnels or disappear into the jungle. During the day, soldiers could see the enemy emerge from their hiding places. The enemy, however, controlled the night. To hunt the Vietcong at night, 'Lieutenant Tahler and Hack [Colonel David Hackworth] have devised this real neat tactic ... out guerrillaing the guerilla. US soldiers would ambush the Vietcong during the night, using machine guns and cobras [AH-1 Cobra attack helicopters]' (Holley, 150).

Ho Chi Minh Trail. (see p. 97 for map which details Ho Chi Minh Trail) The Trail, first used in 1959, was the main supply route between North Vietnam and the Vietcong in the South. In 1961, it was little more than a jungle track. Americans called it the Ho Chi Minh Trail; the North Vietnamese called it the Truong Son Route, because it cut through the Truong Son Mountains, which formed a natural boundary along the border between Laos and North/South Vietnam. Troops moved at night, stopping to pick up weapons discarded by the French who had left in 1954.

If the Ho Chi Minh Trail had been a straight line, it would have been 300 miles long; but because it crossed mountains, it was about 600 miles. And it was not one trail. It split into three

On the Ho Chi Minh Trail.
(Wikipedia)

separate routes into Laos; a fourth trail went through the DMZ – Americans were not supposed to fire across the DMZ, and a trail through the DMZ was a clear violation of a UN mandate (Dunnigan and Nofi 296). Approximately every 12 miles, there would be a cut-off which entered South Vietnam.

The trail was so valuable that it was constantly improved, filling in bomb craters made by US aircraft. During the years of improvement, widening the trail, 100,000 people (mostly women) labored on the trail; local Laotians and Montagnard were often forced to work as porters, bringing supplies down from North Vietnam. Before the trail was wide enough for trucks, porters loaded bicycles with heavy equipment or ammunition and pushed the bikes down the trail. By 1964, the United States estimated 6,000 people had moved down the 600 mile trail. By 1965, it was the main supply route coming from Russia and China with aid for guerilla forces and regular North Vietnamese army troops. By 1967, about 69,000 troops had come down the trail, making sneak attacks across the Cambodian and Laotian borders.

At its peak, in dry weather, the North Vietnamese moved 10,000 troops a month down the Ho Chi Minh Trail, plus over 1,700 tons of food, almost 7,000 weapons, 800 tons of ammunition, and many tons of other supplies. These men and porters were supported by 40,000 troops stationed at or along the Laotian border, with the assistance of 60,000 Laotians, porters and laborers who built and maintained the trail. It was so well thought-out that there were fifty bases along the way for rest, and thousands of trenches and bunkers for protection from bombing once the trucks came – they were much easier to spot than green-clad troops among the mountains, swamps, and jungle.

The United States not only knew early on that a trail was there, but also that the North Vietnamese used the trail to bring weapons and other materiel supplied by the Chinese to the Vietcong in the South. Since the US and North Vietnam had signed an agreement not to involve Laos or Cambodia in any war, the United States was powerless to stop it. Not until August 1967 did the US announce to the public what soldiers on both sides knew long ago, that it had been conducting bombing operations along the Ho Chi Minh Trail in Laos for a while.

At first, the United States dropped anti-vehicular mines onto the trail. The ordinance used was the Claymore, which would be detonated by trip-wire or by timer. The Claymore spread hundreds of steel balls in a conical area to shred whatever was in its path. To protect their troops and the civilians who repaired the trail, the North Vietnamese set up heavy guns to fire at helicopters over the trail. The United States could shut down one or two routes, but the North Vietnamese would simply go to another route. The trail was 10–30 miles wide to accommodate vehicles, and 300 miles long. The interlocking and parallel trails made it about the size of Rhode Island. Later, the US dropped propaganda leaflets on the Vietcong, 'directed against the military and civilian personnel [who were often lonely.] Some leaflets showed the US sympathy for their dislike of the South Vietnamese government and [offered] them land. Once they entered South Vietnam, they were offered safe conduct passes if they were willing to relinquish their communist ties' (quote from Anon; material on Ho Chi Minh Trail summarized from Dunnigan and Nofi, 296-298).

Above left and above right: Safe Conduct passes.

Above left and above right: Propaganda leaflet. (Anon)

Two such poetic leaflets read:[19]

Below is a translation of the first two stanzas of the poem on left above:

A Poem to Mother
A North Vietnamese Youth Spills out his Heart

From the day I left you, mother,
to follow my companions on the trip to
Central Vietnam through Laos,
I have endured the hardships of
Climbing up the green mountains
And marching through rain and shine.

Although with my young age
Life should blossom like a flower.
For the sake of peace I don't mind
   Enduring hardships and danger. (Anon 8)

Other leaflets contained nostalgic poetry, supposedly written by NVA soldiers about their life at home. This poem is entitled 'Sister':

My Sister

I have a little sister,
as beautiful as a poem.
Her name sounds like "dream."
Her husband was drafted away.

For two years, she hoped
to see her man home.
From the far away battlefield
where man go,
but no news from them come back.

She usually wept when alone,
and moaned, reproached, and resented
those who instigated this war.
And caused wives to be parted
from husbands they beloved. (Anon 20).

Tunnels. Although they had air vents and camouflage entrances, these were not tunnels in the ordinary sense of the word. They were tiny villages. The Vietcong believed in fighting first, comfort second. Tunnels had workshops for producing homemade weapons, military storerooms, conference rooms, printing presses, and even temporary

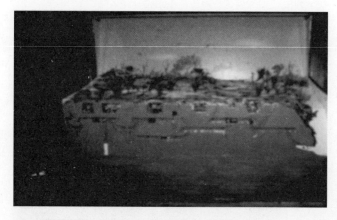

3-D diagram of tunnel system. (E. Brown, Jr)

Above: Tunnel living area. (Courtesy Dr E. Brown)

Left: Vietcong surgical hospital. (Courtesy Dr E. Brown)

graveyards. They built air-raid shelters in such a way that they could hear approaching aircraft. They also had complete living facilities: places for sleeping and eating, latrines, a hospital, a kitchen, and a well. Their kitchens were smokeless, sending smoke through many ducts. Tunnel entrances usually had false entrances, ones that led nowhere. There were hidden entrances, usually a small square one with dirty water and vegetation to cover it up. There were also booby-trapped entrances. To avoid detection, the Vietcong would often reroute their tunnels and change the camouflaged entrances. The Vietcong had to build their tunnels to hide from the enemy above, sometimes on poor soil and even with wooden beam reinforcements that often collapsed under pressure from above caused by tanks, bombs, and mortar shells. 'The Vietcong who hid in these tunnels followed three precepts: "Walk without footprints, cook without smoke, and speak without a sound"' (Brownmiller, 173–174). US attempts to map tunnels proved unsuccessful. Soldiers bulldozed land in a bid to collapse tunnels; entrances were also blown up. By the end of 1970, the US had discovered 4,800 tunnels.

Tunnels
By Yusef Komunyakaa

Crawling down headfirst into the hole,
he kicks the air & disappears.
I feel like I'm down there
with him, moving ahead, pushed
by a river of darkness, feeling
blessed for each inch of the unknown.
Our tunnel rat is the smallest man
in the platoon, in an echo chamber
that makes his ears bleed when he pulls the trigger.
He moves as if trying to outdo
blind fish easing toward imagined blue,
pulled by something greater than life's
ambitions. He can't think about
spiders & scorpions mending the air,
or care about bats upside down
like gods in the mole's blackness.
The damp smell goes deeper
Than the stench of honey buckets.
A web of booby traps waits, ready
to spring into broken stars.
Forced onward by some need,
some urge, he knows the pulse
of mysteries & diversions
like thoughts trapped in the ground.
He questions each root.
Every cornered shadow has a life
to bargain with. Like an angel
pushed up against what hurts,

his globe-shaped helmet
follows the gold ring his flashlight
casts into the void. Through silver
lice, shit, maggots, & vapor of pestilence,
he goes, the good soldier,
on hands & knees, tunneling past
death sacked into a blind corner,
loving the weight of the shotgun
that will someday dig his grave. (138)

Tunnel Rats To counter the tunnel systems, the South employed tunnel rats, soldiers who went into tunnels to find the enemy or discover enemy resources. Each unit had its own tunnel rat, small in stature and thin. He could crawl into a tunnel looking for the enemy or supplies and weapons. A 'Tunnel Explorer Locator System' followed the tunnel rat's progress and mapped the tunnel. Some units employed teams to explore tunnels using CS (or tear gas) first to flush any enemy out. After a tunnel had been searched, it was then destroyed to prevent further use (Hay, 34).

Although the tunnel rat received no extra pay for this dangerous assignment, he was often proud because he found something that he exceled at and liked to do: 'I got to like it after I found out I could be good at it. I've only had to kill two guys I found so far – brought thirteen out alive when I was doing it. I think it was cuz I took the fear out of them, I'd just flash my flashlight on my face when I knew there was one there, and I'd smile – real big, like I'd just knocked off a piece, you know – and they'd come right out. I even brought out two at once one time' (Anderson, *Grunts*, 95).

Tunnel rats had to overcome fear and feelings of claustrophobia in tunnels that were so low they had to bend over to walk, and so narrow they had to walk sideways. Some of the tunnels were so small and narrow that crawling on their belly was the only way to get through. Tunnels were dark, so the sense of smell was critical. Tunnel rats didn't smoke (smoke could be smelled half a mile away), chew gum, eat candy, or even eat anything before going into a tunnel. Most tunnel rats tossed in CS gas before entering, and they carried a knife because the sound of a weapon discharging was painful to the ears in the contained space. Tunnel rats developed a sixth sense – they just knew when Charlie was there. They often felt or smelled the enemy was nearby in one of the cut-outs, just waiting.

Danny Phillips as
tunnel rat. (Courtesy
D. Phillips)

Marine Puller's platoon discovered a tunnel hidden on a hill. Puller was surprised at how many of his men volunteered to investigate, 'since there was no way of knowing what was inside, but the element of the unknown seemed to spark the enthusiasm of some of the men. After a volunteer was selected, we tossed a couple of grenades into the shaft. A volunteer's quick foray produced nothing but some sacks of rice and medical supplies from an American pharmaceutical company. Apparently, the shaft was used only for storage, which was a relief to me but a disappointment to the tunnel rat, who was looking for the in-country R&R that a kill would bring him' (107).

One tunnel rat made the decision not to confront an enemy in a tunnel:

'Then I cautiously raised the upper half of my body into the tunnel until I was lying flat on my stomach. When I felt comfortable … I switched on the flashlight, illuminating the tunnel. There, not more than 15 feet away, sat a Vietcong eating a handful of rice from a pouch on his lap. We looked at each other for what seemed to be an eternity, but in fact was probably only a few seconds … Neither one of us reacted. … To this day, I firmly believe that grunt and I could have ended the war sooner over a beer in Saigon than Henry Kissinger ever could by attending the peace talks.' (Grossman, 1–2)

Other Guerilla Warfare Tactics. Another strategy involved the creation of **booby traps.** Bamboo sticks, called **punji stakes**, sharpened to a point, buried point-up slightly above ground level and camouflaged with dirt, penetrated GIs' combat boots and caused infections, the stakes having been smeared with feces or a poisonous material. Punji stakes were also placed at the bottom of a ditch, covered and camouflaged with sticks and leaves. Combat Paratrooper Gene Woodley jumped off a helicopter right on a well-hidden punji stake. He had no choice but to keep running with the stake sticking out of his boot. His foot swelled. When the mission was over, three days later, they had to cut the boot off his foot (Terry, 244–245). However, according to Dunnigan and Nofi, 'Punji Stakes caused only about 2 percent of American casualties and virtually no deaths' (70).

The traps and snipers which harassed the Americans and South Vietnamese soldiers meant that the South had little chance to confront the enemy, who remained hidden but watchful. Besides punji stakes, the enemy had explosive traps: '**Explosive booby traps** were more common than *punji* pits, especially in the latter stages of the war, and they came in a variety of shapes and sizes.' **Toe poppers** were small explosive charges set in bamboo tubes, hand grenades placed in empty cans or in clay mudballs, or in coconuts strewn along the ground (J. Ebert, 227–228, 237). As James Ebert notes, 'Kicking things was a habit common to Americans that the enemy used to his advantage' (238).

Marine Lewis Puller, Jr, author of the Pulitzer Prize-winning autobiography *Fortunate Son* in 1992, described a booby trap and sent himself a reminder to be more diligent: 'The device consisted of a C ration can holding a grenade with its pin removed so that the grenade's spoon was held in place by the side of the can. … If we had proceeded … in the previous day's twilight rather than stopped to make camp, my point man and perhaps several others would probably have been maimed or killed. I reminded myself that the platoon had to become more disciplined at using probe sticks and staying off trails' (128).

Bouncing Betty (also known as a **Bouncing Bitch**, **the castrator**, or in French *soldat silencieux* ('silent soldier') (G. Rottman, *FUBAR*, 28). This was the booby trap that

Above: Vietcong sticking trap on the trail. (Courtesy Dr E. Brown)

Left: Punji stakes. (Courtesy Dr E. Brown)

was feared the most. It was trip-wired, with a three-pronged primer. When the plunger depressed, a Bouncing Betty would bounce up about 3 or 4 feet and explode:

'The Bouncing Betty, anti-personnel mine, is one of the more brutal products of American military technology.[20] When triggered, it doesn't explode in the ground and take feet off legs. It springs up four feet before it goes off and separates heads and arms from bodies and perforates lungs, stomachs, and intestines. Lance Corporal Epps' Bouncing Betty picked him up and, while he flew through the air, ripped off his clothes, legs, hands, and all of his head but the lower jaw, then dumped him on his back – stumps of thighs and arms raised in supplication to a garish sun. The first man on the scene told a corpsman that he thought he saw a pink mist hanging over the corpse for a few seconds.' (Anderson, *Grunts*, 165)

Overhead mines. Not only did soldiers need to watch where they stepped, but they also had to be aware of what was above them. Mines were hung on trees and released by an electric detonator when a soldier or platoon walked under one.

Point Man. To counter booby traps, the soldiers used a point man, who was the first man on a combat patrol. The man right behind him, called the **slack man**, was the most vulnerable on the trail, as he often missed what the point man saw. The point man would be the first to notice a booby trap.

Point man. (Vets with a Mission)

Sergeant Danny Phillips, a **Fucking New Guy (FNG)**, said he wanted to walk point. Every day, the lieutenant would ask someone else to walk point; but some did not welcome the opportunity, afraid of missing something. Phillips felt that having one person walk point each day would increase the likelihood of spotting dangers as he learned what to look for. 'I think I did a pretty good job, nobody behind me stepped on a mine and I didn't lead my company into any ambushes. I would like to say that I wasn't scared but that would be a big lie. I was scared many times but I kept doing what had to be done' (email to Margaret Brown, 17 June 2009).[21]

Johnny, a Vietnam vet, always walked point with his rifle on automatic. 'It could fire 18 times in three seconds,' he said (Vietnam Vet Program, 4/2/93).

Point Man
By Randy Cribbs

If only I could see
What lurks behind that tree
Or around the next bend,
Enemy or friend.
What waits in the grass so thick;
Some harmless creature
Or that sharpened stick.
Focus, if only I can;
My turn almost up,
Who's next – point man. (35)

Hidden
By Randy Cribbs

What hides in
The elephant grass
There
Beyond the great water buffalo.

Does it live?
as it waits, or
Is it cold,
Metallic?

Go slow,

Today I am first;
My turn
To find the answer,
To feel the hard learn.

Fate awaits
Me to find,
But
What will
It be this time? (108)

The point man and others behind him would use **Probe Sticks**, poking the ground in front of them to discover hidden dangers. Doing this also served as a reminder that they were in enemy territory and to always be aware of what was around them.

Many of the traps created by the Vietcong made use of material discarded by the soldiers. Although we were able to limit supplies carried through Laos and Cambodia and those coming by ship to North Vietnam, we were unable effectively to police our own area before leaving. '**In Vietnam, our soldiers were a major part of the enemy's supply system.** The US soldier, by nature, was rather wasteful, a trait that carried over from his civilian life. He tended to discard anything he considered extra and the idea of policing the battlefield was distasteful to him' (*Distant Challenge*, 273).[22] Even when encamped in remote firebases or while patrolling in the bush, American troops maintained a high standard of living. They generated a lot of trash; and one man's trash is another man's treasure. What passed for garbage among Americans was often immensely valuable to a poverty-stricken Asian. Empty ration tins, old clothing, or dud ammunition could be used not only by the enemy but by the local villagers as improvised explosive devices (IEDs).

An analysis by the US Army determined that the grunts were contributing to its enemy's main source of supplies. This analysis led to a policing action called Operation Baker (19 April to 20 September 1967). 'Found: 174 US grenades recaptured – probably because the US soldiers just left them; 172 booby traps – of these, 35 were found the hard way, 32 men KIA and 70 WIA [wounded in action] – and 24 were made from discarded C-ration cans, 35 from captured US hand grenades, four from US claymores – and others from gun shells, mortar rounds, and naval gun shells' (*Distant Challenge*, 84).

Tin Trap
By Randy Cribb

That peanut butter tin
Became a must keepsake,
Not left for the
Surprise Charlie could make
Never eat it,
Caused too much thirst,
There in the boonies
Nothing worse
But with it
Those C's* you could heat,
By mixing slowly with
A squirt of OD Deet.*

Hot chow for
The whole team;
Important then,
Silly as that
May seem;
And
Better to keep
It now than to
Feel it later in our lap,
Among the innards
Of Charlie's booby trap. (41)

(*A pinch of C4 could ignite a fire. A pinch or two will cook your rations.
*Olive Drab insect repellant.)

United States War Strategy[23]

'The Vietnam War was a limited war, with limited objectives, prosecuted by limited means, with limited public support. Therefore, it was destined to be (and was) a long war, a war so long that public support waned and political decision by Congress terminated our involvement, resulting in a victory by the North Vietnamese Communists.' General William Westmoreland, Vietnam Lessons, 6.

In his Foreword to the *Handbook for US Forces in Vietnam*, General Westmoreland comments on the enemy's strategies: 'The enemy we face in South Vietnam today, both regular and guerilla forces, is challenging us with many old fighting techniques and a few new ones. ...I have summarized in this handbook certain basic techniques and procedures which have evolved out of seven years of combat operations against the enemy.'

This proved to be an important statement of what US troops would face in their fight against communist forces in Vietnam. What made it even more difficult for the soldiers was the rifle they were given, the **M-16**.

The **M-16** was an automatic or semi-automatic assault weapon, also known as the widow maker. It weighed 7.6 pounds, had a twenty-round cartridge and a range of 460 meters. Its automatic firing rate was 650–700 rounds per minute, and its lighter ammunition meant soldiers could carry more and did not have to be resupplied quite as often. The **M-16**, in development when first used in Vietnam in 1965, had not been battle tested.

But grunts didn't trust it, because it was being battle-tested in Vietnam by them and it tended to jam. Soldiers preferred the field-tested **AR-15**, new and improved. Only it wasn't improved. The military decision was to equip both American and South Vietnamese soldiers with the **M-16**. 'The M-16 rifle you are armed with is the best weapon there is for use here in Vietnam' (Captain Paul Von Hoene, *Tropic Lightning News*, 25th Infantry Division, Cu Chi, Vietnam, 3 July 1967; Rottmann, 11).

Rifle, 5.56MM, XM16E1
By Larry Rottmann

The M-16 sure is a marvelous gun.
In a god-awful war
it provides some keen fun.

The bullet it fires appears too small to harm.
But it makes a big hole
and can tear off an arm.

Single shot, semi, or full automatic.
A real awesome weapon,
though often sporadic.

Listen to Ichord[24] and forget that stuck bolt.
You aren't as important
as a kickback from Colt.

So carry your rifle (they don't give a damn).
Just pray you won't need it
while you're in Vietnam.

The M-16 is issue, though we all feel trapped.
More GIs would protest,
but somehow they got zapped. (Rottmann, 11)

118

LRRP Richard Ford was amazed at the equipment that was handed out without a question: 'M-14s, if an M-16 how many rounds of ammunition you want? Grenades? Whatever you want was yours for the asking. We were so in the spirit that we hurt ourself. Guys would want to look like John Wayne. The dudes would just get in the country and say, "I want a .45. I want eight grenades. I want a bandolier. I want a thousand rounds of ammo. I want ten clips. I want the works, right?" We never knew what the weight of this ammo is gon' to be' (Terry, 35).

Retraining. Despite advanced infantry training, when it came to fighting guerillas in the jungle, the US soldiers were unprepared. They had been fighting conventional war tactics in Europe and Korea, and were not prepared for the kind of war the Vietcong were fighting. The United States continued to use conventional means, bombing and 'Search and Destroy' methods, and newer means, with chemicals to defoliate the jungle and sensors to locate the enemy.

> 'In Vietnam the US dropped three times as many explosives as it dropped in all theaters of World War II, even including our nuclear bombing of Hiroshima and Nagasaki.' (Loewen, 243–244)

To help fight the guerilla war, the US armed and trained auxiliary forces, the mountain tribes of Vietnam whose communities were overrun after the war by the North Vietnamese. Not until **Vietnamization** under Nixon and the withdrawal of US forces did the North Vietnamese Army returned to the battlefield. But with the **Tet Offensive** in 1968, all efforts at Vietnamization and the Marines' **Civil Operations and Revolutionary Development Support program (CORDS)** ended. When the **NVA** did fight in a more conventional way early in the war, they lost. Most of the early war years, thus, were fought by the Vietcong, with ambushes, booby traps, and hit-and-run assaults.

The United States could not win the ground war because the enemy knew jungle warfare; it could not win the **hearts and minds** of the people through Vietnamization because all the Vietnamese wanted was peace. They had fought the French from 1945–1954. In this new war, the US controlled the air, but we could not bomb them into submission, even though we could make use of helicopters to create air mobility. Flight surgeon Pendergrass remarks on the difference between the air and ground war: 'The war in the sky had a different dynamic, a different feel from the ground war. If you were shot down, you faced the quick death of combat, the hell of captivity, or the joy of being rescued. You were unlikely to end up in my hospital' (29). Whereas if you were wounded in the ground war, you might just end up in a hospital, maybe have a million-dollar wound, which was your ticket home.

The **Hueys**, the nickname for the Bell UH (utility helicopter), controlled the air. Heavy use of the helicopter was another innovation necessary in this war. 'In a land that favored the easily hidden, lightly loaded foot soldier, the helicopter balanced the odds. Air mobility was a dramatic new dimension, which allowed the precise application of a variety of combat power' (Hay, 3). If you heard a Huey, you knew it belonged to the US. 'Helicopters were the "army mules" of the Vietnam War. ... An important consequence of the Vietnam War was that it hastened the widespread use of helicopters by the armed forces, a trend that was already in evidence' (Dunnigan and Nofi, 109).

The terrain and weather often determined the effectiveness of any operation. In mountainous terrain, 'the transport helicopter can carry about 60% of the load possible in the lowlands' (*Handbook*, 92). In the canopy jungle, landing a helicopter was impossible, so soldiers had to jump to disembark. Helicopter assaults, called eagle flights, were 'especially developed for flat, low lying terrain like that of the delta where lack of roads, great expanses of inundated land, vast networks of tree-lined rivers and canals and widely dispersed populations made fighting the VC on foot a most difficult task' (*Handbook*, 93).

Freelance reporter Michael Herr found himself in a war that was deadly boring one-minute, acute panic the next: 'Fear and motion, fear and standstill ... no way even to be clear about which was really worse, the wait or the delivery. ... Everyone suffered the time between contact, especially when they were going out every day looking for it. ... I can remember times when I went half dead with my fear of the motion, the speed and direction already fixed and pointed one way' (15).

From a North Vietnamese soldier's memoirs: 'In my bedroom, on many nights the helicopters attack overhead, the dreaded whump-whump-whump of their rotor blades bringing horror for us in the field. I curl up in defense against the expected vapor streak and the howling of their rockets. But the whump-whump-whump continues without an attack, and the helicopter image dissolves, and I see in its place a ceiling fan. Whump-whump-whump' (Bao Ninh, 46).

Body Count. Another war strategy was to count dead bodies to prove back home that we were winning the war. Since none of our efforts succeeded in defeating the enemy and we did not have enough troops to win and control territory (there are stories about conquering a hill and then abandoning it), the only true measure of success in this war was the body count. Hence the inflation of numbers for back-home consumption. 'General

Helicopter. (Courtesy D. Phillips)

Westmoreland's strategy of attrition also had an important effect on our behavior. Our mission was not to win terrain or seize positions, but simply to kill. ... Victory was a high body-count, defeat a low-kill ratio, war a matter of arithmetic. ... This led to such practices as counting civilians as Vietcong. "If it's dead and Vietnamese, it's VC", was a rule of thumb in the bush. It is not surprising, therefore, that some men acquired a contempt for human life and a predilection for taking it' (Caputo, xix).

'In a war where capturing territory was not as important as eliminating enemy troops, the success or failure of an operation was often difficult to determine. ... So the army came to evaluate operations on the basis of something called the "kill ratio", that is, the number of enemy troops killed for each friendly soldier lost in action. Thus was born the notorious "body-count". ... In addition, the "kill ratio" was seen as an excellent way to evaluate combat unit commanders' (Dunnigan and Nofi, 75–76).

Although Military Assistance Command Vietnam (**MACV**)[25] set up regulations about whom to count – dead armed people, soldiers or not – on the ground, pilots and/ or observers had to determine kills 'beyond a reasonable doubt' (J. Ebert, 339).

'The body-count was quickly corrupted. ... Even with all the padding, it was still publicly acknowledged that communist troops were not being "killed fast enough", and could not be without the addition of many more American troops and an invasion of North Vietnam. The troops in the field were not very enthusiastic about the body-count process, as they were sometimes ordered to go counting while the enemy was still shooting. This situation did not do much for accuracy in the count. But then, accuracy was never a major factor in the body-count department' (Dunnigan and Nofi, 76).

> 'The [body-count] numbers often seemed so ridiculous that more than
> one veteran commented sarcastically that American soldiers apparently
> killed the whole country' (Ebert, 343)

One of my vets told me that body count became so ridiculous that if they found empty Vietcong food boxes, they assumed that those Vietcong had died and added them to the body count (Vietnam Vet Program (4/2/93). Combat Engineer Harold Bryant said with a straight face: 'And they had a habit of exaggerating a body-count. If we killed 7, by the time it left from Saigon going to Washington, it had went up [*sic*] to about 125' (Terry, 21). A Special Forces captain told Michael Herr all about the body count: 'I went out and killed one VC and liberated a prisoner. Next day the major called me in and told me that I'd killed fourteen VC and liberated six prisoners. You want to see the medal?' (172).

Psychiatrist Robert Jay Lifton interviewed many Vietnam veterans on the psychological effect of the war. One of them told him: 'If it's dead, it's VC. Because it's dead. If it's dead it *had* to be VC. And, of course, a corpse couldn't defend itself anyhow' (64).

'The American practice of "body-counting" enemy casualties in the Vietnam War was mindless in innocently assuming that these deaths had a bearing on North Vietnamese capabilities and willpower' (Seabury and Codevilla, 121). The military was stuck: with no territory to capture and hold, and no prisoners to take, the only strategy was to kill and kill some more.

'We may have enhanced the killing ability of the average soldier through training (that is, conditioning), but at what price? ... But in doing so we have not made them capable of handling the moral and social burdens of these acts' (Grossman, 291–292).

121

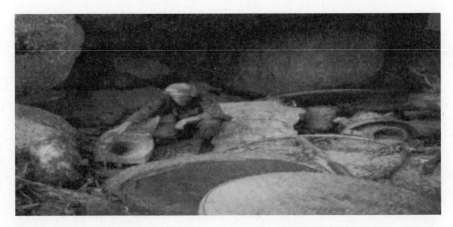

VC supply cave. (Wikipedia)

Another strategy attempted to deprive the Vietcong of rice; this operation was known as **Rice Robbery**. The VC would show up at harvest time for rice. Each year their demands were different. Sometimes, as a tax, they would take a quarter of a harvest, other times nearly all of it. Then 'the peasants were made to carry the product of their own labor into the hills to the secret caches of the Vietcong' (Walt, 51).

Once the Americans arrived, the South Vietnamese peasants no longer had to carry their rice to the VC hideouts, although they still had to pay a tax to them. The VC, in retaliation, told the peasants not to harvest their crops – or else. Without the Marines, the peasants would never have been able to harvest their crop, store it, and plan its distribution. The VC, attempting to make good on its 'or else' threats, were repelled by the Marines whenever a village was threatened. 'The rice denial program of the 3rd/21st, which within the month of Nov netted over 31,875 lbs. of rice was extended into December with the discovery of 10,200 more lbs of rice' (Phillips, 40).

In this way, the South deprived the VC of rice, and the peasants could have what they grew. Marine patrols also searched areas looking for hidden stores of rice. They were successful in finding tons of rice hidden near the fields or in shelters (Walt, 51–53). A South Vietnamese man tells a quite different version of events: 'American soldiers plundered peasants' rice and then rationed it out to refugee peasants as "relief" rice. And the peasants are obliged to receive "gratefully" the rice that they cultivated with their own labor. ... Such an operation cannot but be called "Rice Robbery" equipped with helicopters, automatic rifles, and machine guns' (Honda, 11).

The Vietcong, beginning in 1960, reminded the peasants that the Saigon regime worked for the Americans, not for them, and that they, not Saigon, were attempting to drive the Americans out of Vietnam. They also told the peasants that they were working for the rich landowners, not for themselves. 'This land is yours. If anyone comes to disturb you, we will protect you. In exchange, you must give us your undivided assistance' (Clos).

Since the Americans could not hold territory, they found another way to make an area unlivable. These offensive operations, known as **Search and Destroy**, destroyed enemy forces without maintaining holding actions. By destroying possible enemy

Above left: Searching for Vietcong. (Wikipedia)

Above right: Rescue. (Vets with a Mission)

sanctuaries, they also created fear in those who ordinarily might provide food and shelter for the Vietcong. They had three purposes: 1) locating the enemy and attacking them; 2) clearing enemy forces from populated areas; and 3) securing operations directed against the enemy in the hamlets, who were often farmers by day and Vietcong by night. 'Each of the three missions supported the pacification program'" (Hay, 169–170).

A monograph published by the Department of the Army stated: 'Search and Destroy Operations, by any name, were the *tactics* by which US units engaged the enemy. They were the right operations at the time, and they contributed to the essential function of shielding the pacification effort from the enemy's main forces. Without the shield, the South Vietnamese would not have had the opportunity to rebuild their forces, and the pacification effort in Vietnam would have been impossible' (Hay, 178).

In his six-month duty in the field, Doc Holley learned how the peasants were treated: 'From what I've heard from some of our grunts, these [Search and Destroy] missions can get real hairy because it is so hard to tell who is the enemy and who are the innocent peasant farmers. ... It usually ends up with their hooches being burned by flame throwers and their rice hauled off to the ARVN soldiers. ... I guess it never occurs to them that a rice farmer would have large amounts of grain on hand until he could get it hauled to the market' (48). US soldiers tried to avoid rice farms and their dikes, as they were often booby-trapped.

'The grunts saw the war up close, in its most stark terms: To most of them, missions to "Search and Destroy" seemed much more authentic than "pacification". They were in Vietnam to kill gooks, period, not make friends with the Vietnamese. Some did it well, and some enjoyed it – often making up the rules as they went' (Parish, 46). 'Killing

Rice in Vietnam is grown in terraces. (Encyclopedia Britannica)

comes with a price, and societies must learn that their soldiers will have to spend the rest of their lives living with what they have done … society must now begin to understand the enormity of the price and process of killing in combat' (Grossman, 192).

The US command soon realized that Search and Destroy missions gave soldiers the opportunity to destroy anything and everything in their area, including the inhabitants. Recoilless Rifleman Kirkland oversaw a Search and Destroy mission: 'You just clear the village and burn the hootches because the village is suspected of a Vietnam stronghold or VC sympathizers. A Zippo raid was standard operation procedure when we went into a village … [Kirkland's] platoon did that to 50 to 75 villages. … If we use the figure 50 villages, we found suspects in 12 of them. Maybe 30 suspects in all of them. We very rarely found a real VC' (Terry, 94).

Because soldiers took Search and Destroy literally, it had a bad effect on morale and on winning hearts and minds. 'In April 1968 General Westmoreland … directed that the use of the term be discontinued. Operations thereafter were defined and discussed in basic military terms which described the type of operation, for example, reconnaissance in force' (Hay, 177). Many US soldiers, meanwhile, thought that for South Vietnamese soldiers, Search and Destroy meant 'search and avoid'.

'In the summer of 1967, Marine Lance Corporal Bill Ehrhart [recalls destroying a Buddhist temple] "just because we were bored. … It was stinking hot; we were going nowhere. And we're just looking to pass the time. The temple's there. So let's wreck it. … I took a little vase [that held joss sticks to remind me after forty years] of what I'm capable of' (Ward, 206).

Defoliants. The US sprayed different chemicals, depending on their purpose – see the next two pages for individual descriptions of what these chemicals did. Operation Ranch Hand destroyed jungles that the Vietcong had used to ambush American and South Vietnamese troops. This operation used defoliants, such as **Agent Orange**, to clear the jungles. Spraying defoliants began in 1962 and continued until near the end

Above left: Spraying a defoliant over jungle. (Courtesy D. Phillips)

Above right: Effect of defoliant. (Courtesy D. Phillips)

of the war, reaching their peak in the late Sixties. Their purpose was to defoliate and deforest the land, making it more difficult for the Vietcong to wage guerilla war.

By the war's end, 'Almost twenty million gallons of defoliants ... were sprayed throughout Indochina' (Hastings, 309). Morley Safer explained the consequences of the American failure to understand the effects of defoliants: 'It was chemical warfare pure and simple. Its defenders [the United States military who ordered the operation] had the arrogance to maintain that what would kill trees would not hurt people, or American people any way' (106), even though soldiers set up tents on grounds saturated with Agent Orange and waded in streams polluted with this and other defoliants. But, of course, it led to death and birth defects, not only in the United States but in all the countries whose populations were sprayed with the defoliants. Even more devastating were the leaflets distributed by Americans as a psychological operation which told the Vietcong that Agent Orange would not harm them. They could drink or bathe in water contaminated with Agent Orange with no ill effects. Those who participated liked to think that they did not know Agent Orange's effects, but they probably did (Anon).

George Black, in an article twenty-five years later about the effects of spraying defoliant in Laos during the war, commented: 'Anyone writing about conflict knows that no war ever truly ends; each of them casts a long shadow. Lives are changed forever, and the secrets of wartime can stay hidden for decades. ... The use of the herbicide in the neutral nation of Laos by the United States – secretly, illegally and in large amounts – remains one of the last untold stories of the American war in Southeast Asia. [The defoliant] was in the soil, the food supply and human blood and breast milk, and there were unusual numbers of birth defects in those living in the most heavily contaminated locations [in Laos]. Since there were no industrial sources of contamination in the area, the only possible culprit was Agent Orange' (1, 3).

Agent Orange, like all the defoliants used, were stored in cannisters whose lid determined the nature of the particular defoliant. Agent Orange was 'a known carcinogen [and] ... the most widely used. About 90 percent of it was used for defoliation, about 8 percent for crop destruction [500,000 acres of farmland in Vietnam had been infected by Agent Orange, denying food to the mostly civilian population], and about 2 percent to clear base perimeters, roads and so forth' (Dunnigan and Nofi, 136). 'Agent Orange eventually kills the plant because [the plant] absorbs the agent. Approximately 90% of the missions were to defoliate; 10% for crop destruction. Each mission could drop 700–800 gallons' (Hay, 90).

One of my vets rolled orange-lidded cannisters into planes. Years later he developed raised red splotches and bumps on his arm, which doctors told him, in his many visits to a VA hospital, were poison ivy or an allergic reaction to stress, anything but exposure to Agent Orange. Fortunately, his children were born with no birth deformities associated with this defoliant.

Years later, Brownmiller, a news writer for ABC during the war, discovered the irony of Agent Orange: "Vietnam's doctors and scientists placed a low priority on rigorous, expensive studies of the lasting effects of Agent Orange. They had more pressing national health problems to deal with. Vietnam is an impoverished tropical country beset by malaria, malnutrition, hepatitis B, encephalitis, dengue fever, and parasites, and hampered by a polluted water supply, a Third World sanitation system and an almost total lack of antibiotics' (139).

Both Agent Purple and Agent White were defoliants. Agent Purple was ten times more dangerous than Agent Orange. Even in 1973, the VA recognized Agent Purple caused soft tissue cancer (Johnny Phillips, Vietnam Vet Program, 4/2/93). Agent White was used when Agent Orange wasn't available. **Agent Blue** withered rice crop.

Napalm. Another defoliant, made from gasoline and detergent, napalm is an incendiary chemical stored in 55-pound drums that burns at about 2,000 degrees Fahrenheit. Not only can it cause death by burning, it also 'deoxygenates' the air, creating carbon monoxide gas (Dunnigan and Nofi, 124). Water has no effect on napalm, which can be stored for a long time.

Ironically, because napalm sticks to the skin and burns nerve endings just below, there is not as much pain as if a victim has suffered second-degree burns. It may not cause as much pain, but as Nick Ut (Huynh Cong Ut) showed in his iconic photograph entitled, "Napalm Girl," its effect is quite painful. It was used by both North and South Vietnam during the war.

Bao Ninh, a North Vietnamese soldier and writer, reported on the effect of napalm: 'The enemy sent napalm spraying through the jungle and a sea of fire enveloped [the soldiers], spreading like the fires of hell. Troops in the fragmented companies tried to regroup, only to be blown out of their shelters again as they went mad, became disoriented, and threw themselves into nets of bullets, dying in the flaming inferno' (5).

'In December 1969 the UN General Assembly resolved any use of chemical warfare – including herbicides – violated international law; the United States rejected this resolution as outside the scope of the General Assembly. In August 1971, however,

the US and the Soviet Union jointly submitted a draft ban on biological weapons' (Kutler, 1).

My husband Earl Brown, Jr, and I went to Vietnam in 2007. We expected to see the effects of the defoliants sprayed on the land many years ago. Although we spent most of our time in Ho Chi Minh City and Hanoi, we noticed how lush the countryside was, with grass and trees

Agent Orange kills; exhibited in Hanoi, summer 2007. (Courtesy E. Brown, Jr)

126

everywhere, rice fields irrigated with clean water, and Vietnamese harvesting wheat. The land seemed living and breathing again, seemingly unaffected by the chemicals which saturated its land and rivers.

Another means of defoliation, not used until 1967 in Vietnam, although used in World War II, was the **Rome Plow**, named after Rome, Georgia, where it was manufactured. The Rome Plow, a caterpillar D8 bulldozer, destroyed trees and other jungle flora that could be used by enemy forces. A tank platoon and an infantry company, assigned to each Rome Plow, would ensure the safety of the plow and its operator. After the area had been cleared, soldiers would Search and Destroy enemy camps and tunnels.

Indoctrination. Since Search and Destroy and defoliation had little effect on the enemy's will to win, the US decided to try to win the hearts and minds of the South Vietnamese. The phrase most used by politicians, winning hearts and minds, was first used by John Adams: 'The Revolution was effected before the war commenced. The Revolution was in the hearts and minds of the people' (Olsen, 194). LBJ stated: 'So we must be ready to fight in Vietnam, but the ultimate victory will depend on the hearts and minds of the people who actually live out there' (Olson, 194–195).

The phrase, first used in a *Time Magazine* cover story on 11 May 1962, proved more difficult in Vietnam than in the colonies that had formed the early United States. Many of the soldiers and reporters continually used the phrase in a derogatory manner. Marine Lewis Puller, Jr, said: 'The platoon was in no mood to waste time winning hearts and minds, and when the villagers realized that we were going to be in their midst for several hours, they became inhospitable' (138). Reporter Morley Safer, meanwhile, described the carvings on the desk of a foreign service officer: 'Take them firmly by the balls and their hearts and minds will follow' and 'Join the Marines! Travel to exotic lands … meet exciting people … and kill them' (189).

Many methods were tried to win over the Vietnamese people: Civil Operations and Revolutionary Development Support (**CORDS**), the Civic Action Program (**CAP**), Medical Civilian Action Program (**MEDCAP**), and Nixon's strategy of Vietnamization, turning the war over to the South Vietnamese.

'In May 1967, an organization known as CORDS – Civil Operations and Revolutionary Development Support – was formed to coordinate the US civil and

Taking woman and child to safety. (Vets with a Mission)

military pacification programs. ... It pulled together all the various US military and civilian agencies involved in the pacification effort, including the State Department, the USAID, the USIA and the CIA. ... CORDS civilian/military advisory teams were dispatched throughout South Vietnam's 44 provinces and 250 districts' (history.net/cords-winning-hearts-and minds in Vietnam. html).

Combat Paratrooper Woodley recalled: 'We had the war beat until they started this pacification program. Don't shoot, unless shot upon. The government kept handicapping us one way or 'nother. I don't think America lost. I think they gave up. They surrendered' (Terry, 256). 'The reporters call it "the other war", [a Civic Action Program]. The embassy calls it "pacification". And the politicians call it "winning hearts and minds"' (Anderson, *Other War*, 68). According to the US Army, 'pacification was an unprecedented addition to the commander's mission. Although it was basically a civilian endeavor, the military played a vital and continuous part because the restoration of security in the countryside was a prerequisite to pacification' (Hay, 181).

Each CAP included fourteen Marines who volunteered, one of whom was fluent in Vietnamese, and one Navy corpsman. 'All team members had civilian work experience that could be applied directly to the agricultural economy of the rural Vietnamese village, things like farming, live-stock breeding, construction, and small engine repair' (Anderson, *Other War*, 69). CAP was inexpensive – it required fourteen men per team and was cheaper than keeping these men in the field. They also served another purpose – providing protection from the Vietcong and their demands for produce, especially rice.

CAP did have a major problem, however. Officials in Vietnam (the US Agency for International Development, USAID), with recommendations from military advisors in the field, decided 'what was needed for South Vietnamese Development: "food, grain, medicines, and construction materials, and equipment"' (Anderson, *Other War*, 69). Once ordered, everything went to a safe port, where it was unloaded by Vietnamese, 'then distributed through the Vietnam bureaucracy, down the organization chart from province chief to district chief to village chief and finally to the hamlet chief, who would see that the people who needed the goods got them' (Anderson, *Other War*, 69–70). USAID ended up putting ordered goods into the hands of corrupt Vietnamese, who stole from warehouses and ports and sold everything to the black market, but how could the United States claim its host country was corrupt?

Similar to CAP but offering medical help to local villagers was the Medical Civilian Action Program. The US developed MEDCAP to separate the Vietcong from the civilian population. 'Once a week we take a corpsman out to a vill [village] and give free [medical] treatment. ... There's a lot of skin infections, simple things like that. Villagers can't figure out why they don't heal up but they keep taking baths in the same stream they shit and piss in. We teach them how to use soap but the next time we go back we see the same new bars we gave them. If they got some serious illness or need an operation, we bring them into a hospital in Da Nang' (Anderson, *Other War*, 67).

Doc Holley, after six months in the bush ready, willing, and able to use his weapon, was just learning what his job at the rear would be: 'I will be expected to make three or four trips per week under the MEDCAP program to the local villages to treat their ill, in an effort to "win the Hearts and Minds" of the natives' (21). 'Thousands of doctors, dentists, nurses, and medical technicians spent hundreds of thousands of hours administering modern medicine and teaching basic standards of hygiene, in both large cities and tiny villages, under the Medical Civic Action Program (MEDCAP) of the US Command. Hundreds of clinics, hospitals and schools were built and thousands of Vietnamese trained to staff them. On their own initiative, thousands of American servicemen spent much of their off-duty time working in orphanages and schools' (Anderson, *Grunts*, 203).

'However all the docs I [Doc Holley have] talked to stress the importance of being well armed as they are occasionally mortared or ambushed. What gratitude! Seriously though, this points out one of the biggest problems for any American over here – just who is the enemy, and how can you tell him from the typical peasant farmer who lives out in the paddies and wears black pajamas and thong sandals just like Charlie?' (21).[26] This was not only a problem for doctors in the field, but for everyone in Vietnam.

When all else failed, Nixon decided the answer was Vietnamization, a gradual withdrawal of American forces to leave non-communist South Vietnam forces to establish their own country, with Saigon as the capital. The American plan was to turn over more of the defense of South Vietnam to South Vietnamese trained by Americans. Ironically, the North Vietnamese called this same plan 'de-Americanization' (Safer, 102). To make the South Vietnamese more reliant on themselves, the Americans rebuilt the infrastructure and helped farmers produce more crops. 'These measures helped the government in Saigon double the portion of the South Vietnamese countryside that it controlled. … Despite these achievements, Vietnamization was never as successful as its architects hoped' (Zeitz, 5).

But once the United States became involved in this war, the real reason to continue had little to do with winning hearts and minds. A memo to Secretary of Defense Robert McNamara from the Assistant Secretary of Defense 'set forth American goals in South Vietnam in terms of the following priorities:

'70 per cent – To avoid a humiliating US defeat.
'20 per cent – To keep South Vietnamese territory from Chinese hands.
'10 per cent – To permit the people of South Vietnam to enjoy a better, freer way of life.'[27]

Thus, the official reason given to the American people for the intervention in Vietnam with air power and ground troops made up only one-tenth of the real reason (Stoessinger, 125–126).

Not all of those who went to Vietnam believed in pacification. Some realized that before they came, there was peace and a beautiful country, that had now been destroyed. 'Before me peace … under me peace … over me peace … after me, there must be peace … do we belong here? … We're in harmony with nothing … we scar and crater the earth here … we enhance nothing … in harmony with nothing … nothing … nothing' (Anderson, *Grunts*, 66–67). Duncan, a reporter for *Ramparts Magazine*, discovered that, 'Communist or not, the vast majority of the people were pro-Vietcong and anti-Saigon. I had to accept also that the position "we are in Vietnam because we are in sympathy with the aspirations and desires of the Vietnamese people" was a lie' (91).

Along with the pacification programs, the CIA created the **Phoenix Program** in 1967 to combat insurgency. It was named 'Phoenix' because it was 'a rough translation of *phung hoang*, a mythical Vietnamese bird endowed with omnipotent attributes' (Karnow, 601). Its two goals were: 1) to identify and arrest VC suspects in areas controlled by South Vietnam; 2) to reach a target goal of 3,000 VC suspects per month. Those 3,000 VC suspects were to be arrested and taken to the province interrogation center, where they were to give up information and were then imprisoned. The arresting officers would then provide a dossier to the Provincial Security Council, which decided whether to free the prisoner or to impose a sentence for up to two years. After two years, prisoners were considered rehabilitated (Sperba, excerpted from 2,3,4).

To meet that goal of 3,000 VC a month, many innocent people were charged with being VC. From 1968–1972, about 28,000 people had been captured and imprisoned; another 20,000 were assassinated; 17,000 changed sides from 'maybe VC' to NVA (Karnow, 601). Those frequently targeted were VC organizers, propagandists, and tax collectors; 20,000 were 'neutralized' and 6,187 killed (Karnow, 602).

Captured Vietcong. (Courtesy Vets with a Mission)

Chapter 4

PSYOPS (Psychological Operations)

Both the United States and its allies and North Vietnam used psychology to affect their enemy's emotions, motives, and objective reasoning, and the behavior of governments, organizations, groups, and individuals. One effective psychological operation was to yell or scream at villagers or peasants over a loudspeaker while riding in a helicopter. In one situation, the sound of a baby crying came from the sky. 'You wouldn't have wanted to hear that during daylight, let alone night when the volume and distortion came down through two or three layers of cover and froze us all in place for a moment. And there wasn't much release in the pitched hysteria of the message that followed, hyper-Vietnamese like an icepick in the ear, something like, "Friendly Baby, GVN Baby, Don't Let This Happen to *Your* Baby, Resist the Vietcong Today"' (Herr, 53).

Often, the villagers would hear the name or names of soldiers who had been captured or who had deserted. Herr relates a story by a Belgian mercenary: '"There were a lot of dead VC," he said. "Dozens of them were from the same village that has been giving you so much trouble lately. VC from top to bottom – Michael [Herr], in that village the fucking *ducks* are VC. So the American commander had twenty or thirty of the dead flown up in a sling load and dropped into the village. I should say it was a drop of at least two hundred feet, all those dead Vietcongs, right in the middle of the village."

'He smiled (I couldn't see his eyes).

'"Ah, Psywar!" he said, kissing off the tips of his fingers' (173–174).

SGM Herbert Friedman (Retired) learned from North Vietnamese defectors that Vietnamese loved poetry. '[His] friend Nguyen Tuan Trung explained: From a propagandist point of view, your subject doesn't need much education to understand popular poetry, and a message embedded in such poetry would penetrate a much broader audience, far better than say a Party resolution which typically uses a lot of Chinese-Vietnamese words. Poetry also helps your subject remember the message longer' (H. Friedman, 1).[28]

It was no surprise, then, that 'the Joint US Public Affairs Memorandum 48 dated 15 December 1967 titled Lessons Learned from Evaluation of Allied Psyop Media in Vietnam' encouraged the medium of poetry. 'Do try to make use of the medium of poetry. However, the quality of the Poetry must be at least better than mediocre. More enthusiastic and favorable responses have been obtained from messages in the poetic medium than any other form. Poetry is … a medium … [that has] emotional and/or sentimental appeal. … The resulting product should be field tested before it is distributed' (H. Friedman, 1).[29]

A typical Psyops leaflet depicted a 'North Vietnamese soldier deep in [South Vietnam] thinking of his girl back home' (H. Friedman, 38).

(H. Friedman)

TO THE NVA SOLDIER (first two stanzas)

Oh you, soldier of the North Vietnamese Army!
How very young you still are,
how many springs since you left?
Hear! Spring is here again this year.

Do you still remember the country girl of that evening?
With tears glistening in her eyes,
she bade you farewell.
With hopes of seeing you again when spring comes…(H. Friedman 38)

Another leaflet asks the Vietcong soldier to come home:

'There are a few lines from a longer poem which I
[H. Friedman] will quote

COME BACK

You have followed the Viet Cong since that year
Hamlets and villages were forgotten under evening sunshine
You have been gone about 10 years
Previously, my tears soaked through a dream pillow…
I feel I am alone and my soul is cold
Return to enjoy life…
Come back for a charming and deep love
As anyone else, we need a soon to carry on our hands

(H. Friedman)   (H. Friedman 22)

132

The psychological operations involved more than just leaflets dropped from the air. They also involved what became known as **Chieu Hoi** (Choo Hoy), Vietnamese for 'Open Arms'. The program's purpose was to get the enemy to give up their arms and join the ARVN. A soldier would descend in a helicopter and broadcast these instructions in Vietnamese or drop leaflets after a battle (Terry, 79–80).

One recent defector to the Chieu Hoi program heard that the Joint US Public Affairs Office was looking for poetry that might encourage others to defect. He offered the following poem, sent to me by an anonymous source:[30]

Take a Husband, My Love
By Hoia-Thanh

Take a husband, my love, for my life is ebbing.
Although I must lie to myself when giving you this advice.
But, my darling, I must think of your future …

Have courage, my love, Don't delay
For the fires here in the south burn fiercely (the war rages)
My arm is torn from my body
And with my life's blood I write this last plea …

Please listen, my darling, don't refuse
That I may die in peace without remorse
Darling, please have no anger for me and don't resent your fate
Rather turn your anger and resentment on those
Who have driven me into this senseless war …

Oh, please, do as I say and this is all I ask, Darling
Bury our memories so that our love can melt away with the sinking sun
And my image and all there was of me
Shall fade for ever from my homeland in the North …

Farewell sweetheart, we found no enemies here
Rather it was I who opened fire first
My death is one deserved and I pay for my sin
It is you who remain behind who must suffer …

I am committed
And Eternal bitterness is my lonely fate
Oh, listen to my aching heart
And seek you ideals in LOVE …

The Americans used other means besides poetry to persuade the Vietnamese, especially the Vietcong, to join with them. In a leaflet printed by the Veterans Alliance for

Democracy in Vietnam, Ted Sampley addressed the 'oppressed people of Vietnam'. The following is the opening of the fifteen-page written appeal:

'Democracy for Vietnam
is inevitable;
Join its holy cause.'
by Ted Sampley

Veterans Alliance for Democracy in Vietnam

'Dear oppressed people of Vietnam,
'Stop for a moment and with your whole heart, your whole conscience, your whole body, study what the apostles of Ho Chi Minh's Communist Party have been telling you and learn what a terrible fate those professional revolutionaries have wrought upon you. Their Marxist-Leninist and Ho Chi Minh's "utopian society" ideology is a deadly fraud of which the result is a poverty stricken Vietnam majority forced to live as slaves in one of the poorest countries in the world.'

A surprisingly effective psychological weapon was the **Ace of Spades**. This custom was believed to be so effective that the United States Playing Card Company was asked by Charlie Company, 2nd Battalion 35th Infantry Regiment, and 25th Infantry Division to supply crates of that single card in bulk. The crates were often marked with '*Bicycle Secret Weapon*' ('Bicycle Secret Weapon Playing Card').

To scare the enemy, US soldiers often left the Ace of Spades on dead bodies and even littered the forested grounds and fields with the card. A lot of soldiers 'believed that the ace of spades was a bad omen to the Vietnamese, so…[they] decorated their helmet covers with them' (J. Ebert, 204). Not only was it a bad omen, 'but in Vietnam, it took on a darker and more sinister meaning. The intention was to target the alleged superstitions of the North Vietnamese, by making the Ace of Spades the symbol of death, humiliation, and suffering' ('The Ace of Spades: How American Soldiers used the "death card" as a psychological weapon during the Vietnam War'). If an Ace of

Above left: (Courtesy E. Brown, Jr)

Above right: A deck of Ace of Spades. (Courtesy E. Brown, Jr)

Spades was not available, soldiers used the CBS logo with its eye, although it was not easy to find in Vietnam.

An anonymous source in a 3 November 2023 e-mail debunked the myth of the power of the Ace of Spades: 'The ace of spades was entirely bogus ... the VC had no fear of it'. He continued: 'The army had psychologists and cultural experts [who] said that the ace of spades had no meaning to the Vietnamese. The army published all that but ... like a dog marking its territory, the grunts liked to mark their kills with cards'.

A Japanese reporter, Katsuichi Honda, noted: 'Those things most precious to peasants were not worth a straw in the eyes of these soldiers. But there was one thing which one of them put into his pocket. It was a pack of playing cards found in a shelter. Strangely enough, however, all the cards of the pack were aces' (42–43).

Just as the grunts believed the Ace of Spades spooked the enemy, the North Vietnamese had their own secret weapon – disappearing their dead bodies. American soldiers were shocked, if not spooked, when they returned to the battlefield unable to find any traces of dead VC. Herr said the grunts would go back for a body count after a battle but find no VC casualties. The VC had taken the dead bodies into tunnels, whose entrances were hidden. The grunts learned that the NVA or VC had dragged their dead away which messed with their heads (95).

One night, a patrol was getting ready for a combat assault. The first problem the men encountered was swarms of stinging black ants. Off went all their clothes so that the ants could not get in them and sting. But they knew they were making too much noise, as Mortarman Robert Mountain recounted: 'Here comes Charlie. ... They had to hear us. But they came walking right on up the trail. The patrol still can't understand this. We sprung the doggone ambush in our undershorts, supposedly killed four of 'em. And we don't have no bodies. Haven't got a damn thing to show for it. You can go out there and see where there was some blood. I don't know where these guys go when you kill 'em. It's just that they just vanish. Somewhere. I don't know. Maybe the Twilight Zone' (Terry, 177).

The Vietcong also used poetry as a propaganda weapon: 'This Vietcong poetry leaflet was found in Vinh Long in July of 1966. ... The poem asks the South Vietnamese troops to stop serving with the Americans, because when they lose the war the Americans will all return home. The Vietnamese Army veterans will have nowhere to go. Vietnam is their country. The leaflet argues that the Vietnamese troops should return home to their villages and families. Some of the text is:[31]

YOU WILL EVENTUALLY COME TO LIVE ON YOUR ANCESTRAL LAND

Should the Americans lose, they will go away back to America.
Where will the local village soldiers on the American side go?
Should The Americans lose, they will retreat to America.
And the Viet traitors will swiftly follow.
But you, you are a common low ranking soldier
Where can you go then?
Betrayed, would it b better to remind yourself of your compatriots?
How Can you depart the land of your father, your ancestors?

135

Your wife and children stay here.
Even a falling leaf will stay near the roots, where would you go?
Be considerate and think it over!
Cease to be a soldier, return home!
Your field and garden await you
Your wife and children long too the reunion!
Care for your land laboriously.
Live a life innocent and free of worries! (Anon 49)

Below is the cover of a twenty-four-page anti-government booklet, produced by the National Liberation Front:[32]

'[The cover of] this booklet depicts a Vietcong holding ripped-out barbed wire standing over a caricature of an American soldier and a Vietnamese with a dollar sign on his shirt, obviously their concept of a collaborator. In the background we see a burning building, and this would seem to be a strategic hamlet that the Vietcong have raided and "freed" the prisoners. The entire book is filled with patriotic and anti-Government poems' (Anon 52).

Doc Holley shared one of the leaflets with his wife: 'I am enclosing a VC propaganda leaflet we found in hooch on one of our MEDCAPs to a local hamlet. Can you believe

(Anon 52)

the spelling and grammar? You'd think they would have found someone to do a little better job with the English.

> "'AMERICAN GI's [all errors in the text are VC errors]:
> "'From the 1st to Nov 5th, 1.968. The united states commitec for demand of ending the US aggressive war in Vietnam hold 'the week for united states armymen' which support to your opposing the war movement en demand for repatriation. Don't let american youths go on to south Vietnam and dic uselessly and senselessly. The Vietnam people and youths and students and pupil as well as the World people warmly wellcome and give whole hearted support and response to the creation of the united states committee. GI's … Oppose the US aggressive war Vietnam.
> "'Demand the US government to stop immediately the US aggressive war in Vietnam and it must negotiate directly south Vietnam national front of liberation.
> "'Demand the US government brings home all US troops.
> "'Let the Vietnamese settle themselves their our affairs.
> "'Demand your repatriation refuse to go to the battefiel oppose your going to slaughler the Vietnamese people who are struggling for their independence, freedom and peace. That's the only way for you to defend the honer and pestige of america and save the happiness of your families and yousse lves'" (85).

A black soldier tells Wallace Terry: 'They had us naïve, young, dumb-ass niggers believin' that this war was fought for democracy and independence. It was fought for money. All those big corporations made billions on the war, and then America left' (256). Both the United States and North Vietnam tried to dissuade any more fighting – come join *OUR* side. Leaflets and small booklets were dropped or handed out by both sides.

Another North Vietnam psychological weapon was **Hanoi Hannah** or **Helen**, who became the North Vietnamese propaganda voice to the United States soldiers.[33] Hanoi Hannah read a letter to a particular LRRP that had been in a mail drop from a helicopter that crashed. It was all about how much his wife missed him (Terry, 39). But what really got to the bloods (black soldiers) was what Hanoi Hannah said after Martin Luther King, Jr, was assassinated: 'Soul Brothers, go home. Whitey raping your mothers and your daughters, burning down your homes. What you over here for? This is not your war. The war is a trick of the Capitalist empire to get rid of the blacks' (Terry, 39). LRRP Ford was bothered: "I really thought – I really started believing it, because it was too many blacks than there should be in infantry' (Terry, 39).

Hanoi Hannah
By Yusef Komunyakaa

Ray Charles! His voice
calls from waist-high grass,
& we duck behind gray sandbags.
"Hello, Soul Brothers. Yeah,

Georgia's also on my mind."[34]
Flares bloom over the trees.
'Here's Hannah again.
Let's see if we can't
light her goddamn fuse
this time.' Artillery
shells carve a white arc
against dusk. Her voice rises
from a hedgerow on our left.
'It's Saturday night in the States.
Guess what your woman's doing tonight.
I think I'll let Tina Turner
tell you, you homesick GIs.'
Howitzers buck like a herd
of horses behind concertina.
'You know you're dead men,
don't you? You're dead
as King today in Memphis.
Boys, you're surrounded by
General Tran Do's division.'
Her knife-edge song cuts
deep as a sniper's bullet.
'Soul Brothers, what you dying for?'
We lay down a white-klieg
trail of tracers. Phantom jets
fan out over the trees.
Artillery fire zeroes in.
Her voice grows flesh
& we can see her falling
into words, a bleeding flower
No one knows the true name for.
'You're lousy shots GIs.'
Her laughter floats up
as though the airways are
buried under our feet. (141)

The North Vietnamese soldiers weren't immune to the same psychological fears that Hanoi Hannah provoked in black soldiers. Although many had been smoking *rosa canina* (made from a plant and its flowers), they told stories about smelling their own blood as a prediction of death and monsters chasing them. 'Many said they saw groups of headless black American soldiers carrying lanterns aloft, walking through in Indian file. Others paled in terror as horrible, primitive wild calls echoed inside their skulls in the rainy, dewy mornings, thinking they were the howls of pain from the last group of orangutans said to have lived in the Central Highlands in former times. ... Soon there sprang up tiny altars in each squad hut and tent, altars to the comrades-in-arms' (Ninh, 13–14).

'Many white people are ungrateful for what Black people mean to America, what we have been, what we have done, what we have given them and what we have endured.' (Stewart, 'What White Voters See in Herschel Walker')

One of the more effective propaganda the North employed was to pit black against white Americans. The issue of **race** had long been a problem in the United States, but after President Truman integrated the armed forces on 26 July 1948, it became a problem for the military, never more so than in Vietnam.

Marine Lieutenant Colonel David Tomsky stated that the greatest racial tension he ever encountered as a Marine was during the Vietnam War: 'As a practical matter, you cannot have a racist Marine in an integrated organization and expect to train and fight together as a unit' (Belew, 150).

'I have an intuitive feeling that the Negro Servicemen have a better understanding than whites of what the war is about.' (General William C. Westmoreland, US Army, Saigon, 1967) (epigraph to Terry's *Bloods*).

Even before Hanoi Hannah used the death of Martin Luther King, Jr to urge black soldiers to turn on their oppressors – white soldiers – race was a volatile issue for the

A blood, and bloods with their platoon. (Courtesy D. Phillips)

soldiers in Vietnam. Many soldiers commented on the racial issues. Platoon Leader Biggers 'learned ... you have to take a person for what he feels. ... 'Now my platoon had a lot of Southerners as well as some Midwesterners. Southerners at the first sign of a black officer being in charge of them were somewhat reluctant. But then, when they found that you know what's going on and you're trying to keep them alive, then they tried to be the best damn soldiers you've got. Some of the black soldiers were the worse [*sic*] I had because they felt that they had to jive on me. They wanted to let me know, Hey, man. Take care of me, buddy. You know I'm your buddy. That's bull' (Terry, 111).

Duncan, a reporter for *Ramparts*, served as an NCO for the Special Forces Procurement Office. His commanding officer, General Yarborough, requested that no Negroes be assigned to his unit. 'Our final instructions from the captain directly in charge of the program had some succinct points I stood in shocked disbelief to hear, "Don't send me any niggers. Be careful, however, not to give the impression that we are prejudiced in Special Forces. You won't find it hard to find an excuse to reject them"' (78): meaning they wouldn't pass the written test, wouldn't pass the physical, or would have a criminal record.

In another incident, a black sergeant saved the life of a white man, for which he received the Bronze Star. He stated: 'Hell, he was one of my men. Black or white, I would have done the same even if I got shot to hell in the process' (Terry, 151–152).

Combat Engineer Bryant learned that white soldiers got just as scared as he did. One member in his platoon announced that he was a member of the Ku Klux Klan, but when a black soldier saved him from certain death, he changed his attitude towards blacks. Other black soldiers noticed: 'We didn't have racial incidents like what was happening in the rear area, 'cause we had to depend on each other. We were always in the bush. ... Racial incidents rarely happened in the field but back in base camp, they saw Confederate flags. Although they knew they were not racial statements, still they took the flags personally' (Terry, 38).

Roy Parks, a Vietnam vet, said racial relations 'was a tough situation for lots of people. I wouldn't have called myself prejudiced, but a lot of those boys were when they

Wounded Marine dragged to safety. (Courtesy Vets with a Mission)

got there. One thing is for sure, they weren't for long. It didn't matter who you were, we were in it together and you trusted them with your life' (Kristi Ramsey, 68). They quickly learned that bullets don't discriminate. Bobby Ward, a veteran who attended my Thursday evening program, was asked about racial issues in Vietnam. He said: 'There aren't any races in the Army; we're all one', all helping each other survive (Elkins, 17).[35]

Marine Lieutenant Marlantes amplified that point: 'I saw how [the war] threw together young men from diverse racial and ethnic backgrounds and forced them to trust one another with their lives. It was a racial crucible that played an enormous, if often unappreciated, role in moving America towards real integration' (2).

But it was the death of Martin Luther King, Jr that brought the racial issue in Vietnam to a head. 'But [Hanoi Hannah] didn't unsettle the brothers as much as when she got on the air after Martin Luther King died,[36] and they was rioting back home' (Terry, 39). Reporter Herr didn't underestimate the trouble King's assassination caused: 'The death of Martin Luther King intruded on the war in a way that no other outside event had ever done. In the days that followed, there were a number of small, scattered riots, one or two stabbings, all of it denied officially ... A southern colonel on the general's staff told me that it was a shame, a damn shame, but I had to admit (didn't I?) that he'd been a long time asking for it' (158). Later, Herr met up with a black staff sergeant, a friend who'd ignored him when the news was everywhere.

'"Now what I gonna do?" he said.' Herr responded: 'I'm a great one to ask.' The sergeant continued: 'But dig it. Am I gonna take 'n' turn them guns aroun' on my own people? Shit!'

Herr wrote: 'That was it, there was hardly a black NCO anywhere who wasn't having to deal with that. We sat in the dark, and he told me that when he'd walked by me that afternoon it had made him sick. He couldn't help it' (158–159).

'Dr King's death – and the reaction of some white troops to it – threatened to destroy unity. [Marine Roger Harris recalls that] at Can Ranh Bay, a group of white soldiers hoisted a Confederate flag over the naval headquarters and paraded around in makeshift Ku Klux Klan robes.[37] ... We are supposed to be American soldiers fighting a war in Vietnam. But it seems as though the white man thinks we're still at home' (Ward, 303).

Robert Minter, a black soldier, reported: 'We came off patrol only to learn about Martin Luther King's assassination. Many white officers wanted to disarm the black soldiers as they came in from patrol. We discussed it among our fellow soldiers white and black. We decided we were soldiers here in Vietnam, and needed to be unified, not separated by events in the states. We all agreed to hold on to our weapons' (Baxter, 178).

Report from the Skull's Diorama
[A Diorama is a 3-D representation of scenes from the past:
like Roosevelt charging up San Juan Hill.]
By Yusef Komunyakaa

Dr King's photograph
comes at me from *White Nights*
like Hoover's imagination at work,
dissolving into a scenario
at Firebase San Juan Hill:

our helicopter glides in closer,
down to the platoon of black GIs
back from night patrol
with five dead. Down
into a gold whirl of leaves
dust-deviling the fire base.
A field of black trees
stakes down the morning sun.
With the helicopter blades
knife-fighting the air,
yellow leaflets quiver
but the red-bordered
leaflets tell us
VC didn't kill
Dr Martin Luther King.
The silence etched into their skin
is also mine. Psychological
warfare colors the napalmed hill
gold-yellow. When our gunship
flies out backwards, rising
above the men left below
to blend in with the charred
landscape, an AK-47
speaks, with the leaflets
clinging to the men & stumps,
waving to me across the years. (156)

Captain Norman Alexander McDaniel, a POW, recalled: 'When Dr King was assassinated, they called me in for interrogation to see if I would make a statement critical of the United States. I said no, I don't know enough about it. They wanted all of us to make statements they could send abroad or make tapes they could play to the GIs. They wanted me to tell black soldiers not to fight because the United States is waging a war of genocide, using dark-skinned people against dark-skinned people. I would tell them no, this is not a black-white war. We're in Vietnam trying to help the South Vietnamese. It is a matter of helping people who are your friends' (Terry, 137).

It was a black and white war, according to Staff Sergeant Don F. Browne:

'When I heard that Martin Luther King was assassinated, my first inclination was to run out and punch the first white guy I saw. I was very hurt. All I wanted to do was go home. I even wrote Lyndon Johnson a letter. I said that I didn't understand how I could be trying to protect foreigners in their country with the possibility of losing my life wherein in my own country people who are my hero, like Martin Luther King, can't even walk the streets in a safe manner … [A few days later a white guy said], "I wish they'd take that nigger's picture off the TV" … And we commenced to give him a lesson in when to use that word and when

142

you should not use that word. To play on the sympathy of the black soldier, the VC would shoot at a white guy, then let the black guy behind him go through, then shoot at the next white guy' (Terry, 167).

To many black soldiers, Dr Martin Luther King Jr's 'Declaration of Independence from the War in Vietnam' in April 1967 made them realize that 'none of the things we claim to be fighting for are really involved' (J. Ebert, 292). To fight for the rights of the South Vietnamese and then to come home where their rights were not guaranteed made black realize the hypocrisy which Dr King had spoken about in his 'Declaration'. Although the Civil Rights movement had made improvements in the lives of blacks, they were still not created equal, still not entitled to equal protection under the law, and still unable to realize the American Dream. 'It takes little effort on the part of any member of any race to imagine the deep rage and bitterness a black grunt on patrol in a nameless jungle or sitting in a foxhole must have felt on hearing that thirty-two of his brothers and sisters had been gunned down in the streets of Detroit in 1967, or that in 1968 his most effective leader in the fight against a second class existence in white, "who-needs-niggers" America – Martin Luther King, Jr – had been assassinated. At some point in their tours, most blacks came to feel that in Vietnam they were being used to fight "whitey's war"' (Anderson, *Grunts*, 186).

'American regionalism also contributed to racial tension during the Vietnam War.' Many Southerners felt it was both a duty and an honor to fight for their country. Thus, a larger proportion of the white soldiers came from the South just as a larger percentage of the black soldiers came from the urban North. This inevitably led to many misunderstandings and tensions between young blacks in the lower ranks and white authority figures (Anderson, *Other War*, 154).

But when the black was in authority, a different sort of dynamic occurred. In the 1989 mock documentary, *84 Charlie Mopic* (see media credits for more information on the film, now available in the United States), a cinematographer asks a soldier from South Carolina how he felt having a black lieutenant. He responded that he would do anything for him in Vietnam, even die for him, but back home he wouldn't know him.

The race issue wasn't restricted to black vs white. The attitude of many soldiers, and in fact many Americans, was expressed in Morley Safer's 1966 interview with General Westmoreland, the US commander of the war. Safer asked him about the tremendous losses by the South Vietnamese army. '"Oh yes," he said. "But you must understand that they are Asians, and they don't really think about death the way we do. They accept it very fatalistically"' (35).

Chapter 5

Foreign Alliances

To fully understand the extent of the war in Vietnam and to understand better what was at stake, we need to describe those who fought for each side, starting with those allied with the South.

South Vietnam and its allies. The largest forces in South Vietnam were the United States and the Army of the Republic of South Vietnam (ARVN). ARVN troops often wore yellow kerchiefs for identification and to distinguish them from the Vietcong and the North Vietnamese Army (NVA) (*Vietnam: Special Newsweek Edition*, 27). 'The ARVN were terrible,' said Johnny Phillips, a Vietnam vet who attended my class, during one Thursday program with college freshmen. 'Not behind us. They were doing what they had to do to survive, I was, too. We got to go home to America; they had to stay in rice paddies. They were scared the US would pull out. They knew that if they were captured, they were killed. I couldn't trust them. I didn't know if they were VC or not – they ran from us, maybe because they didn't want to be recognized' (Vietnam Vet Program 2/4/93).

The Ruff-Puffs were volunteer militia. They sometimes joined ARVN on operations but they were not ARVN. Regional Forces (RF or Ruff-Puffs) were under provincial control. Another similar force, Popular Forces (PF), were a rifle platoon led by non-commissioned officers, They were under the control of the village chief (Anon). 'According to [an] intelligence officer, the Ruff-Puffs were politically as well as militarily suspect; their ranks were believed to be riddled with Vietcong or Vietcong sympathizers' (Caputo, 52). 'The[ir] relaxed behavior … indicated one of three possibilities: no one had warned them that an enemy attack was imminent; they had been told, but were such experienced veterans that mere warnings did not alarm them; or they were the worst soldiers in the world' (Caputo, 52).

'American soldiers also viewed the Vietnamese government … with contempt. It was a government most soldiers believed to be corrupt and hardly worth defending, which prompted GIs throughout the war to wonder why they were enduring all that they were' (J. Ebert, 292).

ARVN
By Randy Cribbs

The ARVN did
Not always stay;
Never a surprise when
Smoke cleared and

They had run away;
Maybe nothing new
To them – who can say;
Better to live
And fight another day.

It is not for me to scold,
My lot has always
Been overbold.
And too, for them,
That insane situation
Was their life,
And we, just another
Group, full of advice;
Clearly they had learned
None of us live twice.
Twelve months and we were done.
No need to run
When the end is in sight,
Easier to stay and fight.

But the ARVN, day after day,
Year after year,
Exercising discretion that
We took as fear.
Sometimes they fought,
Sometimes they ran,
It was their life – we
Were only hired hands. (33)

Another group of South Vietnamese who aided the United States were **Kit Carson Scouts**, also known as **Tiger Scouts** – former VC defectors who collaborated with the

Tiger Scouts, Danny Phillips in middle (Courtesy D. Phillips)

Marines. by choice. General Lewis W. Walt of the Marine Corps said: 'We began to accept … these volunteers, cautiously at first because of the obvious danger both to the volunteer and to our own men. We waited for one of them to turn against us or lead a Marine unit into an ambush – it didn't happen. Instead, we found no adequate substitute for their knowledge' (Walt, 42–44). Doc Holley found their knowledge invaluable, helping them avoid traps and other dangers (Holley, 84).

US Military Personnel. The lowest-ranked soldiers in Vietnam were the **grunts**, also known as ground-pounders. Here is one grunt's comment on being a grunt: 'His grandfather was a "Doughboy", his father was a "GI", and he is a "Grunt"; different names, different times, different wars, but the job of the combat infantry remains the same, it's a 24 hour-a-day working, sweating, grunting job. … But believe it or not, he's sort of proud of the name – GRUNT. … The Grunt is a special kind of man. He lives with dirt, danger, and destiny unknown. In the field, he lives in a way most will never experience even in his worst nightmare; the kind of living that has to be experienced and can never be fully imagined' (Phillips, 44).

My Country
By William Simon

I am Whitey; they call me pimples;
eighteen and from Nebraska,
stalking the enemy
in the mud of the Delta. Eyes focused
on the back of my neck.
Flying ants in the food, mosquito sucking the blood on my
wrist, chiggers between my toes, and,
the enemy behind the trees.
There are no wheat fields in the Delta.

They call me Chico because they do not know:
I am Jose Maria of the barrio.
The Texas Captain calls me greaser
and gives me ribbons and medals for killing VC,
little yellow men nobody can see.
I kill to live.
At home I am one they cannot see.

They call me Helicopter Jockey:
Below in the jungle, carpeted
with blood of the men I have killed. I see the
faces of men I have never seen.
Daily riding the clouds, appointed scythe-swinger of
the aluminum age,
silvery engines of slaughter: hellfire raining from above.
Dead and dying are the same.

I am the Texas Captain, Korea's ribbons on my chest;
burn a village and return – a week's ground gained
in a day, lost to the night.
They're still firing, call for the planes.
There's blood on my shirt: a medic. I'm
dying, save me.

I am America.
I am America dying in Asia. (Rottmann, 42)

The grunts were 'babies. The average age of the men was nineteen. They were mostly black and Hispanic city kids and poor midwestern farm boys. ... This was a war of teenagers – poor lower-class men who gave their lives and their limbs' (Harrod, 4). 'We were boys mostly and thought everything was possible' (Caputo, 263). When we put our soldiers on the ground in a little country called Vietnam, most of our soldiers didn't know how to spell it or know where it was. They dragged their bags with them and deplaned at the Replacement Depot **(Repo Depo)**, the place that would give them their orders. Most of them would never see each other again, assigned to different platoons, and to their individual Military Occupational Specialty **(MOS)**.

'The new arrivals [called Newby, FNG (Fucking New Guy) or Cherry] called them grunts you know, the guys from the bush in Nam, and they're supposed to be the gungiest [the most gung-ho] mothers around' (Anderson, *Grunts*, 15). Grunts were always trying to do things for you: 'like the time this grunt tried to give me his mattress to sleep on or the way grunts in Hue one day had tried to give me their helmets and flak jackets because I had turned up without my own. If you tore your fatigues ... you'd have new or at least fresh ones within minutes and never know where they came from. They always took care of you' (Herr, 136–137).

The grunts learned early on that they 'were no longer in a geographical place named Vietnam. They were in a box of adversity and suffering, all the things one could think of to complete the old phrase, "anything but that". But this box had no limits – they would walk but they would never reach the other side, the end. ... They were now the young newly-made old; bodies carrying their own corpses of youth' (Anderson, *Grunts*, 49–

Grunt on the front of a car. (Courtesy E. Brown, Jr)

50). Soldiers were fighting while trying to adjust to the heat and not enough drinkable water. Heat exhaustion was common, even at 9am when the temperature would reach 104° (Anderson, *Grunts*, 112). Other maladies included foot fungus – socks and boots were constantly wet from the rivers and jungle – and a fungus called jungle rot, causing cracks and craters in the skin that oozed pus and rotted. Soldiers asked for baby powder from home and socks to keep their feet dry and protected.

Important Things
By Randy Cribbs

> In youth I
> Dreamed about things
> I could reap;
> Now, all that I
> Would gladly let
> Others keep,
> But for a pair
> Of dry socks, a
> Peaceful night's sleep,
> And for a hooch that
> Does not leak! (113)

The grunts' experience in Vietnam was unpleasant. They received too little mail, too little food, had to carry 80 pounds on their back every day, and had little to no

Time out. (Courtesy D. Phillips)

understanding of US strategy. If that were not enough, fear of death and of the enemy, dealing with the jungle with its razor-sharp grass and its wait-a-minute vines, with torrential rains and high humidity, and with leeches and fire ants, made life miserable. 'Despite all this the grunt did his job well' (http://www.vwam.com/thewaryears.html).

When they had time to write home, they asked for Kool-Aid and Jell-O gelatin to disguise the taste of water that had been treated with chlorine or iodine because of dysentery due to unclean water – and socks, socks, socks, to keep their feet dry.

Life of a Grunt
All days just seemed to blend into the next. What with killing time and the occasional battle, soldiers got used to the daily routine of life in Vietnam: 'Reveille, roll call, calisthenics, morning chow, working parties, noon chow, close order drill, working parties, calisthenics, evening chow, liberty call for those who had liberty, guard mount for those who did not, evening colors, taps, lights-out' (Caputo, 29).

Nurses talking with a platoon. (Courtesy D. Phillips)

Above and left: Life in a platoon. (Courtesy D. Phillips)

Above: China Beach. (Courtesy D. Phillips)

Right: Bob Hope in Vietnam. (Public domain)

Each morning, they had to take a prescribed number of pills: Yellow malaria pills (chloroquine) which caused diarrhea and pink salt tablets which caused nausea. Later soldiers were given weekly doses of Dapsone for malaria. These pills, like Chloroquine, also caused diarrhea (Anderson, *The Grunts* 216, Holley 102).

Their living quarters changed daily. Back at base camp, they lived in barracks; but in the field, they lived in Vietnamese-like hooches or tents.

But there were some benefits – letters from home, beer, and an occasional show back at base camp. Bob Hope, Connie Francis, and other Hollywood stars went to base camps in Vietnam to provide much-needed relief from the soldiers' dreary existence. 'Thanks to Connie Francis and all the other members of her show, we felt close to home for a few moments. ... The personalities who entertained in the war zone will never know how much we appreciated their efforts' (Ketwig, 92).

Once per year, troops had leave, often referred to as Rest and Relaxation (R&R). Many took their leave in Thailand, Japan, Malaya, Taiwan, the Philippines, Singapore, and Australia; some even stayed in Vietnam at resorts like China Beach, but only a lucky few went to Hawaii. Troops referred to it as 'I & I' – intoxication and intercourse.

Doc Holley wrote to his wife about their upcoming reunion in Hawaii: 'I guess you are packing your bags to come see me. So, you probably won't get this letter until you return, but I've been thinking about you and had to write anyway. ... I can't really believe that in three days we will be together. ... I'm still a little concerned about how I will seem to you. I know I've changed some. So much has happened to me and around me since I last saw you' (Holley, 143).

If they weren't meeting their wives or girlfriends, Americans and Australians on R&R went to China Beach – My Khe beach in the City of Da Nang. In 1988, television introduced *China Beach* to the nation. The drama series was set in the fictitious 510th Evacuation Hospital. The cast included actors playing US Army doctors and nurses, as well as those who came to the hospital. The series was based on Linda Van Devanter's experience published in *Home Before Morning*. Unlike *MASH*, which occurred during the Korean conflict, China Beach provided little humor, portraying instead the seriousness of the war and those who fought and were wounded during it.

If you decided to spend your R&R in Saigon, known as 'Sin City', there were always 'boom-boom' girls to be had. On his way to Vietnam, Lieutenant Puller avoided the prostitutes in Okinawa that, according to one of his friends, 'had elevated prostitution to an art form' (75). Wherever there were bases or airports with soldiers travelling, there were prostitutes. Near Sin City, soldiers could buy 'two half-gallons of Gilby's gin for $1.65 each. We take a bottle to papa san. Buy a girl for $5 or $10. Combat Engineer Bryant swears the girls were clean because medical personnel would come check them out and get shots if they [were] needed' (Terry 26). In fact, soldiers learned that girls were available almost everywhere they went.

A visit to the United Services Organization (USO) provided another means to forget the war. 'Established by request of the President [Franklin Roosevelt], the USO [is] a private, non-profit organization providing morale and recreational services to [armed] forces ... and sponsored by the National Catholic Community Service, National Jewish Welfare Board, National Travelers Aid Association, Salvation Army, Young Men's Christian Association, and Young Women's Christian Association' (Rottman, *FUBAR*, 112–113). It operated many centers in and around Vietnam, with goodies such as books, milkshakes, and company. The USO is usually linked to its Christmas show, which for many years featured Bob Hope plus a starlet or two. One such starlet, Sue Thompson – known for such songs as *Sad Movies* and *Norman* – was able to get to more remote bases because she traveled with a trio. She wrote to her parents: 'Tonight we are at Can Tho, a huge American air base. You can see the fighting (flashes from guns), hear the mortars. We're fairly secure most of the time ... but must be aware that things can pop right in our midst.' The trip left her shaken: 'A heartbreaking – and heartwarming – experience ... I'll never be the same again' (Genzlinger, 'Sue Thompson'). The show, welcomed by the troops, was

Boom Boom girl. (Courtesy Danny Phillips)

also a source of danger, as the enemy knew exactly where a large group of soldiers would be (Herr, 7).

At one center, the USO sponsored a Seder for Jewish service members. 'The armed forces shipped 18 tons of "Kosher for Passover" delicacies, including sacramental wine, gefilte fish, matzoh and boiled chicken, to Vietnam for the celebrations. New kitchen utensils were provided for their preparation' (*The New York Times*, quoted in *Vietnam War Diary*, 80). Birthdays, Easter, and Christmas were also celebrated; anything they could do to bring a sense of normalcy to the soldiers' lives.

In an interview with one former USO member, Susan Wimmers, she explained that she wanted to be in Vietnam in some capacity because she was patriotic. 'I was too old to join the Red Cross,' she said with a laugh. 'You had to be between the ages of 22–25 and I was 26. I went to many of the centers in Vietnam. One of them was in a combat

Christmas in Vietnam. (Courtesy D. Phillips)

Outside USO Club. (Courtesy D. Phillips)

zone, although I don't think it was supposed to be. In our club facilities, we offered 13 shops, a restaurant or two, a rec room, a library, and a small chapel. We also had the first base phones to the US. Now we didn't have plumbing; we had a "Squat-a-toilet". We had luncheons for the women in Vietnam. We heard about an ambulance standing around that was a brothel, but I'm not sure about that.'

Books
By Randy Cribbs

Those beat up books.
Passed around
One to another.
Paperbacks:
  Most without a cover.

Stuffed in
Pockets, shirts, packs,
Never left unattended
In the rack.
Torn, dog-eared;
Muddy,
 Bloody.

Selected pages removed
To be read in solitude
When literary worth
  Bordered on Lewd.

Not artistic richness.
No profound truths
  Vomited forth;
Never philosophic doctrine;
  Plain words,
Narrative to free our mind
  Of the here and now;
  To take us from
  That place,
    Somehow. (59)

The men were taken care of in other ways as well. The most welcome was receiving mail from family, friends, and loved ones. Turn-around time for mail was about two weeks. But for grunts on the move, mail had a hard time catching up with them. When a resupply helicopter finally arrived, 'the grunts bent all their attention to their mail. They tore it open and studied over and over the words written by feminine, parental, brotherly, sisterly, or wifely hands. The packages full of Hershey bars and canned hot dogs and peaches and apples and peanuts and homemade cookies and cakes were passed around the hill' (Anderson, *Grunts*, 58). For most, mail was just about the only thing that kept them going. Doc Holley wrote to his wife, Sondra: 'Keep your letters coming. When I don't get one, I hear my men saying, "Well, Doc's got a case of the ass today. He didn't get a letter from Sondra!" People back in the World have no idea what a morale boost mail call is to those of us over here. If I couldn't get letters from you, I think I'd go crazy, really! I read your letters, and for a few minutes, it's almost as if I'm home with you' (103).

Mail Call
By Randy Cribbs

Writing home. (Courtesy D. Phillips)

Easy to tell who did well
  And who appeared
    Under a spell.

Last name called
  And still some linger,
Longing to feel the paper
Between trebling fingers.
Glancing down
  To the ground,
Searching for that
  Not to be found.

Just yesterday, soft
  Words of forever

  Touch again, never.
Seeing her last
  As she turned
And now
  Spurned.

Mail call;
No cookies to share,
  No one to care,
Not even that special one—
  Back there…(55)

Charlie Plumb, a POW for nearly six years, said: 'The V never made us wait for "Dear Johns"' (160). The V did, however, stash mail for POWs, undelivered yet not destroyed. 'Once a POW, alone in the room, found a bushel basket filled with letters from the States. He grabbed a couple of them, concealed them under his sleeve, brought them back to the cell, and passed contents through the walls to their overjoyed owners' (161). Mail was moved by helicopter when resupply was called for or if benefits (**bennies**) were dropped. Lynda Van Devanter, a chagrined nurse, said in a letter home: (150)

'Dear Mom and Dad,
'I hang my head. Mail call just brought six letters from you in addition to the nicest care package I've ever seen. Postmarks go back as far as a month. I don't know what the holdup was, but mail call was bright for the first time in a very long time. I'm sorry I misjudged you. It's hard to keep my spirits up when there's no mail to cheer me, the move to An Khe was canceled again. The rumor mill is still buzzing, but this is supposed to be the final word.'

Mail – a Good Day
By Randy Cribbs

Getting mail now, all those years later
Seems so routine;
Not much excitement about what
Lies within the box, unseen.

But back then, in that land
Way over there,
Mail was hope, fear,
A package of care.

Chow out of a can,
Okay;
Listening to politicians
With nothing to say,
No problem; but mail call –
Do not delay.

A good day was getting mail,
To hear from anyone at all,
Your name yelled out by
The angel doing mail call.

We all knew who was getting
Mail, who was being let down,
The Dear John from
Some far away town. (56)

Sometimes mail did not bring good news – Dear John letters, or those telling the soldier that someone had stolen his girl. Lynda Van Devanter, who was a nurse in training for duty in 'Nam, explained to her friend: 'I overheard a drill sergeant say to one of his men, "Your best friend, Jody, is already pumping your girlfriend, Mary Jane Rottencrotch, asshole. When you walked out the front door, he slipped in the back." It's supposed to help turn the guys into killers' (68).

Letters from loved ones were the most valuable connection to the World; but letter campaigns meant that many veterans received letters and packages from people they did not know: 'Col. Ned Edward Felder was serving in Vietnam when he was surprised by a care package from a stranger. It wasn't the contents that touched him; it was the idea that someone had taken the trouble to send it. ... The Kindness felt enormous' (Svrluga, 1).[38]

The Dear John was the most devastating because that close connection was gone at the worst time of a grunt's life. With that connection broken, comes isolation; it's not the grunt's fault that a controversial war led to 'an increase in Dear John letters. As the war became more and more unpopular back home, it became increasingly common for girlfriends, fiancées, and even wives to dump the soldiers who depended upon them. Their letters were an umbilical cord to the sanity and decency that they believed they were fighting for' (Grossman, 277).

Supplies and benefits (or bennies) also helped take care of the men. As much as grunts could carry on their backs, they still needed resupplies out in the field brought to them on helicopters. 'The blunders, trials and missed chances of the day were set aside in the exhilaration over what the re-supply helicopter had brought – carrots, cucumbers, tomatoes, C-rats, new socks and jungle uniforms, orange juice, grape juice, mail, water, and 300 mortar rounds, many more than the Company could carry. "Hey, B.J., you see them boxes off to the side? Mortar rounds, hundreds of them. That means we stay for awhile, Man!"' (Anderson, *Grunts*, 110–111).

Goody Drop
By Randy Cribbs

Helicopters resupplying troops.
(Courtesy D. Phillips)

Morning,
After a night
Passed with outcry and
Much uproar,
It descends
From the heavens,
Hesitant, then quickly drops
Into our hell.

Briefly outlined against the pale
Daybreak and then
Gone again;
From its bowels
For us fell,
Happiness
In cans of hot chow
And great bags of mail. (39)

'There was mail service [for North Vietnamese soldiers], although because of the American firepower along the Ho Chi Minh Trail and the need to carry the mail much of the way via courier, a lot of it never arrived or took months to do so if it did' (Dunnigan and Nofi, 270–271). This is confirmed by Morley Safer's conversation with a former North Vietnamese soldier. Safer asked him: 'What about mail … messages from home?' The ex-soldier replied: 'For us? No, never for us. Some of us brought along with us letters we received from sweethearts before we left for the South. We passed them among ourselves and read them aloud and laughed and teased each other with some of the things girlfriends say to soldiers going off to war' (45).

Religion also helped relieve some of the tensions of daily grunt life. In 1968, there were about 300 chaplains in Vietnam. Chaplains would remind soldiers that others had similar feelings, that they were not alone. They would also remind soldiers to take pride in themselves, to take care of themselves, to be the best soldier they could be. Then others would respect them. Ketwig recalled one chaplain telling him: 'It's called battlefield religion, son. You'll get over it. You'll do what you have to do, and you'll go home. The worthwhile things in life are never easy, and I want you to feel free to come in and talk with me any time' (95). But that was not all many of them did. Because every day seemed to blend into the next, chaplains often reminded the troops, 'Today is Sunday. Let us pray.' Some chaplains went with the men.[39]

One platoon, while waiting for a helicopter to land to take out some of the heat casualties, was surprised: 'When the helicopter touched down it discharged the last person in the whole division the grunts expected to see – the battalion Chaplain. Chaplains are considered by most Marines to be largely useless appendages on the *corpus militaris*. This day, however, the grunts would change their minds about chaplains, for not only had this one bothered to leave his air-conditioned chapel to come out and try to cheer them up a little, but this member of the general's "God Squad" was actually going to hump with them, share the merciless heat with them' (Anderson, *Grunts*, 53).

Al Davis, a Vietnam vet, said he 'never saw a chaplain' (Vietnam Vet Program, 2/4/93). Grunts had little respect for them – they were quick to note the hypocrisy of blessing men who were going out to kill. They thought there was something wrong with a chaplain 'blessing the troops, their mission, their guns, their killing. As one of the men put it, "Whatever we were doing … murder … atrocities … God was *always* on our side"' (Lifton, 163).

Rifleman Kirkland told Wallace Terry: 'Even the chaplains would turn the thing around in the Ten Commandments. They'd say, "Thou shall not murder", instead of "Thou shall not kill". Basically, you had a right to kill, to take and seize territory, or to protect lives of each other. Our conscience was not to bother us once we engaged in that kind of killing. As long as we didn't murder, it was like the chaplain would give you his blessings. But you knew all of that was murder anyway' (Terry, 91).

Man of God
By Larry Rottmann

The chaplain of the 25th Aviation Battalion at Cu Chi
Prays for the souls of the enemy
On Sunday mornings
And earns flight pay as a helicopter door gunner
during the rest of the week. (Rottmann 24)

Herr understood the situation. A shy Indian boy from Arizona asked him where he could find a chaplain. He'd just volunteered for a 'suicide squad, two jeeps that were going to drive across the airstrip with mortars and a recoilless rifle. It looked bad … It might be bad. He just had a feeling about it, he'd seen what always happened to guys whenever they got that feeling, at least he *thought* it was that feeling, a bad one, the worst he'd ever had. "Listen, though. If it happens … I think it's going to … will you make sure the colonel tells my folks I was looking for a chaplain anyway?" I promised, and the jeeps loaded and drove off' (183). The next morning, Herr learned there had been a small firefight – and that the Indian boy was A-okay.

Fear of losing his own life is not what always draws a military person to a chaplain. Rabbi Arnold Resnicoff, a retired Navy captain, told a story about a colonel in Bosnia. '"Chaplain," he said, "the Army trains me to kill people and break things. Your job, Chaplain, is to keep me from ever getting to a point where I like doing it"' (Sherman, 119).

And Then There Were None
By Stan Platke

Men bled
Many dead

A world safe for democracy
But not for life
Rather funny
In an unfunny sort of way

And the Bible said
That when He came
Everyone was dead
No one left to claim

Men bled
Many dead

Yea as I walk through the valley of death
I shall fear no evil
For the valleys are gone
And only death awaits

And I am the evil. (Rottmann, 101)

Rabbi Mark Goldman shared with his temple a picture of his GI Kit. (Courtesy E. Brown, Jr)

Chaplains had to be willing to assist any person in need of spiritual help, no matter what their religion or rank. Each chaplain was issued a GI kit with religious items that most soldiers could relate to. Rabbi Mark Goldman shared with his temple a picture of his GI kit from the war.

Letters, beer, the USO shows, and religion helped the soldiers relax, but it was **humor** that got them through. If nothing else cheered the men, there was always laughter, practical jokes, and just general nonsense. When you are powerless, you might as well laugh, even if it makes no sense. 'Once in some thick jungle corner with some grunts standing around, a correspondent said, "Gee, you must really see some beautiful sunsets in here", and they almost pissed themselves laughing' (Herr, 10). Johnny, at one of the Vietnam vet Programs, confessed that in a secure area he fired his weapon, everyone landed in the mud, and then he just said, 'Sorry, my weapon misfired' (2/4/93).

'Genuine humor served to take some of the sting out of life in the field. Every unit had its clowns who somehow made the worst bearable and helped everyone endure beyond their limits. Such men were worth their weight in gold in helping to maintain a unit's morale' (J. Ebert, 289).

Doc Holley and his ambulance crew were once fired on. Doc called for some help, because the only way to return to safety was by the same road they came by. But even with the escort of a deuce-and-a-half (a 2½-ton truck) with a machine gun mounted on the top, five shots passed over their heads. 'You could actually hear them whiz over the top of our jeep. Mitch looked over at me, grinning, and said, "That wasn't even close, Doc. Besides, you never hear the one that kills you anyway!" We all burst out laughing. It's really amazing how humor plays along with fear' (46).

The Vietcong also used humor to lighten their lives, as it wasn't only the Americans who needed to laugh. Herr reported a joke from the VC: 'Once after an ambush that killed a lot of Americans, they [the VC] covered the field with copies of a photograph that showed one more young, dead American, with the punch line mimeographed on the back, "Your X-rays have just come back from the lab and we think we know what your problem is"' (35).

Most of their shift, the grunts spent in the **Boonies**,[40] in country, in the bush, in the 'Nam, out in the field, away from the firebase or base camp. Roving reporter Michael Herr described the boonies as a place 'where [the grunts] were deprived of all information except what they'd gathered for themselves on either side of the tree line' (47). Because they did not receive information on where they were going and why they were going there, they often felt that the mission was absurd or useless. The order to 'dig-in' was especially frustrating, as often the platoon leader told them to stop digging. For the grunts, one of the most unpleasant experiences was a change in orders. After humping all day, only to be told that they had to hump some more, led to much bitching and whining. 'Eat the apple, fuck the corps' was a typical reaction to such changes in orders. Then, of course, because their orders had changed, they had to hurry up and wait for helicopters to come and move them somewhere else (Anderson, *Grunts*, 35–36).

Grunts humped in all kinds of weather, never knowing from one moment to the next whether it would be a monsoon, a clear day, or light rain. Marion Lee ('Sandy') Kempner wrote to his parents and a few others about humping: 'I spent a three-day "walk in the sun" (and paddies and fields and mountains and impenetrable jungle and saw grass and ants, and screwed-up radios and no word, and deaf radio operators, and no chow, and too many C-rations, and blisters and torn trousers and jungle rot, and wet socks and sprained ankles and no heels, and, and, and) for a battalion that walked on roads and dikes the whole way and a regiment that didn't even know where the battalion was, finished off by a 14,000-meter forced march on a hard road' (Edelman, 36).

Helicopter unloading troops. (Courtesy with a Mission)

Kempner's 'walk in the sun' didn't mention everything he carried in his rucksack that hung off the straps or belt or around his neck – all of which weighed about half his weight again. What did he carry? O'Brien provides us a list:

> 'They carried USO stationery and pencils and pens. They carried Sterno, safety pins, trip flares, signal flares, spools of wire, razor blades, chewing tobacco, liberated joss sticks and statuettes of the smiling Buddha, candles, grease pencils, The Stars and Stripes, fingernail clippers, Psy Ops leaflets, bush hats, bolos, and much more. Twice a week, when the resupply helicopters came in, they carried hot chow in green marmite cans and large canvas bags filled with iced beer and soda pop. They carried plastic water containers, each with a two-gallon capacity. [Some individuals carried things important to them, starched tiger fatigues, Black flag insecticide, good luck charms, and empty sandbags for extra protection at night.] Some things they carried in common. Taking turns, [they carried] the big PRC-77 scrambler radio, which weighed 30 pounds with its battery. They shared the weight of memory. They took up what others could no longer bear. Often they carried each other, the wounded or weak. They carried infections. ... they carried the land itself – Vietnam, the place, the soil – a powdery orange-red dust that covered their boots and fatigues and faces. They carried the sky. The whole atmosphere, they carried it, the humidity, the monsoons, the stink of fungus and decay, all of it, they carried gravity.' (14–15)

The grunts lived in a world of hurt. Randy Cribbs, a Vietnam vet from Florida, told me ten years after his service ended: 'So I'm in a world of hurt figuring there's a fucking grenade out there with my name on it. I'm scared. I got 104 days left, not even short. I'm so fucking scared I'm walking point so I have some control. ... If somebody's gonna fuck up, let it be me. A guy who got himself a Million Dollar wound gave me his Ace of Spades. I've got it in my pocket. It's a little dog-eared by now, but it kept him safe, well, safe enough. Lost three fingers on his left hand, what the hell, he's right-handed. Maybe his card will keep me safe. I need some boonie magic bad' (interview with Randy Cribbs, January 2008). This attitude affected large numbers of grunts. Herr describes talking with a man worried about his friend: 'So when he told me that he saw ghosts whenever they went on night patrol I didn't laugh. But I got really worried when he said he saw his own ghost, but it was okay since his ghost was behind him. "It's when he goes and moves up in front that you're livin' in a world of hurt"' (252).

To keep from feeling sorry for themselves, grunts used several expressions which became mantras: '**It don't mean nuttin**', '**There it is**', '**It's just a thang**', and '**That's the 'Nam**'. Although the mantras may sound callous, unfeeling, or indifferent, they provided another form of self-preservation, along with drugs, alcohol, DEROS – the end of their time overseas, which they knew down to the minute – and R&Rs.

'It don't mean nuttin' when it really did – the death of another grunt nearby, the war itself, looking at the aftermath of a skirmish or battle, or a 'Dear John' letter from a girlfriend saying she wants to break off the relationship. Being callous, or unfeeling, or indifferent can be protective. Radiotelephone Operator Krehbiel numbed himself to the question about why he was in Vietnam, and to all other questions: 'It doesn't matter. Get home. It's okay. You just numbed out' (Ebert, 288). Tony Anthony, a sergeant in the infantry, covered operations, including secret ones, as a correspondent for the 198th Light Infantry Brigade. He was not worried on patrol. He cut his own trail. He did everything right. He felt ready to help anyone who needed it. 'A shot rings out in the jungle up ahead. The point man's in trouble. I rush ahead to help him. He's hit. He's down. I reach out to cover his wound and suddenly I'm hit in the shoulder. *It don't mean nothin'* (90–91). It was a mantra of acceptance, resignation, and self-preservation.

Don't Mean Nuttin'
By Randy Cribbs

It don't mean nuttin',
Or so we said,
But 'it' was there,
Somewhere in our head.

All that stuff,
Tucked way in the back,
To preserve sanity;
Added to the stack.

We wished it away
And moved on
To confront another
Time, alone.

It don't mean nuttin'.
Death was not real,

Filed away in a place
We could not feel.

To survive
    Was the chore.
To live.
    Nothing more.

No room for
Remorse or pain;
Everything to lose
And nothing to gain.

It don't mean nuttin'.
But we knew it did,
And, now, often,
It creeps from
    Under the lid.

To remind us
That we are here
Alive
With nothing more to fear.

Except all that stuff,
In there,
Year afer year. (74–75)

Even nurses felt this: 'My jaded "so what, don't mean nothing" attitude surfaces when the bullshit comes down from authority figures. … I have a real problem with authority figures who don't know what's happening on the front line' (Harrod, 25). 'But we put on a uniform and so people think we must be different, we must be immune. We're not. It's just as bad for us. And the worst thing someone can say to you is, oh, let it go' (Deaver, 263). Another frequently used phrase, 'There it is', occurred when a grunt saw the unexpected but not surprising given the circumstances: a body bag falling from a helicopter or watching a grunt drop ammo into a stream because he'd asked for too much. 'It's just a thang' was an expression used to signify 'that is just one of those things, you don't know if you are going to make it back or not but … it's just a thang' (Baxter, 109). One soldier, an FNG, reported that when he was dropped off the helicopter, the pilot said to him: 'It's just a thang man, see you if you make it back' (Baxter, 109).

But perhaps the most synonymous phrase reflecting the attitudes of the grunts was 'That's the 'Nam' – a recognition that it could only happen here, a *hope* that it happens only here, in the 'Nam. For example, when a grunt caught in a wait-a-minute vine discharged his weapon as he tried to extricate himself from its thorny streams of vines; or white monkeys that threw sticks at a unit as it passed by; or mud so thick it pulled boots off the grunts.

Although not an expression, a common occurrence was what grunts called a 'thousand-yard stare'. Grunts who had been in 'Nam too long developed a 'thousand yard stare'. Herr reported the first thing he noticed about grunts who had been in 'Nam too long, seen too much: 'He had one of those faces, I saw that face at least a thousand times at a hundred bases and camps, all the youth sucked out of the eyes, the color drawn from the skin, cold white lips, you knew he wouldn't wait for any of it to come back. Life had made him old' (16).

Thousand Yard Stare
(The Siege of Khe Sanh)
By Joseph Greene

Iron falls like rain,
day after day of earth slamming
bone ripping indifference as I watch
one boy after another being smashed
into hash by jagged chunks of death;
it's been falling for weeks –
waiting my turn.

Mirror images: red shadows,
filthy, intimate with rats,
hollow eyes, thousand yard-stare,
gaunt, beyond terror, no black, white or brown,
just sick down to the marrow –
heroes are in myths.

Rockets slam as I run
zigzag playing tag with death
trying to escape the unending barrage
of hatred that leaves meat
scraps strewn over the landscape –
without even a 'by your leave'.

Six marines huddled close for safety
in their own coffin dug in red earth.
I scramble to get in but come up short;
one-hundred-and-fifty-two millimeters
Of revenge with a debt to pay, slams home –
all died but me;
all died but me. (Eichler, 51-52)

Morley Safer noticed that the Vietnamese also had that thousand-yard stare: 'I look away from Van Le's face; it is bent to one side, his eyes focused past me. Again, the thousand-yard stare of boys who aged overnight' (247).

But all those phrases, all those benefits, all those humorous incidents, all those disasters, and all those thousand-yard stares were just attempts to forget for a moment the need to survive:

'Something about war was becoming very clear now. It was not the drama of one side named US against the other side, called the Enemy. ... War was a constant fight to survive against heat, thirst, poisonous centipedes, endless HUMPS, spreading jungle rot, sunburn, chapped and cracked lips and noses, twisted ankles, dehydration, intricate and constant patterns of pain from joints and muscles, unimagined extremes of boredom and exhaustion, stupid rumors about mad tigers that pounce on inattentive Americans at night, too few letters, too little food and booze and women, too much diarrhea, and too much despair that all this shit would never end, that home would never be seen again.' (Anderson, *Grunts*, 55–56)

But if you were lucky, you survived. Experienced grunts looked at everything around them everywhere they went; they prayed; they carried a good-luck charm. 'A grunt in the field is one of the most superstitious varieties of human life. Before he was sent to Vietnam there was a touch of the rational in him ... but during his year on the other side of the world, that rationality was pushed aside by events in which there was little or no reason. Frequent disappointment and disillusion caused by faulty intelligence, continuous word changes, and the ubiquitous uncertainty and fear pushed the grunt to erect around himself elaborate defenses consisting of no more than hopes, fears, and ritual acts' (Anderson, *Grunts*, 79–80). Anderson quotes one grunt saying: 'I bet if I eat this can of peaches now we'll move before noon' (80).

Herr watched what grunts held onto: the ritual moves, carrying their lucky piece, wearing their magic jungle hat. 'Five-pound Bibles from home, crosses, St Christophers, mezuzahs, locks of hair, girlfriends' underwear ... pictures of John Kennedy, Lyndon Johnson, Martin Luther King, Huey Newton, the Pope, Che Guevara, the Beatles, Jimi Hendrix ... an oatmeal cookie ... wrapped up in foil and plastic and three pairs of socks. ... Then there would be a magic grunt. Every unit had one. He was the one who stepped on a dud of a mine or had ESP – he just knew where the VC were. [If] you had special night vision, or great ears, you were magic too' (56–57).

Thanks
By Yusef Komunyakaa

Thanks for the tree
between me & a sniper's bullet.
I don't know what made the grass
sway seconds before the Vietcong
raised his soundless rifle.
Some voice always followed,
telling me which foot
to put down first.

FOREIGN ALLIANCES

Thanks for deflecting the ricochet
against that anarchy of dusk.
I was back in San Francisco
wrapped up in a woman's wild colors,
causing some dark bird's love call
to be shattered by daylight
when my hands reached up
& pulled a branch away
from my face.
Thanks for the vague white flower
that pointed to the gleaming metal
reflecting how it is to be broken
like mist over grass
as we played some deadly
game for blind gods.
What made me spot the monarch
writhing on a single thread
tied to a farmer's gate,
holding the day together
like an unfingered guiter string,
is beyond me. Maybe the hills
grew weary & leaned a little in the heat.
Again, thanks for the dud
hand grenade tossed at my feet
outside Chu Lai. I'm still
falling through its silence.
I don't know why the intrepid
sun touched the bayonet,
but I know that something
stood among those lost trees
& moved only when I moved. (154)

Later in the war, grunts – whether Army or Marine – faced feeling unimportant. It didn't matter what they did and what hearts and minds they tried to win through repairing infrastructure and building hospitals, 'nothing ever got any better. Vietnam stayed as backward and screwed up as it was at the beginning of everyone's tour. The war then became an apolitical and personal project – the struggle to survive it. The only thing the grunts found to win in Vietnam was 365 consecutive days of life' (Anderson, *Grunts*, 232).

This Last Time
By Basil T. Paquet[41]

This last time
the sun dries his lips
and bakes dry his earth,
he sees green rice rows

167

wander towards a white temple,
tin roofs shake their heat at the sun,
water buffalo wander
near a temple.
This last time sun fevers his head
black mynas cry a warning,
fire breaks from the shadows
of a tree line.
The last time sun bursts his eyes
he sees darkly the fall of sparrows
against a shaken sky. (Rottmann, 19)

The troops had to go through 'trial by fire' before they knew how they would react to war. Most grunts thought they themselves weren't heroes, just guys doing their job. Claude Anshin Thomas, (a Vietnam vet, later a Buddhist Monk) said this about the war: 'My job in Vietnam was to kill people. By the time I was first injured in combat (two or three months into my tour), I had already been directly responsible for the deaths of several hundred people. And today, each day, I can still see many of their faces' (20).

Ode to the Grunt
By Bill Person

The thicky growth snarls in withering heat,
And reddish mud clings at my plodding feet,
I labor on through smells that suit me not,
Scarcely inhale this jungle's breath so hot.
Have gone only a mile or several more?
Does lofty MAC-V* really know the score?

The pack straps knife through my quaking flesh
Soaked and caked red, no longer OD** mesh.
Sweat rolls down fast to sting my eye,
My fluids drain, but my mouth is dry.
My canteen tastes of iodine bitter,
The rain pours down a depressing pitter.

My pulse, I feel it in my temple throb,
Steel helmet weighs down my strength to rob.
M-16 in hand on "rock n roll."
Ready to reap a deathly toll.
Short breaths, I take in tiny swallows
I search for death in the bushy hollows.

Then calm is breached with stabs of flame
The grim reaper springs his horrid game,

Grunt. (Vets with a
Mission)

My throat grips fast to my warning shout.
Not a whisper from my lips gets out
Midst screams of pain, men drop to the ground
Charlies' fatal slugs have their target found.

The ambush is answered in blistering volley,
A doubtful hit, tis all in folly.
We're zapped but good, now Charlie's gone
He's slipped back into his safety zone,
We've not but our dead to carry back,
All bagged and tagged in a body sack.

The fallens' tour is done, they're homeward bound
For loved ones there to inter in hallowed ground.
Whilst we suffer on to serve in anguished pain,
Soaked to the soul by monsoon rain.
Two enemies to fight, one real, one fear
The truth be known? I'll know this year! (Eichler, 92–93)

* MAC-V = Military Assistance Command-Vietnam
** OD= olive drab

Besides Grunts, other US personnel included Marines, US Special Forces, A-Team, LRRPs, Tiger Force, nurses and other women who served in Vietnam, rear echelon, and truckers.

When a **Marine** signed up, it was for three years; Army enlistees were for two. 'Marines are not allowed to die without permission; we are government property' (Hasford, 13).[42]

Hey, Marine, have you heard?
Hey, Marine …
L B J. has passed the word.
Hey, Marine …
Say good-bye to Dad and Mom.
Hey, Marine …
You're gonna die in Vietnam.
Hey, Marine, yeah! (Hasford, 25)

'The Marines were well disciplined but were not in very good condition … They were also utterly untrained for the assignment' (Safer, 162). One of the Marines thought otherwise: 'Our real enemy is the jungle. God made this jungle for Marines. God has a hard-on for Marines because we kill everything we see' (Hasford, 150). 'No one seemed to tell them there were "friendlies" around. The decision to put an elite assault force into static positions in a highly populated area [was a mistake]. In Vietnam they were given the worst assignments and the most outdated equipment' (Safer, 162).

Just Another Marine
By Robert Hall

Seek me where the fight was thickest
Where the issue was in doubt
But apart from thee
I shall show my love for things,
Never meant to be.
Where my blood and bone in battle
Stayed the line and stopped the rout.

Seek me where the triple jungle
Formed a cauldron for our host,
Or out where the frozen mountains
Barred our pathway to the coast.

Seek me in the ruined village
Where our cause was sorely tried
Or upon the waste of desert
Where we turned the bitter tide.

Seek me where the fight was thickest
Where they pressed the issue keen,
Gently sleeping, slain in battle,
Lies another dead Marine. (Eichler, 57–58)

Then
By Terry Crosby

Boy scouts was Great!
Pup tents, tying knots, camping
Ya know, Man stuff.
Boyscout, not cubscout,
I was a man.
Not enough, more complicated
Knots required. Thoughts.
Thoughts of my father, he was
in the War, they WON ya know! He
was a real man, fought a war, and won.

The Marine Corps needed a few
good men, I was 17. I joined,
I was a confirmed man, a Marine!
My dad went to War – and won.

I went to Vietnam, a police
action. I was a man, in a

Police action, and Lost!
I could tie real good knots, I
could put up a tent pretty good too.
But I, I had never ya know,
killed anybody, but I was a man
a Marine.
I killed, I cried, I died, soulfully, mentally on my
Honor to do my best, to do my duty to
God and country.
DIED! Sometimes I wish I had.
Boy Scouts was great
I was a boy then. (Eichler 33–34)

The **United States Special Forces** were trained to aid, supply, and enlist locals in guerilla warfare. They also had specialized skills to combat the enemy in unconventional ways. President Kennedy, upon watching increased Vietcong guerilla activity, ordered anti-guerilla training for US troops. The Army Special Forces were known as the Green Berets. Other special forces were the Navy SEALS and CIA operatives. In the Vietnam War, the 'most successful operations against the Vietcong and the North Vietnamese were by small groups of specialists in irregular warfare. These were the Army Special Forces, the navy SEALS, CIA operatives, and several other groups' (Dunnigan and Nofi, 168).

Dallas, a Vietnam vet who talked with students in my course, spoke about his experiences: he told them he was enrolled in a community college in Kentucky when he decided to enlist. Wanting to be a helicopter pilot, he went to Officer Candidate School, graduating as a second lieutenant. Then he went to Fort Bragg to get trained to be in the Special Forces. In December of 1968, he went to Vietnam. He was assigned to Fifth Special Forces Group.

He reminded the students that he wasn't 'Rambo', wasn't a hero, just someone doing his job. During his tour, he was trained in how to protect himself and how to kill face-to-face. 'We were doing counterinsurgency or insurgency in hostile country. These included: area reconnaissance, bomb damage assessment, wiretap, prisoner snatch, road mining, and ambush.'

He told them on a different night that to gather intelligence, you recon the area in a small plane, looking for landing zones. 'The helicopters would take us forward, we'd have to wait for the weather, then get dropped on an LZ, and call for extraction when supplies ran out. We communicated three times a day. Each of us carried two gallons of water, three rounds of ammo, 5 days of food, and 4–5 grenades. Sometimes there'd be flybys, and we could call in airstrikes if we needed to.'

He told them that he was on some unusual missions. His unit measured the level of traffic on the Ho Chi Minh Trail, which he said was more like a highway than a trail. They were also in Cambodia and Laos, 'even though we weren't supposed to be. I saw bunkers, but I didn't see any tunnels – this was *their* territory. Didn't see any civilians. Sometimes we'd be ordered to RON – or remain overnight, also called snooping and pooping. I was always the one to get our supplies. They never got dropped in the right spot. But everybody'd say, "Here comes Rat". And I'd be lugging coolers full of beer and soft drinks in a hill' (Vietnam Vet Thursday Night Program).

The **A-Team** was a twelve-man team of US Special Forces. These elite soldiers mostly fought alone in remote places accessible only by helicopter. They fought guerillas through unconventional warfare, including political subversion and psychological operations. 'Nicknamed the "Green Berets", the Special Forces had been created in the early 1950s with the mission of organizing guerrilla forces behind enemy lines. As a natural corollary to their guerrilla mission, they also began to develop a counter-guerrilla doctrine' (Dunnigan and Nofi, 168). Reporter Michael Herr saw a sign in the Special Forces' A Camp that read: 'If you kill for money, you're a mercenary. If you kill for pleasure, you're a sadist. If you kill for both, you're a Green Beret' (257).

To gather intelligence, the military employed soldiers who did Long Range Reconnaissance patrols, known **as LRRPs**. They were elite teams, usually comprised of five to seven men, who went deep into the jungle to scout and watch the enemy to gather intelligence, called 'poop and scoop' or 'sneaking and peeping'. They dressed tough, acted tough, and took no prisoners. LRRPs also performed anti-guerilla warfare, often referred to as counterinsurgency. After 1969, they were known as Rangers. 'Some of them got down and dirty, and looked like animals' (Johnny, Vietnam Vet Program, 2/1/93).

Colonel David Hackworth created a platoon-sized military unit which he called **Tiger Force**, to apply guerrilla warfare tactics against Vietcong guerrilla fighters. Initially, Tiger Force was a highly decorated small unit in Vietnam which suffered heavy casualties and was awarded the Presidential Unit Citation. Their purpose was to deny the enemy sanctuary and to keep others from helping them, but after Hackworth[43] left Vietnam, the force was accused of atrocities and war crimes.[44]

Women were an integral part of the US Mission in South Vietnam whether as members of the armed forces, nurses, USO staff, or in the rear supporting our troops. According to Dunigan and Nofi, approximately 7,500 women served in the military in Vietnam based on official Department of Defense statistics. "Unfortunately, this conflicts with other more or less official statements," which put the number as high as 10,000 (161). Just like the men, women underwent basic training. But since most of them were going to be nurses or administrative personnel, their training included first aid, medical procedures, basic military discipline, clerical work, map reading, and communication but also included physical fitness. Women joined for many reasons, some like Dee Phillips joined because their father or mother was in the military; some joined because of the words of President Kennedy, "Ask not what your country can do for you, ask what you can do for your country" (Harrod 2); others to escape— broken relationships at home or with boyfriends. But all were volunteers. Some who had special skills, "OR nurses and nurse anesthetists" were recruited. ... Thus the great number of nurse in Vietnam were like me—OR and critical-care nurses (Harrod 2).

"As women in Vietnam, we faced a variety of problems related to our gender that were intrinsic to the military. When boot camp instructors called soldiers 'girls' or 'ladies' to insult them, it is impossible for the same soldiers and their officers to regard women as anything but inferior. In 'this man's army' of 1971, women had a limited role, and the men believed it was their right to determine what that role should be (Powell 142). Some of these problems, not faced by many men, were unwanted sexual advances or peeping toms, harassment and the belief by many men that women didn't belong in the armed forces.

'The gravest sin of women who served in Vietnam is that we haven't told our stories; we have let others tell them for us" (Harrod xi). Several have chosen to write about their experiences, including Bernadette Harrod, Lynda VanDevanter, Mary Reynold Powell and most recently in the fictional account of Frankie McGrath told by Kristin Hannah in *The Women* (2024). But for most the story goes "untold, unrecognized and, for the most part, unknown. My duty as a survivor of the Vietnam War is to inform others about my pain, longing, and sadness" (Harrod xi). Even less reported, according to Dunigan and Nofi, is "the story of American civilian women [serving in Vietnam] as government officials and employees, teachers, relief, development, and aid workers, entertainers, journalists and missionaries" (163). Their names, except perhaps for those who came to entertain the troops, have been forgotten.

Coming home proved just as difficult for women as for men, Mary Reynolds Powell wrote, "[Stephanie, a friend of Powell's who also served in Vietnam] sat in uniform in the Dallas airport for fourteen hours and no one spoke to [her]. By the time [she] got to Mississippi ... [she] had spent four days on the road in the same clothes, and no one, military or civilian, had said 'Welcome Home' or even 'How are you?' Being ignored by military people was harder for me than being ignored by civilians "(154). But perhaps most humiliating was the fact that they were not considered Vietnam Vets. Most were not allowed to demonstrate against the war because it would look as though the demonstrators were "swelling" their ranks with non-vets (Lynda Van Devanter, 231). The Veterans Administration would not extend their counseling and other services to veteran women until forced to by political pressure (Dunnigan and Nofi 162).

Other women also served in the rear. Although often looked down upon, those who lived in Saigon or the base camps were the men and women who kept the soldiers supplied with everything from weapons to food. Often called Pogue (person other than a grunt), Saigon Warriors, Clerks and Jerks or Rear Echelon Mother-fuckers (**REMF**), they were the support staff at the rear. According to John McGrath, approximately 60 per cent of those in Vietnam were support staff or 'tail' (1). McGrath divided support into two categories: logistical support and life support (5). Logistical staff support troops in the field: 'quartermaster, supply, service, maintenance, ordnance, ammunition support, adjutant general, transportation, medical, and small finance detachments. ... [Life support staff] run the base camps and provide ... post newspapers, base infrastructure, theatre [of operations] infrastructure, base construction ... as well as morale, welfare, and recreation activities' and financial and legal matters (McGrath, 5–6). Many of those in support accurately claim that they were in Vietnam, but few Americans would ask them if they fought in the war.[45] Even though they didn't fight, their support was essential to those fighting in Vietnam.

'Eight out of ten Americans in Vietnam never heard a shot fired in anger, never saw a bomb dropped or a village burned. They were the men in combat support and service support units – clerks, cooks, mechanics, MPs' (Ward, 326). A major goal of REMFs was to create a place as much like the World as possible to take their mind off the war, even for just a little while. Like the short-timers, those in the rear would count the days, and when their time got short would forget the promises they had made to themselves to serve their country to the best of their ability, especially after learning that someone with whom they had trained had died or been injured in combat (Anderson, *Other War*, 41). Those in the rear 'appeared slightly bored by their dull work but were content in the knowledge that their rear-echelon jobs gave them what their contemporaries in the line companies lacked: a future' (Caputo, 304).

There was animosity between those in the front lines and those in the rear who created the operational orders but didn't have to carry them out, 'never had to walk that little two-and one-half inches on the map that turned into man-killing three thousand two hundred meters on the ground' (Anderson, *Grunts*, 28).

'I really have a thing about these "Saigon warriors" who think they have been to war and have never left the relative safety of the city. They have never had to undergo the mental and physical strain that is part of a grunt's daily existence, where the highlight of any day is mail call. Half of these REMFs have girlfriends with apartments or villas and live with them' (Holley, 161).

The following lament, popular among GIs, was written by an anonymous grunt:

'Scuse me General Westy, I hate to bother you,
But I've got a couple of problems,
And I don't know what to do.
My air conditioner's broke,
My sedan's outa gas,
Besides all this, well, I can't get a seven-day pass.

I'm a Saigon Warrior, I'm helping fight a war.
Pushin' a pencil, my finger's getting sore.

Well, now, since I've been 'In Country' – that's military
For 'here' – I've learned to speak the language,
I'm winning hearts and minds.

I can say fluently... 'Tudo', 'Saigon
Tea', ... 'I love you too much',
'"massage?', 'Hey, where you go now?'
'Money changed?'
'dee-dee ... you buy for me ...'

I'm a Saigon Warrior, I'm helping fight a war.
Pushin' a pencil, my finger's getting sore. (Safer, 259–260)

Between the support staff and the soldiers were the **road warriors** (truck drivers), who provided supplies that were too heavy for helicopters. Many of them drove 2½-ton trucks. These truckers took war supplies off the ships that landed in heavily fortified ports. Some equipment and soldiers could be transported to bases inland by helicopters or small aircraft, but most of the supplies, equipment, and soldiers had to be trucked in convoys down thousands of miles of roads that had never been cleared of mines and were not patrolled. 'Next to the infantry, the guys who saw the most combat were the long-haul truck drivers' (Dunnigan and Nofi, 95). Truck drivers were armed with M-16s, and some trucks were equipped with machine guns; however, at least one of the trucks in the convoy carried explosive or flammable material. For this reason, those trucks were at the end of the convoy, which was not a secret to the VC.

The VC often ambushed convoys, even though they were heavily guarded by helicopters, armored vehicles, and combat trucks. It was like swinging a red cape in front of a bull. 'The truck companies lost about a quarter of their carrying capacity to these security measures, plus thousands of trucks damaged and destroyed by the

Vietnamese woman walking past convoy of trucks. (Courtesy D. Phillips)

attacks' (Dunnigan and Nofi, 95). Bobby Ward drove a truck: 'You should have seen a thunder run. You got two fools in a tank, going as fast as they can, and hope the mine blows up when you're past it. Now top speed was only 30 mph. But somebody had to clear the roads and take out the bushes near the roads. Those APCs (Armored Personnel Carrier – Tank) were all-terrain' (Vietnam Vet Program, 2/12/93).

Other countries provided troops or supplies, or both, many of them members of the Southeast Asia Treaty Organization (SEATO).[46] Not wanting to be seen as going it alone, the Johnson administration pressured other countries to join in the Vietnam War, much as George W. Bush would later form a 'coalition of the willing' to fight in Desert Storm. From 1964–1972, military personnel from Australia, South Korea, Thailand, New Zealand, and the Philippines assisted the South. From 1966–1972, South Korea provided 47,500 personnel a year; far greater than Thailand's high of 11,586 in 1970; New Zealand's high of 552 in 1969; and the Philippines' high of 2,061 in 1966. Australian support reached a high of 7,661.

Canada was a quiet ally – about 40,000 enlisted in the US armed forces. Other supporters may have been observers, technical advisors, relief workers, and medical personnel: they came from Argentina, Britain, the Republic of China, Spain, and West Germany (Dunnigan and Nofi, 64–65). South Korea was the main US and South Vietnamese partner, providing over 300,000 troops and suffering some 5,000 deaths. The South Korean troops did not have to adjust to the Vietnamese culture and different philosophies of life, since they were themselves believers in the same values. One of their divisions became known as the Tiger division. 'The Koreans sent more troops and much more aggressive troops [than other US allies]' (Vietnam War Combatants).

The United States also had support from local tribes, whose acronym was **FULRO** (Front unifié de lutte des races opprimées – the United Front for the Struggle of Oppressed Races). Resistance organization in the highlands of Vietnam comprised the **Montagnard**, including the Hmong, Cham, Nung, Negritos, and ethnic Khmer.[47] The Montagnard (or Yards), French for Mountain people, may have been the original inhabitants of Vietnam. They farmed, smoked, and sold a lot of marijuana, especially to American soldiers – no wonder they got on well with the US Special Forces. They proved to be more dependable than the ARVNs (Van Devanter, 215). The Yards were fierce fighters and comfortable with Special Forces; many LRRPs and SEALs wore Montagnard bracelets, which were brass, made from bullets.

A favorite catch-and-cook for the Yards was the rat. Because rats hung around food and dirt, Special Forces in underground camps were overrun with the vermin. After shooting the rats, sometimes with shotgun shells filled with rice, the Special Forces brought them to the Yards, who didn't understand why the Americans wouldn't join them to eat (Dunnigan and Nofi, 102). But they also enjoyed fooling Americans into eating 'what looked like dried fruit' but were human ears. Herr had learned that there were a lot more heads than ears in Vietnam, so declined to eat 'the dried fruit' (Herr, 34).

Combat Paratrooper Woodley walked point dressed like a Montagnard: 'I wore a dark-green loin-cloth, a dark-green bandana to blend in with the foliage, and a little camouflage paint on my face. And Ho Chi Minh sandals. … I dressed like that specifically as the point man, because if the enemy saw anyone first, they saw myself. They would just figure I was just another jungle guy that was walking around in the woods. And I would catch 'em off guard' (Terry, 244). Others followed his example, disguising themselves as best they could to remain hidden from the enemy.

Camouflaging the Chimera*
By Yusef Komunyakaa
(*an illusion)

We tied branches to our helmets.
We painted our faces & rifles
with mud from a riverbank,
blades of grass hung from the pockets
of our tiger suits. We wove
ourselves into the terrain,
content to be a hummingbird's target.
We hugged bamboo & leaned
against a breeze off the river,
slow-dragging with ghosts
from Saigon to Bangkok,
with women left in doorways
reaching in from America.
We aimed at dark-hearted songbirds.
In our way station of shadows
rock apes tried to blow our cover
throwing stones at the sunset. Chameleons
crawled our spines, changing from day
to night: green to gold,
gold to black. But we waited
til the moon touched metal,
til something almost broke
inside us. VC struggled
with the hillside, like black silk

wrestling iron through grass.
We weren't there. The river ran
Through our bones. Small animals took refuge
against our bodies; we held our breath,
ready to spring the L-shaped
ambush, as a world revolved
under each man's eyelid. (37)

Although the French referred to them as Montagnard, the **Hmong** were a separate ethnic group. Located in China, Vietnam, and Laos, they made up the bulk of the Laotian Royal Army. After 1973, a number emigrated to the United States; others were slaughtered by the North Vietnamese (Dunnigan and Nofi, 184–185). During the Vietnam War, the United States recruited thousands of Hmong people in Laos to fight against North Vietnam.

North Vietnam and its Allies

All of those who sided with the North Vietnamese had communist forms of government or were sympathetic to Ho Chi Minh and the Viet Minh.

The North Vietnamese Army (NVA), also known as the People's Army of Vietnam (PAVN), did not engage the South immediately, but let the guerilla Vietcong fight. Colonel Huang Dai Hai, who commanded an artillery and aircraft unit, told Morley Safer: 'When you join the army you take seven oaths, the seventh is to swear to live together, die together, and share sorrows as if they were joys. I still maintain that oath, even now … but I have feelings of guilt that we didn't win the war more quickly. … Even though we now want reconciliation with the United States … I still hate those people who thrust war upon our country and those people who committed crimes in our country' (88–89).

The NVA was a military unit with a command structure similar to that of the US. It fought in a similar fashion, with big battles, trench warfare, use of missiles, and stronger firepower than their Vietcong supporters. In contrast, the Vietcong, or **NLF** (**National Liberation Front**), were familiar with the jungle. 'They relied on stealth, on ambush, on their personal skills and wile, as opposed to firepower. They knew it did not pay for them to stand and fight us, so they wouldn't. They'd come back and fight another day. We knew that we could not afford to get careless with them because you pay the price' (Terry, 226).

They fought very hard. '"The dink[48] was not right. There was something not right about him." He kicked the almost naked body over. Two hand grenades were jammed into the soldier's belt, with wires running from his pants to his wrists. By raising his arms to surrender he would have killed us all, and died himself. What

NVA soldiers. (Vets with a Mission)

kind of enemy was this? I was scared. That day I stopped calling them dinks. They were the enemy or Mr Charles' (Laszlo Kondor in Sinaiko, 109).

Mr Charles, the enemy, was part of a larger militia group known as the NLF, established by North Vietnam to conduct an insurgency in South Vietnam. It included the main fighting force, the **People's Liberation Army** (**PLAF**), and the Vietcong, also known as Victor Charlie (hence Mr Charles), the guerilla fighters. 'The term [Vietcong] is a contraction of Viet-nam Cong-san and was the equivalent of "commie". It was originally used by Ngo Dinh Diem, who was President of South Vietnam from 1955 until 1963' (http://mazalien.com/viet-cong.html). Many soldiers could not distinguish South Vietnamese nationals from the VC – how could they? They had no standard uniforms or weapons. The VC conducted its attacks against the South Vietnamese from home bases in Laos and Cambodia, resupplied by locals coming down the Ho Chi Minh Trail.

The Vietcong had a central office (**COSVN**), which divided South Vietnam into six military regions, each controlled by a political leader. The leader in each region coordinated all fighting to ensure unity of effort. In 1969, North Vietnam increased the international status of this organization by naming it the Provisional Revolutionary Government (PRG).

'The simple but effective code of the VC is "when the enemy advances, withdraw; when he defends, harass; when he is tired, attack; when he withdraws, pursue". The VC exhibit great skill in making the most of their enemy's weaknesses' (Handbook, 14).

Master Sergeant Donald Duncan, a member of the Army Special Forces, didn't understand why the Army of the Republic of (South) Vietnam, the ARVN, was criticized as a fighting force, yet the Vietcong were praised. 'I suppose one of the things that bothered me from the very beginning in Vietnam was the condemnation of the ARVN as a fighting force: "the Vietnamese are cowardly … the Vietnamese can't be disciplined … the Vietnamese just can't understand tactics and strategy, etc., etc." But the Vietcong are Vietnamese. … It became obvious that motivation is the prime factor in this problem. The Vietcong soldier believes in his cause. He believes he is fighting for national independence. He has faith in his leaders, whose obvious dedication is probably greater than his own' (91).

Caputo, a platoon commander in the Marine Corps, also had respect for the Vietcong. He and several others moved into a small Vietcong base camp and noticed the squalid conditions in which they lived: 'It took a lot of dedication to live in a place like that where you could hardly see the sun, where the air was dense enough to cut, and mosquitoes rose in clouds from stagnant pools' (116).

'The ability of the Vietcong continuously to rebuild their units and to make good their losses is one of the mysteries of this guerilla war. … Not only do the Vietcong units have the recuperative powers of the phoenix, but they have an amazing ability to maintain morale' (General Maxwell Taylor, from a briefing in November 1964[49]).

Bai Ninh, a North Vietnamese soldier, shares the Vietnamese world view in *The Sorrows of War*. 'To win, martyrs had sacrificed their lives in order that others might survive. Not a new phenomenon, true. But for those still living to know that the kindest, most worthy people have all fallen away, or even been tortured, humiliated before being killed, or buried and wiped away by the machinery of war, then this landscape of calm and peace is an appalling paradox' (193).

Two specialized units of the Vietcong were the **death squads**, who frightened the civilian population by the atrocities they committed on leaders of individual communities, and the **sappers**, armed with explosives, who destroyed American base camps, their trucks, planes, and ships. The sappers' intent was to damage the means of supply and the centralized headquarters. While the death squads would slaughter the civilian population, the sappers would destroy their means of protection.

Other Southeast Asian allies included the **Khmer Rouge** and the **Pathet Lao**. The Khmer Rouge, the Communist Party in Cambodia,[50] was organized by both North and South Vietnamese communists not only to fight in South Vietnam but also to conduct a guerilla war against their own neutral government in Cambodia. The Pathet Lao, the Communist Party of Laos, forced its neutral government to allow the North Vietnamese to move troops and supplies to South Vietnam on the Ho Chi Minh Trail which ran through Laos.

Although the **Soviet Union** and **China** did not provide troops, they did offer materiel support, preferring to stay in the background to avoid escalating the war. Professor Moise[51] wrote that 'if there had been no Chinese or Soviet support, the North Vietnamese could not have won ... pointing out that the US military budget was roughly 30 times greater than the entire gross national product of North Vietnam'. The Russians and Chinese remained almost invisible in the North, and never appeared in the South. 'By contrast, the Americans failed to perceive the damage done by the presence of their own officers at the elbow of every Vietnamese in authority.' Prime Minister Ky called them 'insensitive to appearances' (Hastings, 280).

Chapter 6

The War Years

'The Great ancient Chinese military strategist Sun Tzu taught that warriors who lured
their enemy into a trap should leave a way of escape and avoid
a desperate battle to the death.' (Kilgore)

Phase One (1950–1954): The Domino Theory

By the end of 1950, the United States had provided $133 million dollars in aid to the
French-controlled region of Indochina, although the French were suspicious of our
motives. By 1952, the US was paying for one-third of the cost of the war against Ho
Chi Minh, the rebel leader of Vietnam. Previously Ho Chi Minh had asked for US help
against the French as the Vietnamese fought for its independence, comparing his war to
our war for independence. He reminded the US that he provided military intelligence
while he fought against the Japanese during World War II (Rosenberg 1) and repeatedly
asked for US help against the French as the Vietnamese fought for their independence,
comparing that war to our War of Independence.

'In early 1952, Truman's National Security Council postulated that "the loss of
any of the countries of Southeast Asia to communist aggression would have critical
psychological, political, and economic consequences". It was the first articulation of
the domino theory [the loss of one country to communism would hasten the loss of
another]'[52] (McMaster, 34).

By 1953, the US had spent $400 million dollars in Indochina: new president Eisenhower
thought the US had no choice but to defend the region. The French were defeated in battle
at Dien Bien Phu by General Giap, who was later named Commander-in-Chief of the
North Vietnam Army. Vietnam was then partitioned into North and South Vietnam along
the seventeenth parallel, with free elections scheduled for 1956. Meanwhile, ceasefires
were established in Laos and Cambodia. 'American largesse [to the French, which from
1950–1954 totaled $2.6 billion,] was prompted by communist threats to the stability and
democratic institutions of many [Western European] nations' (Hastings, 32).

The partition of Vietnam was part of the 1954 Geneva Accords, 'endorsed by the
French, British, Chinese and Russians but conspicuously not by the Americans …

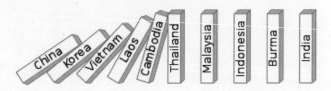

Representation of
Domino Theory.
(Wikipedia)

nor by either of the Vietnamese delegations'. But because the US and South Vietnam refused to sign it, they argued that they were not bound to honor the Geneva Treaty's requirement that Vietnam hold free elections in 1956 (Hastings, 90).

After the peace accords, 'Eisenhower and Dulles [his Secretary of State] ... invested the new semi-nation [South Vietnam] with a sense of legitimacy and importance rooted in the need to calm their constituency at home and restore the administration's self-esteem after failing to save the North [Vietnam, from communism]. South Vietnam, said [Dulles], might yet prosper "free of the tint of French Colonialism" through the instrumentality of Ngo Dinh Diem, a figure whom Washington embraced with an enthusiasm that was somewhat startling, given how little the Americans knew of him' (Hastings, 90–91).

Phase Two (1954–1961): Building Democracy in South Vietnam

By the late 1950s, there were some 1,500 US 'advisors' in the region. French aid to the region stopped: Vietnam's economy was in ruins because of fourteen years of war against the Japanese in World War II and then the French. The United States stopped several coups to unseat the newly appointed but unpopular Premier Diem. American advisors were in South Vietnam trying to build a democracy that would vote against Ho Chi Minh. The strength of Ho Chi Minh led the US to block scheduled elections in 1956 that would have reunified the country under one leader. The United States feared a united Vietnam would become a communist country. [53]

In October 1954, President Eisenhower ordered a 'crash program' of military assistance, and in February 1955, the US Military Assistance Advisory group (**MAAG**) took charge of advising, training, and equipping the Vietnam National Army, known by its French acronym ARVN. 'From 1954 to 1960, Washington provided Diem's government with 444 million [dollars] in military aid and 1.4 billion in economic aid' (Kiernan, 404). 'Some of the huge aid infusion, together with a respite from war, brought happy times to the Mekong Delta in the late 1950s. ... Communist Party membership declined dramatically. There was rice in the fields, fruit in the orchards, pigs snuffling around the yards, fish in village ponds. Wooden houses increasingly replaced huts' (Hastings, 112).

Diem made a crucial mistake in abolishing local elections in South Vietnam that would have named village and provincial officials. Instead, he wanted to appoint his own officials who would be loyal to him. The National Liberation Front, the Vietcong, then vowed to overthrow Diem, whom they considered to be a dictator.

The relocation of the MAAG to South Vietnam made the US solely responsible for training and equipping the ARVN. The Eisenhower administration sought to weaken the North Vietnamese through psychological warfare and covert operations. Meanwhile, Diem, with the help of Catholics, the CIA, and other anti-communists, consolidated his power.

During this period, the communist North realized that since there would no free elections, the only way to reunite Vietnam was through violent struggle, overthrowing the puppet South Vietnam government and forcing the United States to evacuate.

Phase Three (1961–1963): Testing our Determination: Limited Involvement

The number of US 'advisors' in Vietnam grew from 8,000 in late 1961 to 9,000 in late 1962.[54] These Military advisors include engineers, troops, and medical personnel.

> First hints of problems to come: can't tell the Vietcong (South Vietnamese communist guerilas) from civilians. Everyone in South Vietnam is a target.

By 1961, South Vietnam ranked fifth in receiving economic aid from the United States. In the fall of 1961, President Kennedy was unwilling to commit troops to stop what he saw as a civil disturbance, although he did send 'helicopters and 400 green berets and authorized secret operations against the Vietcong' (Vietnam War Timeline). When the Vietcong stepped up attacks in South Vietnam, and Diem wanted more aid to build an army in South Vietnam, Kennedy's advisor, Walt Rostow, visited and warned the situation was now serious. By late 1962, some 9,000 'advisors' were flying combat missions and deploying South Vietnamese troops into battle.

'Although Kennedy was willing to send US military "advisers" into South Vietnam and mount covert operations in North Vietnam, Cambodia, and Laos, he drew the line on US combat units. Kennedy used the word "adviser" to imply that the South Vietnamese would do their own fighting. Any introduction of American combat units risked transforming the war into an American war, raising the specter of high US casualties, and fomenting congressional and public debate over administration policy' (McMaster, 37).

Kennedy increased the number of advisors to combat the increasing presence of the Vietcong. These additional advisors would continue to train South Vietnamese troops and at the same time fly them into battle areas. This seemed to have 'stabilized the situation' in the South, as did Diem's Strategic Hamlet Program, 'consolidat[ing] much of the South Vietnamese rural population into villages in which they theoretically remained insulated and secure from Vietcong activities and influence' (McMaster, 37).

Operation Ranch Hand. Beginning in 1962 and peaking in the late 1960s, Operation Ranch Hand, using Agent Orange and other defoliants, destroyed forests and jungles in which the Vietcong hid. This allowed the United States and its allies to fight a conventional war.[55]

Operation Helicopter. The first US combat mission in Vietnam occurred on 12 January 1962. 'US army pilots fly helicopters to help 1,000 South Vietnamese soldiers sweep a North Vietnamese stronghold near Saigon' (*Vietnam: Special Newsweek Edition*, 7).

Laos. In 1962, the United States and both Vietnams guaranteed the neutrality of Laos. They would respect its borders. However, to bring troops and supplies to the South, North Vietnam broke the agreement. The United States, in response, bombed the Ho Chi Minh Trail. For nine years, the US continued its bombing operation, dropping explosives on average every eight minutes.

After the United States supported a coup against Diem and his brother in November 1963, twelve different governments controlled South Vietnam between 1963 and 1965, as one coup followed another.

Phase Four (1963–1965): Open-ended Commitment
What had been 23,300 US 'advisors' in Vietnam in mid-1964 became 184,000 troops by December 1965.

Three weeks after the coup and the murder of Diem and his brother, JFK was assassinated.[56] Vietnam became a huge problem for the new US president, Johnson, because JFK had reacted to crises instead of planning long-term strategies.

To put a more positive spin on US involvement in Vietnam, President Johnson used what he stated was an attack on two American warships, the USS *Maddox* and *C. Turner Joy*, in the **Gulf of Tonkin** on 2 August 1964, to enter the conflict without a declaration of war at 11am on 5 August 1964. Since Congress had not declared war, and only Congress can do so, this was never technically a 'war'.

Gulf of Tonkin Resolution. Johnson used the incident to win Congressional support[57] for the Gulf of Tonkin Resolution, which allowed him to use 'all necessary measures to repel any armed attacks against the forces of the United States and to prevent further aggression, [in essence] a blank check to run the war'. This marked a major change: the US was no longer defending South Vietnam, instead now responding to North Vietnamese provocations. General William Westmoreland requested the Marines be sent to Vietnam, but General Maxwell Taylor, the US Ambassador to South Vietnam, warned the US was not prepared to fight a guerilla war and that the South Vietnamese would be all too happy to have the US fight its war for them. Johnson personally approved each air strike and target: he deployed 50,000 personnel and promised another 50,000. This was approved on 10 August 1964.

'Subsequent studies have cast serious doubts upon this official version [of the events that took place in the Gulf of Tonkin[58]]. ... [T]he President misled Congress and the people, and through that deception was able to obtain congressional authorization for a war that he had decided on months before while promising the voters peace' (excerpted from Stoessinger, 126). 'Both former US Defense Secretary Robert McNamara and top Vietnamese leaders confirmed retrospectively that reports of an attack were false, based on bad intelligence and misrepresentations of intercepted communications' (Sonnenfeld, 3).

Before the Gulf of Tonkin incident in the summer of 1964, 'the Johnson administration was laying secret plans for an expansion of US military involvement in Vietnam. Any such wider action should have Congressional support, officials determined, [but] the Gulf of Tonkin incident provided the opportunity to secure this authorization', said Fredrik Logevall[59] in an interview on PBS (*American Experience*).

On the evening of 5 August 1964 (Vietnamese time), a young North Vietnamese member of a Youth Brigade, Bao Ninh, attended a vacation camp and rally for 16-year-olds at Do Son on the Gulf of Tonkin. The teenagers pitched their tents and lit a bonfire. Around the fire they sang and drank beer and wine. At night, when most of the teenagers were sleeping, the bonfire was still burning – a sailor with a rifle kicked sand in the fire to put it out. Those still awake asked why.

"'Don't ask why. We got orders tonight. No fires on the beach. No lights. They order it, we carry it out. We aren't allowed to ask why, it's a military order."

"'Is singing banned, too?" asked Phuong, feigning innocence.

'The sailor lowered his gun, softened his stance, and sat down with them. "No. Don't stop singing. That's got to go on at all costs. Sing us a song now," he invited.

> 'Two others from the shore patrol returned ... .
> "'Sing all the same, sister," [the sailor] said sadly. "Sing a farewell song to us. I'll tell you a secret; you'll know tomorrow anyway. It's war. America has entered the war. We're fighting the Americans."'

WHY VIETNAM? REFLECTIONS ON THE EFFECT OF WAR

Phuong's Song

The winds, they are a-changin'.
The harsh winds blow in the world from tonight,
No longer the peace
We were hoping for.
Our loved ones will grieve for those who'll be lost.
No longer in peace
Our children will live.
From this moment on,
The winds, they are a-changin'. (all the above, excerpts from Ninh, 175)

Bao Ninh was one of just ten who survived out of a Youth Brigade of 500. As a 16-year-old, he attended the rally at Do Son, a suburb of Haiphong, where he along with all the others shouted 'War! War!'. 'The sea roared out the message in the small hours of 5 August 1964. A small storm began far out across the Tonkin Gulf and the group looked on as distant forked lightning seemed to signal the start of the war' (175).

In early 1965, President Johnson accused the North Vietnamese of being the aggressor. He reminded the nation of the Domino Theory, espoused by Eisenhower; if South Vietnam fell to the communists, then all Southeast Asia would be next. Johnson therefore moved away from Kennedy's limited response by July 1965. Kennedy's advisors, however, remained with Johnson.

From 1964–1966, the United States and South Vietnam reinforced their troop levels and added more firepower. 'Matching this new escalation, the NLF stepped up its conscription in the South. Recruitments quadrupled: the 1964 tally of 45,000 new Front recruits shot up to 160,000 for 1965' (Kiernan, 439).

Phase Five (1965–1967): Escalation into Ground War

'I see the light at the end of the tunnel.' (Walt Rostow, US National Security Advisor, December 1967)

In December 1966, the US had 385,000 troops in Vietnam; by December 1967, that figure had grown to 485,000.

Morley Safer, a CBS correspondent in Saigon in 1965, recalled: 'Nothing prepared me for what I found in Saigon. Both the physical and psychological terrain was being prepared for a colossal American Intervention. Machismo was in the air. American military advisers – there were no full-scale units – were beginning to strut their stuff. They were giving up their role of bystanders and sideline coaches. The war was ceasing to be a Vietnamese show' (xvi–xvii).

Operation Hastings and Operation Prairie, July 1966 – February 1967. The purpose of both operations was to drive the North Vietnamese north, back across the DMZ. 'On Operation Prairie we [a Marine battalion] were fighting for a long time with very little sleep, low on ammo and no food for three days … Time, since those days, has carried a long chain of these memories into the present, and still with all the suffering

184

and loss and everything that was said of that war over all these years, I can only think of the days spent in that company as the great privilege of my life' (Ned Broderick, in Sinaiko, 33).

> Each face
> will lose his name
>> and time will not defer
>> But there will always
> be the bond
> between what we are
> and where we were. (Broderick, in Sinaiko, 33)

Operation Rolling Thunder. This was the biggest bombing operation of the war, from 2 March 1965 until 31 October 1968. The bombing was supposed to boost the morale of the Saigon government, stop transportation of materiel and supplies from the North to the Vietcong in the South, keep North Vietnamese soldiers from infiltrating the South, and destroy their industry and air defenses. Because of the military and materiel assistance from its communist allies, the bombing did not halt the war nor hinder North Vietnam's support of the Vietcong. According to Pepinsky, Kocher, and Kalyvas,[59A] 'aerial bombing was an ineffective, wrongheaded strategy that drove neutral citizens into the arms of the Vietcong' (Lowery, 1)

During the war, US aircraft dropped approximately 13 million tons of bombs, six times the total dropped by US aircraft in the Second World War. 'The explosive force was sufficient to displace 3.4 billion tons of earth – ten times that evacuated for both the Suez and Panama Canals – that caused an estimated 26 million craters and flattened 200 square kilometers of forest' (Dunnigan and Nofi, 131). Rolling Thunder did not come without cost to the US, as at least 2,317 US aircraft were shot down. Surprisingly, it was 'old-fashioned cannon and automatic weapons fire that accounted for nearly 90 percent of the loss' (Dunnigan and Nofi, 122–123).

Rolling Thunder[60] probably came from the first four lines of the hymn *How Great Thou Art* (words and music by Carl G. Boberg and R.J. Hughes):

> O Lord my God, When I in awesome wonder,
> consider all the worlds Thy Hands have made;
> I see the stars, I hear the rolling thunder,
> Thy power throughout the universe displayed.

Johnson hoped Rolling Thunder would soften the enemy so that they would be willing to negotiate a peaceful settlement. By April 1965, however, the bombing proved to have had little effect on the North, so Johnson offered the following terms: 'vast rural rehabilitation and a flood control program for the Mekong Valley, supported by $1 billion of United States funds in which, after accepting peace, the North Vietnamese would share. ... Rejecting Johnson's overture, Hanoi announced its four preconditions the next day: 1) withdrawal of United States military forces; 2) no foreign alliances or admission of foreign troops by either side; 3) adoption of the NLF (National Liberation

Front or Viet-Cong) program by South Vietnam; 4) reunification of the country by the Vietnamese without interference' (Tuchman, 324). Since the United States had intervened to stop the spread of communism, the United States would not and could not accept the third condition.

'In May 1965, the United States making its own effort, initiated a pause in the bombing which it was hoped might evoke from Hanoi a sign of willingness to talk' (Tuchman, 325). But this did not have any effect on Hanoi's willingness to negotiate. Rolling Thunder then resumed. In June, Johnson authorized 'combat support of South Vietnam by American ground forces'.

The colossal American intervention occurred only because other means to negotiate a peace had failed. President Johnson's authorization to send in combat troops was not for the US to win the war, but for US troops to bolster South Vietnam's defenses until South Vietnam could take over. 'By entering the Vietnam War with no goal to win, Johnson set the stage for future public and troop disappointment' (Rosenberg, 2). Not only were there no goals, but there were limitations established by the army and authorized by the president. **The Rules of Engagement (ROE)** left soldiers in precarious positions. The ROE were formed to keep the war limited to Vietnam. Even though the Ho Chi Minh Trail snaked its way down the borders of Laos and Vietnam, the military command forbade soldiers to fire into Laos or go into Laos. VC supply bases in Cambodia were also off-limits. Banjo, at one of my Thursday evening programs, said if you got wounded in Cambodia, there was no compensation (Vietnam Vet Program, 2/4/93). Within Vietnam, the ROE instructed soldiers to determine who was a VC and who was a civilian before acting. This was established to help calm the tensions between villagers and American soldiers who were combing the area for the VC.

Often accused of not fighting aggressively enough, the US military was severely hampered by the ROE, which favored the enemy. Soldiers in Vietnam could be shot by the VC shooting from Laos, but they were prevented from returning fire.[61] The ROE, however, did prevent any other countries near and surrounding Vietnam from intervening. Because of this, the war remained a 'limited war' (Kutler, 481–483). 'You have to go into war with the intention to win. You can't tie soldiers' hands. In Korea, MIGs could chase you up 'til the Yalu River. The lesson is there. Let generals run the war' (Bowman, Vietnam Vet Program, 2/4/93).

First Lieutenant Joe Biggers had major complaints about the rules. He watched a Marine walk over to a 3-year-old kid running down the street. When the Marine touched him, they both blew up. 'If those guys were low enough to use kids to bait Americans or anybody to this kind of violent end, well, I think they should be eliminated. And they would have been if we had fought the war in such a manner that we could have won the war. ... The people in Washington setting policy didn't know what transpired over here. ... That's why we had all those stupid restrictions. ... If only we could have fought it in a way that we had been taught to fight' (Terry, 110–111).

Even tank drivers complained: 'The fact that we couldn't legally hold land we had won created an extremely weird situation. We had to drive out of that town knowing damn well another group of VC would move in at any time, even against the wishes of the inhabitants. There simply weren't enough ARVN to go around and sooner or later, we'd have to clean it out again' (Zumbro, 54).

Operation Cedar Falls. In January 1967 US Army began an all-out offensive against the communist stronghold of the "Iron Triangle" northwest of Saigon (Nguyen, 1). One US general 'described the Iron Triangle as a "dagger" aimed at the South Vietnamese capital' (Milam, 2). As part of the operation, US forces removed villagers from Ben Suc and destroyed the village. The operation 'followed a so-called hammer and anvil plan. American and South Vietnamese units would be inserted to the north as "hammers" that would drive the enemy into an "anvil"' (Milam, 2). 'The most significant achievement [of the operation], according to military sources, was the confirmation of the existence of a huge labyrinth of tunnels' (Milam, 3).

Those tunnels were built by Mo and other villagers in the Cu Chi area. They were used as barracks, a command center, and communication network (Nguyen, 1). Nguyen, in *As the Earth Shook, They Stood Firm*, writes about the bravery of Mo and her fellow Vietcong in fighting the US forces: 'That poorly equipped, poorly supplied communist forces were able to resist a sustained mechanized onslaught was a testament to the resilience, adaptability, and tenacity of [the Vietcong]' (2). Nguyen quoted a Vietcong colonel on their resilience: '"Although they could not eliminate our leadership, they destroyed our bases, especially our supplies ... and established a secure perimeter for themselves in the northwest of Saigon"' (2).

General Westmoreland, commander of all US forces in Vietnam, in a speech to a joint session of Congress on 28 April 1967, commented on both the limited aims and the rules of engagement: The Vietnam War is a limited war, with limited objectives, prosecuted by limited means, with limited public support. 'We are fighting a war with no front lines, since the enemy hides among the people, in the jungles and mountains, and uses covertly border areas of neutral countries. One cannot measure (our) progress by lines on a map' (Lindsay 6).

From what General Westmoreland told Congress, it was obvious that the US still had no strategy, given the enemy's guerilla tactics, to win the war. Yet he insisted he could see an end to the war if Congress would grant his request for an additional quarter of a million men. But President Johnson and his administration were not as positive as Westmoreland seemed to be. Herr felt, despite Westmoreland's optimism, that the war was barreling out of control. The attempt to control everything – '"arms control, information control, population control, control of the almost supernatural inflation, control of the terrain through the Strategy of Periphery' – was not working (48).

> Contradiction: US wanted a limited war (so nearby non-communist countries were not threatened), but it also wanted a quick war, so critics at home wouldn't try to stop it.

Several assumptions hindered any strategy. The US assumed its equipment superiority mattered and that its optimism mattered; yet it was not optimism but morale that really mattered. By 1967, the cost of the war had been $2 billion per month since 1965.

Problems:

(1) **No strategic guidelines for use of American power**, so the US military fought a conventional war – ignoring jungles, limitations of the South Vietnamese Army, the problems of resupplying troops halfway round the world, and restraints imposed by politicians.

(2) **Although bombing was more palatable at home**, the North Vietnamese responded by keeping open bombed roads and using over 30,000 miles of tunnels built during other wars.

(3) **The impact of weather on planning operations**, from weapons, armored vehicles, planes, and helicopters, down to fatigues, boots, and equipment suitable for monsoons, fog-shielded targets, and targets hidden in a triple-canopy jungle.

(4) **'Body count'** eventually became the only way to measure success because the US was not taking and holding territory. After the war, experts think the body count was inflated by as much as 30 per cent.

(5) **Hanoi showed no signs of weakening.**

(6) **The US split into 'hawks' and 'doves'** – hawks believed that Vietnam was a global struggle against communism; doves questioned the morality of war. On 21 October 1967, over 30,000 people demonstrated outside the Pentagon; The following year, Secretary of Defense Robert McNamara resigned.

The Battle for Khe Sanh. Khe Sanh was located in red clay hills near the DMZ. Marines were under siege there for seventy-seven days. Herr reported on the situation at Khe Sanh, where Marines had been shelled for forty-five days, with no resupplies or

Dug-in before assault. (Courtesy with a Mission)

evacuations possible. Peter Braestrup of the *Washington Post* asked a brigadier general from Marine Headquarters who came to brief reporters on Khe Sanh: "'General, why haven't those Marines *dug in*?' The room was quiet. Braestrup had a fierce smile on his face as he sat down. When the question had begun, the colonel had jerked suddenly to one side of his chair, as though he'd been shot. Now, he was trying to get his face in front of the general's so that he could give out the look that would say, "See, General? See the kinds of peckerheads I have to work with every day?"' (Herr, 150–152).

Hastings states that the siege of Khe Sanh was a distraction to keep the United States from defending other positions later attacked during the Tet Offensive. 'The two NVA divisions around Khe Sanh subjected its Marine garrison … to an intermittent bombardment, rendering the landing strip [the only means of resupplying the base] hazardous. In the course of January and February, harassment of the base became a huge worldwide news story. Westmoreland suggested that Giap [commander of all North Vietnam troops] intended to make this a new Dien-Bien Phu[62] … though the general added that the communists would assuredly fail to match the Vietminh's triumph' (441). Many Marines who lived through Khe Sanh wrote about their experience:

Red Clay (excerpt)
David G. Rogers[63]

So the story is told by the hills themselves
As they speak in jargon unfamiliar today
That a Marine came along stalking the 'cong'
With his rifle to 'Search and Destroy' his prey
His comrades came, too, to render support
Each finding ruggedness causing them to say
These hill are infested with a potent enemy,
These hills of Khe Sanh made of red clay. (Eichler, 110)

Khe Sanh
By Robert Ratkevich

In years to come some Old Gunny will tell
of this place called Khe Sanh, on the border of Hell.

He'll tell some Young Boot bout the 'Old Corps Marines',
The Tough Fighting Men of His Mighty Green Machine.

He'll tell of the days when the sky rained hot lead
Of the Padre who knelt and prayed for our dead.

In years to come some old Gunny will tell
And he'll cliché the words, War Is Hell.

But few will remember and less, less will care
Except for some Jar Head Marines, that were there. (Eichler, 100)

'Johnson sought, in his own words, to do "enough but not too much", hoping that carefully calibrated bombing in the North and the commitment of combat troops in the South would persuade Hanoi to negotiate a peaceful two-state solution. ... Both efforts achieved their immediate goals ... [but] an elusive and resilient enemy avoided contact when necessary. ... By early 1967, the war had become a bloody stalemate' (Herring, 2).

Phase Six (1968): Tet Offensive
By December 1968, some 536,000 US troops were serving in Vietnam.

Early in 1968, Le Duan, the Communist Party secretary, sought to end the stalemate. 'His bold plan called for a series of attacks in remote parts of South Vietnam', leaving cities unprotected (Herring, 3). On 30 January 1968, he launched what became known as the **Tet Offensive**. During the Tet Offensive, Vietcong forces assaulted all major urban areas of South Vietnam, including an assault on the US embassy in South Vietnam: many Vietcong died but the Vietcong come across as winners because they brought war to every place in South Vietnam at the same time. The Tet Offensive included the battle for Hue and the siege at Khe Sanh, from 20 January to 14 April 1968.

The North Vietnamese hoped that this one major attack would encourage the civilian population to rise and fight for freedom. 'The communists guessed wrong. Militarily, the attack was a disaster, with some 50,000 communists dead and many more wounded. This was over ten times American and South Vietnamese losses. The population did not rise in support of the VC' (Dunnigan and Nofi, 258). Because of the heavy losses in the Tet Offensive – 'among the casualties are the Vietcong's best fighters, officers and organizers' (*Vietnam: Special Newsweek Edition*, 7) – North Vietnamese Army troops

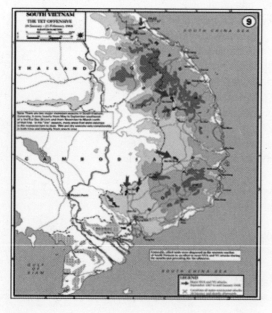

Map showing Tet strikes.
(Wikipedia)

190

were hurriedly sent to South Vietnam to 'refill the depleted ranks of the NLF. ... One draftee remembers being told "to move fast or there will be nothing left to liberate"' (Ward, 313). Radio Hanoi initially announced the success of the Tet Offensive and the support of the civilian population. 'But after a couple of weeks,' one Hanoi resident remembered, 'we didn't hear any more news. The Saigon regime was still there and the US planes were still bombing. It was obvious the radio wasn't telling the truth' (Ward, 314).

The Vietcong were no longer content to fight a guerilla-type war, hiding in jungles and melting into the population of rural villages between attacks. The Tet Offensive struck cities and towns. 'Life changed for the South Vietnamese. Son Dinh Nguyen, an orderly at the Can Tho ARVN Hospital, remarked, "The war had come to us to our town. Suddenly we did not know what the future would bring. We might have a good day and believe everything was normal, but in the middle of the night something might happen"' (Powell, 106).

With the failure of the Tet Offensive to encourage the civilian population to rise up against the oppressive South Vietnamese government, and the loss of so many fighters, the North now realized that a sudden offensive would not win the war. They needed to preserve their military forces for future campaigns. They needed to endure, to be patient, and to seize their opportunities; they realized that 'victory will come to us, not suddenly, but in a complicated and tortuous way' (Ward, 387).

Although the Vietcong losses were heavy, 'the Tet Offensive had an electric effect on popular opinion in the United States. The banner headlines and the television reports of fighting in the cities brought the shock of reality to what was still for many Americans a distant and incomprehensible war. The pictures of corpses in the garden of the American embassy cut through the haze of argument and counterargument, giving flat contradiction to the official optimism about the slow but steady progress of the war' (Fitzgerald, 493).

In response to the Tet Offensive, the US and its allies launched a series of counter-offensives:

1. The 3rd Marine Division's **Operation Kentucky** aimed at preventing enemy infiltration through the Demilitarized Zone in central Quang Tri Province.
2. **Operation Nevada Eagle**, initiated on 17 May 1968 in Thua Thien Province, continued in 1969 as the US 101st Airborne Division continued to defeat enemy personnel and capture rice caches, material, and installations within its large area of operations.
3. Two battalions of the 4th Marine Regiment were engaged in **Operation Scotland II.** Initiated on 15 April 1968, this multi-battalion search and clear operation was centered in and around Khe Sanh.
4. The IV Corps Tactical Zone Dry Weather Campaign began on 1 December 1968 in support of the overall mission to prevent Vietcong units from interfering with pacification efforts. **Operation Speedy Express** interdicted lines of enemy communication and denied him the use of base areas. Although engagements in Speedy Express were typically small, the 9th Infantry Division fought several sizeable engagements with impressive results. (all above excerpted from US Army Center of Military History, 9)

Walter Cronkite
with troops
in Vietnam.
(Public domain)

Walter Cronkite, the voice of CBS News and the most trusted source in the United States, reported after the Tet Offensive that 'past performance gives no confidence that the [South] Vietnamese government can cope with its problems. ... The Tet offensive required the realization ... that negotiations had to be just that, "not the dictation of peace terms"' (Tuchman, 352–353).

This statement shocked members of the US administration, who felt they had lost Walter Cronkite. After his platoon "shelled the South Vietnamese town of Bentre," on 7 February 1968, a US major explained what war tactics were necessary: 'we had to destroy the town in order to save it' (Merton, 489).[64]

Peter Arnett, an AP reporter stationed in Vietnam, wrote his impressions of events at Ben Tre, realizing 'it was [also] the essential dilemma of the Tet Offensive. It became necessary to destroy the town in order to save it. ... At what point do your turn your heavy guns and jet fighter-bombers on the streets of your own city? When does the infliction of civilian casualties become irrelevant as long as the enemy is destroyed?' (256). The statement by the US major in Ben Tre and the Tet Offensive provided the answer. In March 1968, 'Atrocities reached a new level [as] U S soldiers [under the command of Lieutenant William Calley] tortured and murdered around 500 unarmed South Vietnamese civilians' in what later became known as the My Lai Massacre (Rosenberg, 3).

The losses in the war, and the anti-war sentiment led Senator Eugene McCarthy to challenge Johnson in the 1968 Democratic primaries; Senator Robert Kennedy also announced his candidacy for the presidency. Johnson dropped out 31 March 1968 allowing his Vice President Hubert Humphrey to enter the race, losing to Richard Nixon, who promised to end the war in Vietnam. During that year both Robert Kennedy and Martin Luther King, jr. were assassinated.

The administration blamed hostile news media, for all the chaos and anti-war sentiment in the United States, not realizing its own contribution to the public's misunderstanding: the US was unduly optimistic and deliberately deceptive in its assessments of the war. Formal peace talks began in Paris on 13 May 1968: the first order of business was what shape the peace table would take! Around this time, the number of ARVN troops expanded, but many also deserted and officers were in short supply. Many ARVN soldiers were happy that Americans were doing the bulk of the fighting.

In March 1968, 'Atrocities reached a new level [as] U S soldiers [under the command of Lieutenant William Calley] tortured and murdered around 500 unarmed South

Vietnamese civilians' in what later became known as the My Lai Massacre (Rosenberg, 3). Then Robert Kennedy and Martin Luther King, Jr, were both killed. Johnson chose not to run for re-election, and Richard Nixon won the 1968 presidential election.

Phase Seven (1969–1973): Fighting to Win an Honorable Peace
'Let us understand: North Vietnam cannot defeat or humiliate the United States. Only Americans can do that.' Richard M. Nixon (1969)

'We believe that peace is at hand.' Henry Kissinger (October 1972)

President Nixon says, 'The true objective of this war is peace. It is a war for peace.' 'Peace with honor' was the slogan: any pull-out of American troops could not look like defeat; any pull-out had to leave South Vietnam independent with a reasonable chance to survive on its own (11/3/1969).

The number of US troops in theatre began to de-escalate: December 1969 there were 475,000 troops in Vietnam; in December 1970 there were 334,600 troops in Vietnam; in December 1971 there were 175,000 troops in Vietnam; and by December 1972 only 24,200.

'Nineteen hours after the self-imposed week-long Tet truce, 4 February 1968, [North Vietnam escalated the war:] enemy gunners launched coordinated rocket and mortar attacks on more than 100 cities, towns and military installations throughout South Vietnam, including the capital Saigon' (Knauer, 18). These attacks towards the end of 1968 made it even more imperative to get North Vietnam to engage in peace talks to bring this war to an end.

> Peace talks in Geneva in 1969 provided little hope of a truce as delegates argued over whether the table should be round or rectangular: round, all have equal status; rectangular, some delegates from some countries would sit at the head of the table.

With little hope of success in Geneva, Nixon begins a policy called 'Vietnamization',[65] the gradual takeover of the war by the South Vietnamese Army. The number of US troops in country began to de-escalate. In December 1969 there were 475,000, in December 1970 334,600, December 1971 156,800, and by December 1972 just 24,200. By 1970, it had become one of the largest, best-equipped armies in the world. But the US, through its incursion into – really an invasion of – Cambodia on 30 April 1970, continued to support the ARVN troops. With the war nearing its end, demonstrations against the war became more imperative with major demonstrations held on US college campuses, including Jackson State (MS) and Kent State (OH), and 100,000 protesters went to Washington in May.

Operation Menu. From 1969–1973, the United States, under the direction of Henry Kissinger, bombed Cambodia, claiming that Cambodia had become a sanctuary for Vietcong, North Vietnam soldiers, and other communists. This contributed to the Khmer Rouge's four-year reign in Cambodia (Tan, 1–2).

Operation Apache Snow. This was the name given to the operation to take Hill 937, which came to be called Hamburger Hill. Although US forces took the hill, it was only with 272 support sorties (assignments) by the USAF, 450 tons of bombs, 69 tons of napalm, five infantry battalions of 1,800 men, and ten batteries of artillery. Seventy Americans were killed and 372 wounded, while at least 630 soldiers in the North Vietnamese Army were killed. The US forces abandoned the hill soon after defeating the North Vietnamese, who then retook the hill.

'Troops in the 101st Airborne Division (Airmobile) even offered $10,000 to anyone who would kill the officer who ordered the bloody and pointless attack on Hamburger Hill' (Kutler, 175). The outrage reached home. An American soldier tried to put this battle into the perspective of the war: 'It was the bare determination, not to take this hill or that one, but to survive this hell, to outlast that little slant-eyed, rice-powered bastard they chased no matter how many hills had to be humped or how many monsoons or 118° days had to be endured' (Anderson, *Grunts*, 158).

North Vietnamese soldier Bao Ninh, one of only ten to survive from a brigade of 500 men, wrote: 'Often in the middle of a busy street, in broad daylight, I've suddenly become lost in a daydream. On smelling the stink of rotten meat I've suddenly imagined I was back crossing Hamburger Hill in [1969]. Walking over strewn corpses. The stench of death is often so overpowering I have to stop in the middle of the pavement, holding my nose' (46).

Combat Engineer 'Light Bulb' Bryant was never in the fight for Hill 937, but he could see the lunacy of fighting for territory, then letting it go. 'And we weren't gaining any ground. We would fight for a hill all day, spend two days or two nights there, and then abandon the hill. Then maybe two, three months later, we would have to come back and retake the same piece of territory' (Terry, 21). US news reporting focused on a military strategy that appeared to have no purpose – why take a hill and then abandon it at a tremendous loss of life?

The military was sensitive about the operation at Hamburger Hill. Consequently, there were various official word changes and restrictions introduced. There was no more 'hearts and minds'; instead, they were 'developing community spirit'. 'Search and destroy' became 'search and clear', so as to protect the civilians. In all, twenty-two common military terms were dropped, including the much-abused 'body count'. And there were no more 'Five o'clock Follies' (Herr, 99); instead, reporters were briefed. Herr had to shake his head at the new jargon – 'frontier sealing, census grievance, black operations (pretty good, for jargon), revolutionary development, and armed propaganda. I asked a spook [spy] what that one meant and he just smiled. Surveillance, collecting and reporting, was like a carnival bear now, broken and dumb, an Intelligence beast, our own' (52).

Senate revokes Tonkin Gulf Resolution. Nixon continued to withdraw troops; by the end of 1971, only 175,000 were left – just 75,000 were combat troops.

'By 1971, the glory and the innocence of the early days of the Vietnam conflict were gone. The war was a stalemate; both sides were claiming victory, but only the losses were real. More than 50,000 Americans had died, and there were not a lot of war-hungry hawks left (at least, not among those of us chosen to do the fighting). The public still supported the troops on principle, but the conflict itself had been disowned by virtually every segment of society. It turned into a war without end or purpose' (Pendergrass, 18). By the summer of 1971, 71 per cent of the American public believed the US had made a mistake by sending troops to Vietnam; 58 per cent said the war was 'immoral'.

To destroy the Ho Chi Minh Trail through Cambodia and Laos, and to strengthen Kissinger's bargaining power at the negotiating tables, Nixon ordered the secret bombing of the trail and invasions into Cambodia in 1970 and Laos in 1971to try to stop the supply route. 'Yet, no matter what they tried, the Americans never succeeded in seriously disrupting North Vietnamese supply lines' (Vietnam Combatants, #5 & #6).

In March 1972, North Vietnam invaded South Vietnam in what became known as the **Easter Offensive**. Up until then, most of the fighting in the South had been done by the National Liberation Front, known as the Vietcong. In response, Nixon ordered the bombing of Haiphong Harbor and Hanoi and a naval blockade of North Vietnam. Because Nixon and Kissinger had eased tensions with the Soviet Union and the Chinese, and because the 'major North Vietnamese offensive stalled in the Spring of 1972, Hanoi became amenable … to a negotiated settlement' (Lippman, 8). The US agreed to let North Vietnamese troops remain in South Vietnam, for Nguyen Van Thieu to continue to lead South Vietnam, and to accept a tripartite election: the Saigon government, the Vietcong, and neutralists.

In October 1972, South Vietnamese leader Thieu rejected this plan. To reassure President Thieu, President Nixon delivered more than $1 billion in military hardware, after which the South Vietnamese Army had the fourth-largest air force in the world. Nixon also ordered Operation Linebacker II (Lippman, 9).

Operation linebacker II. After the breakdown of peace talks on 13 December 1972, Nixon hoped that massive bombing would cause the North Vietnamese to return to the negotiating table. Over twelve days, between 18 and 30 December 1972, the US military dropped more bombs on North Vietnam than had been dropped from 1969–1971. On 30 December, Nixon halted the bombing. Peace negotiations restarted in January 1973; a negotiated settlement was imposed on South Vietnam.

Phase Eight (1973–present): Post-War

'You have my full assurance that we will respond with full force should the settlement be violated by North Vietnam.' Richard Nixon in a letter to President Thieu (January 1973)

'Today, America can regain the sense of pride that existed before Vietnam. But it cannot be achieved by refighting a war that is finished … These events, tragic as they are, portend neither the end of the world nor of America's leadership in the world.' President Gerald Ford (7 May 1975)

'The good news is the war is over. The bad news is that we lost.' Henry Kissinger

Nixon had three tactics for ending the war: 1) **Vietnamization**; 2) '**Linkage**, an attempt to leverage Moscow into convincing its ally … North Vietnam, to accept some of America's key negotiating positions. … If Nixon could somehow "link" trade and arms control agreements with Soviet cooperation in Vietnam, both sides stood to benefit'; 3) **Escalation**, which he used in the hope of scaring the North Vietnamese into making concessions at the negotiating table. The outcome was the Paris Peace Accords in January 1973. The Accords were the same that the US could have accepted four years earlier (Zeitz). The Paris Accords stipulated the creation of the Council of Reconciliation and Concord – composed of South Vietnamese, neutralists, and communists – who would supervise elections, reunifying Vietnam. 'He [Kissinger] and Le Duc Tho shared the Nobel Peace Prize for the secret negotiations that produced the 1973 Paris agreement and ended US military participation in Vietnam' (Lippman, 1)

'The treaty left the situation on paper no different from the insecure settlement of Geneva nineteen years before. To the physical reality had since been added more than half a million deaths in [the] North and South, hundreds of thousands of wounded and destitute, burned and crippled children, landless peasants, a ravaged land deforested and pitted with bomb craters and a people torn by mutual hatred' (Tuchman, 373).

Operation Homecoming. After the Paris Peace Accords in 1973, North Vietnam released approximately 550 US prisoners of war. In November 1973, Congress passed the War Powers Act: the US President was required to notify Congress within forty-eight hours of any deployment of American troops, and must withdraw them within sixty days unless Congress backed the use of force. In the Fall of 1974, the balance of power shifted to North Vietnam. Then in December, North Vietnam invaded the South; the US failed to respond. Congress authorized $33 million to evacuate Americans and for humanitarian purposes. In 1975, the North Vietnamese Spring Offensive brought about the collapse of South Vietnam and the capture of Saigon, which was subsequently renamed Ho Chi Minh City.

South Vietnam officially surrendered on 30 April 1975. Military strategists and hawks blamed the US administration and the media for dictating the rules of engagement and not letting the military win the war. Many doves responded by saying that the US never should have entered the civil war in the first place, a war that it could never win.

In April 1975, President Ford ordered **Operation Babylift**, a mission to evacuate Vietnamese orphans before Saigon fell. Regina Aune, a US Air Force flight nurse, directed the operation out of Tan Son Nhut airbase. The first mission ended in disaster – the plane crashed soon after take-off, with 130 lives lost, seventy-eight of them orphans – but subsequent missions successfully evacuated more than 3,000 orphans. On 2 July 1976, Vietnam became the Socialist Republic of Vietnam.

Operation BabyLift. (Wikipedia)

SECTION FOUR

Coming Home

'And what about when your warrior's anger goes home? What is it like with his wife and children? Is it useful then, too?' (Cicero)

♦ ♦ ♦

'They went off to fight, they came home, and nothing felt the same. To their thinking, the government abandoned them. Their women had moved on or grown more independent. Their kids were strangers. They didn't know how to make sense of the world going on without them, and they needed someone to blame.' (Slaughter, 338)

♦ ♦ ♦

John Kerry Vietnam War question: 'How do you ask a man to be the last man to die for a mistake?' (T. Friedman)

Introduction

One student who attended my course on Vietnam asked Johnnie Phillips (one of the Vietnam vets): 'How can I get my father to talk about the war?' Johnnie told her to say: 'Welcome home.' She went over to Johnnie and welcomed him home with tears in her eyes. Many of the students were equally touched. I never found out if she did welcome her father home, or, if she did, how he responded.

Whenever my husband, daughter or I see a Vietnam vet, or for that matter any veteran, we always welcome them home. I usually add that my welcome includes the 160 students I taught in my several courses on the Vietnam War. We have learned what words to say and not to say. One phrase we stopped using is, 'we appreciate your service'.

They clearly remember that no one welcomed them home; that they came home one at a time because they each had a different **Date of Expected Return from Overseas (DEROS)**; that their country did not honor them; that no one gave them a parade; that no one in their community felt honored that they had served; that, in fact, many in their community avoided them and referred to them as 'baby-killers'. Many of them have stories to tell of the hatred others felt for them, not realizing their sacrifices. Coming home was both traumatic – the world had changed – and joyful – they had survived. Some 58,000, however, had not.[1]

One who did not return. (Public domain)

INTRODUCTION

'Coming home' meant something quite different for the many South Vietnamese who were escaping Vietnam to live in a foreign country. One such Vietnamese, Hoang Ly, has never forgotten to what extraordinary means Marine Stephen Greene went to save him and his family. Every Thanksgiving and Christmas, he and his family sent letters of thanks to Marine Greene (Free, 1). Not only did these escapees face language and cultural difficulties, but many Americans were not particularly welcoming. These Vietnamese also faced, and still face, many of the problems that returning United States veterans encountered. The United States owes them a debt of gratitude for their contributions to the war: many of them fought side-by-side with US personnel or served as Tiger Scouts, policemen or other administrative functions in the South. When the war was over, many who were unable to escape faced harsh punishments for opposing the North.

Chapter 1

Short-Timers

Going home was so important that the soldiers kept track of how many days they had left before the Freedom Bird would take them home. When they had fewer than 100 days in 'Nam, they referred to themselves as 'two-digit midgets'. They even created an acronym for it: DEROS (Date of Expected Return from Overseas). Each man had a different DEROS, so the war was a matter of coming and leaving alone.

According to psychologist James Goodwin, 'DEROS did its job. For those who had been struggling with a psychological breakdown due to the stresses of combat, the DEROS fantasy served as a major prophylactic to actual overt symptoms of acute combat reaction. For these veterans, it was a hard-fought struggle to hold on until their time came' (J. Ebert, 397). They had calendars; some had them on their helmets, which they would reduce one day at a time. They called themselves 'short-timers', possibly borrowed from prison slang (Hynes, 184).

A short-timer was nearing the end of his tour of duty. He knew exactly how much more time he had left 'in country', almost down to the second. 'I remember when I had two months, seven days, and eleven hours and thought I was short' (Bobby Ward, Vietnam Vet Program, 1/21/93). Many of the troops had a ritual game, 'how short are

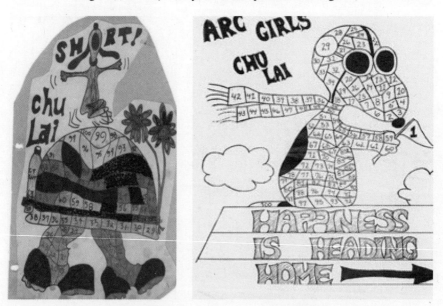

Above left and above right: Short-timer calendars. (Courtesy E. Brown, Jr)

you?' The short-timer would reply with some appropriate remark. '"I'm so short," he would say, "I have to stand on a ladder to tie my bootlaces"' (Van Devanter, 229). Another appropriate remark was: 'I'm so short I'd have to parachute off a dime.'

Many short-timers who were two months from leaving would stick to their base camp and keep a low profile. 'Short-timers still in the field were overly cautious by nature and sought to avoid any condition that might lessen by the smallest fraction their chances of completing their tours intact. Thus, [one man] soon learned that short-timers didn't want to be near a new guy; it was paranoia or bad luck' (J. Ebert, 139). It was only later, much later, that researchers discovered that only 6 per cent of the casualties occurred to men with less than three months to go (Dunnigan & Nofi, 77–78).

'Three weeks. Eternity. Two weeks. Each breath uses time, brings escape closer. Maybe, just maybe I might make it? Can't afford to be careless. Details. So few of the guys around me understand. The ones who understood made it. [And finally] there aren't any more squares on my calendar'[2] (Ketwig, 195).

Reporter Michael Herr saw that 'odd things happen when tours are almost over. It's the **Short-Timer Syndrome**. In the heads of the men who are really in the war for a year, all tours end early. No one expects much from a man when he is down to one or two weeks. He becomes a luck freak, an evil-omen collector, a diviner of every bad sign. If he has the imagination, or the experience of war, he will recognize his own death a thousand times a day, but he will always have enough left to do the one big thing, to Get Out. … In this war they called it "acute environmental reaction", but Vietnam has spawned a jargon of such delicate locutions that it's often impossible to know even remotely the thing being described' (91).

See the End
By Randy Cribbs

Get through one day,
Then think about the next,
Always in our mind
. Like a hex.

As the tour shortened,
We dwelled on it more,
Thinking of
That friendlier shore.

Then so short, can't
Get in the rack,
But more anxious; maybe
We would get back.

One digit midget, days
From the great silver bird;
Think it, but don't say it,
Bad luck.
Not a single word. (53)

'They [25 of my buddies from the 4/39] were very surprised and happy to see old Doc Holley there, and the feelings were mutual. Well, as of tomorrow I will officially become a "two digit midget" with only ninety-nine days remaining until DEROS! Praise the Lord, I'm getting short!' (Holley, 188–189).

'I sure am getting a short-timer's attitude. I don't feel like doing anything but eat, sleep, and drink. I wish I could just go to sleep and wake up one day before DEROS. But it's really best to keep busy, which I am doing with all the troubles at this dump' (Holley, 191). Short-Timer Syndrome became a preoccupation. Infantryman Tom Schultz said: 'You'd been there a long time, but you could have only one day left and make a mistake' (J. Ebert, 398). 'Almost every day the grunts ambled over to Epps' mortar pit, ate C's [combat rations] with him and helped him get things ready to go, as if by thus associating with and helping these short-timers, some of their shortness would rub off and help them get home sooner' (Anderson, *Grunts*, 163).

Not only short-timers were obsessing about time. 'Like every American in Vietnam … he had his obsession with Time. No one ever talked about "When-this-lousy-war-is-over". Only "How much time you got" … This could be seen in the calendar on their helmets' (Herr, 118).

Short Timer
By Randy Cribbs

So short you can't see me.
Days, not weeks, and I am free.

How glorious I begin to feel,
Hot food replacing the OD [olive drab] canned meal.
Not hiding from
The detail man,
Too short, but
Catch me if you can.

A different line of work, no doubt,
Even assembly line widgets,
Things OK to think about
If you are a one digit midget.

No more worry over
Ignition of fuse and primer,
Not for me,
    I'm a short timer! (66)

They called their transport home the **Freedom Bird**. The name for the plane spoke volumes about what going home meant. But 'Freedom Bird' hit a raw nerve with the CBS Bureau's Vietnamese staff, who found the name too casual. '[A]s if their tragedy, their national hemorrhage was nothing more than a stop on a Disney tour' (Safer, 318). It was sixteen hours home with little or no debriefing, no information about how you might be received, nothing about what had changed: your wife running the household, your wife with a job, a baby born while you were in 'Nam. You were no longer the head of the household. While you were away, your wife had been forced to assume those duties to keep herself and her children alive. Your coming home was both a joyous occasion and a disruption of the household routine. Coping with this new routine was difficult. You felt disoriented: your former friends had little in common with you. Often, to help you cope, you drank, either alone or with your vet buddies.

'From life and death to snooty bitches and a pile of rubber, steel, grease and vinyl from Detroit called "Something to Believe in" was too great a distance for the veterans to cover in sixteen hours, or even sixteen days. It could be done physically but not mentally. Few could quickly assimilate that stark dichotomy, few could quickly move away from it and formulate those things their parents call career goals' (Anderson, *Grunts*, 181).

LRRP Ford couldn't absorb the fact that he was leaving: 'I should have felt happy I was goin' home when I got on that plane in Cam Ranh Bay to leave. But I didn't exactly. I felt – I felt – I felt very insecure 'cause I didn't have a weapon. I had one of them long knives, like a big hacksaw knife. I had that. And had my cane. And I had a couple of grenades in my bag. They took them from me when I got to Washington, right? And I felt insecure. I just felt real bad' (Terry, 31). No wonder many slept with a gun beside them or became violent when they heard firecrackers go off.

At the beginning of his tour, Holley said: 'I thank God every day for America and I vow to kiss her good earth the minute I get off that big freedom bird 358 days hence! We have the finest country in the world, and anybody who doubts it should come to Nam for a spell as a grunt' (24). He kept his promise when his tour was over. When his Freedom Bird landed at Travis Air Force Base, he got off, dropped down and kissed the grimy surface. 'I had promised myself I would kiss the good old ground if God would just let me return home' (199).

Going Home
By Randy Cribbs

Glistening leaves,
Like emeralds,
Such a deep green,
But
Maybe here a spot of red;
And here a creature
Of the jungle,
Tentative,
Raising its dazed head.

In the distance,
Delayed
To the ear.
Raising up, bright,
Napalm,
A blooming chandelier.

Thousands of years
Left alone
In this canopy darkness,
Interrupted by death;
The order of things gone.

Movement. Static.
A moan.
Into the Freedom bird.
    Going Home. (Cribbs, 99)

Welcome home. (Public domain)

Chapter 2

Protests

Although many were aware of the anti-war movement, they weren't aware of the growing gulf between those for and those against the war. At first the split wasn't obvious, but as the war dragged on, both sides became more vocal, with factions showing up in Congress and the White House as well. At first, Johnson was concerned about the Hawks (Republicans and conservative Democrats) who wanted to win the war. The Hawks in Congress subscribed to the **Domino Theory**, while the Doves, who wanted peace, questioned how Vietnam was of value to us.

The protests only strengthened after the publication of what became known as the *Pentagon Papers* in June 1971. These papers revealed the government's deceptions in an attempt to encourage young men to fight in Vietnam. The protests also strengthened when some of the soldiers joined them – many did.

Jon Voight, in the 1978 film *Coming Home*, represented many returning veterans who believed that the war had been wrong. These veterans badgered congressmen, marched on the Pentagon, tried to turn themselves in for war crimes and threw their medals over the recently erected fence at the Capitol building. 'Thus, it fell to the Vietnam Veteran himself, the lower-level instrument of the policy ... to articulate the concerns about the widening license of war, as practiced by the American military ... his own dehumanization and brutalization by the environment of Vietnam' (Reston Rift, 183).

In the final scene of the movie, paraplegic Luke Martin, played by Voight, tells high school students that they have a choice; he didn't. They may feel it is patriotic, glorious, a chance to get their licks in, be a war hero. But once they get over there, the situation would be totally different. They would grow up fast. They'd realize that

Vietnam veterans join protest
movement. (Public domain)

killing someone, that having their best buddy die in their arms, were images they'd never forget. He tells them he is ashamed of some of the things he did over there, and he lives with that shame each day. It gives him chills just thinking about it.[3] He reminds them that they have a choice, that they don't have to endure the horrors he witnessed.

But to some Vietnam vets, the actions taken by the veterans against the war and the movie itself, which starred Jane Fonda, betrayed all that they had fought for. They called Fonda 'Hanoi Jane' for her outspoken support of North Vietnam during the war. She travelled to North Vietnam during the conflict to demonstrate her support. In Hanoi, US newspapers showed a picture of her sitting with an anti-aircraft weapon.

They also had no love for the character played by Voight. He was a **Jody**, the name given to the man back in the World who stole the love and affection of the girlfriend or wife of a soldier overseas. That Jody was a vet himself made his actions all the worse; he, too, was a traitor in the movie. He stole the heart of a soldier's wife and chained his wheelchair to the gates of a recruiting center in his own anti-war protest.

'Forgive and forget' was not part of the grunts' philosophy towards Fonda. Even now, after Fonda's years of explanations and apologies for her actions during the war, the veterans and many others forced the QVC shopping channel to cancel Fonda's scheduled appearance on a show. They wrote so many letters vilifying Fonda and threatening to boycott the channel if Fonda appeared that, ultimately, QVC asked Fonda not to appear; and she didn't.

Chapter 3

Problems at Home

'Dr Jonathan Shay, ... a clinical psychologist, ... has written extensively about
[the lasting effects of the war on Vietnam Veterans.] "They returned
home to protesters who accused them of being torturers, perpetrators
of atrocities, and baby killers. For every returning veteran who encountered this
personally, there were many more who saw scenes selected for their dramatic
and/or outrageous qualities in the TV news or heard nth-hand stories.
The media presented a barrage of images portraying the Vietnam Veteran
as crazy, drug-addicted, and violent. For many veterans who had joined up
because they thought it was their duty as citizens, who had grown
up on John Wayne and Audie Murphy, rejection by the Community
was infuriating."' (Chrisinger, 3.)

Coming home meant facing many problems. Because soldiers came home one at a time, each with their own DEROS, there was no debriefing, no parades, no celebrations, no welcome homes, no preparing them to re-enter the world of civilians. During my Thursday evening programs many of the vets talked about not being welcomed home, about their attempts to find their way in this new world, and how the memories of the war continue to affect them. Many assumed menial jobs, much below their abilities, as they were unable to get on with their lives. Some, like Randall, (see the Preface) carried their weapons with them wherever they went. 'The army had no debriefing or adjustment period. A grunt might fly to Oakland or Portland in fatigues he had worn in the bush, still caked with Vietnamese mud. In the Stateside processing center he would grab a shower, a dress uniform, a pay envelope ... and be home that afternoon. There was no orientation; the army did not want to admit your head might be screwed up by Vietnam' (Ketwig, 186).

There were, however, parades in New York City and Dallas for the returning 566 prisoners of war released by the North Vietnamese as part of the agreement between the United States and North Vietnam, known as Operation Homecoming. One of these men, Philip Manhard, the pacification chief in Hué, was the highest-ranked civilian POW in North Vietnam. He remained in solitary confinement for five years until North Vietnam released him as part of the peace Accords (Reston, Sherman, 306–307).

Vietnam veterans protest against lack of jobs. (Public domain)

On a Freedom Bird, coming home.
(Public domain)

The grunts who had come home one at a time were not invited to participate in these parades. This is why most Vietnam veterans felt that they have not yet been welcomed home. Many wives reported that they could not touch their husbands while they were sleeping for fear of being attacked. Many veterans still carry weapons on their person and many take cover when they hear thunder, fearing incoming missiles. The Fourth of July can be hell for some vets. One of my students at my Thursday evening program asked Vietnam vet Johnnie Phillips what he missed most. He said not being welcomed home. She stood up, walked over to Johnnie and welcomed him home.

When Lynda Van Devanter's[4] tour was over, she was dropped off at Oakland Airport in uniform and had to hitchhike to San Francisco. When someone finally picked her up, he spat on her: 'We're going past the airport, sucker, but we don't take Army pigs' (Van Devanter, 247). 'Some veterans still in uniform and back in the World noticed how others viewed them. There was "The look" – as combat nurse, Lynda Van Devanter said. "I was a pariah, a nonperson so low that they believed they could squash me underfoot; I was as popular as a disease and as untouchable as a piece of shit"' (248).

Once home, soldiers dealt with their own memories of the war, feelings that their families couldn't understand. Soldiers were not free. Some suffered from PTSD (Post Traumatic Stress Disorder); others from survivor's guilt. 'Somewhere between Vietnam and a bottle of whiskey my nightmare began. With scratches of line and bursts of color I have tried to rid myself of that nightmare and its long-reaching effects. I have tried to draw a map for myself from the past to the present from sickness and anger to peace and health. Every day I have to work because the truce I have with darkness is delicate and peace requires constant maintenance' (Richard Bartow in Sinaiko, 25).

Kevin Kerney, the fictional New Mexico policeman created by author Michael McGarrity, comes home from Vietnam a changed man, according to his landlord, Erma Ferguson: 'K[evin Kerney] so changed since Vietnam. That warm, open young man now quiet, closed, wary. Tight smile, stingy conversation, long silences, easily distracted' (McGarrity, 96). Several chapters later, his son asks about his killing people in his career as a policeman, but it applies equally well to his days as a soldier in Vietnam. Kerney responds: 'There's no simple way to describe it. You tell yourself it was necessary, that you had no choice. But each time it happens, a little bit of you withers away. … [What withers away is] your innocence, the good inside you – call it what you will. You carry what you did like an invisible yoke' (McGarrity, 137). **Post-Traumatic Stress Disorder.**

> In the television show JAG, about military lawyers, one episode (season 4 (1998), episode 5) depicts the mistreatment of veterans suffering from PTSD and other mental ailments. The show argues for better care of America's military veterans. It reveals the impact budget cuts and poor care have on America's damaged military.

PTSD is what they used to call 'shellshock' in both the First and Second World War. 'The difference between the two is at least they now know something about treating it' (Jones, *Dead of Winter*, 291). 'PTSD is a mental health condition that's triggered by a terrifying event – either experiencing it or witnessing it. Symptoms may include flashbacks, nightmares, and severe anxiety' (Mayo Clinic). It's what causes Vietnam vets to sleep with a gun under their pillow, hide under their bed during Fourth of July celebrations or react violently when touched while asleep. 'I know a little bit about the monsters war can turn men into. The monsters that go bump in the night when we return from war. … Lost causes, lost lives, lost souls. You hate God. Deny Jesus. Screw Abraham and Mohammed and Buddha and Miss America' (Jones, *Dead of Winter*, 291).

Harrod, an army nurse, suffers from a form of PTSD. 'I am very claustrophobic. I don't go into stores where I can't see the exit signs and the lights are too bright. Unexpected sounds make me jump. People who sneak up on me are in for a big surprise. I have frightened a few coworkers with my response' (Harrod, 25). One veteran told Herr: '"I just can't hack it back in the World," he said. He told me that after he'd come back home the last time he would sit in his room all day, and sometimes he'd stick a hunting rifle out the window, leading people in cars as they passed his house until the only feeling he was aware of was all up in the tip of that one finger' (5).

Survivor's Guilt. Others suffered from survivor's guilt. Wounded Marine Lewis Puller, Jr describes the feeling: 'I felt guilty for years that I had abandoned them [the South Vietnamese] before our work was finished. I was to feel even worse that I was glad to be leaving them' (187). 'To make matters worse, I suddenly felt guilty to be feasting on prime rib and drinking chilled wine while real marines were trying only to make it through another day in the arena' (273).

Jail
By Jim Gray

> If life can be thought of as a prison
> In which we serve a term prescribed
> By the ultimate Supreme Court,
> Then surely my solitary confinement
> Is cruel and unusual punishment.
> What I did for love of my country

Was not cold and premeditated,
It was a crime of passion
And I was just a juvenile offender. (27)

North Vietnamese soldiers suffered from survivor's guilt too. In his book *The Sorrow of War*, Bao Ninh wrote: 'What remained was sorrow, the immense sorrow, and the sorrow of having survived. The sorrow of war' (192).

For Lew Puller
By Hoa Binh and Mike McDonell

I remember the first time I ever heard of you, Lew,
it was in the late fall of '67 and word came down
from the lieutenants' net that Chesty Puller's son
was at the Basic School in Quantico and I thought
'The poor sonofabitch' because you were your father's son
and would never be able to fill his boots
and everyone would expect you to.
But I was wrong – you more than filled them –
but in a totally different way
and so
I write to you while you transit between life and legend.
Like you, we knew where you would go: to VietNam and I Corps,
to the 1st Marine Division and the First Marines.
It was written in the stars, the Southern Cross,
under which we fought each night and which surrounded
the blood-red 'One' branded with 'Guadalcanal'.
If Chesty was the Marine Corps' god, then he was the son of the
1st Marine Division: his son would come to us.
'God save him,' I thought and pissed off into the monsoon rain,
stumbling towards Tet, near death and enlightenment.
Four months after I made my bird to El Toro,
you made yours to Danang, as green as I once was;
brown bitterness had not begun its work on you yet
as it had begun on me.
Shuffling papers in Barstow, I heard you were blown away
by a 105 rigged as a mine –
'One of ours got one of ours thanks to them,' I thought
and without looking back, I climbed through
the hole in my soul and never thought of you again
until I emerged from the other side
and found you there before me.
We shared the same wounds to the soul, Lew,
and you showed me how to heal them
one day at a time and in God's time
not mine.

You made us proud and humble,
two contradictory feelings held together
by your example of courage and service
to your brothers and sisters and to God.
Two years ago you dedicated my copy of your book,
thanking me for my service to my country,
welcoming me home and signing it 'Semper Fi'.
You ended by telling me to 'Keep coming back'
and we have come back –
to the World,
to this Wall and the memory of the others
and of you.
Rest in peace and in our hearts,
Fortunate Son.[5]

A New World. Others had a difficult time finding and keeping a job or reintegrating into their communities and families. Basil Paquet speaks to that difficulty:

A Visit
By Basil Paquet

'You don't look bitter,'
she said.
He thought,
'Bitter is a taste',
feeling her words
scrape across
memory's slow healing
like a slow knife.
Did she think she could see
how he felt?
'It don't matter,'
he said and heard
outside voices
in the wind
in humming tires
voices running against
the windows in a heavy rain. (Rottmann, 110)

What they came home to was not the world they had left. 'The veteran's bewilderment at the civilian reaction to the war revealed a large flaw in his observation of those who did not go. … The home-towners were no more interested in Vietnam when the veteran they knew left home than they were when he came back. … But whether there was a flaw in the veteran's thinking, his analysis of civilian America was no less real to him: apathy about the war was still inexcusable' (Anderson, *Grunts*, 182). Anderson also noticed that neither those at home who wanted an explanation as to why we lost nor the veterans, seeking 'consolation and understanding', got what they needed from the other. The grunt couldn't explain the administration's war policy, nor could he understand the deep frustration felt by those at home (184). One veteran said on the fact that 'nobody cared that you had been to Vietnam. … Everybody would be wondering where have you been for so long. They would say "how did you lose your leg? In a fight? A car wreck?" Anything, but Vietnam' (Terry, 181).

For most of the men and women in the 'Nam, there were only two places: the 'Nam and the World.[6] Or maybe in the craziness, you weren't sure just where you were – in-coming, out-going, in-coming, in-coming, out-going. You can read about the war, talk to others about it, but you can't know what it was like unless you've been there – jungle rot, over 100°F every day, mud, and Charlie out there waiting for you to pass. 'And a lot of things that might scare a lot of other people in terms of danger, I can just walk right on through without backing away, shying away, or making compromises that really should not be made. I've been there' (Terry, 142).

'About 2.5 million served in Vietnam … [and] were dispersed within a population of over 200 million [in the United States]. Thus, the Veterans had only about a one percent chance of meeting each other. Back in the World the Veterans were surrounded by persons unable to understand their thoughts, their actions, or even their words' (Anderson, *Grunts*, 176).

'To one vet the World was a 427 Chevelle with cheater slicks and tri-power carbs, parked way at the back of the drive-in, with footprints on the headliner and beer cans under the seat. … The World was where your kid brother lived, and if he ever thought of leaving to come over to this cesspool, you'd chop his toes off with a hatchet. … The World was flush toilets and doorknobs and fishing streams. A mythical, magical place that had existed once, and would again, and had been interrupted by the Vietnam War as a TV show is interrupted by a commercial. … The World existed. All too often the fantasy became clouded over by the day's events. It seemed far away intangible, even alien; but you couldn't let go of the fact that it existed, or you might never make it back.

427 Chevelle, 1967. (Wikipedia)

… Every single thing I had taken for granted in my life was a fantasy. The kitchen. My car. The folks. Clean sheets. Toilet paper. My arms, my legs, my face, even my brain … might not exist ten seconds from now.' (Ketwig, 4–5)

Herr had one conversation with a soldier: '"I ain't never getting hit in Vietnam … cause it don't exist." It was an old joke, but this time he wasn't laughing' (125).

Back to the World
By Randy Cribbs

Back to the world.
Always in our mind.
Waiting for that day,
Putting in our time.

Each day things
Grow more insane
For the pawns in
This political game.

Back in the world
They blame
The warriors for the war,
Those brave youth who
Heeded the call,
Nothing more.

We remind them,
Back in the world, of
Things not right,
Of us and them,
For and against,
Flee or fight.

But still
Over here
Not getting back
To the world
Is our worst fear …(92)

Leaving a rifle behind or out of sight was impossible at the end of a tour. The veterans knew only one thing to do with it. Charlie, one of our vets, was out in the woods the first day of deer hunting, and suddenly he realized that he was looking for a gook to kill: 'I took that rifle straight home and put it away' (Vietnam veterans program 3/4/93).

Caputo, like other Vietnam vets, had problems adjusting. He had symptoms of what he called 'combat veteranitis', 'an inability to concentrate, a childlike fear of darkness, a tendency to tire easily, chronic nightmares, an intolerance of loud noises – especially doors slamming and cars backfiring – and alternating moods of depression and rage that came over me for no apparent reason. Recovery has been less than total' (4). Caputo remembered telling his girlfriend, later his wife, that he needed to get out of a restaurant before he started a fight. He didn't know why he felt that way, but a little later that feeling was 'followed by this black depression' (story excerpted from Chrisinger, 4).

Dean Phillips, awarded the Silver Star and two Bronze Stars as a paratrooper in Vietnam, felt the same way: 'You know one of my best friends is blown in half and I keep thinking about that and here is this fucker sitting over here and the most important thing in his life appears to be whether the Dodgers won the pennant' (Chrisinger, 4).

The US Army provided booklets to parents (which continues today) that included what to expect once their loved ones came home. For those coming home from the 'Nam, parents were told: 'Don't be surprised if: your son grabs a bar of soap, runs outside in the rain and strips. It's a bush shower. They may crave ice cream. Milk. Canned peaches. Long showers. Careful about that weapon under the bed. Hours on the phone' (Van Devanter, 229–230).

Daniel Phillips created his own satirical, but accurate, list of soldiers' deprivations for parents of troops returning to Vietnam:

1. Never allow more than one piece of silverware per meal (a plastic spoon is best …).
2. Don't serve anything but roast beef for thirty to forty days. This is all the cooks [knew] how to prepare. [Call it anything you want, BBQ, pot roast, etc.]
3. Don't serve any milk that is fresher than 6 months old.
4. Before serving coffee in the morning, be sure to throw a cigarette butt in for flavor.
5. Remain calm when he pours gravy on his dessert or mixes peanut butter with his green peas.
6. Each evening after 7PM, open all doors and windows to let in … bugs and insects.
7. At least once a day interrupt his serenity and bliss by yelling 'Snake, Snake'.
8. Never allow the house to be cooler than 95 degrees. … Anything over 95 is fine.
9. When you wash his clothes add one cup dirt to rinse water to maintain that yellow look that he is accustomed to. (47)

Dunnigan and Nofi wrote::

'Vietnam Veterans seem no less well-adjusted than were those of the nation's earlier wars, though perhaps public awareness and tolerance of problems among them has been more acute. There have been a few genuinely objective surveys of Vietnam Veterans. These suggest a considerably different picture from the common one. Some 91 percent of Vietnam Veterans are proud to have served, and 74 percent believed their service was necessary. The overwhelming majority (91 percent) of Vietnam Veterans received discharges that were honorable, the same percentage that had prevailed in the decade before the war. Nor have most of them found adjustment to civilian life unusually difficult.

About 88 percent of them made the transition without difficulty, and the average income of Vietnam Veterans is about 18 percent higher, and their unemployment rate rather lower, than that for their non-veteran contemporaries. Drug abuse patterns among Vietnam Veterans and non-veterans of the same era are not particularly different; remember that it was the era of "turn on, tune in, and drop out". Fewer than 0.5 percent of them have been in jail, in contrast to a national incarceration rate of about 1.5 percent.' (22–23)

'To [the Vietnam Veteran], logic looks absurd, absurdity looks logical. They can't make realistic decisions about the future because they are no longer sure what reality is. … Now for the confused veterans the mad play of life on the planet Earth goes on, bouncing back and forth between reality and illusion. … Action is okay, passivity is okay, brutality is okay, love is okay – they're all okay, they're all worthless, "who gives a shit?"' (Anderson, *Grunts*, 231). Even men who served after Vietnam had similar problems returning to the world: 'I knew what I had to do in the army but it's "Easy to lose your way back in the world, man. And I think I've been losing mine"' (Jones, *August Snow*, 172). 'As with many men who return from war, I'd lost my faith in God. It's a helluva thing to realize the fallacy of both God and country in one fell swoop' (Jones, *Dead of Winter*, 289).

Lost Ideals
By Randy Cribbs

Too Many of us were
Leaders too young to lead,
And soldiers too full
Of adventure and then
Of bitterness over
   Ideals unfulfilled.
Our knowledge of the
World was torn
Away and replaced with
Thoughts of only surviving.
Life in that place
   Trying to stay sane.
Somehow,
The great adventure
   Went awry
And with it the
   Best of our youth. (125)

'[Doc Holley is] tired of hating. I want to return to a place where people don't hate so much, but I can't help hating **CHARLIE**. He is so ruthless and has killed so many of my friends. Baby, I know I will never forget Vietnam, but I do hope I will be able to put it way back in a distant corner of my mind. All this hatred and killing have really brought out the worst in me.' Two pages later, Holley writes: 'I may come home without any visible scars, but I can assure you there are many scars way down deep inside me that may never heal. You can't be exposed to all that I have seen, felt, smelled and heard and not have it affect you' (Holley, 151, 153).

Charles Strong, a black soldier who in Vietnam was a **Blood**, said he had seen 'many people back here stateside killing as many people as they were killing in Vietnam. Vietnam really gave me a respect for human life. I value people. ... And I don't feel inferior anymore. ... See, I found out from reading about my past before slavery – my ancestors built the pyramids that still stand today ... I learned that as a black man the only problem I had was that I wasn't exposed to things. I feel equal to everyone, and I walk humbly among men. I'm studying to be a computer programmer, but that doesn't make me better than a garbage man' (Terry, 61).

Clemency. For deserters and civilian draft evaders, coming home presented a different set of problems. On 16 September 1974, President Ford announced a clemency program. Marine Lewis Puller, Jr, badly wounded in the war and highly decorated, asked to be on the program's committee. President Ford increased the size of the committee from nine to eighteen members; Puller and three others were the only Vietnam veterans. Over the summer of 1975, Puller read about 5,000 case histories. He explains: 'We read the summaries. [Then met as a three-member panel.] If the panel recommendation was not unanimous, the dissenting member could refer the case to the full board. ... Usually the only issues to be decided were whether the applicant should be granted clemency and, if so, whether a period of alternative service should be required as a condition of receiving clemency. As a result of our deliberations, we granted clemency in almost 95 percent of the cases we evaluated' (337).

Puller came to realize that the problems he faced on the committee were 'a terribly unfair conscription system and a tragic war that never should have been fought. Out of the general population of draft-age men during the Vietnam era, fewer than one in ten ever served in Vietnam' (338, 342). He hoped that the committee 'did some good' for those who applied, 'but that good was insignificant when weighed against the irreparable harm caused by the four administrations that mired us in Vietnam and then refused to acknowledge any wrongdoing or culpability'. He believed that the committee 'were determining the guilt of the wrong people. It was for me as shattering an experience as the loss of my legs and a dozen good friends in Vietnam to discover face-to-face the arrogance and the blindness that so often passed for leadership during the Vietnam era' (342–343).

Chapter 4

MIA/KIA

Missing in Action. 'And we tended to list the people as MIA as opposed to KIA until we were absolutely certain. We held out hope that they would be recovered, captured, anything but dead' (Terry, 194).[7]

The North Vietnamese had an MIA team (not the same as the US MIA) to find, identify, recover and then bury the dead. To many North Vietnamese, the dead became shadows, or they became sounds. One MIA team was haunted by a song each claimed to hear; following the sound, the team came across a shallow grave, with nothing but bones and a guitar. After the burial, the song ended forever.[8] Vietnamese soldier Bao Ninh, who was there, said: 'True or not? Who's to know? The yarn became folklore. For every unknown soldier, for every collection of MIA remains, there was a story' (91).

Chapter 5

Postwar Reflections

(All of these reflections are either direct quotes or excerpts from soldiers who were there.)

'It's time that we recognized that ours was in truth a noble cause.'
(Ronald Reagan, October 1980)

'What we need now in this country, for some weeks at least and hopefully for some months, is to … put Vietnam behind us and to concentrate on the future.'
(Henry Kissinger, 29 April 1975)

'The Change that the Vietnam defeat brought in the way Americans perceive themselves is denied and suppressed by the leaders who produced the defeat.' (Reston, Sherman, 38)

'Those who forget the past are doomed to repeat it.' (Santayana)

One of the enduring myths of the war was that blacks died at a disproportionate rate in Vietnam. According to Captain Marshal Hanson, a retired researcher for the US Naval Reserve, '86% who died in Vietnam were Caucasians; 12.5% were black … a figure proportional to the number of blacks in the US population at the time and slightly lower than the proportion of blacks in the Army at the close of the war' (Pedigo, 2). This is backed up by Dunnigan and Nofi – 'black Americans were not disproportionately represented in the ranks in Vietnam' (7).

> "'The fundamental blunder with respect to Indochina was made after 1945," wrote Secretary of State John Foster Dulles, when "our Government allowed itself to be persuaded" by the French and British "to restore France's colonial position in Indochina."' (Loewen 248)

Many postwar experts tried to explain the war. In an interview, Colonel Harry Summers, Jr, who wrote *On Strategy: The Vietnam War in Context*, analyzed what the United States did wrong in Vietnam. Over the years, he said, there were too many political objectives, none of them attained: 'The great tragedy of the Vietnam War was all of this military effort, great bravery and sacrifice and everything else, was totally unfocused because of the lack of a goal. And because it was unfocused, it failed to achieve the objectives of the US foreign policy' (Kreisler, tape recording).

218

Nurse Mary Powell, in *A World of Hurt*, agrees with Summers, saying that no clear objectives kept the military from waging a winnable war: 'Military commanders saw what I saw: that Vietnam was a primitive country, peopled by villagers concerned not with an abstract ideology but with the source of their next meal, that our presence was destroying the people we had come to save, that the government we backed was corrupt, and that poor leadership was wasting GIs.' While many careerists resigned, 'disheartened by the ethical disintegration of the armed forces ... the grunts had no voice and no escape' (160).

As General Westmoreland (the US general in charge of overall tactics in Vietnam from 1964-1968) reported to Congress, 'the war was a limited, defensive struggle to maintain the integrity of South Vietnam, not to unify the country through attacks in the North. The United States and South Vietnamese Military were ordered not to cross into Laos or Cambodia to stop the Ho Chi Minh Trail supply route and not to cross the DMZ to invade the North.' Because of these orders, 'the best we could hope for was a stalemate', maintaining the status quo with the DMZ dividing the two nations (Kreisler, 2).

Colonel David Hackworth, US Army (Ret.), who earned over 30 medal including two Distinguished Service Crosses during his service in World War II, Korea and Vietnam commented in a Preface to Mary Powell's *A World of Hurt* on postwar reflections: 'I suspect the historians have tried to bring clarity, understanding and a certain tidiness to a conflict that ripped America apart and that will probably not go away until those who lived through that decade of fire have gone to their maker. ... But the generals and their men – rationalizers and revisionists for the Vietnam War ... have tried to spin the disastrous defeat into victory. They say there really was "light at the end of the tunnel" and that we did in fact win the war. In reality, it was a war that was as unwinnable, at least the way their bosses fought it, as it was morally wrong' (x).

Fred Barnes, a political commentator who frequently appears on Fox News, thinks otherwise. He believes we were right to be there to stop the spread of communism; if we hadn't, the world would be a much worse place. He says that Westmoreland's methods of fighting the war, his defensive strategy, his search and destroy missions and his attempt to win by attrition, would never work. But when General Creighton Abrams replaced him, the US had a chance to win the war if it weren't for the lack of support in America (Hackworth, Powell, x–xi).

Neither Hackworth nor Barnes, despite their concerns about the viability of the war, were concerned with its lasting effects on those who fought and those who heard reports about the fighting. Reston, however, worries what might be its lasting images: 'Will the legacy of Vietnam be that image of crazed ruthlessness from *Apocalypse Now* and *The Deer Hunter* and *Coming Home* forever *be* Vietnam? Or are these images mistaken, wholly or partially?' (Sherman, 7). This legacy became known as Vietnam War Syndrome. 'The Vietnam War Syndrome was open to many interpretations but more than anything, it was the belief that any large-scale American military intervention abroad was doomed to practical failure – and perhaps also to moral iniquity' (Dionne). 'Reverend J. Bryan Hehir, a professor of ethics and international relations at Georgetown University, believes that ... the syndrome is exaggerated. To the extent that the syndrome is defined as a revulsion against protracted and uncertain commitments', it has not kept the United States from other foreign entanglements – Grenada, Panama, Kuwait, Iraq and Afghanistan (Dionne).

Kathleen Belew, author of *Bring the War Home*, sees its lasting effect quite differently: 'On both the right and the left of the political spectrum, the war worked to radicalize and arm paramilitary groups' (20). Left-leaning veterans worked to promote labor unions and racial equality. Those on the right joined forces with other right-wing groups, the KKK and neo-Nazis. They believed the government betrayed them – leaving soldiers behind – and that the public, especially those anti-war, 'spat on their service and [did] not appreciate [their] sacrifice' (20). As Belew's title suggests, they 'brought home the war as [they] fought it and dedicated [their] lives to urging others to "bring it on home"' (20).[9]

In their attempts to keep the country from becoming radicalized, Presidents Ford and Carter tried various means to forget and forgive, to pardon and offer amnesty to those who avoided the draft, moved to Canada, protested the war or committed minor atrocities while in Vietnam, but most declined the offer. Many Vietnam veterans, because of their disillusionment with the government, became radicalized after their return from the war. Many joined white power movements, culminating in extreme actions such as the bombing in Oklahoma City (*NY Times* Editorial Board). On 30 May 1979 President Carter 'proclaimed that the nation was, at last, ready to change its heart and mind toward the Vietnam soldier and recognize his valor, sacrifice, and commitment. [Quoting Phillip Caputo's and his] moving tribute to a fallen comrade: "You were a part of us and a part of us died with you. … your courage was an example to us. … Nothing can diminish the rightness of what you tried to do. Yours was the greater love"' (Reston, Rift, 18).[10]

Southerners in Congress also objected to any amnesty or pardons for those who left the United States or found other ways to avoid the draft. President Reagan, in a speech to the Veterans of Foreign Wars in 1980, proclaimed: 'A small country newly free from colonial rule sought our help in establishing self-rule and the means of self-defense against a totalitarian neighbor bent on conquest. … We dishonor the memory of 50,000 young Americans who died in that cause[11] when we give way to feelings of guilt as if we were doing something shameful' (Reston, Sherman, 263).

Lewis Puller, Jr, marine, Pulitzer prize winner for *Fortunate Son*, and an attorney, wrote: 'If I could now summon the courage to forgive my government, to forgive those whose views and actions concerning the war differed from mine, and to forgive myself, I could perhaps move into the present, attain a degree of serenity, and find the reason for which I had been spared, first in Vietnam and then a second time, an alcoholic death' (*Rappahannock Record*, 'Area's "Fortunate Son" Dies', 19 May 1994).

Even after fifty years, many questions remain unanswered or controversial. James Loewen says that 'simply to list the questions [below] is to recognize that each of them is still controversial':

> Why did the United States fight in Vietnam?
>
> What was the war like before the United States entered it? How did we change it?
>
> How did the war change the United States?
>
> Why did an antiwar movement become so strong in the United States?
>
> What were its criticisms of the war in Vietnam? Were they right?
>
> Why did the United States lose the war? [Did they lose the war?]

What lesson(s) should we take from the experience? (Loewen, 248)
'All gave some. Some gave all. US Military Vets. Never forgotten'
(words seen on a T-shirt)

Above: Memorial to those from Memphis who died in Vietnam. (Courtesy E. Brown, Jr)

Right: Tupelo, Mississippi Memorial Park. (Courtesy E. Brown, Jr)

Coda

To Come Full Circle

The United States' involvement in Vietnam occurred gradually, from support of the French – until they lost in 1954 – to military advisors and then combat troops, from Eisenhower's belief in the Domino Theory to the Kennedy assassination, then to Johnson's and Nixon's attempts to find ways to bring the North Vietnamese to the conference table to negotiate a peace. There were many opportunities to leave without losing face. The United States chose none of them. The most simplistic answer came from Dr George Wald, a Nobel Prize-winning scientist. He said: 'People ask me how to get out of Vietnam? So I tell them, by ship.'

Instead, we fought a defensive battle trying to maintain the borders of the Republic of South Vietnam without crossing the Demilitarized Zone or openly sending troops into Cambodia and Laos to halt the flow of materiel and soldiers along the Ho Chi Minh

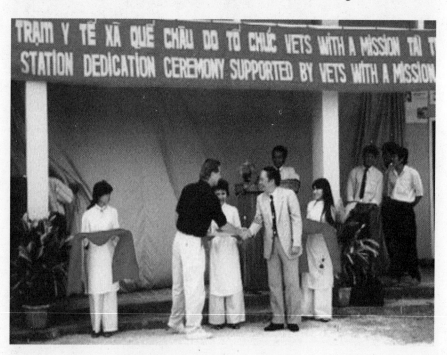

Vets with a Mission setting up health clinics in Vietnam, 1989–1999. (Vets with a Mission)

Trail into the South. Ours was a war of containment – its purpose: to keep the war from widening into a larger global conflict between democracy and communism; in other words, to keep the USSR and China from sending troops to aid the North Vietnamese.

Back home, the Vietnam War caused great turmoil, with demonstrations and riots in the streets. Unlike the so-called 'peace and prosperity' of the 1950s, the 1960s were a time of anger and frustration: the Civil Rights movement; the drug counter-culture; the assassinations of President Kennedy in 1963, then Senator Kennedy and the Rev Martin Luther King, Jr., in 1968; the riot at the Chicago Democratic Convention in 1968; the destruction of files in at least two Draft Board offices in the late 1960s; the killings of students at Kent State University in 1970; *The Pentagon Papers* in 1971; and President Nixon's resignation over the Watergate scandal in 1974. The wounds have not healed.

Post-war reflections from both the Vietnamese and the American point of view reveal the conflict inherent in this war which was not technically a war.[1] Did we win? 'There is no North Vietnamese flag flying over the White House,' as one soldier stated. Did we lose? Or were we forced to leave because of lack of support at home? Vietnam is now one country. There were no free elections, which was part of the 1954 Geneva Peace Accords, of which the United States and South Vietnam were not signers. Was the support worth the cost financially, militarily, the loss of young men's lives and deep divisions back home? Even some fifty years later, many of these questions have not been answered. Maybe they never will.

A 'No-Bullshit' War Story
By Jim Gray

We went to Vietnam
And some of us came back.
That's all there is –
Except for the details. (21)

SECTION FIVE

Appendices, Credits, Works Consulted, End Notes, Acknowledgements

Appendix A

Chronologies of the War[1]

Vietnam: Special Newsweek Edition (pages 6–7) provides the following condensed chronology of the war (extracted from original text):

1954 May 7	The French surrender at Dien Bien Phu.
July 21	Geneva Accords.
1955 January	The first direct military aid to South Vietnam arrives.
1959 March	Ho Chi Minh declares a people's war to unite North and South.
1961 December 11	JFK orders more US assistance; 400 personnel and helicopters arrive.
1962 January 12	Operation Helicopter, first US combat mission.
1963 November 22	JFK assassinated. [LBJ] takes office.
1964 August 4	Gulf of Tonkin incident; later proved to be false. LBJ orders retaliation.
August 7	Congress passes Gulf of Tonkin resolution.
November 1	The Viet Cong launches its first attack on US troops.
1966 April 12	B-52 bombers are used for the first time against North Vietnamese.
1967 November 29	Secretary of Defense McNamara resigns after release of Pentagon Papers. [Pentagon Papers were not released until 1971. Defense Secretary McNamara resigned in 1967 after commissioning a Task Force to write an encyclopedic history of the Vietnam War, known informally as the Pentagon Papers.]
1968 January 31	Tet Offensive.
March 16	My Lai Massacre.
November 1	Operation Rolling Thunder ends, after three and a half years.
1972 December 18	Nixon orders Operation Linebacker, a 12-day bombing campaign.
1973 January 8	Peace talks resume.
January 27	A ceasefire is reached between all combatants.
March	Last combat troops leave South Vietnam.
1975 April 30	Saigon falls. All American personnel evacuate.

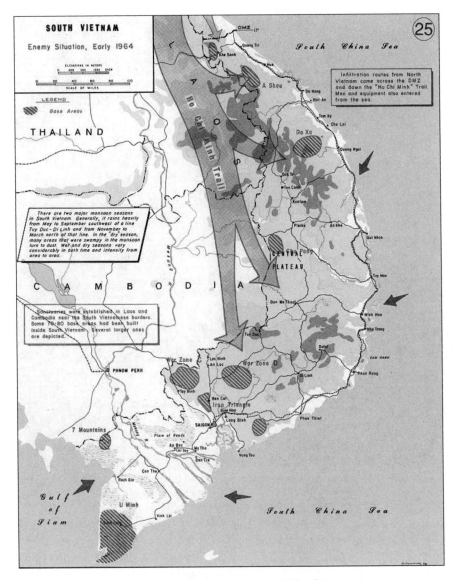

South Vietnam in 1964 (Ho Chi Minh Trail in dark gray). (Wikipedia)

The US Army Center of Military History provides a more detailed chronology of the army's involvement in the war history.army.mil/html/reference/armyflag/vn.html

Advisory, 15 March 1962 – 7 March 1965: Advisors in the field rose from 746 in January 1962 to over 3,400 by June to 11,000 … by the end of the year to 11,000 including 29 US Army special forces detachments. (2)

Defense, 8 March 1965 – 24 December 1965: During this campaign the US objective was to hold off the enemy while gaining time to build base camps and logistical facilities. (2)

Counteroffensive, 25 December – 30 June 1966: American forces for the remainder of 1965 and well into 1966 sought to keep the enemy off balance while building base camps and logistical installations. This involved search and destroy operations. Of particular concern ... was the protection of the government and people of South Vietnam. (3)

Counteroffensive, Phase II, 1 July 1966 – 31 May 1967: Operations ... were a continuation of earlier counteroffensive campaigns. ... The Joint Chief of Staff declared that American military objectives should be to cause North Vietnam to cease its control and support of the insurgency [the Vietcong] in South Vietnam and Laos ... and to assist South Vietnam in pacification extending government control [of] its territory. (4)

Counteroffensive, Phase III, 1 June 1967 – 29 January 1968: The Conflict in South Vietnam remains ... unchanged. South Vietnamese Armed Forces become more active and capable under US advisors. (5)

Tet Counteroffensive, 30 January 1968 – 1 April 1968: Determined enemy assaults [attacked] northern and central provinces ... Saigon and the Mekong Delta. Some 84,000 VC and North Vietnamese ... fired upon 5 of 6 autonomous cities, 64 of 242 district capitals and 50 hamlets [as well as] a number of military installations. (6)

Counteroffensive, Phase IV, 2 April 1968 – 30 June 1968: During this period friendly forces conducted a number battalion-size attritional operations against the enemy. US Army ... reach a peak of nearly 360,000 men. (7)

Counteroffensive, Phase V, 1 July 1968 – 1 November 1968: During this period a country-wide effort was begun to restore government control of territory lost ...[in] the Tet offensive. (7)

Counteroffensive, Phase VI, 2 November 1968 – 22 February 1969: In November 1968 the South Vietnam government with American support began a concentrated effort to expand security in the countryside. ... [Newly elected President Nixon announces] a coming end to US combat in Southeast Asia and a simultaneous strengthening of South Vietnam's ability to defend itself. ... Truce negotiations began in Paris January 25, 1969. (8)

Tet 69/Counteroffensive, 23 February 1969 – 8 June 1969: The enemy ... tried to sustain an offensive ... [but were repelled by] aggressive allied ground operations. (9)

Summer–Fall 1969, 9 June 1969 – 31 October 1969: Conduct of operations increasingly turned over to Vietnamese [as] US troops withdrew in greater numbers amid reaffirmations of support for the Republic of South Vietnam. (9)

Winter–Spring 1970, 1 November 1969 – 30 April 1970: An increase in enemy-initiated attacks … signaled the first phase of the communist winter campaign … highlighted by intensified harassment incidents and attacks throughout South Vietnam. (10)

Sanctuary Counteroffensive, 1 May 1970 – 30 June 1970: This campaign was mainly concerned with the Allied incursion into Cambodia [due to] enemy's strength in the sanctuaries inside Cambodia. [Anti-communist Lon Nol] appealed to the US for help. (11)

Counteroffensive, Phase VII, 1 July 1970 – 30 June 1971: Fighting continued in Cambodia … before and after South Vietnam began its US aided drive in Laos. (11)

Consolidation I, 1 July 1971 – 30 November 1971: This period witnessed additional progress in the Vietnamization program which included turning the ground war to South Vietnam, sustaining the withdrawal of US troops, but also continuing air strike on enemy targets. … US troops dropped to 191,000, lowest level since May 1967. (12)

Consolidation II, 1 December 1971 – 29 March 1972: The US continued to reduce its ground presence … but American air attacks increased while both sides exchanged peace proposals. (12)

Cease-Fire, 30 March 1972 – 28 January 1973: On 30 March 1972 the North Vietnamese Army launched its greatest offensive of the entire war … in a major effort to end the war with conventional forces. … Recapture of Quang Tri City … marked the complete failure of the enemy to hold any of the targeted provincial capitals. The US ground role in Vietnam was totally replaced by the RVNAF [Republic of Vietnam Air Force]. … The US policy of Vietnamization continued as the army continued its withdrawal of troops. (12–13)

Note: 1973 did not mark the end of the war but the end of major army involvement as all troops were withdrawn by March 1973. The war continued until the fall of Saigon in 1975.

Appendix B

Military Rules of Conduct
and Other Codes

Issued by the Armed Forces Information, Education and the Department of Defense

Do be courteous, respectful, and friendly;
Don't be overly familiar with the Vietnamese.
Do learn and respect Vietnamese customs;
Don't forget you are the foreigner.
Do be patient with the Vietnamese attitude toward time;
Don't expect absolute punctuality.
Do appreciate what the South Vietnamese have endured;
Don't give the impression the US is running the war.
Do learn some useful Vietnamese phrases;
Don't expect all Vietnamese to understand English.
Do be helpful when you can;
Don't insist on the Vietnamese doing things your way.
Do learn what the South Vietnamese have to teach;
Don't think Americans know everything.
(From *A Pocket Guide to Vietnam* by the Armed Forces Information and
Education & the Department of Defense, 5 April 1966, 94.)

Nine Rules

Assistance Command, Vietnam
For Personnel of US Military

The Vietnamese have paid a heavy price in suffering for their long fight against the
Communists. We military men are in Vietnam now because their government has asked
us to help its soldiers and people in winning their struggle. The Viet Cong will attempt
to turn the Vietnamese people against you. You can defeat them at every turn by the
strength, understanding, and generosity you display with the people. Here are the nine
simple rules.

Remember we are special guests here; we make no demands and seek no special
treatment.

Join with the people! Understand their life, use phrases from their language, and honor their Customs and Laws.

Treat women with politeness and respect.

Make personal friends among the soldiers and common people.

Always give the Vietnamese the right of way.

Be alert to security and ready to react with your military skill.

Don't attract attention by loud, rude, or unusual behavior.

Avoid separating yourself from the people by a display of wealth or privilege.

Above all else you are members of the US military forces on a difficult mission, responsible for all your official and personal actions.

Reflect honor upon yourself and the United States of America.

(Armed Forces Information and Education, Department of Defense, *Vietnam*, iii)

Guidelines for American Vietnamese Rapport
Religions of South Vietnamese in Faith and Facts
US Navy, Bureau of Naval Personnel, Chaplains Division (1967)
(at sacred-texts.com)

Be prepared for difference in thought, behavior, customs, etc.

Be patient, persistent, consistent, acceptable, and accepting.

Be interested in people as individuals.

Be alert to areas of agreement rather than disagreement.

Be aware of possible long-range consequences of gifts, actions, and reactions.

Be adaptable when moral principles are not involved.

Be prepared to treat Vietnamese as you would desire to be treated.

Be aware of your attitudes. Your actions will produce good or bad for you, your buddies, and those who follow you.

Be understanding, compassionate, and concerned.

Determine to be the best American example possible.

Soldier's Creed

(https://www.army.mil›values›soldiers)

I am an American Soldier.
I am a warrior and a member of a team.
I serve the people of the United States, and live the army values.
I will always place the mission first.
I will never accept defeat.
I will never quit.
I will never leave a fallen comrade.
I am disciplined, physically and mentally tough, trained and proficient in my warrior tasks and drills.
I always maintain my arms, my equipment and myself.
I am an expert and I am a professional.
I stand ready to deploy, engage and destroy the enemies of the United States of America in close combat.
I am a guardian of freedom and the American way of life.
I am an American Soldier.

Rules of Engagement

The United States is a party to the following conventions pertinent to warfare on land:

1. Hague Convention No. III of 18 October 1907, Relative to the Opening of Hostilities …
2. Hague Convention No. IV of 18 October 1907, Respecting the Laws and Customs of War on Land …
3. Hague Convention No. V of 18 October 1907, Respecting the Rights and Duties of Neutral Powers and Persons in Case of War …
4. Hague Convention No. IX of 18 October 1907, Concerning Bombardment by Naval Forces in Time of War …
5. Hague Convention No. X of 18 October 1907, for the Adaptation to Maritime Warfare of the Principles of the Geneva Convention …
6. Geneva Convention Relative to the Treatment of Prisoners of War of 27 July 1929 …
7. Geneva Convention for the Amelioration of the Condition of the Wounded and Sick of Armies in the Field …
8. Treatment on the Protection of Artistic and Scientific Institions [*sic*] and Historic Monuments of 15 April 1985 …
9. Geneva Convention for the Amelioration of the Condition of Wounded and Sick in Armed Forces in the Field of 12 August 1949 …
10. Geneva Convention for the Amelioration of the Condition of Wounded and Sick and Shipwrecked Members of the Armed Forces at Sea of 12 August 1949 …
11. Geneva Convention Relative to the Treatment of Prisoners of War of 12 August 1949 …

12. Geneva Convention Relative to the Protection of Civilian Persons in Time of War of 12 August 1949 ...
13. Geneva Protocol for the Prohibition of the Use of Asphyxiating, Poisonous or Other Gases and of Bacteriological Methods of Warfare of 17 June 1925 ...

(US Marine Corps 12–13)

Appendix C

The Vietnam Memorial, Washington, DC

'The Wall'

Dedicated 13 November 1982

'The Healing Stone. A Shrine of Reconciliation. The Wall. America's Vietnam Veterans Memorial has been given many names.' (Scruggs, Ezell, 9)

'The beginning of the end of war lies in remembrance.' (Herman Wouk, Ezell, 10)

'War drew us from our homeland in the sunlit springtime of our youth. Those who did not come back alive remain in perpetual springtime, forever young, and a part of them is with us always.' (anonymous, Longley, 5)

What is the purpose of a memorial? To honor those who bravely fought or made some important contribution to the world? To remind us of the event itself? Or, as many of the books written about the Holocaust remind us, to say, 'Never

The Wall. (Picture appeared in Gabriel Bell's article)

Again'? Recently, the United States has been engaged in a discussion of Civil War monuments. Is it appropriate to honor those who fought for the Confederacy? Should we honor those who we defeated or whose deaths we caused? Hugh Gusterson, in an article entitled 'Reconsidering How We Honor Those Lost to War', wonders if we should have memorialized not only those soldiers who died in Vietnam but also those Vietnamese who lost their lives during the war: 'The Vietnam Memorial is rightly honored as the most aesthetically bold and emotionally powerful memorial in Washington. But imagine if, in addition to the $58,000^2$ names of Americans soldiers lost in Vietnam, the memorial found some way to recognize the even greater suffering of the Vietnamese people, who may have lost 2 million of their number in the war' (5).

What memorials do is allow us 'to express emotions that might otherwise remain bottled up. They are an essential element of our lives, especially when they enable us to come to grips with strong emotions, such as grieving'[3] (Ezell, 27).

This attitude led to the idea for a Vietnam Memorial, conceived by Jan Scruggs in 1977 while doing graduate research at American University on the psychological problems facing many fellow Vietnam veterans. Scruggs had served in the 199th Light Infantry Brigade from 1969–1970; he was wounded and earned a medal for gallantry. He wrote a proposal for a Vietnam Memorial and gave it to the Senate. When Scruggs had heard nothing for two years, he decided to build it with private funds. After six weeks, he had collected $144.50. After national publicity, veterans eventually raised $8.4 million. Scruggs envisioned the memorial near the Mall, not near Arlington National Cemetery. Because the Vietnam War produced no major battle to commemorate, nor did it have a hero who emerged from the war, Scruggs saw the memorial as a list of names of those who died in an undeclared war.

Scruggs put out a call for submissions and assembled a group to judge them. The judges received over 1,400 designs from every part of the country, from veterans, artists, housewives. The designs were submitted anonymously. Designs were to contain the names of the dead and to be neutral about the results of the Vietnam War or anything else political. Scruggs saw the memorial as one way to assuage the millions who needed a positive sign that their sacrifices would never be forgotten. 'But the healing balm did not emerge from the ferocious fight over what manner of public art would serve the purpose. Indeed, the reverse was true. It was as if the Vietnam War was being fought all over again' (Reston, Rift, ix).

Because of the uncertainty of its reception, '[the] effect [it] would have on the survivors and on the nation' and the fact that ceremonies welcoming the Vietnam veterans home were postponed, this uncertainty delayed any thoughts of a memorial until several years after the war ended (Ezell, 27). Many Vietnam veterans, however, wanted and needed some sort of recognition, a memorial, for their service to their country and to honor those who died in the war. No one needed to see the memorial built more than Lt Lewis Puller, Jr, a Marine so severely wounded that he was moments from death on 11 October 1968 when medevac'd to the naval hospital in Da Nang (187). Since 1981, Puller had 'followed with keen interest the vicissitudes of the Vietnam Veterans Memorial. On a positive side, funding for the memorial topped eight million dollars, the majority of which came in individual contributions of ten dollars or less. ...

I was most proud that the government that had shattered the lives of so many of us had not been called upon to contribute one red cent. ... I thought it particularly fitting that it now be excluded from taking any credit for such a powerful symbol of the healing process' (423–424). Puller couldn't have anticipated the reaction to the chosen design.

Lewis Puller, Jr. Age 48, Dies by His Own Hand –
A Casualty of The War
By Constance Lee Menefee

> Faces of friends rise like tears,
> as I read the headline;
> should I phone them all, tonight?
> see if any called in fire
> on his own position, too?
> Overrun ... but not going down
> Easy.
>
> Will we now
> build monuments to the men
> who lost their lives,
> but did not die,
> In Viet Nam? (Vietvet.org/Menefee)

The selected design was announced in 1981. It was submitted by Maya Lin, a 20-year-old born in the United States of Chinese immigrants. Upon first seeing the design, some called it 'a black gash', a 'black gash of shame' or a 'tombstone'. Why did it look like a V – for Vietnam? Did it mean we won or lost? Why was it black when so

Dedicated to the men who fought by Frederick Hart (Courtesy E. Brown, Jr)

Dedicated to the Nurses by Glenna Goodacre (Courtesy E. Brown, Jr)

many memorials near it were white? Why did it have no statues? No famous quotations, no height, no columns? 'Many of those who disputed the winning design did so on the grounds that the completed memorial would fail to evoke healing because it was not, in effect, a *traditional* monument' (Beattie, 44). If the chosen design would evoke 'a reconciliation of the grievous divisions wrought by the war' – part of the charge given to those who planned to submit a design for the memorial (Beattie, 44) – many couldn't see how. 'To many interpreters the names... [have] the potential to redirect the meaning of the memorial away from unity toward sorrow and loss' (Beattie, 45). The public reactions included 'The waste', 'Such a waste' and 'Oh God, the waste' (John Lang, quoted in Beattie, 45). But Maya Lin, in moving away from the traditional to 'privileges of names' (Beattie, 46), allowed for private reactions – touch a name on the smooth, shiny black granite, slide your fingers down a row of names, rub in paper that precious name, leave a personal tribute (a letter, a rose, a flag, a teddy bear, a photograph, a boot).

Names on a plain black wall. Despite opposition, the project went forward, and Maya Lin's design – the design that memorialized no war, that offered no important battle and that had no conquering hero – took shape.

1. 140 polished black granite panels in the shape of a chevron; black granite to reflect your image to make you a part of the wall of names:

East Side   **West Side**
1959–May 1968   **May 1968–1975**

2. West points to the Lincoln Memorial; east points to the Washington Monument;
3. Each panel holds engraved names (middle initial, not middle name) of those KIA or MIA;

4.. Each name (one-half of an inch high) is separated from another by ●;

5. Names listed in alphabetical order consecutively over time;

6. When a visitor comes to a name not following the previous alphabetically, this indicates a new day in the war;
   example: last name SANDERS ● followed by last name HENRY ● The names are not in alphabetical order but by date died; so SANDERS ● marks the end of one day of death in the war; HENRY ● then, begins a new day of death in the war;

7. The total length is 500 feet;

8. The memorial begins eight inches high at each end; it rises to ten feet at the center.

9. The names of the first and last killed have a prominent place: 'The names etched in the stone begin at the vertex … with the name of the first casualty, Dale R. Buis, in 1959, and run east "in the order taken from us". The list resumes at the low, west end of the Wall, and runs to 1975, where the last casualty, Richard Vande Geer [died 15 May 1975 in the last combat of the Vietnam War which took place on the *Mayaguez*, an American ship commandeered by the Khmer Rouge after the fall of Saigon] is listed, making the ten-foot high "fold" in the Wall the place where the killing begins and ends' (Meyer, 10).[4] The architects, the officers of the Vietnam Veterans Memorial Fund, and her name, Maya Lin, appear at the top of the Wall. (For information on individuals who died, see the Vietnam Veterans Memorial Fund website www.vvmf.org.)

At the dedication of the memorial on 13 November 1982, there were 58,183 names on 'The Wall', as it came to be called. One-third of the names on The Wall were draftees; there were eight female names; over 1,000 names were marked with a † to indicate 'MIA' status; after time, some were declared 'KIA', so ◊ was put around the cross.

Those who died after their service in Vietnam, who may have died indirectly because of their service, are not mentioned at The Wall. One such soldier was Lewis Puller, Jr.

In a Foreword to *Reflections on the Wall*, General William Westmoreland wrote: 'I am proud and honored to pay tribute to the gallant Vietnam veterans who served their country, especially those who gave their lives maintaining freedom. Few have experienced the anguish that I have felt for those men and women who died in Vietnam what the leadership of the country asked them to do – and did it well – and who in return were ignored and often abused by their fellow countrymen' (Ezell, 15). One such woman, Commander Elizabeth (Dee) Barrett, was the first woman to hold a command in a combat zone in Vietnam, serving as Commanding Officer of the Naval Advisory Group in Saigon. She is quoted in *Stars and Stripes* as saying: 'Some critics of women's liberation say if women want equal rights, then they should be subject to a draft. I say, yes, that's fine. Others say women are too frail to do a man's job. I agree that some women may be too frail but are you going to deny the woman who isn't too frail?' (from her 2021 Obituary).

Many, including Ross Perot, a major funder of the design competition, would have preferred a more traditional memorial. US President Ronald Reagan, in his acceptance speech, helped meet that need by 'reinterpret[ing] the memorial as a reflection of nearby traditional monuments' (Beattie, 44–45). That need was later met by a compromise: two statues – one dedicated to the men who fought, sculpted by Frederick Hart, the other to the nurses, sculpted by Glenna Goodacre – were installed near the memorial. As part of the compromise, a flagstaff was installed with 'the addition of a brief inscription to the memorial itself' (Beattie, 45–46).

Gabriel Bell, in an article entitled 'Maya Lin's Vietnam Veteran's Memorial Changed How We Process War', wrote: 'The story of the Vietnam War … is one about resetting how we remember, how we view war and history, and how we live with the wounds we inflict. … The Vietnam War was … primed for forgetting. The conflict that divided family members and generations from each other didn't simply run counter to the stories America told itself, it detonated them. Vietnam was the spark that turned long-smoking conflicts over race, culture, class, gender, government, economics, and patriotism into unavoidable firestorms' (3).

Scruggs wrote about those who visit The Wall: 'During a visit to the Memorial you may see a grown man weeping. Or a young woman leaving flowers. Or a child placing a poem near one of the names. These individual moments make the Memorial special' (Ezell, 9).

Three-and-a-half million visitors come to the Vietnam Veteran's Memorial, The Wall, each year. In their own way, they say: 'Welcome home.' But many vets have a hard time visiting The Wall. One such individual was Johnnie Phillips, a vet who attended my Thursday evening program. Johnnie said he'd been to DC a number of times intending to visit The Wall, but never could. During our cla visit, he and a student held hands as they walked to The Wall. The student told me that Johnnie ran his hand along The Wall, trying not to step on the treasures (teddy bears, letters, necklaces, children's drawings) that are collected everyday by the National Park Service and stored, or in some cases become part of the Museum Collection. He then said: 'They're all my brothers.' I have chills when I think about that experience.

Wallace Terry, in *Bloods*, wrote about one vet who was distressed to see General Westmoreland at The Wall: 'And it really hurt me to see Westmoreland at the memorial, 'cause he said that we had no intentions of winning the war. What the hell was we over there for then?' (quote by Ford, 52).

Addendum

'If you got there, you could hardly avoid the chubby old man stretching to reach for a name just off his fingertips, a woman with her eyes closed crouching with one finger on a name, two men hugging in front of a panel, a young soldier in full dress uniform saluting a panel, a ten-year-old boy sitting on a man's shoulders to get a rubbing of a name way high up. So much pain not just on the faces but evident from the teddy bears, the roses, the flags, the letters, the medals, and the photographs left each day, maybe left for someone you might have known. Was that chubby old man Mad Dog's Dad? The grieving woman Lucky's wife who bore his child long after he was dead? Your private demons pop up, you don't even know why you came, what made you believe anyone who told you that you had to do this, that it healed them, that the healing began after this pain ripped you loose from your moorings, names, and names, and names and

I don't remember none of them' (part of a letter written to me by a veteran who wishes to remain anonymous, 1974).

That remains the terrible irony of The Wall. In platoons, the soldiers went by nicknames based on a physical feature, where he was born, what MOS (job) he did, how he was regarded. In a platoon of sixty or seventy, grunts rarely knew each other's names. First, it wasn't good to be close to a guy who might be dead next week. Secondly, the rotations in and out meant almost every grunt had a different DEROS – some were newbies with their whole term to serve; some were already counting down the days on their short-timer's stick. Those grunts who had been around for a few months didn't have a particular reason to try to know newbies.

As with any nickname, it reflected something about **appearance** – Dog Face, Whiskers, Shorty, Pencil (tall and skinny like a …), Porky (who'd eat anything nobody else wanted); or about **some peculiarity** – Fruitcake (who carried around his grandmother's fruitcake, no doubt oblivious to the thought that would become her grandson's nickname, and who would be safe from everyone, even Porky), Postman (who wrote a letter to his girlfriend every day), Peaches (he'd swap you almost anything for your can of peaches), Klutz (did everything wrong), Cowboy (for his gung-ho attitude), Magic ('cause he had that good set of ears and intuition, so he *always* knew if Charlie was hanging around), Einstein; and then **where a newbie came from** – Okie, Beach Boy, Dee-troit, I-away; or **a favorite team or favorite player** – Red Socks, Redskin, Yankee, Bull Dog, Stretch, Hank, Yogi; and **music** – Elvis, Stones, Lobo, Crystal, Soldier Boy; and sometimes by **ethnicity** – Chico, Bandit, Bro, Brother Willy (idea from J. Ebert, 140–142). "According to veteran Roger Hoffman, nicknames were bestowed as an indication of acceptance as a new man moved up the infantryman's social ladder' (J. Ebert, 140). (Note: this would be a real irony when vets went to the Vietnam Memorial – The Wall – much later; could a vet find Okie or Beach Boy or Dee-troit on the Wall? Maybe. A database there allowed a search for all PFCs from Oklahoma, or all men killed from Detroit.)

Maybe you could find someone. Making it more difficult still, each soldier had a different number of days left, so that one soldier who pushed you into a bunker just in time might be 'Red' – and that's all you know because he was three days from his Freedom Bird. 'All our vets said they didn't remember any names' (Ann Olek, Vietnam Vet Program, 4/15/93).

'You can't view the Wall without becoming a piece of it. You are there in the past. There is no denying that fact. Our vets have been to hell and they survived. They took themselves back to the memories at the Wall; how will we ever be able to thank them for what they did for us' (Dora Perada, Vietnam Vet Program at The Wall, 1993).

'As haunting as the memorial is, when you get there, you can hardly avoid the hawkers' selling deluxe brass POW bracelets (only $7.95), T-shirts ($16.95), buttons ($1), memorial pins and bumper stickers ($3), military patches ($3), books (any price) and mugs ($5), tie clips ($4.95), lighters (from $15.95), postcards ($1) and posters (from $5 to $50), belt buckles ($9.95), dog tag key rings ($4.95), an aircraft made out of beer cans ($20), videotapes of combat ($29.95) and license plate frames ($9.95). 'All sold by guys adorned with buttons ("POW/MIA WANTED DEAD OR ALIVE"; "POWS NEVER HAVE A NICE DAY"; "I GUESS YOU HAD TO BE THERE"; "REMEMBER

VIETNAM VETS"), infantry patches, ribbons, medals on their T-shirts ("WAR IS A 24-HOUR JOB") or camouflage shirts, faces older than their years. Flags everywhere, for sale, of course. Had those dudes really been to the 'Nam or were they just jerking everybody around?' (part of a letter written to me by a vet who wished to remain anonymous, 1974). All these hawkers are keeping alive the memories of those who may remain MIAs or POWs.

Rolling Thunder also helps keep those memories alive.

Rolling Thunder, an annual Memorial Day parade in Washington, DC, reminds the United States that it can leave no one behind. The parade for POWs and MIAs draws bikers from nearly every state. The route begins at the Pentagon and ends at the Vietnam Memorial. As many as 400,000 bikers clog up the capital to remind the nation of POWs and MIAs that may be alive, as many as 400,000 American flags, too. (Note: When I attended Rolling Thunder, I saw hundreds, if not thousands of Harleys. The noise was shattering.)

'Some had ridden across the US in a pilgrimage to "The Wall", the name given to the stark yet moving monument that records the names of the 58,000 US servicemen who died in Vietnam' (Anne Davies, www.theage.com, 5/30/97). The ponytails might have greyed, and they're not as lithe as they were 40 years ago, but for the Harley-riding Vietnam veterans who descend on Washington for Memorial Day, it's a chance to remember and reflect on the war that changed their generation.

'An estimated 400,000 motorcyclists swarmed the capital at the weekend for the 20th Rolling Thunder event. Many were veterans sporting leather vests advertising

Rolling Thunder. (Wikipedia)

their platoon, their tour of duty, fallen comrades – and their devotion to their Harley-Davidson. They are sometimes called "Nam Knights", even with their middle-aged potbellies' (Davies). In a Vietnam Veterans of America chapter in south-west Virginia, a company usually loans them a flatbed truck to haul their motorcycles. Sometimes you think you're in a convoy of pick-up trucks full of motorcycles, motorcycles riding side-by-side, no helmets, with American flags in stickers, license plate holders, bandanas, painted on trucks, and American flags of all sizes hanging from houses and businesses along the route.

In 2012, a member of the United States Congress 'commend[ed] Rolling Thunder and its founders ... for the 25 years of Memorial Day weekend events to honor America's POWs and MIAs, veterans and the men and women who currently serve in the United States military' (First Trip, 9).

Veterans History Project

'I urge all Americans to participate in the Veterans History Project. Capturing stories of those who served in uniform in their own words will provide the inspiration future generations need when it is their turn to defend the nation Abraham Lincoln once called, "the last best hope on earth"' (Anthony Principi, Secretary of Veterans Affairs).

'It is in the nation's best interest to collect ... oral histories of American war veterans so that ... Americans will always remember those who served in war and may learn first-hand of the heroics, tediousness, horrors, and triumphs of war' (Public Law, 106-380).

If there is an organization or institution that is an official partner of the Veterans History Project in your state, you can contact them and volunteer to assist in the creation of their oral history project and collection. A list of official partners is available on their website at www.loc.gov/folklife/vets/partners/partners.html.

Information:	Veterans History Project	Telephone: (202) 707-4916
	American Folklife Center	Fax: (202) 252-2046
	Library of Congress	web: www.loc.gov/folklife/vets
	101 Independence Ave, SE	message line: 1-888-371-5848
	Washington, DC 20540-4615	E-mail: vohp@loc.gov

Appendix D

Who is a Vietnam Vet?

(Song heard on Long Binh Post, 1971)
He's a convoy truck-drivin' man
He shoots all the gooks that he can
Even doin' brave deeds, he's strung out on speed
He's a convoy truck-drivin' man.

He's an infantry ground-poundin' man
He lives with a gun in his hand
He has faith, he has hope, and then he has dope
He's an infantry ground-poundin' man.

He's an artillery shell-firin' man
Loves shooting his cannon when he can
His rushes they bloom, his cannon goes boom
He's an artillery shell-firin' man.

He's a rear echelon supply man
He smokes every chance he can
He'll always be stoned until the day he goes home
He's a rear echelon supply man. (Powell 81)

These were the Vietnam vets. Each had his own MOS (Military Occupational Specialty) but despite their training for that MOS, it meant little once they arrived in Vietnam. Bobby Ward, who attended my Thursday evening programs, trained as a cook, but ended up driving a truck. Each man had a role to play whether it was driving a truck to supply the troops in the field or those in the rear making sure the supplies were available. But myths surround just who went to war. They had an average age of 19, were mainly draftees, with an abundance of minorities, uneducated, prone to suicide once home, homeless when they got home, divorced once or twice, constantly unemployed, suffering from PTSD or the effects of Agent Orange or alcohol or other drugs. There are many images of homeless vets in tatters crouched on a street corner begging for money, a bedraggled, whiskered man bent over and sobbing at The Wall – these myths are reinforced by books, magazine articles, pictures and movies.

So who went? Volunteers made up two-thirds of the 9,087,000 military personnel who served during the Vietnam era. Of that number, 2,709,918 served in uniform in

243

Vietnam. Their average age was actually 22; 97 per cent were honorably discharged; 91 per cent were glad they served their country; 74 per cent would serve again. But that leads to another problem: what is the Vietnam era? Defining that has been a problem. 'The Veterans' Improvements Act of 1996 (Public Law (PL) 104-275, Section 505 enacted October 9, 1996)' (Hanafin, 1) changed the date of the Vietnam era into two dates, depending on where the veteran served: either (1) Vietnam era vets must have served in the Republic of Vietnam at any time between 28 February 1961 and 7 May 1975; or (2) Vietnam era vets must have served at any time between 5 August 1964 and 7 May 1975. The legal status and the access to veterans' benefits impact a veteran who served at any time from 1961 to 1964. That veteran will now be a 'Vietnam era vet' if he served within the Republic of Vietnam. This change allows for a longer period to be a Vietnam era vet (1961–1975) for those men who served in-country; but this change allows for a shorter period to be a Vietnam era vet (1964–1975) for those men who served elsewhere [Germany, South Korea, or the United States] (Hanafin, 1).

Were they prone to suicide, homelessness, divorce, unemployment or suffering from PTSD (Post Traumatic Stress Disorder), alcohol or other drugs misuse after they returned home? Some did suffer from PTSD: 'Virtually all the veterans expected that their settling back into familiar places and routines would be one of the most pleasurable experiences they would ever know. But most found the process to be a succession of painful adjustments to a way of life which contrasted sharply with the one they left behind in Vietnam' (Anderson, *Grunts*, 175).

Some certainly turned to dope or alcohol to lessen the pain, but the majority did not. Some beat their wives, committed suicide, stood in unemployment lines, but again the majority did not. 'Few had any illusions how the war would shape the rest of their lives, but they also pined for their old normal existence. ...They hid their emotional scars ... though they bore the added injury of an angry, often disrespectful America. They were forced to carry the weight of political and military decisions, to answer for Johnson and William Westmoreland. ... This, in a way, is where the stereotype of the fragile veteran finds some truth – not in the war itself, but in the reception, back home' (Longley, 4).

In *Vietnam Facts vs. Fiction*, Bobbie G. Pedigo, former Commanding Officer of the 68th AHC (Assault Helicopter Company), with the help of research by Captain Marshal Hanson, USNR (Ret), amplifies what Kyle Longley wrote about the returning veteran. According to Hanson's research, Vietnam veterans have done well. In their age group, Vietnam vets have a lower unemployment rate than non-vets, and their personal income exceeds non-Vietnam vets by 18 per cent. A Veterans Administration Study concluded that drug usage in this age group is the same, whether veteran or not. They are less likely to be in prison; only 0.5 per cent of Vietnam vets have been jailed. According to Hanson's research, '85 per cent have made a successful transition from military to civilian life' (Pedigo, 1–2).

But Wallace Terry, in his introduction to *Bloods*, writes: 'America owed the black veterans of the war a special debt. ... But what can be said about the dysfunction of Vietnam veterans in general can be doubled in its impact upon most blacks; they hoped to come home to more than they had before; they came home to less. Black unemployment among black veterans is more than double the rate for white veterans. The doors to the Great Society have been shut' (xv).

What about suicide? Some vets did commit suicide, but not between 50,000 and 100,000; more like 9,000. During the first five years after discharge, the Vietnam vet was 1.7 times more likely to commit suicide than the same age group of non-vets. After those five years, however, the rate was less than that of non-vets (Pedigo, 3).

Another myth that will not go away concerns the number of black men who were killed in the war. Black fatalities (12 per cent) represent the percentage of blacks in the United States at that time. Eighty-six per cent of the men who died were Caucasian. Approximately 70 per cent of those killed in Vietnam were volunteers (Pedigo, 3).

Hanson, in his *Vietnam War Fact vs. Fiction*, made two main points. One, the United States did not lose the war; two, 'a surprising high number of people who claim to have served there, in fact, DID NOT' (Pedigo, 1). Some people are still convinced the United States lost a war it should have won. But the United States did not lose the war. As one of my vets, Bobby Ward, said: 'Do you see the flag of Vietnam flying at the White House?' Researcher Hanson needs no convincing: 'How could we lose a war we had already stopped fighting? We fought to an agreed stalemate. The peace settlement was signed in Paris on 27 January 1973. It called for release of all US prisoners, withdrawal of US forces, limitation of both sides' forces inside South Vietnam and a commitment to peaceful reunification. The 140,000 evacuees in April 1975 during the fall of Saigon consisted almost entirely of civilians and Vietnamese military, NOT American military running for their lives' (Pedigo, 5).

The Wall Within

Even CBS fell into the myth about veterans and suicide. In an hour-long CBS documentary, *The Wall Within*, Dan Rather claimed, without giving a source, that '[p]ossibly as many as one hundred thousand vets had been driven to suicide over the war' (Burkett and Whitley, 88).

This 1988 documentary about Vietnam vets played to Americans who had 'grown to believe about the Vietnam War and its veterans: They routinely committed war crimes. They came home from an immoral war traumatized, vilified, then pitied. Jobless, homeless, addicted, suicidal, they remain afflicted by inner conflicts, stranded on the fringes of society' (Burkett and Whitley, 87).

The documentary was introduced by Walter Cronkite. Dan Rather called the six vets with him 'outcasts, broken spirits' (88) willing to tell their stories. These six men did not lie about being in service in uniform during the Vietnam War, but at least five of them grossly enhanced the experiences they described to Rather and the TV audience: assassinating Vietnamese under orders from the hush-hush 'Phoenix Program'; forced into skinning alive fifty Vietnamese of all ages; traumatized by seeing a friend on the flight deck walk into a moving propeller. Burkett knew that war crimes had no statute of limitations, so why were two of the men telling of incidents they could be arrested for? Rather never gave his sources of information; half of them said they were on 'secret' missions or were highly trained Special Forces. Secret missions and Special Ops allowed men an excuse not to talk about what they did – 'It's a secret, you know. If I tell, someone will die.' Whatever the reason, Burkett took it upon himself to determine if the so-called documentary was fact or fiction. He surprised himself by finding information about the six with phone calls and requests for military records under the FOI (Freedom of Information Act), something CBS fact-checkers failed to do. After reviewing the military records, Burkett concluded that only one of the six vets could be called a 'true combat grunt. He was the recipient of the Purple Heart and the Combat Action Ribbon, which for Marines demonstrates at least 30 days under active fire' (Burkett and Whitley, 91).

The veteran who supposedly skinned people alive under orders as part of covert ops served for three-and-a-half years, but spent 300 days either AWOL or in the stockade; upon his return, he had been diagnosed as schizophrenic, not something that was war-related. But he does receive money from the government for PTSD (94–95). The man who claimed he was 16 when he became a SEAL was an 'internal communication repairman who went AWOL six times; the only special training he received was not training to become a SEAL, but training in motion picture operations' (92–94).

The vet who saw his friend walk into a propeller was a repairman on the *Ticonderoga* and part of a secret mission (96). But he was not listed as being on the flight deck when he said it happened – and access to a flight deck is strictly controlled. An incident that he described did occur, but at midnight, a time a repairman was unlikely to be on the deck. Burkett reports that this man is receiving money from the government for PTSD disability for a story he heard happened (97). One of the men served his tour as a guard with a USMC helicopter unit, instead of being a grunt 'walking point'. He received 'no valorous combat decorations or Combat Action Ribbon' (91–92). The last of the six held a friend who died in his arms. The only man with the name the vet gave to Rather died in Vietnam 100 miles from where the vet was stationed; the man's death in 1968 occurred months before Rather's vet arrived in country (92). All of the six, however, reported flashbacks, hostile behavior, drug or alcohol addictions and PTSD.

So CBS shows us one type of Vietnam vet: exaggerating what happened or what they heard happened, relating horrifying incidents people expect to hear, showing their own pain and suffering, their ruined lives, while sometimes making themselves appear important because they were on special or secret missions. They were playing a victim of the war racked with PTSD, and in some cases profiting from it.

The Effect of Misconceptions

Vietnam vets and long-time researchers in the National Archives, B.G. Burkett and Glenna Whitley, award-winning investigative reporters, wrote *Stolen Valor* in 1998. Burkett saw first-hand what others thought about Vietnam vets, when other professionals were surprised that he was both a professional (a stockbroker) and a Vietnam vet. '"You're kidding me," [a long-time client of his] said, looking at me as if I had just confessed, I had syphilis. Another said, "Hell, I've dealt with you for years, and I never figured you were a Vietnam Veteran." I was confused. How was it supposed to show?' (42).

But he knew how it was supposed to show – because of the public's misconceptions about Vietnam vets. 'They were losers, bums, drug addicts, drunks, derelicts – societal offal who had come back from the war plagued by nightmares and flashbacks that left them with the potential to go berserk at any moment' (42). But from his own experience, he knew differently, and in trying to raise money for a Texas Vietnam Veterans Memorial, he saw what a challenge he faced. He had to ask for money to memorialize veterans stuck in an offensive stereotype, so if he was to be successful, he had to change the public's notion that the okay vet (as in not going berserk) or the surprise vet (as in 'Gee, I never would have guessed') was not an 'exception' (43) – that he was not an exception.

A series of setbacks in Burkett's fundraising attempts gave him time to wonder if Vietnam vets 'because of their experience in the war, [were] more likely than their peers who didn't go to Vietnam to suffer problems or commit crimes?' (46). He knew many men had come home from the war able to function. Of course, some had problems, but those problems were not anything out of the ordinary. Divorce and alcoholism were not limited to Vietnam vets. But Burkett heard from others whenever a Vietnam vet was involved in a crime or accused of a crime. Bobby Ward, one of our veterans, said if he was 80 and robbed a bank, the headlines would scream 'Vietnam Vet Suspect in Robbery'.

Vietnam era Vets vs Vietnam Vets vs Wannabes

Another 'who' is determined by definitions: an infantryman who fought in the bush, or crawled down into a tunnel with a knife and a rope, or carried out search and destroy missions, or a LRRP who spied, targeted and killed? Or engineers who built roads or kept them clear, who built or rebuilt bridges, who worked without weapons and were easy targets for snipers?

The engineers had one of the highest mortality rates of any other MOS (military occupational specialty). Vietnam vets? How about COs (Conscientious Objectors)? Some of them go to war without a gun for religious or moral reasons. Basil Paquet, who gave a presentation to my students and whose poems are in this book, told them that he would not carry a gun but felt it was important to his self-esteem to volunteer. He served in Vietnam as a medic. Vietnam vets? What about the eight people it took to keep one grunt in the field? Vietnam vets? The cooks on the base? The servers at officers' nightclubs? The resupply guys? The helicopter pilot who flew dead bodies to a Graves Registration Point? And nurses stationed in combat areas? USO employees who came to combat zones to make a homey place at a base camp? Then there were the Vietnam era vets who served in Germany in hospitals. Or chaplains of any religion who went where called. Around five million Americans served somewhere during the Vietnam War.

Nurse Lynda Van Devanter, when she got home, went to a Vietnam Veterans of American chapter meeting but was not welcomed. She was not considered a Vietnam vet because she was only a nurse. Yet the hospital was under attack at times, and there were serious and fatal injuries among the personnel. Vietnam vets? Van Devanter explains: 'There were only a few women in that room. They seemed lost. Some clustered together; others, like me, stood alone, not yet knowing anyone well enough to feel comfortable. When we moved outside to line up, I took a place near the front. However, one of the leaders approached me. "This demonstration is only for vets," he said apologetically.

"'I am a vet," I said. "I was in Pleiku and Qui Nhon."

"'Do you have a sign or something I can hold?" I asked.

"'Well," he said uncomfortably, "I … uh … don't think you're supposed to march."

"'But, you told me it was for vets."

"'It is," he said. "But you're not a vet."

"'I don't understand."

"'You don't look like a vet," he said. "If we have women marching, Nixon and the network news reporters might think we're swelling the ranks with nonvets'" (271–272).

Because of that snub, Lynda Van Devanter founded the Vietnam Veterans of America Women's Project in 1980 and worked with Diane Carston Evans, RN, and Glenna Goodacre to create the Vietnam Women's Memorial, which was placed near the wall. It was dedicated on 11 November 1993 to the nurses and women of the United States who served in the Vietnam War.

And then there are the wannabes and virtual vets.

'In 1984 Connecticut representative Robert Sorensen assured everyone that – although he was opposed to a proposal to open each session of the legislature with the Pledge of Allegiance – he was patriotic. Sorensen's proof? "My patriotism should not be questioned by anyone because when it was necessary, and when my country called me into service, I fought in Vietnam," the thirty-two-year-old Sorensen said on the floor of the state house.' Forced by his opponent, he admitted to fellow legislators that he had lied (Burkett and Whitley, 173).

He then had the chutzpah to claim he really was a Vietnam vet because he watched television. "'For the first time ever, the American public had before them a war in their living rooms," he said. "Every single person in this United States fought in that war in Vietnam. We were all a part of that war in Vietnam because of what was coming to us, what we were feeling, what we were seeing. We all felt the pain. We all felt the anguish that those people felt. So in a sense a part of us was there with every single person that fought there. So in a sense I was there'" (Burkett and Whitley, 173).

Unfortunately, his explanation was not unique. Here's another TV-Vietnam veteran. Five million out of a population of 200,000 million served. Can you pick out those millions? That's the worst problem. Of course, you can't pick them out. Not by their T-shirts, their caps, their medals, their patches or wounds. There are wannabes out there. Most books say that 80 per cent of those you meet who claim to be a Vietnam vet are a wannabe. They claim to be POWs. They share the incident that won them a Silver Star. They go to The Wall and find the location of friends, leave tokens, or letters, or flags, or a can of peaches. Vietnam Veterans of America doesn't check up on who wants to be a member. Wannabes can see dozens of movies, read dozens of 'I Fought in the War' books, read history books and glossaries so they can talk the talk. They pass.

Why does anyone claim to be part of an unpopular war? To be seen as someone who answered the call of his country? To be seen as someone who endured the spitting of peaceniks? To be called 'baby killer'? Why? When doing so, they take money and resources earned by others: VA medical care, money for incapacitating injuries, money for retraining, lower rates for mortgages.

A wannabe is viewed as a hero or a villain. It depends on the reaction he wants. He can claim to have survived a stretch of time at the Hanoi Hilton, telling others' stories as his own or making up his own. He must be a John Wayne, but John Wayne didn't lie.

To sum it all up, listen to Charles Anderson, in *Vietnam: The Other War*, explain the behavior of Vietnam era soldiers:

'For those who, after their return to the States, felt the need to present themselves as something they were not, there was a real advantage to serving in units like 3rd MPs. There was built into each man's assignment to the rear the means of covering up not only that assignment but also all the embarrassing reordering of values and the frantic searching for excuses it had provoked. At the end of their tours these warriors far from the war could go back to the States and say they were in Vietnam during the war. That statement would, of course, be technically true, but not completely true.' No one would dare to ask if you were in combat. Although these rear-echelon personnel performed much-needed tasks, supplying those in combat with what they needed to continue to fight, they themselves never saw combat. But claiming to be in combat was a sign of manhood, a sign of courage, which no one dared question (41–42).

Vets Today

Many vets today, both American and Vietnamese, visit The Wall. Morley Safer, in an interview with Bui Tin, a colonel in the People's Army of Vietnam, was surprised to learn that the colonel had been to The Wall:

'I [Morley Safer] ask him if he has heard or read about the Vietnam Memorial in Washington, DC.

"Yes, yes, I have been to it ... also the memorial in New York."

'I am jolted by this piece of information. I wonder what those veterans who still visit the wall in their old Vietnam fatigues would have done, or thought, had they known that the squat man in the beret near them was possibly responsible for the presence of some of those fifty-eight thousand names on the wall.

"It is very important, the wall,' [the Colonel continues]. "All the memorials. You must remember all those young men. ... You must also remember the kind of bravery those young men had. They may not have had much understanding of the aims of that war. But the sacrifice, so much sacrifice, must not be forgotten. The spirit of young people must not be forgotten."' (Safer, 39–40).

In a similar manner, many American Vietnam vets return to Vietnam. They remember the beauty of the country. 'A group of American veterans, from an outfit called "Vets with a Mission", are in Ho Chi Minh City [formerly Saigon]. They have been touring the country, more as an attempt to heal themselves than out of any curiosity about Vietnam' (Safer, 68–69).

In 1988, Vets with a Mission supported the opening of a health clinic in Vietnam (see the picture below).

One such American who returned to Vietnam wrote the following: 'Looking back, it sometimes seems that things would have been a lot simpler for everyone if the Vietnamese had just let us win the war. ... More than 2.5 million Americans served in the Vietnam War. When some veterans came home, the war came with them. ... Nearly a half-century later, an honest reckoning shows that the bad far outweighed the good. What remains is a terrible sense of waste; a tragedy for both sides. ... War has the ability to make fools of everyone. ... It's often difficult to make sense of life in a war zone. Why do some people die, some people live? ... The great losses of the conflict cast a certain shadow over the Vietnam War, but they do not diminish the bravery and courage of the men who served' (Pendergrass, 227, 235, 239, 240).

In an interview with Bill Baldwin, a former Marine, Safer learned why Baldwin returned to Vietnam. 'I think all veterans are drawn back here. ... Everybody has a sense of unfinished business. I've longed for Vietnam ever since I came home. I've longed for it. I've dreamed about it. I think when I go home, the chapter will be over' (Safer, 76).

First Mission, 1989

Vets with a Mission.

Baldwin and other Vietnam veterans have begun to finish the 'business'. In 1998, a group of Vietnam veterans formed Vets with a Mission© (VWAM). 'VWAM has continued its service in Vietnam as a ministry and humanitarian organization respected by the Vietnamese Government and medical professionals in Vietnam and Southeast Asia, the United States, and Canada' (Vets with a Mission).

Van Le, a North Vietnamese, wrote the following poem about American GIs returning to Vietnam:

There's an American soldier
Who returns to northern Cu Chi
He bends his back to the tunnels
What does he see? What does he think?

There's a Vietnamese hero
Now a grandfather.
He asks the American to share wine
Outside the tunnel.

Each man is silent
As he looks into the other's eyes.
Something is rising like a deep pain.

The war was terrible
All that time past.

WHO IS A VIETNAM VET?

The dead lost their bodies
The living lost their homes.

How many American soldiers
Died in this land?
How many Vietnamese
Lie buried under trees and grass?

The pain still lingers.
Why should we remember it?
We are old, our era past.
Our mistakes belong to bygone days.

Now the wineglass joins friends in peace.
The old men lift their glasses.
Tears run down their cheeks. (Safer, 250–251)

If you are a veteran suffering from PTSD or having trouble adjusting, please consider calling the Veteran's Crisis Hotline: 800 273-8255.

Above left and above right: Both pins from Vets with a Mission website.

Appendix E

Government Report on Casualties

The following provides a context for the Vietnam War. Below are the major wars in which the United States participated. The dates range from 1775, the beginning of the Revolutionary War, to 30 August 2021, when the last US serviceman left Afghanistan. Some figures are not known but have been estimated, such as Confederate deaths during the Civil War. Military personnel killed in the Vietnam War will change when newly discovered evidence is found. The format of this information is the writer's. The second spreadsheet will list Vietnam War casualties by branch of service.

Principal Wars in which the United States Participated from 1775–2021

War & Date	# Serving	Deaths	Non-Fatal
Revolutionary War (1775–1783)	217,000*	4,435	6,188
War of 1812 (1812–1815)	286,730	2,260	4,505
Mexican War (1846–1848)	78,718	13,283	4,152
Civil War (1861–1865), Union	2,213,363	364,511	281,881
Confederacy	1,050,000*	698,000*	unknown
Spanish–American Wars (1898)	306,760	2,446	1,662
First World War (1917–1918)	4,734,991	116,516	204,002
Second World War (1941–1945)	16,112,566	405,399	671,846
Korean War (1950–1953)	5,720,000**	36,574	103,284
Vietnam Conflict (1964–1973)	8,744,000***	58,209	153,303
Gulf War (1990–1991)	2,225,000****	383	467
Afghanistan War (2001–2021)	775,0005	2,218	20,093

*   estimates. 2nd estimate (number of deaths) based on estimate published in The Proceedings of National Academy of Sciences, 18 November 2024
**   total serving in Korea 1,789,000
***   total serving in Vietnam 3,403,000
****   total serving in Gulf 694,500

Source: https//www.va.gov/opa/publications/factsheets/fs_americas_wars.pdf
Source for information on Afghanistan: https://www.defense.gov/casualty.pdf

Vietnam Conflict Only

Casualty Type	Total	Army	Air Force	Marines	Navy
Killed in Action (KIA)	40,932	27,047	1,080	11,501	1,304
Died of Wounds	5,289	3,604	51	1,482	152
Missing In Action (MIA) Declared Dead	1,085	261	589	98	137
Captured – Declared Dead	116	45	25	10	36
Total Hostile Deaths	47,424	30,957	1,745	13,091	1,631
Missing – Presumed Dead	123	118	0	3	2
Other Deaths	10,662	7,143	841	1,746	932
Total Non-Hostile Deaths	10,785	7,261	841	1,749	934
Total In-Theater Deaths	58,209	38,218	2,586	14,840	2,565
KIA No Remains	622	181	221	123	97
MIA Declared Dead – No Remains	737	216	366	75	80
Captured – Declared Dead – No Remains	53	32	7	4	10
Non-Hostile Missing – Presumed Dead – No Remains	97	92	3	2	0
Non-Hostile Other Deaths – No Remains	336	70	30	37	199
Total – No Remains	1,845	591	624	242	388
Wounded – Not Mortal	153,303	96,802	931	51,392	4,178
Number Serving Worldwide (b)	8,744,000	4,368,000	1,740,000	794,000	1,842,000
Number Serving SE Asia (b)	3,403,000	2,276,000	385,000	513,000	229,000
Number Serving S Vietnam (b)	2,594,000	1,736,000	293,000	391,000	174,000

Source: **http://web1.whs.osd.mil/mmid/CASUALTY/vietnam.pdf.** Prepared by Washington Headquarters Services, Directorate for Information Operations and Reports.

a. **Inclusive dates are 1 November 1955 to 15 May 1975.** Casualty dates after the end date represent service members who were wounded during the period and subsequently died as a result of those wounds and those service members who were involved in an incident during the period and were later declared dead.
b. **Estimated figures**. The National Archives and Records Administration (NARA) has published statistics derived from its Southeast Asia Casualties Current File. This includes tables on Vietnam casualty data by branch of service, race, religion, state, and other categories: http://www.archives.gov/research_room/research_topics/ vietnam_war_casualty_lists/statistics.html.
c. The Women in Military Service to America Memorial (WIMSA) presents casualty data on women in principal wars as researched by its historian's office: **http://www. womensmemorial.org/historyandcollec tions/history/lrnmreqacasualty.html.**

Cost of Major US Wars[6]
(This information is based on Daggett's chart which only goes through 2011. I have updated some of the information on Afghanistan)

War	Cost ($)	Cost ($) 2011	War cost as % of GDP peak war year
American Revolution (1775–1783)	101 million	2,407 million	n/a
War of 1812 (1812–1815)	90 million	1,553 million	1813 2.2%
Mexican War (1846–1849)	71 million	2,376 million	1847 1.4%
Civil War (Union) 1861–1865	3,183 million	59,631 million	1865 11.3%
Civil War (Confederacy)	1,000 million	20,111 million	n/a
Spanish–American War (1898–1899)	283 million	9,034 million	1899 1.1%
First World War (1917–1918)	20 billion	334 billion	1919 13.6%
Second World War (1941–1945)	296 billion	4,104 billion	1945 35.8%
Korean War (1950–1953)	30 billion	341 billion	1952 13.2%
Vietnam Conflict (1965–1975)	111 billion	738 billion	1968 9.5%
Gulf War (1990–1991)	61 billion	102 billion	1991 0.3%
Iraq (2003–2010)	715 billion	784 billion	2008 1.0%
Afghanistan/other (2001–2010)	297 billion	321 billion	2008 0.7%

For more information, including detailed description of costs, source of data and inflation adjustments, see Stephen Daggett, 'Costs of Major US Wars', Congressional Research Service **(https://www.researchgate.net/publication/235211847_Costs_of_Major_US_Wars).**

Appendix F

Government Report on Dog Tags

MIA Facts Site
SSC Report
Private Efforts Section, Part 2
1 July 1991
(From the Senate Select Committee on POW/MIAs)
www.miafact.org/money.htm

'Dog Tag' Reports

(All quotes refer to the Report of the Senate Select Committee, unless otherwise noted.)

Over the past ten years, the agency administering POW/MIA cases has received more than 6,300 reports about missing soldiers, known as dog tag reports. In most cases the Vietnam person sending the report claims to have found the body of a missing soldier. 'As proof, they offer data copied from military identification tags (dog tags), tracings or photographs of dog tags, authentic dog tags or other identification documents.'

Most of these reports are fraudulent. Only 3% of the reports refer to men who actually fought in Vietnam and are still missing. For instance, two of the men whose remains, and dog tags several persons claim to have found, are in fact former POWs who returned alive – their dog tags had been kept by their captors. Although the agency provides no rewards or incentives for reports of MIA/KIA soldiers, many of those reporting hope that this will help them resettle in America.

Between 1954 and 1967, dog tags had notches in them; beginning in 1968, they had no notches.

The agency, however, believes that these reports do not come from individuals. 'Throughout the war the communists enforced a policy to find and bury Americans killed in action and to send to central authorities a report of the burial site along with the personal effects and identification taken from the body. They continually stressed that this was important to the "political struggle". Thus, the governments of Vietnam and Laos should have knowledge of the missing men whose names have appeared in dog tag reports.' The agency also believe that the governments of Vietnam and Laos are exploiting the POW/MIA issue. Despite these facts, the agency thoroughly investigates each report. The full report is available at http://1cweb2.loc.gov/frd/pow/senate_home/pdf/report_S.pdf.

Operation Pocket Change. 'A 1981 plan by the Reagan administration to rescue POWs from Laos, tantamount to admission by American officialdom that GIs had indeed been left behind after combat operations closed' ('Vietnam: Special Newsweek Edition', 93). 'A vocal group of POW/MIA activists maintains that there has been a concerted conspiracy by the Vietnamese and US governments since then [1973] to hide the existence of these prisoners' (Wikipedia). Despite Operation Pocket Change, the US continues to deny that there are prisoners of war in Vietnam and that the US government has not covered up their existence. But were they left

behind or did they choose to stay behind. Although talks continue with Vietnam to this day, there are no indications that any servicemen who want to return to the United States are still left in Vietnam. But of course there is no way to be sure; hence the continuing efforts of loved ones to find out about their missing family members.

Appendix G

US Army Units

Field Army: 50,000+ soldiers commanded by 4-star general[7]
Corps: 2+ divisions commanded by 3-star general
Division: 3 brigades commanded by 2-star general
Brigade or Regiment: 3–5 battalions commanded by 1-star (brigadier) general or colonel
Battalion: 3–5 companies commanded by lieutenant colonel
Company, Battery or Troop: 3–4 platoons commanded by captain, 1st lieutenant or major
Platoon: 3–4 squads commanded by 2nd lieutenant
Squad: 6–10 soldiers commanded by sergeant

'The US Army, Vietnam (USARV) controlled all US Army service and logistical units in South Vietnam until May 1972, when it merged with the Military Assistance Command Vietnam (MACV) to become USARV/MACV Support Vietnam' (Knight, 3).
   During the Vietnam War, three men commanded USARV/MACV:

1964–1968	General William Westmoreland
1968–1972	General Creighton Abrams
1972–1973	General Frederick Weyland[8]

Marine Corps Ranks and Pay grade

Pay grade	Rank	Abbreviation
E-1	Private	Pvt
E-2	Private First Class	PFC
E-3	Lance Corporal	LCpl
E-4	Corporal	Cpl

Appendix H

Treatment of Prisoners[9]

THE ENEMY IN YOUR HANDS

AS A MEMBER OF THE US MILITARY FORCES, YOU WILL COMPLY WITH THE GENEVA PRISONER OF WAR CONVENTIONS OF 1949 TO WHICH YOUR COUNTRY ADHERES. UNDER THESE CONVENTIONS:

YOU CAN AND WILL

DISARM YOUR PRISONER
IMMEDIATELY SEARCH HIM THOROUGHLY
REQUIRE HIM TO BE SILENT
SEGREGATE HIM FROM OTHER PRISONERS
GUARD HIM CAREFULLY
TAKE HIM TO THE PLACE DESIGNATED BY YOUR COMMANDER

YOU CANNOT AND MUST NOT

MISTREAT YOUR PRISONER
HUMILIATE OR DEGRADE HIM
TAKE ANY OF HIS PERSONAL EFFECTS WHICH DO NOT HAVE
SIGNIFICANT MILITARY VALUE
REFUSE HIM MEDICAL TREATMENT IF REQUIRED AND AVAILABLE

ALWAYS TREAT YOUR PRISONER HUMANELY

KEY PHRASES.

ENGLISH	VIETNAMESE
Halt	Dung lai
Lay down your gun	Buong sung xuong
Put up your hands	Dua tay len
Keep your hands on your head	Dua tay len dau
I will search you	Tai kham ong
Do not talk	Dung noi chuyen
Walk there	Lai dang kia
Turn right	Xay ben phai
Turn left	Xay ben trai

The Courage and skill of our men in battle will be matched by the magnanimity when the battle ends. And all American military action in Vietnam will stop as soon as aggression by others stop.

21 August 1965   Lyndon B. Johnson

American soldiers were also advised in a separate document 'The Enemy in Your Hands':

1. Handle him firmly, promptly, but humanely.
2. Take the captive quickly to security.
3. Mistreatment of any captive is a criminal offense. Every soldier is personally responsible for the enemy in his hands.
4. Treat the sick and wounded captive as best you can.
5. All persons in your hands, whether suspects, civilians or combat captives must be protected against violence, insults, curiosity and reprisals of any kind.
   Leave punishment to the courts and judges. The soldier shows his strength by his fairness, firmness and humanity to the persons in his hands. (excerpted from http://webdoc.sub.gwdg.de/ebook/p/2005/www.army.mil/cmh-pg/books/vietnam/law-war/law-apph.htm)

The Fog of War, created by Margaret C. Brown. (Courtesy E. Brown, Jr)

Appendix I

Military Awards and Honors

The United States military awarded soldiers for the following: bravery, heroism, gallantry in action, wounded or died in action and combat.

Medal of Honor. Highest military decoration awarded to members of the armed forces. President Biden honored four Army Vietnam Veterans with the Medal of Honor in a ceremony on 5 July 2022. The veterans were Spec 5th Class Dwight Birdwell, 'who led an armored unit through an ambush in 1968'; Major John J. Duffy, 'who fought off an attack on his firebase in 1972'; Spec 5th Class Dennis M. Fujii, 'who directed airstrikes on advancing forces while under fire in Laos and after surviving a helicopter crash', and Staff Sergeant Edward N. Kaneshiro, 'who singlehandedly cleared a trench of enemy fighters … in 1967'. All four had previous awards upgraded (Lamothe).

Medal of Honor.

Distinguished Service Cross. Second-highest decoration. Awarded for extraordinary heroism. The Army, Navy and Air Force have their own Distinguished Service Cross.

Silver Star. Third-highest military decoration. Awarded for gallantry in action.

Bronze Star. Given not always for an act of heroism, but excellence over a long period of time, two or three years. If for an act of heroism, a star is awarded to be placed on the medal. For a period of consistent excellence, but not quite as memorable as a feat deserving the Bronze Star, the Army Commendation Medal (Anon). The Bronze Star can also be awarded to civilians. UPI reporter Joe Galloway was awarded a Bronze Star 'for rescuing a badly wounded soldier under fire at Battle of Ia Drang in 1965' (Wikipedia).

Distinguished
Service Cross.

Silver Star.

Bronze Star.

Purple Heart. Awarded to soldiers wounded or killed in battle. A United States Military Decoration awarded in the name of the President to those who have been wounded or killed while serving on or after 5 April 1917 with the US military. 'To increase morale and enhance the careers of lifers', the system of awarding military honors had been lowered to become almost meaningless (Dunnigan and Nofi, 12–13). 'There was an unwritten policy … that the second Purple Heart was supposed to be a free ticket out of the bush, but the policy, of course, did not apply to officers' (Puller, 151).

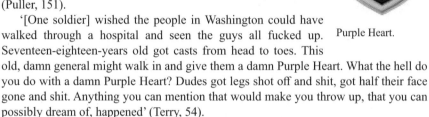

Purple Heart.

'[One soldier] wished the people in Washington could have walked through a hospital and seen the guys all fucked up. Seventeen-eighteen-years old got casts from head to toes. This old, damn general might walk in and give them a damn Purple Heart. What the hell do you do with a damn Purple Heart? Dudes got legs shot off and shit, got half their face gone and shit. Anything you can mention that would make you throw up, that you can possibly dream of, happened' (Terry, 54).

The Purple Heart
By Jim Gray

> Frankly, I prefer the likeness of George Washington
> On a dollar bill rather than the one on this medal.
> The Purple Heart, given by a grateful nation
> To those crippled, unemployed 'True Sons'
> Who zigged when they should have zagged. (25)

Byron Holley, a surgeon in Vietnam, was insulted by a corpsman at the 3rd Field Hospital who offered to put him up for a Purple Heart for a minor wound. Holley suggested that the corpsman go into the combat zone and see what real valor was (Holley, 146).

Combat Infantryman Badge (CIB). Awarded to those who fought in active ground combat. The US Army's combat service recognition decoration awarded to soldiers – enlisted men and officers (commissioned and warrant) holding colonel rank and lower, who personally fought in active ground combat. This badge, worn proudly by a grunt, "identifies the different kind of man who has lived through hell. … The CIB is his fraternity pin' (Phillips, 45).

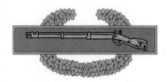

Combat Infantry Badge.

Poetry Credits

Picture Credits

Brown, Dr Earl
Brown, Earl Jr
Dorling Kindersley
Farquhar, Dudley
Hoa Lo Prison, Historic Vestige Brochure
Phillips, Sgt Danny
Sheridan, Autumn
Vets with a Mission

Works Consulted

American Experience: 1964, Part 2 (Boston, MA: WGBH Educational Foundation, 2014).

Anon. E-mails to Margaret Brown, November 2023. Source would prefer not to be named.

'Army Colonel Harry G. Summers, Jr. 67', *Washington Post*, Obituary, 19 November 1999.

Baumgaertner, Emily. "Civil War Toll Much Worse in Confederate States, New Estimate Show." *New York Times*: 19 November 2024.

'Bicycle Secret Weapon Playing Cards', https://www.vanishingingmagic.com/playing-cards/bicycle-secret-weapon-playing- cards/.

'Bill Clinton and the Draft', *Roanoke Times*, 21 September 1992, A10.

Charlie Ration Cookbook (Avery Island, LA: McIlhenny Co., 1966).

CherriesWriter.com/2013/11/14/remember c-rations.

'C. Religious Discipline and Concepts Affecting Behavior', http://www.sacred-texts.com/asia/rsv/rsv/16.html.

'CORDS', historynet.com/CORDS-winning-hearts-and-minds in Vietnam.html.

'First Trip to Vietnam by a US Secretary of Defense Since End of War Yields Big Results', *Vietnam*, October 2012, 8–9.

Handbook for US Forces in Vietnam (Washington: Department of Defense, 10 June 1966).

'How to Make Napalm', http://howany.com/how-to-make-napalm.

'Jungle Rations and Delivery Systems especially by Radio Guided Parafoils', http://www.junglesnafus.com/chapter17.html.

'Jungle Warfare. Jungle Warfare', encyclopedia.com/history/encyclopedias-almanacs-transcripts and maps.

Lindsay, James. The Vietnam War in Forty Quotes. https://www.cfr.org/blog/vietnam-war-forty-quotes.

'List of United States Army MOS', http://absoluteastronomy.com/topics/List_of_United_States_Army_MOS.

'Missing Americans in Indochina', *Roanoke Times*, 29 January 1994, A4 from AP dispatch.

'Operation Phoenix Program: How it Roots Out Vietcong Suspects', *NY Times* Digital Archives, 18 February 1970, 2.

'Press Releases: PBS Announces Broadcast Premiere for THE VIETNAM WAR', www.pbs.org/about/blogs/news/pbs-announces-broadcast-premiere-for-the-vietnam-war, 12 April 2017.

'Public Papers of the Presidents of the United States: Lyndon B. Johnson, 1966' (Washington, DC: Government Printing Office, 1966), 394–399, from Michael H. Hunt (ed.), *The World Transformed, 1945 to the Present: A Documentary Reader* (New York: Bedford/St Martin's, 2004).

Quonset-hut.blogspot.com/p/Quonset-hut.html.

Ruck For Miles, 'What does a soldier carry in his backpack going into battle', http://www.ruckformiles.com/guides.

'The Ace of Spades: How Americans soldiers used "the death card" as a psychological weapon during the Vietnam War', www.thevintagenews.com/2018/03/29/death-card-vietnam-war.

'The American Presidency Project', www./presidency.ucsb.edu/Lyndon B. Johnson/People/President/Lyndon-B-Johnson.

'The Presidency Never Recovered After Vietnam', *The Atlantic Magazine* (October 2017).

Time 1969 (NY: Time, 1969).

US Army Survival Manual (NY: Barnes and Noble, 1992).

USAMM.com, 'The US Military Code of Conduct', https://www.usamm.com/blogs/news/the-u-s-militarys-code-of-conduct.

'USO® Until Everyone Comes Home®', http://www.uso.org/other-services.aspx 2011.

Vets with a Mission, https://www.vetswithamission.org/about-us.

'Vietnam: America's Conflict', 4-DVD set (Mill Creek Entertainment, 1969).

'Vietnam: Endless War', *Monthly Review* 20 (April 1969), 1–11.

Vietnam Lessons. https://www.chicagotribune.com/1988/06/01/vietnam-lessons/.

Vietnam War Diary (NY: Military Press, 1990).

'Vietnam: Special *Newsweek* Edition', *Newsweek* (November 2017).

'Vietnam War Combatants', https://www.history.com/news/vietnam-war-combatants.

'Vietnam War Timeline', https://www.history.com/topics/vietnam-war/vietnam-war-timeline.

'Viper's Vietnam Veterans Pages, Military Wannabe's [*sic*], Fake's [*sic*], and Fraud's [*sic*]', http://vietnam-veterans.us/wannabes.

Wikpedia.

'Women Veterans Bravely Served during the Vietnam War', Vantage Point (14 March 2021), https://blogs.va.gov/VAntage/86001/women-veterans-bravely-served-vietnam-war/.

Books/Articles

Ackerman, Diane, *An Alchemy of Mind* (NY: Scribner, 2004).

Alfano, Roger, 'Grunts', http://www.leatherneck.com/forums/archive/index.php/t-1036.html.

Anderson, Charles, *Grunts* (NY: Berkeley Books, 1976).

Anderson, Charles, *Vietnam: The Other War* (NY: Random House, 1990).

Anon, 'Numbers Chosen in Draft Lottery', *The New York Times* (9 March 1973), 30.

Anthony, Tony, *Life is War But You Can Win* (Wayne, PA: Morgin Press, 1994).

Anzenberger, Joseph Jr. (ed.), *Combat Art of the Vietnam War* (Jefferson, NC: McFarland and Co., 1986).

Applebaum, Anne, 'There are no Rules', https://www.theatlantic.com/international/archive/2023/10/israel-war-hamas-terrorism-ukraine-russia/675590/.

Appy, Christian, 'What was the Vietnam War About?', *The New York Times* (26 March 2018).

Armes, Chris. 'Courage', *Final Papers on Vietnam* (ed. Margaret Brown) (Radford University, Radford, VA: Radford University Honors Program, Spring 1963), 1–12.

Arnett, Peter, *Live from The Battlefield* (Norwalk, CT: The Easton Press, 1994).

Ashby, Hal (director), *Coming Home* (Paramount Pictures, 1978).

Baldwin, James, 'The War Crimes Tribunal', in *War No More* (ed. Lawrence Rosenwald) (NY: Literary Classics of the United States, 2016), 427–431.

Baxter, Randall, *Vietnam: On the Outside Looking In* (Port Saint Lucie, FL: Westwood Books Publishing LLC, 2021).

Beattie, Keith, *The Scar that Binds: American Culture and the Vietnam War* (NY: New York University Press, 1998).

Becker, Elizabeth, 'Public Lies and Secret Truths', *The New York Times* (9 June 2021), Section F 2.

Belew, Kathleen, *Bring the War Home* (Cambridge, MA: Harvard University Press, 2018).

Bell, Gabriel, 'Maya Lin's Vietnam Veteran's Memorial Changed How We Process War', Surfacemag.com/articles/maya-lin-vietnam-veterans-memorial/ (27 May 2019).

Beltrone, Art and Beltrone, Lee (ed.), *Vietnam Graffiti* (Charlottesville, VA: Howell Press, 2004).

Bender, David, *The Vietnam War: Opposing Viewpoints* (St Paul, MN: Greenhaven Press, 1984).

Bender, David and Dudley, William, *The Vietnam War: Opposing Viewpoints* (2nd edition, revised) (St Paul, MN: Greenhaven Press, 1990).

Black, George, 'One of the Last Best Secrets of the Vietnam War', https://www.aspeninstitute.org/wp-content/uploads/2021/04/2021-3-19-George-Black-NY-Times-At-War-.pdf.

Blight, David, 'Was the Civil War Inevitable?', www.nytimes.com/2022/12/21/magazine/civil-war-jan-6.html.

Boot, Max, 'The Taliban defeated America. Let the blame game begin', *Washington Post* (12 July 2021).

Bowman, John (ed.), *The Vietnam War: Day by Day*, Introduction by Fox Butterfield (NY: Bison Books, 1985).

Boylan, Jennifer, 'Vietnam on the Reel-to-Reel', *The New York Times* (20 September 2017), A23.

Bradley, Doug, 'I Served in Vietnam. Here's My Soundtrack', *The New York Times* (13 March 2018), www.NYTimes.com/column/Vietnam_67.

Brown, Margaret C., 'English 102 Honors, The War in Vietnam' (Radford University, Radford, VA, Spring 1993, 1994, 1995 & 1996). The four courses, 20 students each, included a film series and weekly meetings with members of the Vietnam Veterans Association as well as other events: including a trip to The Wall and Rolling Thunder with these veterans, and guest speakers Tim O'Brien, Basil Paquet and Adrian Cronauer.

Brown, Margaret C., Conversation with Dr Earl Brown (24 December 1970).

Brown, Margaret C. (ed.), *Final Papers on Vietnam. English 102H, Spring 1993* (Radford, VA: Radford University Honors Program, 1993).

Brown, Margaret C., Interview with Randy Cribbs (29 January 2008).

Brown, Margaret C., Interview with Susan Wimmers (January 2011).

Brown, Margaret C., Interview with Anon (3 November 2023).

Brownmiller, Susan, *Seeing Vietnam: Encounters of the Road and Heart* (NY: HarperCollins, 1995).

Burana, Lily, 'The Quiet Side of Being a Soldier's Other Half', *The New York Times* (11 November 2010).

Burkett, B.G. and Whitley, Glenna, *Stolen Valor: How the Vietnam Generation Was Robbed of its Heroes and its History* (Dallas, TX: Verity Press, 1998).

Butler, Robert Olen, *A Good Scent from a Strange Mountain* (NY: Henry Holt, 1992).

Caputo, Philip, *A Rumor of War* (NY: Ballantine Books, 1977).

Carroll, Andrew (ed.), *War Letters* (NY: Scribner, 2001).

Casto, Heather, 'A Quest for Truth', *Final Papers on Vietnam* (ed. Margaret Brown) Radford University, Radford, VA: Radford University Honors Program, Spring 1963), 13–28.

Chapman, Robert, *American Slang* (New York: Harper and Row, 1987).

Charters, Ann (ed.), *The Portable Sixties Reader* (NY: Penguin, 2003).

Chittenden, Varick (ed.), *Vietnam Remembered: The Folk Art of Marine Combat Veteran Michael D. Cousino, Sr* (Jackson, MS: University of Mississippi Press, 1995).

Chivers, C.J., 'A Sampling from Six Months' Worth of Small-Arms Accidents in Vietnam', *The New York Times* (18 February 2007).

Clark, Gregory, *Words of the Vietnam War: The Slang, Jargon, Abbreviations, Acronyms, Nomenclature, Nicknames, Pseudonyms, Slogans, Specs, Euphemisms, Double-Talk* (Jefferson, NC: McFarland Publishing, 1990).

Clos, Max, 'The Strategist Behind the Vietcong', https://www.nytimes.com/1964/08/16/archives/the-strategist-behind-the-vietcong-north-vietnams-commander-in.html.

Connelly, Michael, *The Wrong Side of Goodbye* (NY: Grand Central Publishing, 2016).

Crawford, Neta, 'Calculating the costs of the Afghanistan War in lives, dollars and years', http://The Conversation.com/Calculating-the-costs-of-the-Afghnaistan-War-in-lives-dollars-and-years.

Cribbs, Randy, *Were You There: Vietnam Notes Birth, Death, Infinity* (Jacksonville, FL: OCRS, Inc, 2003).

Cronauer, Adrian, Talk on his experience in Vietnam, Radford University (16 September 1992).

Cummings, Dennis, *The Men behind the Trident* (NY: Bantam, 1997).

Daggett, Stephen, 'Cost of Major US Wars', https://www.researchgate.net/publication/235211847_Costs_of_Major_US_Wars.

Daly, James and Bergman, Lee, *Black Prisoner of War: A Conscientious Objector's Vietnam Memoir* (Lawrence, KS: University Press of Kansas, 2000).

Daniel, Clifton (ed.), *Chronicle of the 20th Century* (Mt Kisco, NY: Chronicle Publications, 1987).

Daugherty, Leo and Mattson, Gregory, *Nam: A Photographic History* (NY: Barnes & Noble, 2004).

Davies, Anne. 'Thunder rolls, tears rain on Vietnam Vets' parade', theage.com.au/news/world 29 May 2007.

Deaver, Jeffrey, *The Goodbye Man* (NY: G.P. Putnam's Sons, 2020).

DeMille, Nelson, *Upcountry* (NY: Warner Books, 2002).

Dickson, Paul, *War Slang*, 2nd ed (NY: Bristol Parks, 2007).

Dionne, E.J. Jr., 'Kicking the Vietnam War Syndrome', https://www.washingtonpost.com/archive/politics/1991/03/04/kicking-the-vietnam-war-syndrome/b6180288-4b9e-4d5f-b303-befa2275524d/.

Dorland, Peter and Nanney, James, *Dust Off: Army Aeromedical Evacuation in Vietnam* (Washington: US Army, 1982).

Doyle, Edward *et al.*, *The Vietnam Experience*, 18 vol, Robert Manning, editor-in-chief (Boston: Boston Publishing Co., 1981).

Drake, Ben, 'Hall of Shame', http://www.marine-family.org/.../wannabes.html.

Du Lan Le Anh Dung, *The Three Teachings in Cao Dai*, http://www.nhipcaugiaoly/post?id=34.

Duncan, Donald, 'The Whole Thing Was A Lie', *Ramparts, Vietnam Primer* (San Francisco: Ramparts, 1966), 76–97.

Duncan, Patrick Sheane, director, *84 Charlie Mopic* (1989).

Dunnigan, James and Nofi, Albert, *Dirty Little Secrets of the Vietnam War* (NY: St Martin's Press, 1998).

Duong, Thu Huong, *Novel without a Name* (trans. Phan Huy Duong and Nina McPherson) (NY: William Morrow and Co., 1995).

Dutton, George E., Werner, Jayne S. and Whitmore, John K. (eds), *Sources of Vietnam Tradition* (NY: Columbia University Press, 2012).

Durrance, Dick, *Where War Lives: A Photographic Journal of Vietnam* (NY: Noonday Press, 1988).

Ebert, James, *A Life in A Year. The American Infantryman in Vietnam, 1965–1972* (NY: Ballantine Books, 1993).

Ebert, Roger, 'Review of "Charlie Mopic"', *The Chicago Sun Times* (28 April 1989).

Edelman, Bernard (ed.), *Dear America: Letters Home from the Vietnam War* (NY: Pocket Books, 1985).

Edwards, Owen, 'This Artwork Recognizes the Sacrifices made by Native Americans Soldiers in Vietnam', Smithsonian@mail.Smithsonian.com (30 May 2022).

Eichler, Thomas and Fecarotta, Diana (eds),. *Khe Sanh Veterans Book of Poetry.* (Wauwatosa, WI: Khe Sanh Veterans, 2005).

Elliott, David, 'What Trump Needs to Learn from Vietnam', *The New York Times* (16 September 2017), SR 5.

Emanuel, Ed, *The Soul Patrol* (NY: Ballantine Books, 2003).

Ezell, Edward Clinton, Introduction and Narration, *Reflections on The Wall: The Vietnam Veterans Memorial* (Harrisburg, PA: Stackpole Books, 1987).

Fall, Bernard, 'This Isn't Munich, It's Spain', *Ramparts Vietnam Primer* (San Francisco: Ramparts, 1966), 58–70.

Fallows, James, 'Chickenhawk in Chief', www.theatlantic.com/politics/archive/2017/08/what-did-you-do-in-the-twitter-war-daddy/536184/.

Fallows, James, 'The New Series on the Vietnam War and the Mysteries of Historical Resonance', http://www. atlantic.com/notes/2017/09/the-new-series-on-the-vietnam-war-and-the-mysteries-of-historical-resonance/540144/.

Farb, Peter, *Word Play* (NY: Bantam, 1975).

Farquhar, Dudley, 'Americal', poem written in 1982 after attending the dedication of the Vietnam Veterans Memorial in Washington, DC. Given to me by Sgt Farquhar.

Fitzgerald, Clare, 'Project 100,000: The Controversial Recruiting Program of the Vietnam War', www.warhistoryonline.com/vietnam-war/project-100,000.html.

FitzGerald, Frances, *Fire in the Lake.* (NY: Vintage Books, 1989).

Ford, Nick, *Language in Uniform* (Indianapolis, IN: Odyssey Press, 1967).

Free, Cathy, 'He rescued a family from Vietnam in 1975. On Thanksgiving they thank him', https://www.washingtonpost.com/lifestyle/2023/11/21/thanksgiving-vietnam-war-escape-marine/.

French, David, 'The Grim Reality of Waging War against Hamas', https://www.nytimes.com/2023/10/12/opinion/israel-hamas-isis-gaza.html.

French, David, 'There is no Way to Escape the Moral Challenge of War', https://www.nytimes.com/2023/10/15/opinion/gaza-israel-war-morals.html.

Friedman, Sergeant Major Herbert (retired), 'Poetry as Propaganda in Vietnam', psywarrior.com/VNPoemLeaflets.html.

Friedman, Herbert, E-mails to Margaret Brown (3–6 November 2023).

Friedman, Thomas, 'We Don't Yet Know How the Ukraine War Ends', *The New York Times* (21 September 2022), Section A23.

Gardner, Lloyd, *Approaching Vietnam* (NY: Norton, 1988).

Gaylin, Willard, 'What Clinton, Quayle Did Was the Collegiate Norm', *LA Times* (29 October 1992), B7.

Genzlinger, Neil, 'Sue Thompson', *The New York Times* (28 September 2021), Obituary page.

Gerstel, David, 'A Pale Smoke', *The New York Times* (30 March 2018), www.NYTimes.com/column/Vietnam_67.

Ghose, Anna, Managing Editor, *Eyewitness Travel Vietnam & Angkor Wat* (NY: Dorling Kindersley, 2007).

Goldman, Peter and Fuller, Tony, *Charlie Company: What Vietnam Did To Us* (NY: Ballantine Books, 1983).

Goodman, Paul, 'A Young Pacifist', in *War No More*, ed. Lawrence Rosenwald (NY: Literary Classics of the United States, 2016), 432–443.

Gray, J. Glenn, *The Warriors: Reflections on Men in Battle* (Lincoln, NE: University of Nebraska Press, 1998).

Gray, Jim and Olson, Richard, *War Poems: a Collaboration* (Gainesville, GA: Georgia Printing Co., 1986).

Green, Joey, *Joey Green's Encyclopedia of Offbeat Uses for Brand Name Products* (NY: Hyperion, 1998).

Greene, Graham, *The Quiet American* (NY: Penguin, 1956).

Greene, Joseph (ed.), *The Essential Clausewitz, Selections from On War* (Mineola, NY: Dover Pub, 2003).

Grossman, David, *On Killing* (NY: Little Brown and Co, 1995–96).

Guinta, Peter and Cribbs, Randy, *Illumination Rounds* (Jacksonville, FL: OCRS, Inc, 2005).

Gusterson, Hugh, 'Reconsidering How We Honor Those Lost to War', *Sapiens Magazine* (6 July 2017), https://www.sapiens.org/column/conflicted/war-memorials/.

Haass, Richard, 'The West Must Show Putin How Wrong He Is to Choose War', *The New York Times* (24 February 2022), Op Ed section.

Hanafin, Bob, *The Definition of a Vietnam Era Veteran*, http://www.veteranstoday.com (28 July 2009).

Harris, Mark, 'The Flowering of the Hippies', *Atlantic Magazine*, September 1967 issue.

Harrod, Bernadette, RN, *Fort Chastity, Vietnam, 1969* (Bloomington, IN: iUniverse, 2015).

Hasford, Gustav, *The Short-Timers* (NY: Bantam Books, 1979).

Hastings, Max, *Vietnam: An Epic Tragedy, 1945–1975* (NY: HarperCollins Publishers, 2012).

Hay, John Jr., *Vietnam Studies: Tactical and Materiel Innovations* (Washington: US Army, 1974).

Hayslip, Le Ly, with Wurts, Jay, *When Heaven and Earth Changed Places: Vietnamese Woman's Journey from War to Peace* (NY: Random House, 2003).

Hendrickson, Paul, *The Living and the Dead: Robert McNamara and Five Lives of a Lost War* (NY: Vintage, 1996).

Herman, Edward and Chomsky, Noam, *Manufacturing Consent: The Political Economy of the Mass Media* (NY: Pantheon Books, 1988).

Herman, Elizabeth, 'The Greatest War Photographer You've Never Heard of', *The New York Times* (28 March 2017), opinion page.

Herr, Michael, *Dispatches* (NY: Vintage Books, 1991).

Herring, George, 'The Road to Tet', *The New York Times* (27 January 2017), opinion page.

Hilsman, Roger, 'Vietnam: The Decisions to Intervene', *Superpowers and Revolution*, ed. Jonathan Adelman (NY: Praeger Publishers, 1986), 112–141.

History.com, Editors, 'The 1960s History', https://www.history.com/topics/1960s/1960s-history.

History.com, 'Kent State Shooting', https//www.history.com/topics/Vietnam-war/kent-state-shooting.

History.com, 'Woodstock', https://www.history.com/topics/1960s/woodstock.

Holley, Dr Byron, *Vietnam 1968–9: A Battalion Surgeon's Journal* (NY: Ballantine Books, 1993).

Holmes, Richard, *Acts of War: The Behavior of Men in Battle* (NY: Free Press, 1985).

Holzwarth, Larry, 'Here is the Intense Training Soldiers Went Through During the Vietnam War', 23 September 2019, https://historycollection.com/here-is-the-intense-training-soldiers-went-through-during-the-vietnam-war/ .

Honda, Katsuichi, *Vietnam: A Voice from the Villages* (Tokyo: Committee for the English Publication of Vietnam, 1968).

Hoover, Paul, *Saigon, Illinois* (NY: Vintage, 1988).

Howell, Terry, 'Court Expands Coverage for Vietnam Vets', http://www.military.com (22 August 2006).

Huynh, Dien, 'The End of South Vietnam', *The New York Times* (30 March 2018), www.NYTimes.com/column/Vietnam_67.

Hynes, Samuel, *The Soldiers' Tale: Bearing Witness to Modern War* (NY: Penguin Group, 1997).

Iles, Greg, *Blood Memory* (NY: Scribner, 2005).

Isaacs, Arnold, *Vietnam Shadows* (Baltimore, MD: Johns Hopkins University Press, 1997).

Isserman, Maurice, *Witness to War: Vietnam* (NY: Penguin Group, 1995).

Jensen-Stevenson, Monika and Stevenson, William, *Kiss the Boys Goodbye: How the US Betrayed its own POWs in Vietnam* (Toronto: McClellan and Stewart, Inc, 1990).

Johannessen, Larry, *Illumination Rounds: Teaching the Literature of the Vietnam War* (Urbana, IL: NCTE, 1992).

Johnson, Theodore, https://www.thebulwark.com/no-the-u-s-military-is-not-being-weakened-by-wokeness/ (30 November 2022).

Johnson, Theodore, 'The Military's Secret Weapon is … humor', https://qoshe.com/washington-post/theodore-r-johnson/the-military-s-secret-weapon-is-humor/167339453.

Joint Chiefs of Staff, *Dictionary of United States Military terms for Joint Usage* (JCS Pub 1) (Washington, DC: Department of Defense, 1964).

Jones, Stephen Mack, *August Snow* (NY: Soho Press, 2017).

Jones, Stephen Mack, *Dead of Winter* (NY: Soho Press, 2021).

Kanon, Joseph, *The Good German* (NY: Henry Holt and Company, 2001).

Karnow, Stanley, *Vietnam: A History* (NY: Penguin, 1984).

Katakis, Michael, *The Vietnam Veterans Memorial* (NY: Random House, 1988).

Ketwig, John, *… and a hard rain fell* (Naperville, IL: Sourcebooks, Inc., 2002).

Kiernan, Ben, *Viet Nam: A History from the Earliest Time to the Present* (NY: Oxford University Press, 2017).

Kilgore, Ed, 'GOP Hard-liners Overplayed Their Hand Against McCarthy', Intelligencer, hello.intelligencer@e.nymag.com (2 October 2023).

King, Martin Luther, Jr., 'Beyond Vietnam', in *War No More*, ed. Lawrence Rosenwald (NY: Literary Classics of the United States, 2016), 407–424.

Kissinger, Henry, 'Lessons for an Exit Strategy', *Washington Post* (12 August 2005), A19.

Knauer, Kelly (ed.), '1969: Woodstock, the Moon, and Manson: the Turbulent End of the '60s' (NY: Time, Inc, 2009).

Knight, Christina, 'US Army Units Explained: From Squads to Brigades to Corps', https://www.thirteen.org/blog-post/u-s-army-units-explained-from-squads-to-brigades-to-corps/ (31 July 2020).

Komunyakaa, Yusef, *Neon Vernacular* (Middletown, CT: Wesleyan University Press, 1993).

Kreisler, Harry and Barnes, Thomas, interviewers, 'Conversation with Harry G. Summers, Jr', globetrotter.Berkeley.edu/conversations/summers3.html.

Kubey, Craig *et al.*, *The Viet Vet Survival Guide* (NY: Ballantine Books, 1985).

Kutler, Stanley (ed.), *Encyclopedia of the Vietnam War* (NY: Macmillan, 1996).

Laderman, Scott, 'See Beautiful Vietnam!', *The New York Times* (12 September 2017), www.NYTimes.com/column/Vietnam_67.

Lamb, David, 'Revolutionary Road', *Smithsonian* (March 2008), 57–66.

Lamothe, Dan, 'Biden to Award Medal of Honor to Soldiers for Valor in Vietnam', *Washington Post* (27 June 2022), https://www.washingtonpost.com/national-security/2022/06/27/medal-of-honor-vietnam-dwight-birdwell-biden/.

Lanning, Michael Lee and Stubbe, Ray William, *Inside Force Recon: Recon Marines in Vietnam* (NY: Ballantine Books, 1989).

Lawrence, Mark, 'Was the Vietnam War Necessary?', *The New York Times* (29 March 2018), www.NYTimes.com/column/Vietnam_67.

Lerer, Seth, *Inventing English* (New York: Columbia University Press, 2007), 246–257.

Lifton, Robert, *Home from the War* (NY: Simon & Schuster, 1973).

Lippard, Lucy (ed.), *A Different War: Vietnam in Art* (Seattle: The Real Comet Press, 1990).

Lippman, Thomas, 'Henry Kissinger, who shaped world affairs under two presidents, dies at 100', https://www.washingtonpost.com/obituaries/2023/11/29/henry-kissinger-dead-obituary/?utm_campaign=wp_todays_headlines&utm_medium=ema.

Loewen, James, *Lies My Teacher Told Me* (New York: Touchstone, 1966), 240–249.

Lowenfels, Walter (ed.), *Where is Vietnam? American Poets Respond* (NY: Doubleday, 1967).

Lowery, George, 'US bombing in Vietnam drove civilians to Viet Cong' (Ithaca, NY: Cornell Chronicle), 2 March 2011.

Lucas, Jim, *Dateline: Vietnam* (NY: Award House, 1966).

Maclear, Michael, *Vietnam: A Complete Photographic History*, photographs edited by Hal Buell (NY: Tess Press, 2003).

Maga, Thomas, *The Complete Idiot's Guide to the Vietnam War* (NY: Penguin, 2000).

Maraniss, David, *They Marched into Sunlight* (NY: Simon & Schuster, 2003).

Marlantes, Karl, 'Vietnam: The War That Killed Trust', *The New York Times* (7 January 2017), op ed page.

Mason, Bobbie Ann, *In Country* (NY: Harper & Row, 1985).

McGarrity, Michael, *Residue* (NY: W.W. Norton and Company, 2019).

McGrath, John, 'The Other End of the Spear: The Tooth-to-Tail Ratio (T3R) in Modern Military Operations' (Fort Leavenworth, KS: Combat Studies Institute Press).

McMaster, H.R., *Dereliction of Duty* (NY: HarperPerennial, 1997).

Quarrie, Christopher, writer and director, *Jack Reacher*, Paramount Pictures (2012), movie based on novel *One Shot* by Lee Child.

Menefee, Constance Lee, 'LEWIS B PULLER, JR., AGE 48, DIES BY HIS OWN HAND – A CASUALTY OF WAR', https://www.vietvet.org/menefee.html.

Merton, Thomas, 'War and the Crisis of Language', in *War No More* (ed. Lawrence Rosenwald (NY: Literary Classics of the United States, 2016), 489–491.

Meyer, Peter and editors of *Life Magazine*, *The Wall: A Day at the Vietnam Veterans Memorial* (NY: Thomas Dunne, 1993).

Milam, Ron, '1967: The Era of Big Battles in Vietnam', *The New York Times* (10 January 2017), opinion page.

Miller, Henry, 'The Alcoholic Veteran with the Washboard Cranium', *The Wisdom of the Heart* (NY: New Directions, 1960), 103–140.

Mohr, Charles, 'Officers Blamed in Vietnam Defeat', *The New York Times* (17 March 1985), section 1, p.7.

Molotsky, Irvin, 'Levittown 30 Years Later', *The New York Times* (2 October 1977), section L1, p.1.

Mooney, James and West, Thomas (eds), *Vietnam: A History and Anthology* (St James, NY: Brandywine Press, 1994).

Moore, General Harold and Galloway, Joseph, *We Were Soldiers Once and Young* (NY: HarperTorch, 1992).

Nelson, Charles, *The Boy Who Picked the Bullets Up* (NY: William Morrow, 1981).

New York Times Editorial Board, 'Extremists in Uniform Put the Nation at Risk', *The New York Times* (13 November 2022), Op Ed page.

Nguyen, Hai, 'As the Earth Shook, They Stood Firm', *The New York Times* (17 January 2017), opinion page.

Nguyen, Kien, *The Unwanted: A Memoir of Childhood* (NY: Little Brown and Co., 2001).

Nguyen, Lien-Hang, 'In Vietnam, the Pentagon Papers Are History Written by the Defeated', https://www.nytimes.com/2021/06/09/us/vietnam-pentagon-papers-history-hanoi.html.

Nguyen, Viet Thanh, 'A Disturbing Book Changed my Life', *The New York Times* (30 January 2022), section SR, p.4.

Nightingale, Colonel Keith (ret.), *Just Another Day In Vietnam* (Havertown, PA: Casemate Publishers, 2019).

Ninh, Bao, *The Sorrow of War: A Novel of North Vietnam* (trans. Phan Thanh Hao) (NY: Pantheon Books, 1993).

Niven, Doug and Riley, Chris (eds), *Tim Page, Another Vietnam: Pictures of the War from the Other Side* (Washington: National Geographic Society, 2003).

Novak, Marian Faye, *Lonely Girls with Burning Eyes* (NY: Ballantine Publishing Group, 1991).

The New York Times, 'Vietnam 67'. From 17 January 2017 to 30 March 2018, *The New York Times* published a series of articles on the war in Vietnam, written by historians, veterans and journalists.

O'Brien, Tim, *If I Die in a Combat Zone, Box Me Up and Ship Me Home* (NY: Dell, 1973).

O'Brien, Tim, *The Things They Carried* (NY: Penguin, 1991).

O'Brien, Tim, 'The Violent Vet', *Esquire* (December 1979), 96–104.

Olson, James (ed.), *Dictionary of the Vietnam War* (Westport, CT: Greenwood Press, 1988).

Orwell, George, 'Politics and the English Language', *The Collected Essays,Journalism and Letters. Vol. IV*, eds Sonya Orwell and Ian Angus (NY: Harvest, 1968).

Page, Tim, *Mindful Moment* (New York: Thames and Hudson Inc, December 2001).

Palmer, Laura, *Shrapnel in the Heart: Letters and Remembrances from the Vietnam Veterans Memorial* (NY: Random House, 1987).

Paquet, Basil, Talk and poetry reading at Radford University (April 1973).

Parish, Dr John, 'An Autopsy of War', *Vietnam* (October 2012), 44–49.

Pedigo, Bobbie, former commanding officer of the 68th AHC (ed.), *Vietnam Facts vs. Fiction*, researcher Captain Marshal Hanson, http://www.68thahc.com/K Vietnam_facts_Truth.

Pendergrass, John, *Racing Back to Vietnam* (USA: Hatherleigh Press, 2017).

Phillips, Danny, E-mail correspondence with Margaret Brown (14–17 June 2009).

Phillips, Danny, *Black Death* (Unpublished manuscript).

Phillips, Thanh and Phillips, Charles (trans.), *Chieu Hoa* (Program Brochure, 2008).

Pinker, Steven, *How the Mind Works* (NY: Norton, 1997).

Plumb, Charlie, as told to Glen DeWerff, *I'm No Hero* (Independence, MO: Independence Press, 1983).

Poniewozik, James, 'The Eve of Destruction as seen on TV', *The New York Times* (15 September 2017), page C1.

Powell, Mary, *A World of Hurt. Between Innocence and Arrogance in Vietnam* (Cleveland: Greenleaf, 2003).

Prochnau, William (ed.), *Once Upon a Distant War: Halberstam, Sheehan, Arnett – Young War Correspondents and their early Vietnam Battles* (NY: Random House, 1995).

Puller, Lewis Jr., *Fortunate Son* (NY: Bantam Books, 1993).

Redmon, Jeremy. "Fifty Years After Their Release, Former Vietnam POWs Journey Back to Vietnam." *Smithsonian Magazine,* November 2023, 44-55.

Reed, David, 'Vietnam Theories Revisited', *Roanoke Times* (17 September 1993).

Reinberg, Linda, *In The Field: The Language of the Vietnam War* (NY: Facts on File, 1991).

Rempel, John, MD, 'A GI looks at Vietnam' (unpublished diary, September 1966).

Rempel, John, MD, Letter to Margaret Brown (7 April 2013).

Richard, Moriah, 'Building Better Worlds', *Writer's Digest* (May/June 2022), 76–77.

Ridley, Susan, 'What Exactly is a Hero', *Final Papers on Vietnam*, ed. Margaret Brown (Radford University, Radford, VA: Radford University Honors Program, Spring 1963), 29–42.

Reston, James Jr., *A Rift in the Earth: Art, Memory, and the Fight for a Vietnam War Memorial* (NY: Arcade Publishing, 2017).

Reston, James Jr., *Sherman's March and Vietnam* (Lincoln, NE: iUniverse.com.inc, 2000).

Roache, Rebecca, 'The Secret Power of Swearing', https://www.nytimes.com/2023/11/01/opinion/swearing-language-power.html#:~:text=The%20Secret%20Power%20of%20Swearing,-Nov.&text=Dr.%20Roache%20is%20a%20senior,which%20this%20essay%20is%20adapted.

Rosenberg, Jennifer, *A Short Guide to the Vietnam War* (Thought Co, 9 September 2021), thoughtco.com/Vietnam-war-s2-1779964.

Rosenwald, Lawrence, 'Introduction' to Statement by Student Non-Violent Coordinating Committee, in *War No More*, ed. Lawrence Rosenwald (NY: Literary Classics, 2016), 383.

Rosenwald, Michael, 'Operation Babylift: A frantic Saigon rescue efforts is echoed in Kabul's chaos', www.washingtonpost.com (29 August 2021).

Rottman, Gordon, *Fortress 48: Viet Cong and the NVA Tunnels and Fortifications of the Vietnam War* (Botley, England: Osprey Press, 2006).

Rottman, Gordon, *FUBAR Soldier Slang of WWII* (NY: Metro Books, 2010).

Rottmann, Larry, Barry, Jan and Paquet, Basil (eds), *Winning Hearts and Minds.* (New York: McGraw-Hill Book Company, 1972).

Roy, Jules, *The Battle of DienBienPhu*, trans. Robert Baldick (NY: Pyramid Books, 1966).

Ryan, Maureen, 'The Long History of the Vietnam Novel', *The New York Times* (17 March 2017), opinion page.

Sacquetry, Troy J., PhD, 'We're Not in Kansas Anymore', https://arsof-history.org/articles/v10n1_not_in_kansas_page_1.html.

Safer, Morley, *Flashbacks* (NY: St Martin's Press, 1990).

Sajak, Pat, E-mail to author (11 August 2010).

Salah, Michael, 'The Tiger Forces Atrocities', https://www.nytimes.com/2017/09/26/opinion/vietnam-tiger-force-atrocities.html.

Sampley, Ted, 'Democracy for Vietnam is inevitable; join its holy cause', trans. into Vietnamese by Phuc Truong Dao (Veterans Alliance for Democracy in Vietnam).

Santoli, Al, *Everything We Had* (NY: Ballantine Books, 1981).

Scheer, Robert, 'A View from Phnom Penh', *Ramparts Vietnam Primer* (San Francisco: Ramparts, 1966), 37–50.

Scheer, Robert, 'The Winner's War', *Ramparts Vietnam Primer* (San Francisco: Ramparts, 1966), 70–76.

Schell, Jonathan, 'The Village of Ben Suc', *The New Yorker Magazine* (15 July 1967), 28–92.

Schrynemakers, Bob, Master Sergeant, 'In the Line of Duty', *New Yorker* (16 April 2007).

Schultz, Owen, letter responding to article by C. Bassford, 'Vietnam Protesters Distrusted those who Romanticized War', *Roanoke Times* (3 December 1990).

Seabury, Paul and Codevilla, Angelo, *War: Ends and Means* (NY: Basic Books, 1989).

Seemayer, Zach, 'What It Was Like Training For The Vietnam War', www.ranker.com/list/what-was-training-for-vietnam-war-like/zach-seemayer (updated 7 August 2019).

Shafer, Michael (ed.), *The Legacy. The Vietnam War in the American Imagination* (Boston: Beacon Press, 1990).

Shanken, Andrew, 'Monuments with Mission Creep', www.laphamsquarterly.org/roundtable/monuments-mission-creep.

Shawcross, William, Introduction, *Tim Page's Nam* (NY: Alfred Knopf, 1983).

Sheehan, Neil, *A Bright Shining Lie* (NY: Vintage, 1988).

Sheehan, Neil, *After the War was Over: Hanoi and Saigon* (NY: Random House, 1992).

Sherman, Nancy, *Stoic Warriors* (NY: Oxford University Press, 2005).

Sinaiko, Eve (ed.), *Vietnam: Reflexes and Reflections, National Vietnam Art Museum* (NY: Harry Abrams, 1998).

Slaughter, Karin, *The Last Widow* (NY: HarperCollins, 2019).

Smith, Everett Newman, Colonel, Tape provided by daughter Evangeline Smith, 'Thoughts on Vietnam'.

Sonnenfeld, Jeffrey and Tian, Steven, 'Opinion: "Remember the Maine" History Shows How Lies Can Trigger Wars', cnnopinionfeedback@newsletters.cnn.com.

Sorley, Lewis, *A Better War* (NY: Random House, 1999).

Sorley, Lewis, 'The Vietnam War We Ignore', *The New York Times* (18 October 2009).

Soukhanov, Anne, *Word Watch: Stories behind the Words of our Lives* (NY: Henry Holt, 1995).

Souter, Gerry and Souter, Janet, *The Vietnam War Experience* (NY: Barnes & Noble, 2007).

Spiker, David, 'Oil Find Reported by South Vietnan [*sic*]', *The New York Times* (29 August 1974), Page 1.

Sperba, James. "The Controversial Operation Phoenix: How It Roots Out Vietcong Suspects, https://www.nytimes.com/1970/02/18/archives/the-controversial-operation-phoenix-how-it-roots-out-vietcong.html.

Staff, Infantry Magazine, *A Distant Challenge: The US Infantryman in Vietnam 1967–70* (Fort Benning, GA: Infantry Magazine, 1971).

Starry, Donn, General, *Armored Combat in Vietnam* (NY: Arno Press, 1986).

Steinman, Ron (ed.), *The Soldiers' Story: Vietnam in their own Words* (NY: Barnes and Noble, 1999–2000).

Stengel, Richard, Managing Ed, *Time 1969* (NY: Time Books, 2009).

Stewart, Dante, 'What White Voters See in Herschel Walker', https://www.nytimes.com/2022/12/02/opinion/warnock-walker-runoff-georgia.html.

Stoessinger, John, *Why Nations Go to War* (NY: St Martin's Press, 1978).

Student Non-Violent Coordinating Committee, 'Statement on American Policy in Vietnam', in *War No More*, ed. Lawrence Rosenwald (NY: Literary Classics of the United States, 2016).

Summers, Harry Jr., *On Strategy: The Vietnam War in Context* (Carlisle Barracks, PA: US Army War College, 2002).

Summers, Harry Jr., *The Vietnam War Almanac* (NY: Ballantine Books, 1985).

Svrluga, Susan, 'A Soldier in Vietnam and a Girl wrote letters. Decades later, they finally met', https://www.washingtonpost.com/dc-md-va/2023/11/25/vietnam-war-soldier-care-package-letters/.

Takiff, Michael, *Brave Men, Gentle Heroes* (NY: Perennial, 2004).

Tan, Rebecca and Cabato, Regina, 'Henry Kissinger's central role in the US carpet bombing of Cambodia', https://www.washingtonpost.com/world/2023/11/30/henry-kissinger-cambodia-bombing-war/.

Taylor, Telford, *Nuremberg and Vietnam: An American Tragedy* (NY: Bantam, 1971).

Terry, Wallace, *Bloods* (NY: Ballantine Publishing Group, 1984).

Thomas, C. David (ed.), *As Seen by Both Sides: American and Vietnamese Artists Look at the War* (Boston: Indochina Arts Project of the William Joiner Foundation, 1991).

Thomas, Claude Anshin, *At Hell's Gate: A Soldier's Journey from War to Peace* (Boston: Shambala Publications, Inc, 2004).

Thomas, Evan *et al.*, 'In God They Trust', *Newsweek* (7 May 2007), 27–34.

Thomason, John, *Fix Bayonets* (NY: Scribner, 1970).

Tripp, Nathaniel, *Father, Soldier, Son. Memoir of a Platoon Leader in Vietnam* (South Royalton, VT: Steerforth Press, 1996).

Tuchman, Barbara, *The March of Folly* (NY: Knopf, 1984).

Tully, Matthew, 'Less-than-honorable discharge does not have to be permanent', http://www.armytimes.com/community/ask_lawyer/military_askthelawyer_092208w.

Tzu, Sun, *The Art of War*, trans. Samuel Griffith (NY: Oxford University Press, 1963).

US Army Center of Military History, 'The Vietnam War Campaigns', http://history.army.mil/html/reference/army_flag/vn.html.

US Marine Corps, United States Government, 'Field Manual FM 27-10 MCRP 11-10B.1 Formerly MCRP 5-12.1A The Law of Land Warfare' (2 May 2016).

Van Devanter, Lynda, *Home Before Morning* (NY: Time Warner, 1983).

Van Devanter, Lynda and Furey, Joan (eds), *Visions of War, Dreams of Peace: Writings of Women in the Vietnam War* (NY: Warner Books, 1991).

Van Zyl, Meesa, Project Editor, *The Smithsonian Vietnam War* (New York: DK Publishing, 2017).

Walt, Lewis, *Strange War, Strange Strategy* (NY: Funk and Wagnalls, 1970).

Ware, Lawrence, '"Boyz N the Hood" at 30: A vivid Examination of Racism at Work', *The New York Times* (12 July 2021), Section C, 3.

Weber, Joe, *Rules of Engagement* (NY: Jove, 1992).

Wells, Tom, *The War Within: America's Battle over Vietnam* (Berkeley: University of California Press, 1994).

Welsh, Douglas, *The History of the Vietnam War* (London: Bison Books, 1981).

Wilson, Christopher, https://www.smithsonianmag.com/smithsonian-institution/what-its-a-wonderful-life-teaches-us-about-american-history-180979223/.

Zabecki, David, Major General, US Army (ret.), 'Basic Training Vietnam War', https://www.historynet.com/long-basic-training-vietnam-war.html.

Zaroulis, Nancy and Sullivan, Gerald, *Who Spoke Up? American Protest Against the War in Vietnam 1963–1975* (NY: Holt, 1984).

Zietz, Joshua. 'Joe Biden's Kabul is not Gerald Ford's Saigon'. https://www.politico.com/news/magazine/2021/08/17/kabul-biden-afghanistan-ford-saigon-505552.

Zumbro, Ralph, *Tank Sergeant* (NY: Pocket Books, 1988).

Media Credits

The following movies and DVDs contributed to my understanding of the Vietnam Conflict. I have indicated those well worth seeing with ▶.

▶*Apocalypse Now* (1979), directed by Francis Ford Coppola.

Born on the 4th of July (1989), directed by Oliver Stone.

▶*Coming Home* (1978), directed by Hal Ashby.

▶*Dear America: Letters Home from Vietnam.*

Deer Hunter (1978), directed by Michael Cimino.

▶*84 Charlie MoPic* (1989), directed by Patrick Duncan (written, directed by Vietnam Vet).

> "'*84 Charlie MoPic* deserves a place by itself among the films about Vietnam. It is a brave and original attempt to record nothing more or less than the actual daily experience of a unit on patrol, drawn out of the memories of men who were there. I've never seen a combat movie that seemed this close to actual experience, to the kinds of hard lessons that soldiers are taught by their enemies. The filmmakers have earned their right to shoot with a subjective camera – because the eyes we are really seeing through are their own" (Wikipedia, review written by Roger Ebert for *The Chicago Sun Times*, 28 April 1989).

Full Metal Jacket (1987), directed by Stanley Kubrick.

▶*Gardens of Stone* (1987), directed by Francis Ford Coppola (respecting and burying the dead).

Good Morning Vietnam (1987), directed by Barry Levinson.

▶*Go Tell the Spartans* (1978), directed by Fred Post (early military advisors).

Hamburger Hill (1987), directed by John Irvin.

▶*Hearts and Minds* (1974), directed by Peter Davis.

▶*In Country* (1989), directed by Norman Jewison.

Indochine (1992), directed by Regis Wargnier.

Inside The Vietnam War, VHS, National Geographic.

The Killing Fields (1984), directed by Roland Joffe.

My Lai, (2010), DVD, PBS.

Platoon (1986), directed by Oliver Stone.

▶*Southern Comfort* (1981), directed by Walter Hill (Vietcong as Cajuns; grunts as National Guard).

The Roots of the Vietnam War. The Nation Archives (31 August 2010), http://www.thenation.com/print/learning-pack/roots-vietnam-war.

▶*The Scent of Green Papaya* (1993), directed by Hung Tran Anh.

Vietnam: On the front Line, four-part series, The History Channel (2001).

Vietnam: The Women Who Served (1993).

▶*Vietnam War. A Documentary Film* (aired from 17 September 2017 on PBS), written and edited by Ken Burns and Lynn Novick, ten parts, DVD available.

For those we couldn't welcome home. (Wikipedia)

Acknowledgements

Thanks to the Department of English and the Honors Program at Radford University who gave me the opportunity to teach several honors sections of "Research and Reading" on the Vietnam War for several years. This has culminated in two books: *That Time, That Place, That War,* self-published in 2011, named History Book of the Year by the Military Writers Society of America and the book you just finished. My thanks to the Vietnam Veterans of America Chapter 138 who taught my students and me about their experiences in Vietnam and who graciously answered all our questions: George Albright, Jim Bowman, Al Davis, Randall Fletcher, Frank Longaker, Johnny Phillips, James Ratcliffe, Lee Thacker, Bobby Ward, and Banjo Williams.

My thanks also to the wives and children of these veterans who wanted their own time to talk with my class about their experiences: Kathy Bowman, Carolyn Parsons, Diane and Dee Phillips,

And to my students who asked the questions, who wrote about their understanding of the war – some of their comments are embedded in this text – and who took what they called "our vets" to the Wall. To Chris Armes who asked each Veteran, "How did the War change you?" To Heather Casto who walked over to Johnny Phillips and welcomed him home – a moment which still brings tears to my eyes, and to Chris Shell who taped that moment and many others during our Thursday evening meetings with the Veterans. My 160 students who enrolled in my courses on Vietnam are still welcoming Veterans home.

I too welcome all Vietnam Veterans home from Doc Holley who provided important feedback, to Randy Cribbs who talked with me about his experiences and gave me permission to use his poetry, to Susan Wimmers, not a veteran but who, while working at a USO in Vietnam, provided insight into women's roles in Vietnam, to Rabbi Goldman for sharing his experiences as an Army Chaplain, and to SGM Herb Friedman who showed me another side of the war, the real attempt to win hearts and minds. His understanding of the mind of the Vietnamese people provided much needed insights. Special thanks to Danny Phillips who gave me permission to use his photographs, taken with a brownie camera, and to use his unpublished memoir. To all the other Vietnam Veterans who fought for our country, my thanks, and the thanks of all Americans.

Thanks to my support staff, my family, friends and publisher: Thanks to Ron and Marian Link for supplying me with books on Vietnam, to Amy Collins who served as my contract consultant. Without her help, I would not be writing acknowledgements. Thanks too, to the staff at Pen and Sword for publishing my book. Special thanks go to Tara Moran and Harriet Fielding for their generosity, their kind assistance, and for being there to answer my queries and solve my problems. And, finally, to Tony Walton who read my manuscript. All the errors are still mine but thanks to Tony, they are much fewer.

To my family: to my husband Earl and, my daughter Emily. They kept me fed, laughing and provided critical insights which made my book stronger.

Finally, my thanks to you, my readers. I hope your journey into the 1960s and 70s enriched your understanding of the war, Vietnam, and the United States.

Margaret C Brown

Continuation of Copyright Page

Stan Platke. "And Then There Were None," from *Winning Hearts and Minds* copyright © 1972 by 1st Casualty Press. Used by permission of McGrawHill

Basil Paquet, "Night Dust-Off," "A Visit," "This Last Time," In a Plantation," from *Winning Hearts and Minds* copyright © 1972 by 1st Casualty Press. Used by permission of McGrawHill

Jan Barry, "Memorial for Man in Black Pajamas," "Autumn is an Illusion," from *Winning Hearts and Minds* copyright © 1972 by 1st Casualty Press. Used by permission of McGrawHill

W.D. Ehrhart, "Full Moon," from *Winning Hearts and Minds* copyright © 1972 by 1st Casualty Press. Used by permission of McGrawHill

SGM Herbert Friedman for permission to use 'Poetry as Propaganda and Vietnam" as well as correspondence and personal interview.

Randy Cribbs for permission to use any of his poetry from his book *Were You There: Birth, Death, Infinity.* Jacksonville, FL: OCRS, Inc, 2003. I have taken advantage of his kind offer and used many of his excellent poems. Margaret Brown would also like to thank Randy Cribbs for allowing her to publish material from an interview she had with him on 29 January 2008

From Chieu Hoa Program Brochure, Translated by Thanh and Charles Phillips, copyright © 2008. Used by permission of the translators.

From a tape entitled, Thoughts on Vietnam, by Colonel Everett Smith. Used by permission of his daughter, Evangeline Smith.

From an interview with Susan Wimmers. January 2011. Used by permission of Susan Wimmers

Dudley Farquhar "Americal Division" and picture of the Vietnam Memorial Wall. Used by permission of the author.

From *Vietnam 1968-1969: A Battalion Surgeon's Journal*, copyright © 1993 by Dr. Byron Holley. Used by permission of the author.

From Vietnam: An Epic Tragedy 1945-1975, copyright © 2018 by Max Hastings. Used by permission of HarperCollins.

Danny Phillips for permission to use e-mail correspondence, unpublished memoir and pictures

John Rempel, MD, for permission to use unpublished memoir.

CONTINUATION OF COPYRIGHT PAGE

Caputo, Philip. *Rumor of War.* NY: Ballantine Books, 1977.

Dunnigan, James and Albert Nofi. *Dirty Little Secrets of the Vietnam War*. NY: St Martin's Press, 1998.

Eichler, Thomas and Diana Fecarotta, eds. *Khe Sanh Veterans Book of Poetry.* Wauwatosa, WI: Khe Sanh Veterans, 2005.

Gray, Jim. "Frozen in the Now," "Sleeping," "Mama-San," "The Purple Heart," "Rain," "Jail," "A No Bullshit War Story," from *War Poem: A Collaboration* copyright © Georgia Printing Company

From "I Feel Like I'm Fixin' to Die Rag." Words and music by Joe McDonald. Copyright © 1965-renewed 1993 by Alkatrz Korner Music Co BMI.
Puller, Lewis, Jr. *Fortunate Son*. NY: Bantam Books, 1993.

Reston, James, Jr. *A Rift in the Earth: Art, Memory and the Fight for a Vietnam Memorial*. NY: Arcade Publishing, 2017.

Reston, James, Jr. *Sherman's March and Vietnam*. Lincoln, NE: iUniverse.com, inc., 2000.

Van deVanter, Linda. *Home Before Morning*. NY: Time Warner, 1973.

Endnotes

Section 1

1. The term 'gook' was originally used to describe people in the Philippines, who were referred to as '*gugu*'. Gook was used in both Korea and Vietnam to describe the enemy. (Belew, 80)
2. Idea from 'Introduction' to Clark's *The Sleepwalkers*, quoted in Josipovici, Hamlet Fold on Fold, 12–13.
3. Not really so easy. I have oversimplified it in the introduction. A more detailed explanation of the 'how' is discussed in the first and third sections of this book.
4. The NBA doesn't believe that their/our community approves of swearing. 'It's simply a matter of "decorum".' Within the last year, it has started fining players who swear excessively during press conferences. Michael Adams, author of *In Praise of Profanity*, disagrees: '[Profanity] is simply a natural element of language – a useful tool for the moments we require "those expressive extremes".' (*Sports Illustrated*, July 2022, 13–14)
5. For further discussion on the importance of humor, see Johnson, *The Military's Secret Weapon.*
6. The Vietcong would often drag their dead through camouflaged tunnel entrances – just to mess with grunts' heads.
7. DEROS, acronym for Date of Expected Return from OverSeas.
8. Actual meaning: if he died, the insurance money his parents/wife received would pay off the mortgage on the farm. In other words, bought the farm.
9. Kristi Ramsey, a student in my course, wrote about trust.
10. General Westmoreland stated, in a speech given in 1968, that there were only two ways to win this war: attrition or annihilation.
11. 'For the birds', an expression meaning no longer possible.
12. Goodman died mountain climbing in 1967.
13. Connelly's fictional hero, Hieronymus (Harry) Bosch, had been a tunnel rat in Vietnam.
14. See Government Report in Appendix E for totals of death and casualties for every war Americans have participated in, from the Revolutionary War to Afghanistan.
15. Although not well-known or publicized, many Native Americans volunteered to fight in Vietnam. One artist created a tableau, memorializing those who fought. (Edwards, 1–2)
16. Both Jim Bowman and Bobby Ward attended my Thursday evening programs often to answer questions posed by my students.

17. The idea 'that it is right and proper' to die for one's country is a Roman phrase (*dulce et decorum est pro patria mori*). It is also the title of a poem written by Englishman Wilfred Owen, serving his country in France during the First World War. He died during the war.
18. In 1950, Congress passed and President Truman signed the Uniform Code of Military Justice – a description of military law.
19. See Section 3, War, for a detailed description of this code.
20. Soldiers in the army, however, wore solid green.
21. See Appendix F, the Government's report on dog tags found in SE Asia.
22. Military Payment Certificates were issued instead of money; in fact, they were used as money on base camps. Soldiers could buy TVs and send them home.
23. The United States claimed their destroyers were fired upon, creating a reason to put boots on the ground.
24. Loewen notices the cadence of the speech (244), which I attribute to the parallel structures and the use of 'and'.
25. This surcharge was levied to help pay for the Vietnam War.
26. Poem was given to me by Sgt Farquhar. For further information on the wall, see Appendix C: The wall was privately funded mostly by vets.
27. Origin of the term is uncertain. Many thought it referred to the Beatniks who were in the know or 'hip'.
28. Dee Phillips also commented on why she joined the Army and basic training; see page 58.
29. Lynda Van Devanter was instrumental in getting a Vietnam memorial that became The Wall.
30. Puller, Jr, won the Pulitzer Prize for best autobiography in 1992 (*Fortunate Son*), graduated from law School in 1974, ran for Congress in 1978 in Virginia and served as a lawyer for the Pentagon, which he gave up to accept a teaching position at George Mason University. He committed suicide in 1994.
31. 'James Quay, a Conscientious Objector from the Vietnam War era. He is Executive Director of the California Council for the Humanities' (Ezell, 20).
32. For more information on Armed Forces Radio Vietnam (AFRVN) and Adrian Cronauer, see AFRVN below.
33. In Desert Storm 1, all reporters had to be escorted and their stories often censored. They could no longer roam freely, as had those who covered the Vietnam War.
34. Morley Safer and a photographer witnessed the destruction of Cam Ne in Quang Nam Province, a VC stronghold, in August 1965. The bombing of the US Airbase in Da Nang in July 1965 by the VC forced the US to extend their area of responsibility southwest into Da Nang Province. Unlike My Lai, in March 1968, few civilians were injured. Because Safer was there to report on it, the destruction became a major story in the US.
35. I recently saw a man wearing a hat that said 'Cold War veteran'. I welcomed him home. He told me that even though he had served in Germany, when he came home in 1971, some members of his family called him a 'baby killer'. He said: 'It still hurts.'
36. One playing card company offered a deck with nothing but Aces of Spades. The Vietcong also thought the CBS logo, an eye, was a bad omen.

37. Second World War movies often depicted Japanese pilots with evil grins on their faces, so American soldiers already had an image of non-Westerners which may have contributed to the atrocities.
38. Thanks to Sergeant Major Herbert Friedman for telling me about this song.
39. See Armed Forces Radio Vietnam (AFRVN) below.

Section 2

1. Kanon in *The Good German* was writing about soldiers in Germany immediately after the Second World War, but his notion equally applies to the veterans in Vietnam who yearned for the *American Graffiti* world they had left behind. Herr expresses a similar idea: 'Vietnam is what we had instead of childhoods' (244).
2. See Section One.
2.5 This poem comes from a booklet entitled Patriotic poems. This poem and two others were printed by the United States Information Agency (USIA) Regional Service Center in Manila to "promote identification with love for their country by the citizens of the Republic of Vietnam [South Vietnam]" (H. Friedman 31).
3. The population of the United States at that time was more than 346 million.
4. Annamese refers to the people who inhabited Vietnam. Annam became a French protectorate in 1887, part of French Indochina, along with CochinChina and Tonkin. The word, meaning 'Pacified South' in Sino-Vietnamese, was used in the West to refer to Vietnam.
5. Tet is a shortened form of Tet Nguyen Dan, the first morning of the first day of the new period. See Tet Offensive in Section Three.
6. For lists of these rules, see Appendix B.
7. Many of us who watched the tv show *MASH* heard Radar bartering with other MASH units, a form of cumshaw.
8. Although in Japan it is not a polite or honorary way to refer to a man or woman.
9. The Office of Strategic Services, forerunner of the CIA, created by William Donovan during the Second World War.
10. The pin pictured above was awarded to those who fought at Dien Bien Phu. My husband bought it from a street vendor.
11. See Rice Robbery in Section Three.
12. This information was provided by a Vietnam vet who wished to remain anonymous; about $11,000 in today's money.
13. In fact, given the poverty, this amount and the amount for other damages were considered generous.
14. French philosopher, political commentator and photographer.

Section 3

1. President, The Council on Foreign Relations.
2. The American Civil War was a war of necessity to keep the Union intact. The United States' participation in the conflict in Vietnam was for some a war of choice, to others a war of necessity to keep communism contained.

3. Tape provided to Margaret Brown by Colonel Smith's daughter, Vangie Smith.
4. Another reason the body count would seem important is that we were taking no territory, capturing no enemy combatants, with nothing to show that we were winning. The more dead bodies counted, the fewer Vietcong would remain to fight, a war of attrition.
5. These are not types of wars, except counter-insurgency, but strategies.
6. See Appendix D.
7. Chris Shell, a student in my class, wrote an essay entitled 'Just War or Responsible War'.
8. The article appeared in the *American Journal of Political Science*, Vol 55 (February 2011), issue 2, 201–218.
9. For additional information on the Rules of Engagement, see US Marine Corps, The Law of Land Warfare, Field Manual, especially Chapters 1 and 2.
10. Lewis Puller, Jr, was awarded the Pulitzer Prize for Biography/Autobiography in 1992 for *Fortunate Son*. He was awarded the Silver Star Medal, the Navy and Marine Corps Commendation Medal, two Purple Hearts and the Republic of Vietnam Gallantry Medal.
11. Lieutenant William Calley, along with others, was convicted in March 1971 for the My Lai Massacre, killing over 500 villagers on 16 March 1968. US Army officers covered up this atrocity for one year.
12. See *The Law of Land Warfare Field Manual*, especially Chapter 3. Also see Appendix B
13. All non-English phrasing is that of translator.
14. See Section 3.
15. Emphasis added.
16. Emphasis added.
17. A village in the Iron Triangle near Saigon. Taken several times by both South and North Vietnamese allied forces. In January 1967, during Operation Cedar Falls, US forces removed most of the villagers and destroyed the village. Jonathan Schell, in an article entitled 'The Village of Ben Suc', wrote about what he called 'A Tragedy in Vietnam' in the 15 July 1967 issue of *The New Yorker*.
18. Henry Miller, in an essay, remarked that what was important was that it be a good story; its truth didn't matter. 'When a story is good I listen. And if it develops afterwards that it was a lie why so much the better – I like a good lie just as much as the truth. A story is a story, whether it's based on fact or fiction' (Miller, 134).
19. The propaganda leaflet and the translation are from Friedman's article. Some of the propaganda leaflets were written by a Vietnamese couple, now living in Jacksonville, FL. The wife would write the leaflet; the husband would fly the airplane and drop the leaflets from the sky.
20. Actually created by the Germans during the Second World War.
21. Note: Sergeant Danny Phillips walked point for six months until he was wounded. He received the Purple Heart and was awarded the Bronze Star for Valor during his one-year tour in Vietnam. Many of the photographs in this book were taken by Danny Phillips.
22. Emphasis added.
23. For more information on strategy, hygiene, geography, weather and political organizations of the Republic of Vietnam and the Vietcong, including pictures of

aircraft, boats, tunnel systems and enemy traps, see the *Handbook for US Forces in Vietnam*.

24. Reference unknown. I did find a reference to Representative Richard Ichord, who served as a member of Congress from Missouri during the 1960s and '70s. He chaired the House UnAmerican Activities Committee from 1969–1975 and was 'a significant anti-communist political figure'. He co-authored a book entitled *Behind Every Bush: Treason or Patriotism* (Wikipedia).

25. Notice the word 'Assistance'. The US provided 'military assistance' to the South Vietnamese. Thus they themselves were not really fighting this war, only assisting.

26. See also Holzwarth, 22, on the need to arm doctors because of ambushes.

27. These priorities can be found in *The Pentagon Papers* published by Quadrangle Books, page 263.

28. I am indebted to SGM Herbert Friedman for his article 'Poetry as Propaganda'.

29. All that follows is excerpted from Freidman's article

30. Thanks to SGM Herbert Friedman, for bringing the letter and poem to my attention.

31. All that follows is excerpted from Friedman's article.

32. All that follows is excerpted from Friedman's article.

33. She was the Vietnamese counterpart to Axis Sally and Tokyo Rose.

34. Komunyakaa is referring to Ray Charles' refusal to perform before a segregated audience in Georgia in 1961. The Georgia State legislature apologized to Charles in 1979 and later made Charles' version of 'Georgia on my Mind' the state song.

35. Susan Elkins, a student in my course, wrote an essay for *The Search for Peace* Symposium, sponsored by the Radford University Honors Program in 1994

36. See Hanoi Hannah's quote earlier in section.

37. A similar incident occurred at Da Nang when MPs refused 150 black soldiers' requests to attend chapel.

38. Ned Felder finally met Kristina Olson in 2023 (Svrluga, 2).

39. Nearly a dozen chaplains were killed in action and more than a hundred wounded during the war. Three were recipients of the Medal of Honor, two posthumously: LT J.G. Vincent R. Capodanno and USN Major Charles J. Watters. The survivor to receive the Medal of Honor was CPT Charles J. Litkey. All three of these chaplains were Catholic (Dunnigan and Nofi, 164).

40. From a Filipino word meaning 'rugged area'.

41. Basil Paquet came to Radford University to read his poetry and discuss his experience in the war.

42. There is no such thing as an ex-Marine. A Marine may retire, but he's still a Marine. Their motto is *semper fi*, 'always faithful'.

43. Colonel Hackworth received over 90 US and foreign military awards, including the Distinguished Service Cross – the second-highest United States military decoration – for extraordinary heroism. In later life, he often wore a CIB pin. He died from bladder cancer in 2005, caused, many believed, by Agent Orange. He also kept Doc Holley from missing his Freedom Bird.

44. For more information on the atrocities, see Michael Salah, 'Tiger Forces Atrocities', *The New York Times*, 26 September 2017.

45. See Appendix D.

46. See SEATO in Section 1 for a more complete explanation of the treaty.

47. FULRO is still resisting communist attempts to subjugate the indigenous people who make up the organization.
48. Dink = Vietcong soldier.
49. See also Francis Fitzgerald, *Fire in the Lake*, 173.
50. The Khmer are the primary ethnic group of Cambodia and its official language.
51. Edwin Moise, Professor of History at Clemson University, wrote two books on the Vietnam War: *The Myths of Tet: The Most Misunderstood Event of the Vietnam War* and *Tonkin Gulf and the Escalation of the Vietnam War*. It was his opinion that the North Vietnamese won the war. Others felt differently.
52. If one country in South-east Asia becomes communist, like dominoes, they all will fall into communist hands.
53. See previous page for an explanation.
54. I use the word loosely. They were flying combat missions dropping the South Vietnamese Army into battle areas.
55. See a more complete account of the effect of Operation Ranch Hand see Defoliants earlier in this section, p.124.
56. Note: Charles McCarry claims that Diem's family had Kennedy assassinated in a fictionalized account called *Tears of Autumn*.
57. The Senate voted approval by 48–2 in ten hours; the House took forty minutes.
58. See description of the Study and Observation Group in Section 1, John Wayne High School.
59. Frederik Logevall, Laurence D Belfer Professor of International Affairs, Harvard Kennedy School Professor of History, wrote a Pulitzer Prize-winning book on Vietnam, *Embers of War: The Fall of an Empire and the Making of America's Vietnam*.
59A. Professors Pepinsky, Kocher, and Kalyas wrote an article entitled: "Aerial Bombing and Counterinsurgency in the Vietnam War," published in the *American Journal of Political Science*, 2011, vol. 55, issue 2, 201-218.
60. For more on Rolling Thunder, see Appendix D.
61. Because of the Rules of Engagement, soldiers were forbidden to fire into Laos or Cambodia. But being forbidden didn't always stop them, just as it didn't stop the US from bombing the Ho Chi Minh Trail.
62. The battle that ended the French control of Indochina.
63. Served with the 13th Marines at Khe Sanh, August–mid-October 1967.
64. You can hear the statement in the film documentary *Hearts and Minds*, released in 1975, winner of an Academy Award for best documentary, directed by Peter Davis.
65. A way for the United States to gradually leave without losing face, a realization that continuing to fight was futile.

Section 4

1. See Appendices C (The Wall) and E (Government Report on Casualties).
2. A similar calendar is created in the 1989 movie *Major League*. The team hates the new owner, a woman, who wants to move it from Cleveland to Miami but can only do so if attendances are quite low. They create a calendar, a picture of her fully

dressed. After every win, they peel off one more square from her body, exposing more and more of her skin as attendance keeps rising, frustrating the owner.

3. It also still gives me chills listening to Tim Buckley's 'Once I was (a Soldier)', with the refrain 'will you ever remember me', as a backdrop to Voight's speech.
4. Lynda Van Devanter, a nurse in Vietnam during the Vietnam War, wrote *Home Before Morning*.
5. Note: The last line, *Fortunate Son*, is the title of Puller's Pulitzer Prize-winning autobiography. This poem was written after Lew Puller's suicide on 11 May 1994. The poem appeared in the Fall 1994 newsletter of the Memorial Day Writers' Project.
6. The 'Nam meant in Vietnam; in the 'Nam; in the bush. The World meant both the USA and home.
7. See Appendix E.
8. See War Stories in Section 3.
9. For more on Belew's view of the impact the Vietnam War had on veterans, see pages 1–32 of her book.
10. Caputo, *Rumor of War*, Part 3, Chapter 13, p.213. His remarks concern the death of First Lieutenant Levy in 1965.
11. Notice the word 'cause'. In that same speech, he used the term 'noble cause', hearkening back to the South's view that its attempt to leave the Union was a 'noble cause'.

Coda

1. Although the Gulf of Tonkin Resolution, passed by Congress on 7 August 1964 and enacted on 10 August 1964, gave free reign to President Johnson to pursue the conflict, only Congress can declare war.

Section 5

1. For an even more detailed description of the chronology than those presented below, see https.//www.historyplace.com/unitedstates/vietnam/index-1965.html.
2. For more information on the rules governing the conduct of wars, see *The Law of Land Warfare, Field Manual*, especially Chapters 1, 2, 3 and 5.
3. In 2004, the Vietnam Veterans Memorial Fund created a plaque to honor those who fought in the war but later died from other causes: suicide, PTSD, Agent Orange and other causes related to their service. The plaque reads: 'In Memory of the men and women who served in the Vietnam War and later died as a result of their service.' It sits on the grounds of The Wall.
4. Ezell's quote refers to ceremonies, not memorials, but in many ways they evoke similar emotions.
5. The first actual casualty was US Air Force technician Richard B. Fitzgibbon. who died on 8 June 1956. The Buis name was moved in 1999 so that Fitzgibbon's name would appear first.

6. Dan Lamothe, 'How 775,000 US Troops fought in One War: Afghanistan military deployments by the numbers', *Washington Post*, 11 September 2019.
7. 'All estimates are of the costs of military operations only and do not reflect costs of veterans' benefits, interest on war-related debt, or assistance to allies' (Daggett, 2). All the information on war costs comes from an article written by Stephen Daggett, https://www.researchgate.net/publication/235211847_Costs_of_Major_US_Wars, published on 29 June 2010.
8. Field army last used in 1991 in Desert Storm.
9. All of the above excerpted from Knight, 'US Army Units Explained: From Squads to Brigades to Corps'.
10. See *The Law of Land Warfare*, Chapter 3.